Social and Behavioral Research and the Internet

Advances in Applied Methods and Research Strategies

EUROPEAN ASSOCIATION OF METHODOLOGY

The European Association of Methodology (EAM) serves to promote research and development of empirical research methods in the fields of the Behavioural, Social, Educational, Health and Economic Sciences as well as in the field of Evaluation Research.

Homepage: http://www.eam-online.org

The purpose of the EAM book series is to advance the development and application of methodological and statistical research techniques in social and behavioral research. Each volume in the series presents cutting-edge methodological developments in a way that is accessible to a broad audience. Such books can be authored, monographs, or edited volumes.

Sponsored by the European Association of Methodology, the EAM book series is open to contributions from the Behavioral, Social, Educational, Health and Economic Sciences. Proposals for volumes in the EAM series should include the following: (1) Title; (2) authors/editors; (3) a brief description of the volume's focus and intended audience; (4) a table of contents; (5) a timeline including planned completion date. Proposals are invited from all interested authors. Feel free to submit a proposal to one of the members of the EAM book series editorial board, by visiting the EAM website http://eam-online.org. Members of the EAM editorial board are Manuel Ato (University of Murcia), Pamela Campanelli (Survey Consultant, UK), Edith de Leeuw (Utrecht University) and Vasja Vehovar (University of Ljubljana).

Volumes in the series include

Das/Ester/Kaczmirek: Social and Behavioral Research and the Internet: Advances in Applied Methods and Research Strategies, 2011

Hox/Roberts: Handbook of Advanced Multilevel Analysis, 2011

De Leeuw/Hox/Dillman: International Handbook of Survey Methodology, 2008

Van Montfort/Oud/Satorra: Longitudinal Models in the Behavioral and Related Sciences, 2007

Social and Behavioral Research and the Internet

Advances in Applied Methods and Research Strategies

Edited by

Marcel Das

CentERdata and
Tilburg School of Economics and Management
Tilburg University, the Netherlands

Peter Ester

Rotterdam University, the Netherlands

Lars Kaczmirek

GESIS – Leibniz Institute for the Social Sciences
Mannheim, Germany

Routledge
Taylor & Francis Group
New York London

Routledge
Taylor & Francis Group
270 Madison Avenue
New York, NY 10016

Routledge
Taylor & Francis Group
27 Church Road
Hove, East Sussex BN3 2FA

Printed in the United States of America on acid-free paper
10 9 8 7 6 5 4 3 2 1

International Standard Book Number: 978-1-84872-816-5 (Hardback) 978-1-84872-817-2 (Paperback)

Library of Congress Cataloging-in-Publication Data

Social and behavioral research and the internet : advances in applied methods and research strategies / edited by Marcel Das, Peter Ester, Lars Kaczmirek.
p. cm. -- (European Association of Methodology series)
Includes bibliographical references and index.
ISBN 978-1-84872-816-5 (hardcover : alk. paper) -- ISBN 978-1-84872-817-2 (pbk. : alk. paper)
1. Social surveys--Methodology. 2. Internet surveys. 3. Surveys--Methodology--Technological innovations. 4. Social sciences--Research. I. Das, Marcel. II. Ester, P. III. Kaczmirek, Lars.

HM538.S63 2011
300.72'3--dc22 2010032326

Visit the Taylor & Francis Web site at
http://www.taylorandfrancis.com

and the Psychology Press Web site at
http://www.psypress.com

Contents

Part III Data Quality: Problems and Solutions

Preface

These are exciting times for survey researchers. Their discipline has matured and is well grounded in theory, methodology, and practice. Survey research has become the dominant data collection method by which social scientists explore and test their hypotheses, regarding both fundamental and applied issues. Especially in the last decade, survey research developments have progressed enormously. The key factor, undoubtedly, has been the vast advancement and diffusion of Internet surveys. Surveys using the Internet quickly became a most competitive data collection method for survey researchers. They are relatively inexpensive, are able to reach large populations, are not subject to interviewer bias, enable respondents' self-control of questionnaire completion, and data become available almost in real-time. But there are also still major shortcomings such as problems related to coverage, self-selection, and difficulties in reaching specific groups such as the elderly and immigrants. Fortunately, scholars all over the globe are involved in common efforts to address these shortcomings and to explore ways of improvement. Results look promising. Moreover, various highly innovative studies have been launched to advance the design, software, applicability, and reach of Internet surveys. Outcomes from these studies increasingly find their way into mainstream Internet surveys. Internet surveys are here to stay. Besides, professional Internet survey institutes have successfully distanced themselves from all kinds of quick-and-dirty providers of Internet surveys. The market of Internet surveys—hopefully also in the eyes of clients—has become more transparent.

The main aim of this book is to report on the state-of-the-art of Internet surveys, their strengths and weaknesses, their results and promises, and their past and future applications. We have brought together a highly qualified group of scholarly Internet survey experts from both Europe and the United States who report on a wide variety of salient theoretical, methodological, and applicability issues involved in surveys using the Internet. The scope, structure, and topics of the book, as well as the various chapter drafts, were discussed in several rounds of intensive author discussions. The nature of how this book was conceived and written was a matchless experience and we hope it shows. We were not just a number of scholars interested in Internet survey research but became a *group*, in the true sense, of researchers intrigued by this new venue for Internet survey studies. The interactive way in which this volume came about, in combination with its rationale and contributions by renowned specialists, gives the book a distinctive nature. We hope that the book will soon be recognized as providing a unique niche in the field, a key reference among Internet survey researchers.

The book itself is structured around three major themes. Part I focuses on the current state of Internet survey methodology, Part II outlines advanced Internet survey methods and applications, and Part III reviews major issues related to data quality of Internet surveys. For classical but important topics, chapters were included with a focus on reviewing and summarizing the state of the art, while other chapters specifically expand on special problems and new developments. Themes include the development of the Internet survey, its pros and cons, sources of survey error, mixed-mode designs, representativeness, Internet survey panels, ethical issues, visual design and feedback procedures, interaction with respondents, socially sensitive survey topics, mode and context effects, paradata, eye-tracking techniques, and biomarker data collection. The first chapter gives a more detailed outline of the separate chapters.

The book aims at both the academic survey research community and Internet survey practitioners. We sought the right balance between theory and practice, between methodology and application, between design and implementation, between problems and solutions, and between mainstream approaches and innovative methods. We feel that the book will find its way to seminars and courses on Internet surveys. The issues discussed are of prime importance to researchers from a broad spectrum of academic disciplines: psychology, sociology, economics, political science, education, health studies, epidemiology, and to professionals in public opinion and market research. We want to provide the interested reader with a broad insight into the possibilities and challenges of Internet surveys. We are convinced that Internet surveys are about to become the prime method of social survey data collection. But we also want to point at highly interesting combinations of Internet surveys with traditional surveys (face-to-face interviews, telephone interviews, paper and pencil interviews): mixed-mode data collection methods. We anticipate that the book will prove helpful to researchers and practitioners who are involved in learning the craft of Internet survey research. All contributing authors share a fascination for Internet surveys but are also strongly convinced that designing, implementing, and conducting Internet surveys is a scientific craft.

The accelerating development of Internet surveys in the first decade of the 21st century, makes this a great era for survey researchers. This is particularly true for cross-country survey studies. The comparative nature of various important Internet surveys highlights the international ambiance and challenges of our discipline. The book reflects this international scope, in terms of both authors and themes.

A book project like the current one can only be successful if the contributing authors share the same passion about the topic as we as editors do. We were in the luxurious position of having such a group of authors and we are grateful to all of them for their innovative, authoritative, and fascinating contributions.

We would like to thank GESIS – Leibniz Institute for the Social Sciences (Mannheim, Germany) – for providing a budget that allowed the two authors' meetings in Mannheim. These meetings gave the authors the opportunity to present ideas and first draft papers, and to share their thoughts and findings. We thank Margit Bäck for her help in organizing the first meeting. A number of chapters are based on tailored experiments that were carried out in the LISS panel, administered by CentERdata (Tilburg University, the Netherlands). We want to express our gratitude to the Netherlands Organization for Scientific Research (NWO) for their financial support of the Measurement and Experimentation in the Social Sciences (MESS) project, of which the LISS panel is the core element. We gratefully acknowledge the MESS Board of Overseers for giving advice on and reviewing the various experiments, the CentERdata staff for conducting the experiments (i.e., programming of questionnaires, fieldwork support, and data delivery), and last but not least the LISS panel respondents who spent time to fill in the questionnaires. We are indebted to Routledge/Taylor & Francis for their professional assistance, responsiveness, and support. Thanks go also to Joop J. Hox and Vasja Vehovar from the Editorial Board of the SRI Book Series. Finally, we would like to thank Josette Janssen of CentERdata who carefully helped us with copy-editing. Her patience and accuracy are highly appreciated.

Marcel Das, Peter Ester, and Lars Kaczmirek

1

Introduction

Marcel Das
CentERdata and Tilburg School of Economics and Management
Tilburg University
Tilburg, the Netherlands

Peter Ester
Rotterdam University
Rotterdam, the Netherlands

Lars Kaczmirek
GESIS—Leibniz Institute for the Social Sciences
Mannheim, Germany

Technological developments are opening up unique new possibilities for empirical research in the social sciences. Among these developments is the fast diffusion of Internet research. The Internet is rapidly developing into a major instrument of data collection for the social sciences.

The fast development in Internet research can be explained by three factors: the increasing market share compared to other survey modes, the public's increasing access to the Internet, and the costs associated with this method of data collection. The market share has steadily increased over the years. For example, the share for online interviewing grew from 5% in 2002 to 31% in 2008 for the generated turnover of member institutes of the German market research association (ADM, 2008). With respect to Internet use, about two thirds of surveyed European Union citizens use the Internet for personal use. "The proportion of citizens who had used the Internet for personal purposes in the past three months ranged from 41% in Romania to 91% in Denmark . . . . Other countries at the higher end of the ranking were Sweden, the Netherlands, Luxembourg, Finland, and the UK" (European Commission, 2008, p. 15). And finally, in terms of costs, according to the Global Prices Study by ESOMAR (2007), online research is the least expensive mode of data collection in most of Western Europe, the United States, Japan, and Australia. The results of a comparison of 592 participating research agencies show that in most cases online research is about three quarters of the price of telephone interviewing, which is often about three quarters of the cost of face-to-face interviewing.

Internet interviewing bears several similarities to other kinds of interviewing such as paper-and-pencil interviewing (PAPI), computer-assisted personal interviewing (CAPI), and computer-assisted telephone interviewing (CATI). In many ways it can be seen as a combination (or an extension) of these conventional interview modes. However, data collection via the Internet offers a number of advantages over traditional methods. Besides being less expensive, the Internet offers the possibility of graphical or animated presentation, such as a display of probabilities through pie charts or exploding scales. Furthermore, for some subpopulations, the response rate to an Internet survey is higher than to a traditional survey: Very busy or active people are more willing to do an interview at the time and place of their choosing. Moreover, the possibility of dividing interviews into short sections and spreading these over longer periods reduces respondent burden and actually allows for the collection of much more information from a respondent than would otherwise be possible. In addition, due to the absence of an interviewer, Internet surveys are less subject to social desirability bias. And finally, data collected via the Internet can be made available very quickly, even in real time.

This book brings together leading social scientists from both Europe and the United States to share experiences on Internet survey research and to report and discuss data collection through the Internet. The objectives of this book are to exchange views on the representativeness of Internet-based methods, to discuss how to reach difficult target groups, and to explore innovative applications of and promising experiments with Internet surveys (e.g., visual displays, interactive features, biomarkers, eye tracking, and noninterview data). Attention is also paid to mixed-mode designs, context effects, usability, the setup of Internet panels, and ethical considerations in Internet surveys.

The book project was facilitated through GESIS—Leibniz Institute for the Social Sciences (Mannheim, Germany), a leading European research and service center on innovative survey methods, together with CentERdata (Tilburg, the Netherlands), one of the main academic Internet survey institutes in Europe. GESIS facilitated a number of expert meetings in Mannheim, inviting scholars from both sides of the Atlantic. During two workshops participating researchers presented papers on their experiences with Internet surveys, shared research results, and exchanged views on the future of the Internet as a prime source for data collection in the social sciences. CentERdata conducted a number of small-scale experiments using its innovative Internet panel. Several chapters in this book are based on these experiments.

The main target groups of the book are academic and professional survey researchers, graduate students, and market researchers who use the Internet for data collection. Moreover, the book can be used in graduate courses on data collection methods and Internet use. What distinguishes this book from other sources on Internet surveys is the collaboration of leading Internet survey experts from around the world. The book includes the most pressing and current issues in Internet survey methodology. It contains comprehensive reviews and assessments on traditional issues such as strengths and weaknesses of Internet surveys, mixed-mode approaches, representativeness, and questionnaire design. Apart from theoretically grounding the topics, these chapters ensure high applicability by including specific guidance on how to do things right and best-practice examples when conducting Internet surveys. Other chapters focus on current issues (ethics, interactive probing, open-ended versus closed questions, paradata, hard-to-reach groups, context effects, usability) and promising new developments (probability-based Internet panels, eye tracking, biomarkers).

The book consists of three parts. Part I provides an overview of Internet survey research methodology, its strengths and challenges, and best practices. Part II focuses on Internet survey design, describing advanced methods and applications, and Part III discusses problems and solutions with respect to data quality and provides research insights into new promising applications.

Part I starts with a chapter by Jolene D. Smyth and Jennie E. Pearson that reviews the state of the art in Internet surveys and provides a snapshot of the current climate of Internet survey methodology. It starts with a brief history of Internet surveys and an assessment of their current uses, including why the Internet is such an appealing tool for conducting surveys. The strengths and weaknesses of Internet surveys are outlined with respect to the four main sources of survey error: coverage, sampling, measurement, and nonresponse error. The chapter also presents innovative ways researchers have begun to attempt to minimize each of these sources of error in Internet surveys, and discusses potential directions for future research and development.

The chapter by Edith D. De Leeuw and Joop J. Hox provides a theoretical background on mixed-mode designs for online research with an empirical knowledge base on the implications of mixed mode for data integrity, questionnaire design, and analysis. Mixed-mode designs promise better coverage and higher response rates but may lead to problems of data integrity, as the goal in mixed-mode studies is to combine data from different sources. The chapter discusses central issues for equivalence of measurement, gives an empirical review of existing studies comparing Internet surveys with traditional data collection methods, and focuses on data integrity issues. Furthermore, survey researchers can benefit from the guidance it provides about incorporating a mixed-mode approach in their own surveys.

Annette C. Scherpenzeel and Marcel Das describe the methodology to set up a panel that combines the technology of Internet surveys with a "true" longitudinal and probability-based sampling design. Not many long-running scientific panels in Europe and the United States are online panels; most use face-to-face or telephone interviews to collect data. But online interviewing has become a widespread method for access panels and volunteer panels. However, these panels often lack what is scientifically required for true longitudinal and probability-based panels. Nevertheless, the authors show that it is possible to combine the scientific standards for a true longitudinal and probability-based panel with the advantages of online interviewing as method of data collection. The chapter explains how such a panel can be built and maintained, taking the Dutch LISS panel as an example.

Annette C. Scherpenzeel and Jelke G. Bethlehem's chapter shows how the sampling and coverage problems from which many Internet panels suffer can be avoided or corrected. Many online panels rely on self-selection by respondents in constructing and maintaining their sampling frame. Therefore estimates can be seriously biased. Advanced adjustment weighting procedures to improve the quality of survey estimates are discussed. The LISS panel is an illustration of how a probability sample and traditional recruitment procedures can be used to build and maintain an Internet panel. The authors analyze how closely the LISS panel resembles the population using statistical information available at Statistics Netherlands.

In the final chapter of Part I, by Eleanor Singer and Mick P. Couper, the focus is on ethical requirements relating to informed consent in Internet surveys, specifically relating to data security and the collection of paradata. Internet surveys routinely capture user metrics such as browser characteristics, response latencies, changes in answers, and so on. Partial data from break-offs are also often used in analyses. Respondents' rights to make informed decisions requires disclosure about the collection of paradata, especially where respondents are identifiable. The authors argue that it is possible to frame this information so as not to adversely affect the research process and tested their assumptions in an experiment. Advice is presented together with a review of the existing literature on ethical standards in Internet surveys.

Part II, on advanced methods and applications of Internet surveys, opens with a chapter by Vera Toepoel and Don A. Dillman on the visual design of answer formats and the impact of visual design on the interpretability of survey questions. The chapter begins with a review of the accumulated knowledge of the last decade on how visual layout of questions in surveys influences respondent answers. The authors then systematically develop the theoretical background of processing visual information before continuing with a literature review covering challenges and solutions in everyday questionnaire design. The chapter also identifies additional issues that need to be addressed and ends with thirteen dos and don'ts with regard to visual design in survey questions.

Lars Kaczmirek's chapter deals with attention and usability in Internet surveys and its connection to how respondents answer survey questions. The author explains how concepts drawn from usability theory can be applied and tested in survey research. More specifically, an experiment presented in this chapter applied the concept of feedback to the question-answering process and tested the impact of different types of feedback on data quality. The results show that tailoring feedback to the answering process in a set of rating scales can improve data quality in Internet surveys.

Marije Oudejans and Leah Melani Christian, in their chapter, show how Internet surveys can utilize various types of design features to increase the interaction with respondents. They examine how the interactive nature of Internet surveys can help improve the quality of responses to open-ended questions. In an experiment the authors show how motivational statements and interactive probing influence whether people provide a response to open-ended questions, and explore how this affects the quality of responses.

Overall, survey design can benefit greatly from the interactive design possibilities in Internet surveys.

Peter Ester and Henk Vinken analyze the role of Internet surveys in studying highly sensitive social issues. Here, the absence of an interviewer is one of the greatest advantages of self-administered Internet surveys. The anonymous interview setting diminishes social desirability bias effects and has an advantage in revealing underlying motivations and feelings compared to traditional survey methods. Attitudes toward controversial issues are related to question ordering (e.g., consistency and contrast effects) and to open-ended versus closed question measurements. The chapter discusses the main outcomes of an Internet survey study on controversial issues with respect to different ordering of open-ended and closed questions.

Part III, on data quality and new research strategies, focuses on sample selection, measurement and nonresponse error, and new approaches for collecting and understanding online survey data.

Corrie M. Vis and Miquelle A. G. Marchand address the vital issue of underrepresentation of certain groups in Internet panel research. People with a lower income, people living in urbanized areas, and single people are examples of groups who are hard to reach in survey research. Internet panel surveys are no exception and create even higher thresholds for participation. The authors discuss why some groups are underrepresented in panels and which measures may be effective to reduce underrepresentation. The chapter includes various recommendations, based on concrete experience with the LISS panel, on how to (re)balance survey compliance and participation.

The chapter by Arthur van Soest and Arie Kapteyn is on mode and context effects in measuring household assets. Differences in answers in Internet and traditional surveys can be due to selection, mode, or context effects. The chapter exploits unique experimental data from the U.S. Health and Retirement Study (HRS) to analyze mode effects, controlling for arbitrary selection. Moreover, exploiting the panel nature of the data, the quality of core and Internet answers are compared. The chapter focuses on economic variables such as household assets, for which mode effects in Internet surveys have rarely been studied.

Dirk Heerwegh's chapter is on a highly topical issue: paradata. Paradata, also termed "process data," contain information about the primary data collection process (e.g., survey duration, interim status of a case, navigational errors in a survey questionnaire, etc.). Paradata can provide a means of additional control over, or understanding of, the quality of the primary data (the responses to the survey questions). The chapter describes how paradata can be collected in Internet surveys, some of its uses, and data preparation issues that may need to be addressed before paradata can be analyzed. The main focus is on paradata in the process of completing an Internet survey.

Mirta Galesic and Ting Yan discuss the use of eye-tracking techniques in survey research. Eye-tracking data are highly important in studying survey response processes. The chapter outlines a number of research questions that eye tracking can help to answer and presents an overview and history of eye-tracking techniques. The authors go into the comparative methodological, technical, and analytical advantages and disadvantages of eye tracking over more traditional, indirect methods for tracking respondents' behavior (such as measuring response times, recording changes in answers, and tracking mouse clicks and movements). The chapter furthermore provides a summary of a series of recent experiments in which respondents' eye movements were tracked while they were completing a CASI survey.

The chapter by Mauricio Avendano, Annette C. Scherpenzeel, and Johan P. Mackenbach examines the advantages and disadvantages of collecting biomarker data in population surveys, discusses the available methods for doing so, and explores the feasibility of collecting these data in an Internet panel. The authors report the results of a pilot that tested the feasibility of collecting data on blood cholesterol, saliva cortisol, and waist circumference in a subsample of the LISS panel. Collecting biomarker data in an Internet panel is feasible, but specific conditions need to be met for collecting, storing, and analyzing these data.

The final chapter, by Marcel Das, Peter Ester, and Lars Kaczmirek, draws the main conclusions of the book, puts these into perspective, and discusses the consequences for the research agenda on the use of Internet social surveys.

REFERENCES

ADM. (2008). *Jahresbericht 2008*. Frankfurt: Arbeitskreis. Deutscher Markt- und Sozialforschungsinstitute e. V. Retrieved from http://www.adm-ev.de/ pdf/Jahresbericht_04.pdf

ESOMAR. (2007). *Global Prices Study 2007*. Amsterdam: ESOMAR.

European Commission. (2008). *Flash Eurobarometer 241: Information Society as Seen by EU Citizens*. Retrieved from http://ec.europa.eu/public_opinion/flash/fl_241_en.pdf

Part I

Methodology in Internet Survey Research

2

Internet Survey Methods: A Review of Strengths, Weaknesses, and Innovations

Jolene D. Smyth
Survey Research and Methodology Program
Department of Sociology
University of Nebraska–Lincoln
Lincoln, Nebraska

Jennie E. Pearson
Socratic Technologies, Inc.
San Francisco, California

2.1 INTRODUCTION

Much like Earth's climate, the recent climate of survey methodology is in constant flux as advances in technology both bolster and challenge our beliefs about traditional data collection tools. Today, we have more methods for collecting data at our fingertips than ever before and an increasing ability and willingness to mix data collection modes within a single survey. However, there are few measures at our disposal that fully explain how the climate is changing, what forces are driving the changes, and what the final consequences may be. The rate and nature of change in the technologies that affect survey methodology are such that before we can fully understand one change, others are already under way. Moreover, it is virtually impossible to make reliable predictions about the state of the climate in the future. This perpetual state of change has existed from the first use of e-mail surveys in the 1980s through the development of full-fledged Internet surveys in the 1990s and early 2000s, and it will likely continue as the Internet and related technologies continue to develop.

In this chapter we will attempt to provide a snapshot of the current climate of Internet survey research. We will first examine where Internet surveys have come from and how they have developed to their current state. We will then turn to a discussion of the strengths and weaknesses of Internet surveys, organized by the sources of survey error: sampling and coverage error, measurement error, and nonresponse error. In doing so, we will discuss both situations in which the Internet seems ideally suited as a data collection tool and those in which it falls short. In addition, for each error type, we will highlight some of the exciting innovations that are currently being developed and deployed to improve our ability to conduct surveys via the Internet.

2.2 A BRIEF HISTORY OF INTERNET SURVEYS

Internet surveys have come a tremendous distance since their inception in the 1980s. In particular, a series of changes in the 1990s led to the shift from electronic mail surveys to surveys hosted on the Internet as we now know them. First, computer technology improved drastically and computers became more widely available and more commonly used for computer-assisted survey information collection (Couper & Nicholls, 1998). Second, the World Wide Web was developed in the early to mid-1990s. The World Wide Web is a network within the larger set of networks that we refer to as the Internet. What made the Web a suitable host for conducting surveys, as well as varied other uses, is that it used a standard protocol (hypertext transfer protocol or HTTP) that, in essence, served as a shared language allowing users to communicate with one another electronically from anywhere within the network. Third, the first browsers that allowed text and graphics to be displayed together (www.w3.org) and that facilitated the more widespread availability of the Web were developed. Finally, the development of programming languages, starting with HTML in the mid- to late 1990s, greatly expanded the utility of the Web and made it possible for surveyors to develop and post Web questionnaires.

In the simplest terms, an Internet survey consists of a researcher programming a questionnaire using a common programming language (e.g., HTML or others) and placing it on a server that is connected to the Internet. A respondent, located anywhere in the world, can then enter the URL (uniform resource locator or, less formally, Internet address) of the questionnaire into his or her browser software and access the questionnaire, which is translated from the complex programming language stored on the server to a viewable Internet page by the respondent's browser. Using the browser, the respondent can then enter answers to the survey questions. The answers the respondent provides are sent back to a database located on a server where they can be retrieved by the researcher (for a more detailed explanation, see Couper, 2008).

Unlike the development of other survey modes, the ability to build and field Internet surveys spread quickly from the experts to the general population. By 2000, Internet surveying was fully under way, including both probability Internet surveys and non-probability surveys and polls. With such rapid development and spread of Internet surveys, debates quickly arose as to whether the Internet would supplant the traditional survey modes or ruin the survey as we know it by making the ability to conduct surveys widely available with no quality control, regulations, or standards (Couper, 2005). In the ensuing nine years, Internet surveying has developed in ways likely unimagined by those who conducted the first electronic mail surveys, including the widespread availability of free Internet survey software and hosting services online so that anyone with an Internet connection and a computer can build and deploy an Internet survey. Needless to say, the debates continue to be waged.

While the bulk of Internet surveying has shifted to surveys hosted on servers and accessed by respondents using browsers and URLs, it is worth noting that the Internet continues to be used as it originally was—that is, as a means for electronically delivering questionnaires directly to respondents. The Internet has long been used to deliver e-mail surveys (Schaefer & Dillman, 1998), but more recently software has been developed that makes sending questionnaires as attachments to e-mails possible. In some cases, the attached questionnaires are Microsoft Word or Excel forms that can be answered and then returned via e-mail for data entry. Other software programs are also available in which a questionnaire can be designed as an Adobe PDF form that can be delivered as an e-mail attachment. The returned questionnaires are then aggregated and the software compiles the responses from them into a data set, thus eliminating data entry. While these data collection efforts certainly take advantage of the Internet as a convenient and speedy delivery method, the main focus of this chapter is on the use of the Internet as a means for hosting Internet surveys.

2.3 STRENGTHS AND WEAKNESSES OF INTERNET SURVEYS

Using the Internet to host surveys has several immediately recognizable advantages. One very appealing advantage is that Internet surveys can often be conducted at considerable cost savings compared to other survey modes. Purchasing the computers, servers, and software (i.e., the infrastructure) is perhaps the most costly factor in conducting Internet surveys, but once a questionnaire and its database are programmed and placed on a server, there is little to no further cost for collecting data from additional respondents. In contrast, additional respondents to a mail, telephone, or face-to-face survey mean additional printing and postage costs, data entry costs, interviewer wages, telephone charges, and/or travel costs. Moreover, Internet questionnaires have the distinct advantage of not being limited by geography in the same way as face-to-face, mail, and telephone surveys. In other words, there are few additional costs associated with surveying respondents who are spread over wide geographic areas such as across state or national boundaries, whereas postage, long-distance telephone rates, or travel costs accrue for mail, telephone, and face-to-face surveys conducted over such large geographic areas (Dillman & Bowker, 2001).

Another distinct advantage of Internet surveys is their potential to provide very timely data, in some cases even real-time data. If a survey request is sent via e-mail or to an Internet-enabled mobile device (see below for more discussion of mobile devices), responses can start coming back almost immediately, thus eliminating the postal mail delivery and return time that often slows down mail survey returns or the interviewer travel time that is part of face-to-face surveys. In addition, a large number of responses can be submitted quite quickly on the Internet, unlike telephone surveys, where the number of responses is directly tied to the number of interviewers making calls. Moreover, unlike mail surveys, responses to Internet surveys are already in electronic form, thus eliminating the additional time and effort needed for data entry and verification. Thus, preliminary analyses and reports can often be generated considerably more quickly with Internet surveys. For a comparison of the timing of return rates in mail and Internet surveys, see Dillman, Smyth, and Christian (2009, p. 258).

In addition to these practical advantages, Internet surveys also offer several design advantages. For example, respondent burden can be reduced through the automation of complex skip patterns in much the same way as in computer-assisted personal interviewing (Couper & Nicholls, 1998). Similarly, Internet surveys allow for the randomization of questions or response options and the utilization of real-time data verification tools (Peytchev & Crawford, 2005). That the survey is largely handled by computers offers another advantage: reduction of human effort and the potential for human processing errors (assuming, of course, the programming is correct to begin with). As a result of these types of design advantages, Internet questionnaires can be much more complex than self- or interviewer-administered paper-and-pencil questionnaires without additionally burdening respondents, interviewers, or key coders. In addition, unlike mail surveys, which are finalized when they are printed, Internet surveys allow for changes to be made if problems are caught early in the fielding period. Aside from these immediately attractive features, the Internet has a number of other strengths and weaknesses that are perhaps best discussed within the context of the four main sources of survey error: coverage, sampling, measurement, and nonresponse (Groves, 1989).

2.3.1 Coverage and Sampling

Coverage and sampling limitations have always been and continue to be the primary factors limiting the usefulness of the Internet as a survey mode, especially for general population surveys. Despite concerted efforts by several national governments, every country has considerable gaps in Internet coverage rates. For example, at the extreme low end of the continuum, less than 1% of the populations of many developing countries has Internet access. Internet surveys clearly have very limited utility in these countries, as they can only be used to survey incredibly specialized populations. At the other end of the continuum are a number of countries with relatively high Internet coverage. For example, according to a survey conducted as part of the Gallup World Poll, in June 2008, 88% of households in Norway had Internet access (Gallup WorldView, 2008). This is the same percentage reported by Internetworldstats.com based on information from the International Telecommunication Union from September 2007. Penetration rates in the United States appear to be slightly lower, with the Consumer Population Survey (CPS) estimating that in October 2007 nearly 62% of U.S. households had an Internet connection and the Pew Internet and American Life Project estimating the percentage at 65% in

May 2008. However, both the CPS and Pew data estimate that just over 70% of adults in the United States have access to the Internet from any location (e.g., home, libraries, work, etc.; Pew Internet & American Life Project, 2008). Internet penetration rates in the United States appear to be increasing over time, but at considerably lower rates than the explosive growth that occurred between 1995 and 2002, when access rates (from anywhere) grew from less than 15% to about 60% (Pew Internet and American Life Project, 2009).

The fact that Internet coverage rates range from 60% in some countries to nearly 90% in others might generate a fair amount of optimism that the Internet can compete with traditional survey modes in those countries. However, a closer look at coverage rates within these nations reveals several challenges that might temper some of that optimism. One such challenge is that the Internet access some have might not be appropriate for completing Internet surveys, either because the way the Internet can be used by individuals is restricted or because the Internet connection itself is not of high enough quality. As one example, according to Pew Internet and American Life Project tracking data collected in February and March 2007, nearly 2% of Internet users accessed the Internet only from work. Moreover, 8% of users accessed the Internet mostly from work, meaning they accessed it from home or somewhere else less than three to five times per week but from work three to five times per week or more (Pew Internet and American Life Project, 2007). These patterns of Internet access matter because many workplaces limit the ways employees can use their Internet and computing resources. Perhaps even more limiting though is that not everyone with Internet access has broadband access, which provides the quality of connection needed to complete many Internet surveys efficiently. For example, according to the most recent Pew Internet and American Life Project estimates from April and May 2008, only about 55% of U.S. adults have broadband access, although this is up from 47% the previous year (Horrigan, 2008a).

Another challenge Internet surveyors face is that Internet coverage is correlated with a number of important demographic and social factors. In the United States, for example, only 35% of those ages 65 and over have Internet access, while 90% of those ages 18–29 have access. In addition, non-Hispanic blacks are underrepresented, with only 59% having access, while 75% of non-Hispanic whites and 80% of English-speaking Hispanics have Internet access. Those who live in rural places and those with low education are also considerably underrepresented among Internet users in the United States (Pew Internet and American Life Project, 2008). The United States is by no means unique in this situation; similar trends exist elsewhere as well, although there is some variation between countries with respect to the dimensions Internet access is related to.

Such uneven Internet access means that certain populations will be severely underrepresented in Internet surveys, even in the countries with high Internet coverage overall. For studies where the measures of interest are not related to the dimensions along which Internet coverage is distributed, these gaps in coverage will not be problematic. However, because these dimensions are such basic aspects of social life, such coverage gaps are likely to pose problems for many survey topics.

While this chapter is primarily concerned with Internet surveys, it is also important to consider how Internet coverage compares to coverage in other survey modes. For example, it is now estimated that only 78% of households in the United States are covered by random-digit-dialing (RDD) landline telephone surveys (down from over 90% in the 1970s), and those who are excluded are more likely to be young adults, living with unrelated roommates, in poverty, or living in the South or Midwest (Blumberg & Luke, 2009). Moreover, the percentage of the population that has only cell phone service (i.e., no landline service and therefore not included in landline RDD surveys) has grown steadily in recent years and is expected to continue to do so in the near future. With the new availability of the U.S. Postal Service Delivery Sequence File (DSF; to be discussed in more detail below), coverage rates for mail surveys are believed to be considerably better—upward of 95% based on initial evaluations (Iannacchione, Staab, & Redden, 2003).

However, even if Internet coverage is judged to be adequate for the purposes of a particular survey, there are other challenges that must be overcome when it comes to sampling. One of the most frustrating challenges is that no country we are aware of has an adequate general population sampling frame, or list of Internet users and/or their e-mail addresses. Likewise, e-mail addresses lack standardization, making it impossible to develop an algorithm for random selection from among all possible addresses (as with RDD for the telephone).

In addition to these challenges, it is considered unethical in some countries to send e-mails requesting survey participation to people if the surveyor does not have a preexisting relationship with the recipient

(Council of American Survey Research Organizations, 2007). So, for example, a business owner could ethically send e-mail survey invitations to customers who have shared their e-mail address with the business, but a surveyor who wants to survey a more general population would likely not have the same right to send e-mail invitations due to the lack of a preexisting relationship with potential respondents.

The primary implication of these coverage and sampling limitations is that the Internet is limited for general population surveys in ways that other modes are not; however, when the target population is more specific, the Internet might be just as appropriate as another survey mode. Some notable examples include establishment surveys, employee surveys, online vendor customer satisfaction surveys, and surveys of university students or certain professional groups. In all of these cases, Internet penetration is often quite high and a relatively updated and exhaustive list of e-mail addresses can often be obtained for use as a sample frame.

2.3.1.1 Coverage and Sampling Innovations

Survey researchers have developed a number of innovative ways to address the types of coverage and sampling limitations discussed above. One of the earliest innovations was the development of Internet panels. Internet panels consist of survey respondents who are willing and able to answer more than one questionnaire online over some amount of time. The overriding goal behind Internet panels is to recruit large numbers of such respondents so that they are available to participate in intermittent surveys on a variety of topics, thereby circumventing many of the difficulties discussed above.

Generally speaking, there are two types of Internet panels: voluntary (or "access") and probability-based panels. Voluntary Internet panels use non-probability sampling methods, often relying on banners posted on popular Internet sites or mass advertisements posted online or in newspapers to catch the attention of potential respondents. Those who are interested can visit the Web site of the panel and sign up to participate. However, such voluntary participation means that these Internet panels are not representative of the general population. People with no Internet access have no chance to become members, and the fact that some people will respond to the advertisements while others do not introduces a strong self-selection effect. As such, voluntary Internet panels fall outside of probability-based surveys, thereby limiting their usefulness mainly to exploratory research. For a more complete discussion of volunteer Internet panels, see Bethlehem and Stoop (2007) or Dillman et al. (2009, pp. 336–343).

Probability-based Internet panels use decidedly different recruitment strategies in an attempt to recruit and maintain a sample that is representative of the general population. For example, the Internet panel that forms the backbone of much of this book, the LISS panel, consists of 5,000 households that were recruited to be representative of the Dutch population. The households were initially selected from a sample frame of Dutch households in close collaboration with Statistics Netherlands and were then contacted by a face-to-face or telephone interviewer and asked to join the panel. Those who did not have Internet access, and therefore would have been left out of a voluntary Internet panel, were provided with access, extensive support, and training so they could participate (for more information about the LISS panel, see Chapter 4). By bringing the sampling methods of a different mode (i.e., face-to-face) to bear on developing an Internet panel, developers of the LISS panel were able to overcome many of the coverage difficulties of conducting Internet surveys of the general population. In addition, they have a probability-based sample of households that have committed to completing several surveys a month.

While the development of Internet panels represents an innovative response to the difficulties of coverage and sampling in Internet surveys, they are not without challenges. In fact, they share several challenges with more traditional longitudinal surveys, in which the same sample of respondents is surveyed multiple times. In both cases, retention and the potential for conditioning effects are very salient, as either of these can undermine results. On one hand, low retention rates threaten the representativeness of the panel. On the other hand, surveying the same people over and over has the potential to influence their responses, either because it changes the way they interact with the survey (i.e., measurement error) or because answering questions about behaviors might lead the respondents to change those behaviors (i.e., they are no longer like the general public because of the survey experience itself). As such, panel retention and conditioning effects are both topics of high research importance to those operating or using data from Internet panels (for more information on panel attrition and conditioning, see Toepoel, 2008).

Within the United States, researchers working outside the Internet panel model have borrowed ideas from those operating Internet panels in renewed efforts to survey the general public using Internet surveys. The innovation here is in their use of alternative modes with better coverage and/or sampling frames to invite respondents to complete an Internet survey. The availability of the U.S. Postal Service's DSF, in particular, has provided a catalyst for this type of research. The DSF is a list of every postal delivery drop point (i.e., address) serviced in the United States, and preliminary investigations into its quality as a sample frame have been promising (Iannacchione et al., 2003; Link, Battaglia, Frankel, Osborn, & Mokdad, 2008). With this sample frame, researchers have shown that it is possible to select a sample of households, mail them an Internet survey invitation (including instructions for in-house selection of a respondent), and obtain a reasonable response. For example, in one study researchers sent households in a small metropolitan region in northern Idaho and eastern Washington a postal mail letter requesting that the household member with the most recent birthday complete an Internet survey containing 51 questions. The letter emphasized the desire to receive responses via the Internet so that results could be summarized more quickly, but also explained that a paper version of the questionnaire would be sent in about two weeks so that responses could be obtained from respondents who do not have access to the Internet. Using this implementation strategy, the researchers obtained responses from 41% of sampled households via the Internet and an additional 14% via the paper version, for a final response rate of 55% (Dillman et al., 2009, pp. 234–236; Dillman, Smyth, Christian, & O'Neill, 2008).

2.3.2 Measurement

From the perspective of understanding and minimizing measurement error, Internet surveys have a number of strengths and limitations. From a questionnaire design point of view, the Internet offers the advantage of being able to utilize complex questionnaires and employ skip patterns that might be sources of error in a mail survey. From a respondent perspective, because it is a self-administered rather than interviewer-administered survey mode, the Internet provides a certain amount of privacy, which may lead to more honest reporting on sensitive questions (De Leeuw, 2005, 2008). In addition, respondents to Internet surveys have more control over the pace of the survey so, if they are motivated, they can slow down and think through their responses more thoroughly or take the time to consult records, more so than might be the case in a telephone survey, where the interviewer largely sets the pace of the survey (De Leeuw, 2008).

However, the Internet is also a more dynamic medium in the sense that it is not uncommon for Internet users to flit from one task or screen to another (De Leeuw, 2008). For example, a 2004 Kaiser Family Foundation survey of a nationally representative sample of U.S. students in 3rd to 12th grade found that 39% of children ages 8 to 18 reported engaging in multiple computer activities such as e-mailing and instant messaging "most of the time" that they are using a computer, and an additional 25% reported doing so "some of the time." Only 14% reported never engaging in multiple computer activities, and 19% reported doing so "little of the time" (Roberts, Foehr, & Rideout, 2005, p. 54). While answering an Internet survey, respondents have an incredible array of possible distractions at their fingertips. Moreover, as is also the case with mail surveys, the absence of an interviewer means there is less social pressure to finish the survey, which can translate into decreased motivation to continue and increased likelihood of breaking off.

There are also considerable advantages and disadvantages associated with the questionnaire design flexibility introduced by Internet surveys. On one hand, surveyors have more capabilities for including color, graphics, and other visual features than in mail surveys, where the costs of printing largely inhibit their use. Surveyors can even integrate pictures, video, and sound into their Internet surveys. The flexibility of Internet surveys in this regard is perhaps best illustrated by research examining the feasibility and consequences of utilizing animated agent interviewers (Cassell & Miller, 2008; Person, D'Mello, & Olney, 2008). We might say that designers are limited with respect to these features only by their imaginations and computer programming abilities (or budgets). In fact, this relatively affordable design potential has been a significant factor underlying many researchers' excitement about the Internet as a survey mode.

On the other hand, the development of new design features for Internet surveys can quickly outpace surveyors' ability to research and learn about their consequences for data quality. As such, there is much that we do not yet know about how Internet survey design features influence responses. The research that has been done to date shows that, when used intentionally and strategically, some design features can improve measurement in Internet surveys, but it also suggests a need for caution in using many design features, as they may lead to unintended measurement effects. Some examples will help illustrate these points (for more, see Chapter 7 in this volume).

In one example, Christian, Dillman, and Smyth (2007) demonstrate how a series of visual and symbolic manipulations of answer spaces to a question asking students to report the date they began their studies improved the percentage of students reporting in the proper format (two digits for the month and four digits for the year) from 45% to 96%. Using visual design in this way has great potential for helping respondents get answers right the first time and avoid the unpleasant experience of receiving repeated error messages. In another example, Smyth, Dillman, Christian, and McBride (2009) were able to motivate late respondents to an Internet survey (i.e., those who responded in the second half of the fielding period and who are, therefore, possibly the least motivated) to provide more information in open-ended questions by increasing the size of the answer box provided to them. Presumably, the increased size of the answer box communicated to these respondents that more information was desired from them. For more information on how design features specific to Internet surveys affect response, see Dillman et al. (2009) or Couper (2008). These studies have demonstrated how visual design can be used strategically to improve responses. However, other studies have demonstrated how visual design can influence responses in unintended ways.

In an experiment on the effects of pictures included in Internet surveys to supplement the question text, Couper, Tourangeau, and Kenyon (2004) asked Internet respondents how often they did six activities (took overnight trips in the past year, attended sporting events in the past year, went out to eat in the past month, attended live music events in the past year, listened to recorded music in the past week, and took shopping trips in the past month). Respondents were randomly assigned to receive these questions with (1) no accompanying picture, (2) a low-frequency picture, (3) a high-frequency picture, or (4) both pictures. For example, for the shopping trip question, the low-frequency picture was of a department store selling clothing and the high-frequency picture was of a grocery store. For all six questions, there were significant differences between the four versions, and in four of the six questions the high-frequency version led to significantly higher reporting of the activity. In the shopping trip example, the mean number of trips reported was 7.73 for those who received the picture of the department store selling clothing compared to 9.07 for those who received the picture of the grocery store. Additional information collected in the survey suggests that the content of the pictures affected both how narrowly or broadly respondents interpreted the question and what memories they recalled as they formulated their answers. In later work, Couper, Conrad, and Tourangeau (2007) showed that pictures can also trigger contrast effects in Internet surveys. In this experiment they found that respondents presented with a picture of a sick woman in a hospital bed rated their health significantly higher than respondents who were presented with a picture of a fit woman jogging (means of 3.30 and 3.05, respectively, on a 5-point scale when the picture was placed in the question area). Thus, it appears that what constituted good health for respondents was affected by the picture accompanying the question. Both of these studies show that pictures, which are often inserted into Internet surveys to help capture respondents' interest and motivate them, can have considerable effects on responses.

Other research has shown that even more subtle visual design cues can affect responses. For example, Smyth, Dillman, Christian, and Stern (2006) found that using spacing and headings to organize response options into subgroups by topic significantly affected how respondents interpreted the response task. In this study, college students were asked about the benefits of a new student recreation center and provided with a list of six possible benefits. In one version, the benefits were grouped into "health benefits" and "academic benefits" and in the other version there was no such grouping. Results indicated that when the options were grouped, respondents were more likely to select answers from each grouping (70% did so) than when the options were not grouped (41%). In a third experimental treatment, respondents received the grouped response options as well as an instruction to select the best answer. In this treatment respondents remained more likely to select answers of both types than in the ungrouped version (66% did so), but they were also more likely to limit their selections to one item within each group than were respondents in the grouped version with no instruction. This finding suggests that the visual grouping influenced how the instruction to select the best answer was interpreted (i.e., it seems to have been interpreted as an instruction to select the best answer *from each group*). Thus, a visual design decision that is sometimes made to help respondents more efficiently process response options was shown to influence how they interpreted the intent of the question and thereby to influence their responses. These studies along with a handful of others (Christian, 2003; Christian, Dillman, & Smyth,

2008; Christian, Parsons, & Dillman, 2009; Couper, Tourangeau, Conrad, & Crawford, 2004; Potaka, 2008; Toepoel, 2008; Tourangeau, Couper, & Conrad, 2004, 2007) demonstrate both some of the potential and some of the dangers of using certain visual elements in Internet surveys.

While many aspects of visual design, such as those discussed above, can be easily controlled by the Internet survey designer, others cannot. One of the biggest practical challenges for Internet surveyors is that respondents can access Internet surveys using a broad array of hardware, software, and Internet connection configurations, each of which can affect how the survey appears to the respondent. At the ideal extreme is the respondent who accesses the Internet on an up-to-date computer with a high-speed Internet connection and who uses a common screen resolution and a widely used, fully updated browser with client-side scripting such as JavaScript, Java, and Flash enabled. For example, Kaczmirek and Thiele (2006) found that nearly all online applicants to the University of Mannheim in Germany had JavaScript enabled on their computers, 93% to 95% had Java enabled, and nearly 94% had Flash enabled. Designing for these respondents is less challenging because their configuration of technology most closely matches the technology that is likely being used by the Internet programmer. In other words, what the programmer sees is very likely what the respondent will see. At the other extreme are respondents who access an Internet survey through small, mobile handheld devices such as cell phones when it was intended to be answered using a computer. Designing for these respondents is complicated by the fact that what usually goes on an entire computer screen has to be reduced to only a few square inches. In between these two extremes are the bulk of respondents who have computers of various ages, an array of types and speeds of Internet connections, and a wide assortment of browser software programs, some of which likely have never been upgraded. Moreover, respondents can, and many do, change their own user settings. All of these factors can influence the way an Internet survey appears to the respondent in ways unanticipated by the surveyor, and any such changes have the potential to affect measurement in unforeseen ways.

As just one example, Google's new browser, Chrome, which was released in the summer of 2008, provides an illustration of how innovation in browser software raises new questions for Internet survey designers. In Chrome, the user can modify the size of open-ended text boxes by clicking and dragging the lower right corner of the box. This new capability on the part of respondents is potentially important inasmuch as previous research has shown that the size of the answer box influences the amount of information respondents provide (Couper, Traugott, & Lamias, 2001; Smyth et al., 2009). Penetration of Google Chrome is still very small, around 4%; however, this browser innovation is a good example of how technological advances in Internet computing and programming can raise new questions and challenges for Internet survey researchers.

2.3.2.1 A New Measurement Challenge: Handheld Internet Surveys

According to the most recent report by the Pew Internet and American Life Project (Horrigan, 2008b), 75% of Americans own either a cell phone or a personal digital assistant (PDA). In addition, almost two-thirds of Americans (62%) report using their mobile device for non-telephony-related activities, including accessing the Internet, sending/receiving e-mail, texting, taking pictures or video, and searching maps or for directions (Horrigan, 2008b), and 19% of cell phone/PDA users report having ever used the device for sending or receiving e-mail. Of these, 8% say they send or receive e-mail using a cell phone/PDA on a typical day. As the Internet connection capabilities for mobile devices continue to improve (e.g., the availability of 3G [third-generation] technology), these numbers are likely to increase such that more and more activities that can be performed on a personal computer, including Internet surveys, are increasingly done using handheld devices.

Electronic portable devices are already widely used in health studies for quality of life measurements and pain assessments (Caro, Caro, Caro, Wouters, & Juniper, 2001; Marceau, Link, Jamison, & Carolan, 2007; Palmblad & Tiplady, 2004; Peters et al., 2000) and in survey research and marketing research within Europe and Asia (Okazaki, 2007). Clinics and hospitals are also rapidly adopting portable electronic devices to assist health care providers in diagnosis (Coopmans & Biddle, 2008) and new physician training. Currently, handheld devices are being used for research in four ways: (1) responding to online surveys that were never intended to be viewed via a mobile phone, (2) responding to online surveys intended to be taken via a mobile phone (Fuchs, 2008; Okazaki, 2007; Peytchev & Hill, 2008), (3) sending reminders via text messaging (e.g., SMS) for non-mobile-based surveys (Balabanis, Mitchell, & Heinonen-Mavrovouniotis, 2007; Fuchs, 2008; Steeh, Buskirk, & Callegaro, 2007), and (4) conducting surveys

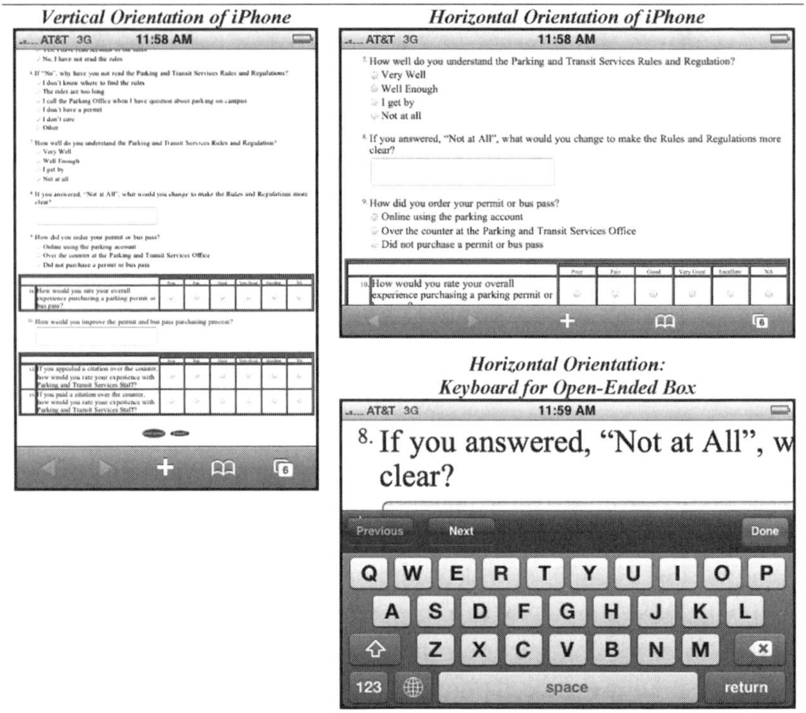

FIGURE 2.1
Survey screenshots from an iPhone.

designed for use on a mobile device that is not connected to the Internet or telephone except for uploading data at the end of data collection (Caro et al., 2001; Marceau et al., 2007; Palmblad & Tiplady, 2004; Peters et al., 2000).

The implications of the use of mobile devices in these four ways are only beginning to be understood in survey research. The ease and speed of collecting data through handheld devices is a great benefit to survey researchers and respondents, and indeed opens up new possibilities such as experience sampling, but the impact on survey costs and total error is an area in need of more exploration. Figure 2.1 demonstrates some of the most obvious design challenges raised by the use of mobile devices. These screenshots were taken on an iPhone, which has one of the largest screens available among cell phones (3.5 inch diagonal). The survey used a scrolling design in which all 13 questions appeared on one page. The questions shown here were selected because they represent one of each type of question used in the survey. The upper-left screenshot shows how the survey is displayed in vertical format, while the screenshot in the upper right of the figure shows the same survey in horizontal format. The advantage to the horizontal format is that the material does not have to be as small, but this format requires considerably more vertical scrolling (and is only available on certain mobile devices). Finally, the screenshot in the bottom right shows that it is possible to zoom in on questions to make them more readable, but doing so cuts off part of the question and makes it necessary to scroll horizontally to see the rest. This screenshot also demonstrates how invoking the keyboard to answer the question reduces the visible portion of the survey even further, in this case almost entirely hiding the answer box that the respondent is typing in. As these examples illustrate, fitting an Internet survey onto even a relatively large mobile phone screen requires a considerable amount of condensing and shrinking of information and the use of only the simplest question formats and designs.

Because of these design challenges, the issue with mobile devices that should be of greatest concern to market and survey researchers in the short term is probably the ability of respondents to access online surveys via their mobile phones when the survey itself was not designed for those devices. Previous research has consistently shown the visual design and layout of questionnaires has a significant impact on the answers respondents select (for a review, see Dillman et al., 2009), but when respondents use their mobile devices to access Internet surveys that were only intended to be viewed using a computer, it is unclear what visual stimulus they will receive.

There are several ways designers might approach this problem. One way is to create all Internet surveys in the simplest way possible by eliminating extra graphical features and using only the most basic question types and formats. Another option is to design a mobile-Internet version of online questionnaires to be fielded simultaneously with the regular computer version in the same way that many Internet sites have alternative versions of their Web pages designed specifically for mobile devices (e.g., the *New York Times*, Yahoo, Flickr, Kayak, and others). A third alternative is to restrict the surveys to computer access only and exclude mobile users who cannot or will not access it using a computer.

Unless the third option of excluding mobile users is used, it is important to understand how differences in the appearance of the survey across devices might affect responses. Research into these effects is scarce, but Peytchev and Hill (2008) have found that images and pictures had very small, if any, effect on responses, whereas they have been found to have larger effects in Internet surveys (Couper et al., 2007; Couper, Tourangeau, & Kenyon, 2004). Likewise, they found that the presentation of multiple items on one page versus items spread over multiple pages did not appear to increase interitem correlations for those answering on mobile devices as has sometimes been found to occur in computer Internet surveys (Couper et al., 2001; Tourangeau et al., 2004). These different findings on mobile devices might occur because the screen is so small that it makes certain visual features insignificant to respondents. On the other hand, Peytchev and Hill (2008) identified several other design features such as scale frequency ranges and question order that had very similar effects among mobile-device users as have been reported in Internet surveys completed through computers.

2.3.2.2 Measurement Innovations

As mentioned above, one of the major challenges with Internet surveys is that different hardware, software, and user settings affect the way Internet surveys look to the respondent. This is problematic because research has shown that even small changes in the visual appearance of questionnaires can affect the way questions are interpreted and answered. Thus, it is desirable from a measurement perspective to ensure that all respondents receive similar visual stimuli, although this need should be balanced with accessibility needs of users (for more information about designing for accessibility, see http://www.w3.org/WAI and http://www.webaim.org). Over the years, Internet survey programmers have learned more and more about how to standardize the visual appearance of surveys across respondents. One way this is currently being done is through the use of cascading style sheets (CSS), which can be used to apply different styles (i.e., fonts, font sizes, colors, widths, etc.) based on user settings such as screen resolution in order to minimize variation in the visual appearance of the survey across users without changing the survey content itself.

Internet survey designers have also found they can take advantage of HTML tables with the column widths set as proportions of the screen, rather than fixed widths, to help control what respondents see (Couper, 2008, pp. 199–201; Dillman et al., 2009, p. 201). The use of the tables ensures that content is not off the screen and out of view when users have small screens, have low monitor resolutions, or have shrunk their browser windows. In essence, using proportional-width columns ensures that the content of the screen maintains its position and proportion relative to other content under varying screen and window conditions.

Others have taken advantage of the flexibility of the Internet to design more interactive features that can help respondents complete some of the more complex survey tasks we often request of them. Questions that ask respondents to rank order items provide one example of a complex survey task that can be simplified on the Internet. Ranking questions are often difficult for respondents because they require them to remember and consider a lot of information at one time. In addition, in paper-and-pencil formats, respondents have to mentally keep track of which items they have placed in their ranking and which ones still need to be ranked. One study found that nearly a quarter of respondents to a paper-and pencil-survey committed errors in responding to a question in which eight items were to be ranked (Stern, 2006). In contrast, Internet survey designers can use scripting languages that allow the respondent to drag and drop the ranked items into the order they would like (Neubarth, 2008). This technique allows the respondent to physically locate each item relative to the others and provides a visual reminder both of the ordering they have provided and of which items still need to be incorporated into the ranking. With this visual record, the respondent does not need to hold nearly as much information in working memory. In addition, editing the response may be easier because the items remain visible as they are shifted around (in contrast to editing with paper and pencil, which requires erasing information and then reentering it).

Another question format that is receiving research and development attention in Internet surveys is the visual analog scale. A visual analog scale typically consists of a horizontal line with verbal labels anchoring it at each end. To provide a rating on the scale, respondents move a marker along the line and place it where they would like their rating to be. Recent research has shown that visual analog scales are comparable to more traditional ordinal scales with respect to response distributions (Couper, Tourangeau, Conrad, & Singer, 2006) and validity (Thomas & Couper, 2007), and some argue that the interval level measurement made possible by visual analog scales is a great advantage (Funke & Reips, 2008). These studies also consistently show that these scales take longer for respondents to complete, a finding that has been interpreted by some as an indication of increased respondent burden. However, Funke and Reips (2008) argue that the increase in completion time may in fact be due to deeper cognitive processing of the visual analog scale compared to a categorical scale.

A number of other features have also been developed and researched in Internet surveys. One early example is the drop-down menu (Couper, Tourangeau, Conrad et al., 2004; Heerwegh & Loosveldt, 2002a). Other features include links to definitions or examples (Conrad, Couper, Tourangeau, & Peytchev, 2006), automatic calculation tools (i.e., fixed summation validation) (Couper, 2008, pp. 121–123; Peytchev & Crawford, 2005), progress indicators (Crawford, Couper, & Lamias, 2001; Heerwegh & Loosveldt, 2006), and open-ended question probes (Holland & Christian, 2007, and Chapter 9 in this volume). Each of these features has the potential to help respondents through the response process, but they do not come without costs. First, many of them rely on respondents having client-side scripting (e.g., JavaScript, Java, or Flash) enabled on their computers. The percentage of browsers with JavaScript disabled is estimated to be around 5% to 6% (http://www.w3schools.com/browsers/browsers_stats.asp and http://www.thecounter.com/stats/2008/June/javas.php, respectively). Depending on the population of interest, this may or may not have significant impact on the overall survey results. Second, use of these features requires complex programming, although some survey software programs are available that make implementation of them easier. Nevertheless, anytime such features are used, extra testing is needed to ensure that they work appropriately across various hardware and software configurations. Third, how the features themselves are designed can significantly affect their likelihood of being used as well as the responses they obtain. Thus, while these features represent innovative approaches to using the Internet as a survey mode, they should be used with caution and considerations of both the positives and negatives. For more in-depth reviews and considerations of each such feature, see Couper (2008) and Dillman et al. (2009).

Another innovation comes with the application of Internet survey data collection using mobile devices for time-sensitive topics. For example, researchers and practitioners in the health and medical sciences have been able to take advantage of such devices to improve measurement of pain and other health symptoms because they allow real-time data collection (Stone & Broderick, 2007). In other words, whereas other survey modes, including Internet surveys accessed using computers, are subject to memory and recall biases associated with retrospective reporting, mobile handheld devices allow researchers to collect nearly instant responses, thus minimizing such biases. For more information about this special case of Internet surveying, see the 2007 special edition of *Pain Medicine* devoted to real-time data collection.

A final measurement innovation is the use of Internet survey experiments to better understand various aspects of measurement. In part because of the cost and time savings associated with fielding Internet survey experiments compared to paper-and-pencil survey experiments, the Internet has become a central component of experimental survey methodology research. In fact, Internet survey experiments have been central to the rapid development of visual design theory in the past decade. An additional feature of the Internet that has helped provide new understanding of the effects of visual design as well as other Internet survey design features is the availability of paradata. Paradata are extra data that can be collected during the survey about the response process itself as opposed to the actual responses (Heerwegh, 2003; Stern, 2008; and Chapter 13 in this volume). Examples include how much time respondents spent on each page and records of mouse clicks they made on pages irrespective of their final responses. Examination of paradata has helped uncover mechanisms underlying some reported Internet survey effects such as subtraction effects in multiple-answer questions (Stern, 2008). Table 2.1 provides a summary of the measurement research areas discussed in this chapter with suggested references.

2.3.3 Nonresponse

In a meta-analysis of 68 Internet surveys reported in 49 studies, Cook, Heath, and Thompson (2000) reported a mean response rate of 39.6%. A more recent meta-analysis reported in 2007 showed a mean response rate of 32.7% (calculated from Table 1 in Lozar Manfreda, Bosnjak, Berzelak, Haas, & Vehovar, 2008). However, perhaps more informative is that in the Cook et al. (2000) analysis, the mean response rate had a standard deviation of 19.6%. As these numbers indicate, response rates to Internet surveys are highly variable. It is not uncommon to hear of some Internet surveys with response rates in the single digits and others that produce response rates quite comparable to survey modes such as mail and telephone (Dillman et al., 2009, pp. 234–236; Kaplowitz, Hadlock, & Levine, 2004). However, overall, Internet surveys can be expected to yield response rates ranging from 6 to 15 percentage points lower than other survey modes (Lozar Manfreda et al., 2008).

TABLE 2.1

Summary of Measurement Research Areas and Suggested References

Research Area	Suggested References
Animated agents	Cassell & Miller, 2008; Person et al. 2008
Automatic calculation	Couper, 2008; Peytchev & Crawford, 2005
Drag-and-drop ranking	Neubarth, 2008
Drop-down menus	Couper et al. 2004; Heerwegh & Loosveldt, 2002a
Grids/matrices	Couper et al. 2001; Tourangeau et al. 2004
Images	Couper, 2008; Couper et al. 2004; Couper et al. 2007
Mobile Internet surveys	Fuchs, 2008; Peytchev & Hill, 2008
Link definitions	Conrad et al. 2006
Open-ends/interactive probes	Holland & Christian, 2007; Smyth et al. (2009)
Paradata	Heerwegh, 2003; Stern, 2008
Programming strategies	Couper, 2008
Progress indicators	Crawford et al. 2001; Heerwegh & Loosveldt, 2006
Visual analog scales	Couper et al. 2006; Funke & Reips, 2008
Visual design	Dillman et al. 2009; Tourangeau et al. 2004
General overview	Couper, 2008; Dillman et al. 2009

One reason for such wide variation is that Internet survey response rates vary considerably over different target populations. Internet surveys of specialized populations tend to produce higher response rates (Dillman et al., 2009; Kaplowitz et al., 2004), while those of more general populations tend to yield lower response rates (Vehovar, Batagelj, Lozar Manfreda, & Zaletel, 2002). Two factors likely contribute to these differences. First, it is easier to tailor the survey topic to specialized populations, thus increasing the salience of such surveys for sample members (Groves, Presser, & Dipko, 2004; Groves, Singer, & Corning, 2000), thereby increasing response rates (Cook et al., 2000). Second, when surveyors opt to use Internet surveys rather than other survey modes for a specialized population, it is often because they know that the population they are targeting has acceptable Internet access and is fairly proficient at using computers and the Internet. Within the general population, there is much more variation in Internet access, skill levels of users, and willingness to share information online.

Another factor that strongly affects the final survey response rate is the recruitment protocol that is used. For example, the cost savings associated with using only e-mail contacts are one feature of Internet surveys that make them so desirable, but there are several reasons e-mail contacts by themselves may not be sufficient for Internet surveys. Foremost among them is the high likelihood that the e-mail will never reach the respondent. Even the smallest errors or typos in e-mail addresses will result in non-delivery (Vehovar et al., 2002). Likewise, e-mails often get caught in spam filters or routed to bulk mail folders that are rarely, if ever, checked. Another reason e-mail contacts may lack effectiveness is because e-mail is a vehicle for many Internet scams. As a result, many Internet users are rightly very suspicious of e-mail invitations, especially those containing links to other Web sites, as is the case with most Internet survey invitations.

Other aspects of the contact protocol have also been shown to affect response rates. In their meta-analysis, Cook et al. (2000) found that among the biggest predictors were the number of contacts used and personalization of contacts. With respect to the number of contacts used, they showed that additional reminders considerably increased response rates. In fact, a more recent study showed that using four reminders as opposed to none increased response rates by 37 percentage points (Olsen, Call, & Wygant, 2005). However, Cook et al. (2000) also show that the number of contacts can reach a point of diminishing returns, and they warn that additional contacts might become a nuisance rather than an inducement to non-respondents. Personalization of contacts also increases response rates. One study found that personalizing e-mail invitations sent to students by using their first and last names in the salutation ("Dear [first name] [last name]") rather than a general salutation ("Dear student") increased response rates by nearly 8 percentage points (Heerwegh, 2005). Likewise, Joinson and Reips (2007) found that personalization of the e-mail salutation increased the odds of a response by nearly 4.5 percentage points.

The use of incentives is another feature of the recruitment protocol that strongly affects response rates. However, because cash, which is the most effective incentive in mail surveys (Church, 1993; Dillman, 2000; James & Bolstein, 1992), cannot be sent over the Internet, researchers have begun to examine the effectiveness of alternative incentives. Examples include electronic gift certificates, gift cards, or monetary incentives provided through such services as PayPal (Birnholtz, Horn, Finholt, & Bae, 2004). Incentives such as these have been shown to increase response rates compared to sending no incentive but do not increase them as much as a prepaid cash incentive. Birnholtz et al. (2004), for example, showed that a cash incentive sent via postal mail resulted in considerably higher response rates (57%) than either a gift certificate sent by postal mail (40%) or an electronic gift certificate sent via e-mail (32%). Thus, cash still seems to be the most effective survey incentive and, in fact, has been shown to reduce nonresponse bias (Groves et al., 2006). Nonetheless, because of the challenges of delivering prepaid incentives in Internet surveys, many surveyors have instead opted to utilize a lottery or prize drawing as the incentive. While this is a very popular alternative, the research shows that it is fairly ineffective at increasing response rates (Brennan, Rae, & Parackal, 1999; Cobanoglu & Cobanoglu, 2003; Göritz, 2006; Porter & Whitcomb, 2003; for an exception, see Bosnjak & Tuten, 2003). However, Tuten, Galesic, and Bosnjak (2004) demonstrated that prize drawings and lotteries might be made more effective by structuring them so that respondents receive notification of their win/loss status immediately after they complete the survey rather than at a later date.

Another factor specific to Internet surveys that has been shown to affect response rates is the method given to respondents to gain access to the survey. From a data quality perspective, it is highly desirable to take steps to ensure that only sample members can gain access to the survey and that they can complete the survey only once. In order to ensure these two things, sample members are generally assigned unique identifiers that have to be used to access the survey. There are two ways this can be done. In manual login, sample members are provided with an access code that must be entered on the survey's first page to gain entrance to the rest of the survey. By comparison, automatic login consists of embedding each respondent's unique access code into the survey URL that is sent to them (so each respondent receives a slightly different URL). When a sample member clicks on or enters his or her URL, the member is automatically logged in to the survey. Research has shown that automatic login significantly increases response rates (by nearly 5 percentage points) over manual login, perhaps because it is less burdensome to sample members (Crawford et al., 2001; Heerwegh & Loosveldt, 2003). However, several studies have found evidence that respondents who manually log in to surveys provide more complete data (i.e., answer more questions and use fewer nonsubstantive answer categories; Heerwegh & Loosveldt, 2002b, 2003).

2.3.3.1 Nonresponse Innovations

Because Internet surveying is so new and much of the research regarding contact and implementation strategies is relatively new within Internet surveying, many of the discoveries discussed above might still be considered recent innovations. However, we want to focus on three other innovations that have been developed in hopes of overcoming some of the nonresponse challenges discussed above.

The first of these innovations involves employing a different mode to contact sample members and invite them to participate in Internet surveys. This strategy was discussed above in the coverage and sampling section because it allows researchers to use sampling frames usually used in other modes that have better coverage than any Internet sample frames. However, using a different contact mode also represents an innovation with respect to nonresponse because it allows surveyors to overcome many of the problems associated with e-mail contacts that limit response rates compared to other modes. Examples include e-mail not reaching its intended recipients; e-mail being perceived as somehow illegitimate, inauthentic, or even dangerous; and the inability to utilize prepaid token cash incentives with e-mail. All of these problems can be overcome by using a different contact mode either to supplement or as a replacement for e-mail. As one example, between spring 2003 and spring 2007, five Internet surveys of undergraduate students at Washington State University (WSU) produced response rates ranging from 50 to 59% (Dillman et al., 2009, p. 39). In each of these surveys, the implementation protocol started with an advance letter sent to students by postal mail. The advance letter was followed by supporting e-mails that provided students with a clickable link to the survey as well as additional postal reminders consistent with the tailored design method (Dillman, 2000). In this case, the decision to start the implementation with a postal mail advance notice was initially made because e-mail addresses were available for only about two thirds of the students in the sample frame (i.e., a coverage problem). However, the use of the postal letters also provided another means for notifying students about the survey when their e-mail addresses did not work for the reasons discussed above. In addition, the postal letter, printed on university stationery, provided evidence as to the legitimacy and authenticity of the survey request, so when the e-mails began arriving, they were less likely to be mistaken for a scam or as spam. Finally, the use of the postal mail advance letter allowed the surveyors to include a $2 bill in the mailing as an advance token incentive (Dillman et al., 2009, p. 39).

Another innovative line of research that is being undertaken is aimed at finding ways to reduce the perceived burden and difficulty of answering

Internet surveys for those who are less familiar with computers and the Internet. For example, in the community survey reported by Dillman et al. (2009), a set of instructions were included with the survey request that walked the respondent step by step through the process of finding the survey, logging in, and answering questions. An example of the instructions used and a more thorough discussion of its design can be found in Dillman et al. (2009, pp. 286–287). While data assessing the success of such an instruction is not yet available, this procedure seems promising, as it has the potential to increase response rates among the least likely respondents and thus perhaps reduce nonresponse bias. At the very least, it makes the question of how to overcome computer and Internet skill deficiencies much more central to survey methodologists and starts what we hope will be an ongoing area of research into implementation methods that might minimize or solve this practical problem.

The final nonresponse innovation to be discussed here is the practice of minimizing survey branding, which typically consists of putting the survey sponsor front and center in contacts and/or the questionnaire itself, and replacing it instead with elements intended to personalize the questionnaire to the target population. Once again, we draw on the general population community study reported by Dillman et al. (2009). In the design of this survey, considerable effort was made to personalize the letters and questionnaires to the area in which the target population resided. This effort was undertaken, in part, because the sample frame did not contain respondent names, which are the most common source of personalization. As a result, it was felt that different ways were needed to help the respondents feel that the survey was relevant to them. In the final design, a photograph of the community under study was included on the opening screen of the survey and in all contact materials; also, photos of widely recognizable community landmarks were included in the banner of the individual screens thereafter. In addition, special care was taken to include questions with particular relevance to the community (see Dillman et al., 2009, Chapter 7, for examples). Finally, the sponsor of the survey was identified, but this information was always secondary to elements of personalization to the community. One caveat to this discussion is that these design features were not tested in an experimental way. Thus, while the success of the data collection effort is encouraging, it is impossible to separate the effects of this type of personalization from other features of the survey, such as the advance notice, incentive, extra instruction, and survey topic. Moreover, the danger of such strategies is that they may only appeal to certain types of respondents, thus perhaps increasing nonresponse bias (Groves et al., 2006). While further testing is definitely needed, the search for new ways to personalize surveys to increase response rates on the otherwise notably unpersonalized Internet seems necessary.

2.4 CONCLUSIONS

The prospect of conducting surveys via the Internet has always been and continues to be an exciting one that has evoked much enthusiasm because of the immense possibilities for survey design combined with the efficiencies and, in many cases, relatively low costs of fielding Internet surveys. Indeed, some of the possibilities of the Internet are just now beginning to be widely recognized. One example is the survey possibilities of the mobile Internet, and especially the prospect of using experience sampling and real-time data collection with mobile devices. Despite its coverage and sampling limitations and some of the challenges of minimizing measurement and nonresponse error, the Internet as a survey mode has grown immensely and continues to expand.

As this chapter has demonstrated, surveyors have been incredibly innovative in addressing the challenges of Internet surveying. To overcome sampling and coverage limitations, some have developed probability Internet panels, and others have used the sampling and implementation methods of other survey modes for cross-sectional Internet surveys. To overcome additional coverage and nonresponse challenges, some have supplied hardware and Internet access to those who do not have it or have offered them another mode in which to respond to the surveys. Others have begun to explore additional ways to assist less experienced Internet users in finding and completing the survey and have explored the effects of replacing survey sponsor branding with personalization elements.

While surveyors have been able to overcome challenges, questions about the effects of Internet survey design and implementation decisions still remain. Some examples include:

- Do aspects of personalization in Internet surveys appeal to some respondents more than others, and how can we decide which personalization strategies are best?
- How can we get people who are uncomfortable with the Internet because of low skill levels, discomfort, or fear to give our surveys a chance?
- How do the measurement effects previously found in computer-based Internet surveys manifest themselves on the tiny screens of mobile Internet-enabled devices?
- From a survey error perspective, is it better to offer non-Internet users the hardware and connection to complete surveys on the Internet or is it better to provide them with an alternative survey mode such as mail or telephone in which to respond?
- What are the consequences of panel attrition and panel conditioning, and what is the best panel management strategy to minimize these?

These are just some of the many unknowns about Internet surveying. A considerable amount of research and experimentation on vital methodological issues is still needed, as are meta-analyses to summarize the research that has been done. However, as this book will illustrate, such research is currently being undertaken in a variety of creative ways by those who seek to maximize the potential of the Internet as a survey mode.

Nevertheless, perhaps the most overarching conclusion that can be drawn about the Internet is that by itself it is a great survey mode for certain populations but is not yet suitable for others. In fact, two recent studies in the United States have shown that Internet surveys alone collect less accurate data than when Internet surveys are supplemented by mail surveys. The first of these studies consisted of an analysis of a Gallup Panel survey in which respondents are encouraged to respond by Internet, but those who prefer not to or do not have access are given the opportunity to respond by mail. This study showed that even after weighting the Internet responses, they were less accurate than those obtained using both Internet and mail modes (Rookey, Hanway, & Dillman, 2008). The second study consisted of analysis of the general population survey of residents in a small metropolitan region of northern Idaho and eastern Washington that was discussed previously in this chapter. This analysis showed that the 41% of respondents who completed the survey via the Internet were considerably different both demographically and in their attitudes and opinions from the 14% who answered by mail. However, when data from the Internet and mail respondents were combined and compared to a separate treatment that obtained a 71% response rate by mail alone, there were very few differences (Dillman et al., 2008). Thus, it appears that, at least in the United States, the Internet is approaching the point where it can be used to survey the general population if it is supplemented by another survey mode.

One final Internet survey issue that is worthy of some consideration is the increasing ability for anyone with Internet access to create and deploy an Internet survey. This ability might be a double-edged sword. On one hand, such widespread ability allows people who were previously unable to conduct Internet surveys to do so, rather than concentrating this resource in the hands of a few organizations. For example, many graduate students and researchers who were previously limited to secondary data analysis now have the means to collect original data that might better measure the constructs in which they are interested. On the other hand, this widespread ability enables the creation and implementation of poor-quality surveys with little to no oversight. It is unclear to what extent respondents can discern between good- and poor-quality research or how poor-quality research might influence people's willingness to complete surveys in the future and their belief in the legitimacy of Internet survey data (and perhaps all survey data) as a source of credible and useful information. In the short term, the growing occurrence of poor-quality surveys means that surveyors have to work harder to designate their surveys as legitimate and important. In the long term, research is needed to examine the impact of such surveys on the survey industry as a whole.

With this chapter, we have attempted to provide an overview of the strengths and weaknesses of conducting surveys via the Internet as well as some of the challenges researchers face and the innovations developed to overcome these challenges. The remainder of this book will explore some of these issues and others in greater depth.

REFERENCES

Balabanis, G., Mitchell, V.-W., & Heinonen-Mavrovouniotis, S. (2007). SMS-based surveys: Strategies to improve participation. *International Journal of Advertising, 26*, 369–385.

Bethlehem, J. & Stoop, I. (2007). Online panels—a paradigm theft? In M. Trotman, T. Burrell, L. Gerrard et al. (Eds.), *The challenges of a changing world: Proceedings of the fifth international conference of the Association for Survey Computing* (pp. 113–137). Berkeley, UK: ASC.

Birnholtz, J. P., Horn, D. B., Finholt, T. A., & Bae, S. J. (2004). Cash, electronic, and paper gift certificates as respondent incentives for a Web-based survey of technologically sophisticated respondents. *Social Science Computer Review, 22,* 355–362.

Blumberg, S. J. & Luke, J. V. (2009). *Wireless substitution: Early release of estimates from the National Health Interview Survey, July-December 2008.* National Center for Health Statistics. Retrieved from http://www.cdc.gov/nchs/nhis.htm

Bosnjak, M. & Tuten, T. L. (2003). Prepaid and promised incentives in Web surveys: An experiment. *Social Science Computer Review, 21,* 208–217.

Brennan, M., Rae, N., & Parackal, M. (1999). Survey-based experimental research via the Web: Some observations. *Marketing Bulletin, 10,* 83–92.

Caro, J. J., Sr., Caro, I., Caro, J., Wouters, F., & Juniper, E. F. (2001). Does electronic implementation of questionnaires used in asthma alter responses compared to paper implementation? *Quality of Life Research, 10,* 683–691.

Cassell, J. & Miller, P. (2008). Is it self-administration if the computer gives you encouraging looks? In F. G. Conrad & M. F. Schober (Eds.), *Envisioning the survey interview of the future* (pp. 161–178). Hoboken, NJ: John Wiley & Sons.

Christian, L. M. (2003). *The influence of visual layout on scalar questions in Web surveys.* Unpublished master's thesis, Washington State University. Retrieved from http://www.sesrc.wsu.edu/dillman/papers.htm

Christian, L. M., Dillman, D. A., & Smyth, J. D. (2007). Helping respondents get it right the first time: The influence of words, symbols, and graphics in Web surveys. *Public Opinion Quarterly, 71,* 113–125.

Christian, L. M., Dillman, D. A., & Smyth, J. D. (2008). The effects of mode and format on answers to scalar questions in telephone and Web surveys. In J. M. Lepkowski, C. Tucker, J. M. Brick et al. (Eds.), *Advances in telephone survey methodology* (pp. 250–275). Hoboken, NJ: John Wiley & Sons.

Christian, L. M., Parsons, N. L., & Dillman, D. A. (2009). Designing scalar questions for Web surveys. *Sociological Methods and Research, 37,* 393–425.

Church, A. H. (1993). Estimating the effect of incentives on mail survey response rates: A meta-analysis. *Public Opinion Quarterly, 57,* 62–79.

Cobanoglu, C. & Cobanoglu, N. (2003). The effect of incentives in Web surveys: Application and ethical considerations. *International Journal of Market Research, 45,* 475–488.

Conrad, F. G., Couper, M. P., Tourangeau, R., & Peytchev, A. (2006). Use and nonuse of clarification features in Web surveys. *Journal of Official Statistics, 22,* 245–269.

Cook, C., Heath, F., & Thompson, R. L. (2000). A meta-analysis of response rates in Web- or Internet-based surveys. *Educational and Psychological Measurement, 60,* 821–836.

Coopmans, V. C. & Biddle, C. (2008). CRNA performance using a handheld, computerized, decision-making aid during critical events in a simulated environment: A methodologic inquiry. *American Association of Nurse Anesthetists Journal, 76,* 29–35.

Council of American Survey Research Organizations (2007). *CASRO code of standards and ethics for survey research.* Retrieved March 17, 2008, from http://casro.org/pdfs/CodeVertical-FINAL.pdf

Couper, M. P. (2005). Technology trends in survey data collection. *Social Science Computer Review, 23*(4), 486–501.

Couper, M. P. (2008). *Designing effective Web surveys*. New York: Cambridge University Press.

Couper, M. P., Conrad, F. G., & Tourangeau, R. (2007). Visual context effects in Web surveys. *Public Opinion Quarterly, 71,* 623–634.

Couper, M. P. & Nicholls, W. L., II. (1998). The history and development of computer assisted survey information collection methods. In M. P. Couper, R. P. Baker, J. Bethlehem et al. (Eds.), *Computer assisted survey information collection* (pp. 1–21). New York: John Wiley & Sons.

Couper, M. P., Tourangeau, R., Conrad, F. G., & Crawford, S. D. (2004). What they see is what we get: Response options for Web surveys. *Social Science Computer Review, 22,* 111–127.

Couper, M. P., Tourangeau, R., Conrad, F., & Singer, E. (2006). Evaluating the effectiveness of visual analog scales: A Web experiment. *Social Science Computer Review, 24,* 227–245.

Couper, M. P., Tourangeau, R., & Kenyon, K. (2004). Picture this! Exploring visual effects in Web surveys. *Public Opinion Quarterly, 68,* 255–266.

Couper, M. P., Traugott, M. W., & Lamias, M. J. (2001). Web survey design and administration. *Public Opinion Quarterly, 65,* 230–253.

Crawford, S. D., Couper, M. P., & Lamias, M. J. (2001). Web surveys: Perceptions of burden. *Social Science Computer Review, 19,* 146–162.

De Leeuw, E. D. (2005). To mix or not to mix data collection modes in surveys. *Journal of Official Statistics, 21,* 233–255.

De Leeuw, E. D. (2008). Choosing the method of data collection. In E. D. de Leeuw, J. J. Hox, & D. A. Dillman (Eds.), *International handbook of survey methodology* (pp. 113–135). New York: Lawrence Erlbaum Associates.

Dillman, D. A. (2000). *Mail and Internet surveys: The tailored design method* (2nd ed.). New York: John Wiley & Sons.

Dillman, D. A. & Bowker, D. K. (2001). The Web questionnaire challenge to survey methodologists. In U.-D. Reips & M. Bosnjak (Eds.), *Dimensions of Internet science*. Lengerich, Germany: Pabst Science Publishers. Retrieved September 25, 2008, from www.sesrc.wsu.edu/dillman/papers.htm

Dillman, D. A., Smyth, J. D., & Christian, L. M. (2009). *Internet, mail and mixed-mode surveys: The tailored design method* (3rd ed.). Hoboken, NJ: John Wiley & Sons.

Dillman, D. A., Smyth, J. D., Christian, L. M., & O'Neill, A. (2008). *Will a mixed-mode (mail/Internet) procedure work for random household surveys of the general public?* Paper presented at the annual conference of the American Association for Public Opinion Research (AAPOR), New Orleans, Louisiana.

Fuchs, M. (2008). Mobile Web surveys: A preliminary discussion of methodological implications. In F. G. Conrad & M. F. Schober (Eds.), *Envisioning the survey interview of the future* (pp. 77–94). Hoboken, NJ: John Wiley & Sons.

Funke, F. & Reips, U.-D. (2008). *Visual analogue scales versus categorical scales: Respondent burden, cognitive depth, and data quality.* Paper presented at the General Online Research conference (GOR '08), Hamburg, Germany.

Gallup WorldView (2008). *Home has access to Internet summary statistics.* Retrieved January 8, 2009, from https://worldview.gallup.com

Göritz, A. (2006). Cash lotteries as incentives in Web surveys. *Social Science Computer Review, 24,* 445–459.

Groves, R. M. (1989). *Survey errors and survey costs.* New York: John Wiley & Sons.

Groves, R. M., Couper, M. P., Presser, S., Singer, E., Tourangeau, R., & Acosta, G. P. (2006). Experiments in producing nonresponse bias. *Public Opinion Quarterly, 70,* 720–736.

Groves, R. M., Presser, S., & Dipko, S. (2004). The role of topic interest in survey participation decisions. *Public Opinion Quarterly, 68,* 2–31.

Groves, R. M., Singer, E., & Corning, A. (2000). Leverage-saliency theory of survey participation: Description and an illustration. *Public Opinion Quarterly, 64,* 299–308.

Heerwegh, D. (2003). Explaining response latencies and changing answers using client-side paradata from a Web survey. *Social Science Computer Review, 21,* 360–373.

Heerwegh, D. (2005). Effects of personal salutations in e-mail invitations to participate in a Web survey. *Public Opinion Quarterly, 69,* 588–598.

Heerwegh, D. & Loosveldt, G. (2002a). An evaluation of the effects of response formats on data quality in Web surveys. *Social Science Computer Review, 20,* 471–484.

Heerwegh, D. & Loosveldt, G. (2002b). Web surveys: The effect of controlling survey access using PIN numbers. *Social Science Computer Review, 20,* 10–21.

Heerwegh, D. & Loosveldt, G. (2003). An evaluation of the semiautomatic login procedure to control Web survey access. *Social Science Computer Review, 21,* 223–234.

Heerwegh, D. & Loosveldt, G. (2006). An experimental study on the effects of personalization, survey length statements, progress indicators, and survey sponsor logos in Web surveys. *Journal of Official Statistics, 22,* 191–210.

Holland, J. & Christian, L. M. (2007, October). *The influence of interactive probing on response to open-ended questions in a Web survey.* Paper presented at the annual conference of the Southern Association for Public Opinion Research, Raleigh, North Carolina.

Horrigan, J. B. (2008a). *Home broadband adoption 2008.* Retrieved October 2, 2008, from http://www.pewInternet.org/pdfs/PIP_Broadband_2008.pdf

Horrigan, J. B. (2008b). *Mobile access to data and information data memo March 2008.* Retrieved October 2, 2008, from http://www.pewInternet.org/pdfs/PIP_Mobile.Data.Access.pdf

Iannacchione, V. G., Staab, J. M., & Redden, D. T. (2003). Evaluating the use of residential mailing addresses in a metropolitan household survey. *Public Opinion Quarterly, 67,* 202–210.

James, J. M. & Bolstein, R. (1992). Large monetary incentives and their effect on mail survey response rates. *Public Opinion Quarterly, 56,* 442–453.

Joinson, A. N. & Reips, U. (2007). Personalized salutation, power of sender, and response rates to Web-based surveys. *Computers in Human Behavior, 23,* 1372–1383.

Kaczmirek, L. & Thiele, O. (2006). *Flash, JavaScript or PHP? Comparing the availability of technical equipment among university applicants.* Paper presented at the General Online Research conference (GOR '06), Bielefeld, Germany.

Kaplowitz, M. D., Hadlock, T. D., & Levine, R. (2004). A comparison of Web and mail survey response rates. *Public Opinion Quarterly, 68,* 94–101.

Link, M. W., Battaglia, M. P., Frankel, M., Osborn, L., & Mokdad, A. (2008). A comparison of address-based sampling (ABS) versus random-digit dialing (RDD) for general population surveys. *Public Opinion Quarterly, 72,* 6–27.

Lozar Manfreda, K., Bosnjak, M., Berzelak, J., Haas, I., & Vehovar, V. (2008). Web surveys versus other survey modes: A meta-analysis comparing response rates. *International Journal of Market Research, 50,* 79–104.

Marceau, L., Link, C., Jamison, R. N., & Carolan, S. (2007). Electronic diaries as a tool to improve pain management: Is there any evidence? *Pain Medicine, 8*(S3), S101–S109.

Neubarth, W. (2008). Online measurement of (drag & drop) moveable objects. In S. S. Gosling & J. A. Johnson (Eds.), *Advanced methods for behavioral research on the Internet.* Washington, DC: American Psychological Association (APA).

Okazaki, S. (2007). Assessing mobile-based online surveys: Methodological considerations and pilot study in an advertising context. *International Journal of Market Research, 49,* 651–675.

Olsen, D., Call, V., & Wygant, S. (2005). *Comparative analyses of parallel paper, phone, and Web surveys with and without incentives: What differences do incentive and mode make?* Paper presented at the annual conference of the American Association for Public Opinion Research (AAPOR), Miami Beach, Florida.

Pain Medicine (2007). Special issue: Computer and information technology in the assessment and management of patients with pain. *Pain Medicine, 8*(S3), S83–S198.

Palmblad, M. & Tiplady, B. (2004). Electronic diaries and questionnaires: Designing user interfaces that are easy for all patients to use. *Quality of Life Research, 13,* 1199–1207.

Person, N. K., D'Mello, S., & Olney, A. (2008). Toward socially intelligent interviewing systems. In F. G. Conrad & M. F. Schober (Eds.), *Envisioning the survey interview of the future* (pp. 195–214). Hoboken, NJ: John Wiley & Sons.

Peters, M. L., Sorbi, M. J., Kruise, D. A., Kerssens, J. J., Vergaak, P. F., & Bensing, J. M. (2000). Electronic diary assessment of pain, disability and psychological adaptation in patients differing in duration of pain. *Pain, 84,* 181–192.

Pew Internet & American Life Project (2007). February–March 2007 tracking survey [Data file]. Retrieved from http://www.pewInternet.org

Pew Internet & American Life Project (2008). *Demographics of Internet users.* Retrieved September 12, 2008, from http://www.pewInternet.org/trends/User_Demo_7.22.08.htm

Pew Internet & American Life Project (2009). *Internet adoption: Percentage of U.S. adults online.* Retrieved May 27, 2009, from http://www.pewInternet.org/Data-Tools/Download-Data/Trend-Data.aspx

Peytchev, A. & Crawford, S. (2005). A typology of real-time validations in Web-based surveys. *Social Science Computer Review, 23,* 235–249.

Peytchev, A. & Hill, C. A. (2008). *Mobile Web survey design.* Paper presented at the annual conference of the American Association of Public Opinion Research (AAPOR), New Orleans, Louisiana.

Porter, S. & Whitcomb, M. E. (2003). The impact of lottery incentives on student survey response rates. *Research in Higher Education, 44,* 389–407.

Potaka, L., (2008). Comparability and usability: Key issues in the design of Internet forms for New Zealand's 2006 Census of Populations and Dwellings. *Survey Research Methods, 2,* 1–10.

Roberts, D. F., Foehr, U. G., & Rideout, V. (2005). *Generation M: Media in the lives of 8–18 year olds.* Publication 7251. Henry J. Kaiser Family Foundation, Menlo Park, California. Retrieved March 18, 2009, from http://www.kff.org

Rookey, B. D., Hanway, S., & Dillman, D. A. (2008). Does a probability-based household panel benefit from assignment to postal response as an alternative to Internet-only? *Public Opinion Quarterly, 72,* 962–984.

Schaefer, D. & Dillman, D. A. (1998). Development of a standard e-mail methodology: Results of an experiment. *Public Opinion Quarterly, 62,* 378–397.

Smyth, J. D., Dillman, D. A., Christian, L. M., & McBride, M. (2009). Open-ended questions in Web surveys: Can increasing the size of answer boxes and providing extra verbal instructions improve response quality? *Public Opinion Quarterly, 73*(2), 325–337.

Smyth, J. D., Dillman, D. A., Christian, L. M., & Stern, M. J. (2006). Effects of using visual design principles to group response options in Web surveys. *International Journal of Internet Science, 1,* 6–16.

Steeh, C., Buskirk, T. D., & Callegaro, M. (2007). Using text messages in U.S. mobile phone surveys. *Field Methods, 19,* 59–75.

Stern, M. J. (2006). *How use of the Internet impacts community participation and the maintenance of core social ties: An empirical study.* Unpublished doctoral dissertation, Washington State University, Pullman.

Stern, M. J. (2008). The use of client-side paradata in analyzing the effects of visual layout on changing responses in Web surveys. *Field Methods, 20,* 377–398.

Stone, A. A. & Broderick, J. E. (2007). Real-time data collection for pain: Appraisal and current status. *Pain Medicine, 8*(S3), S85–S93.

Thomas, R. K. & Couper, M. P. (2007). *A comparison of visual analog and graphic ratings scales.* Paper presented at the General Online Research conference (GOR '07), Leipzig, Germany.

Toepoel, V. (2008). *A closer look at Web questionnaire design.* CentER for Economic Research Dissertation Series, no. 220. Tilburg University, the Netherlands.

Tourangeau, R., Couper, M., & Conrad, F. (2004). Spacing, position, and order: Interpretive heuristics for visual features of survey questions. *Public Opinion Quarterly, 68,* 368–393.

Tourangeau, R., Couper, M., & Conrad, F. (2007). Color, labels, and interpretive heuristics for response scales. *Public Opinion Quarterly, 71,* 91–112.

Tuten, T. L., Galesic, M., & Bosnjak, M. (2004). Effects of immediate versus delayed notification of prize draw results on response behavior in Web surveys. *Social Science Computer Review, 22,* 377–384.

Vehovar, V., Batagelj, Z., Lozar Manfreda, K., & Zaletel, M. (2002). Nonresponse in Web surveys. In R. M. Groves, D. A. Dillman, J. L. Eltinge, & R. J. A. Little (Eds.), *Survey nonresponse* (pp. 229–242). New York: John Wiley & Sons.

3

Internet Surveys as Part of a Mixed-Mode Design

Edith D. de Leeuw
Department of Methodology and Statistics
Utrecht University
Utrecht, the Netherlands

Joop J. Hox
Department of Methodology and Statistics
Utrecht University
Utrecht, the Netherlands

3.1 INTRODUCTION

In 1788, Sir John Sinclair conducted the first documented survey. Lacking funds for a full statistical census, Sinclair mailed out questionnaires to ministers of all parishes in the Church of Scotland with more than a hundred questions about their parish. He pursued them relentlessly using a mixed-mode strategy, with "statistical missionaries" to hurry up late responders, and follow-up letters of which the last was written in blood red to suggest with "the draconian colour of his ink" what would happen to the nonrespondents. It took 23 reminders, but Sinclair achieved a 100% response, and his study is thereby one of the first examples in which a mixed-mode strategy is highly successful in reducing nonresponse. By using a mixed-mode strategy for contact and reminders only (i.e., follow-up letters via mail and in-person "statistical missionaries"), but keeping the data collection itself restricted to one mode (i.e., the written accounts of Scottish ministers), Sinclair also made sure that mode effects would not threaten data integrity. The results were published between 1791 and 1799 in the Statistical Account of Scotland, and these accounts are still part of the online National Data Centre at the University of Edinburgh. This account contains not only demographic statistics such as age distributions, life expectancies, and estimates of the total population, but also data on social statistics and lifestyles. Thanks to Sinclair, we now know that in the 18th century the women of Inveresk organized football matches between the married and unmarried women, and the former invariably won (Hacking, 1990; Heiser, 1996).

Surveys are part of the ever-changing cultural and technological context of society, and survey methodology changes over time. We no longer write to clergymen and use them as informants about their parishioners; instead, we survey people directly using today's technology. Still, common to all surveys—then and now—is that they require a two-way dialogue and that certain assumptions for the collection of valid data remain unchanged. These assumptions can be summarized in the four cornerstones of data quality: good coverage of the intended population, probability sampling, low nonresponse error, and accurate measurements (Groves, 1989; Biemer & Lyberg, 2003; De Leeuw, Hox, & Dillman, 2008a). Groves (1989) also added cost efficiency to the desiderata of good surveys. Like Sinclair, we usually lack the funds to do a census or even a large-scale interview survey, and one of the major attractions of online research is its low cost per completed questionnaire. But the Internet as data collection medium offers more advantages, such as the potential for using complex questionnaires and visual and auditory stimuli, and the quick turnaround time (e.g., De Leeuw, 2008; Chapter 1 in this volume).

While acknowledging the immense potential of Internet surveys, Couper (2000) pointed out that coverage error and nonresponse error are the biggest threats to inference from Internet surveys; see also Chapter 5 in this volume.

Although Internet coverage is growing, we get a very diverse picture when we look internationally. In his extensive inventory of Internet access at home across Europe, Blyth (2008a, 2008b) cites percentages ranging from 86% in the Netherlands and 83% in Sweden to 15% for Turkey and 21% for Bulgaria. These data are based on the Eurobarometer 2007; the Eurobarometer has been collecting data on access to technology EU-wide on a regular basis, using *personal interviews* with adults. For the United States, the percentage of households with Internet access is estimated at around 62% (see Chapter 1 in this volume). The differences in coverage across countries are so large that Blyth (2008a) argues that in order to provide cost-effective international measurements, we must embrace a mixed-mode strategy. But even in countries with high Internet penetration, there may be a substantial risk of coverage bias because online access varies widely across demographic groups; thus a mixed-mode strategy may be called for. For instance, in the Netherlands—a country with coverage of over 80%—Internet access is unevenly distributed over the population, with highly educated, younger, and native Dutch people more often having Internet access (Bethlehem, 2008). Similar indications of a digital divide have been found in other countries; for instance, for the United States, Rookey, Hanway, and Dillman (2008) report that Internet users are younger, have higher incomes, and have more education; Couper, Kapteyn, Schonlau, and Winter (2007) find similar differences in socioeconomic status and age. That the digital divide can be substantial is shown by Couper (2008, p. 86) using data from the Pew Internet and American Life Project: while 91% of college graduates have Internet access, only 40% of those with no high school degree have access to the Net.

Besides noncoverage, nonresponse and its associated potential for nonresponse error are a threat to data quality (Couper & De Leeuw, 2003). Unfortunately, Internet surveys do not achieve high response rates, as recent meta-analyses show. In an early study, Cook, Heath, and Thompson (2000) report an average response rate of 34.6% (SD = 15.7%) based on 56 Internet surveys reported in 39 studies with complete data on (non)response. When Internet surveys are compared to other modes of data collection, they produce overall lower response rates than other modes. Shih and Fan (2008) summarized 39 comparisons of Internet and postal mail surveys that were published in the last 10 years. They found that the unweighted average response rate of paper mail surveys was about 10% higher than that of Internet surveys, which had an average response of 34%. This is in the same range as the results of Lozar Manfreda, Bosnjak, Berzelak, Haas, and Vehovar (2008), who compared Internet surveys to different modes of data collection (e.g., mail, telephone, face-to-face, fax). When analyzing 45 published and unpublished experimental comparisons, they found that Internet surveys yield on average an 11% lower response rate. There are several ways to improve the response rate of a single Internet survey, including incentives and reminders (for an overview, see Chapter 1 in this volume). Switching modes—that is, following up with nonrespondents using a different mode of data collection—can be very effective in increasing response rates to Internet surveys (Couper, 2008, p. 342). However, the mode sequence should be planned by the researcher, going from most affordable to more costly methods; offering potential respondents a choice between methods does *not* increase the overall response (Dillman, Smyth, Christian, & O'Neill, 2008).

The above data all refer to response in cross-sectional (ad hoc) Internet surveys; no detailed overviews are available for response rates in Internet panels. A first attempt was made by Willems, Van Ossenbruggen, and Vonk (2006), who performed an extensive study of online panels in the Netherlands. They extensively analyzed the results of a comparative survey that was hosted by 19 commercial Dutch online panels. The questionnaire used was an omnibus, completion took on average 12.9 minutes, and no reminders were sent. The response varied between 18% and 77%, with an average response of 51%. Although response rates as high as 70% can be reached in an online panel, one should take into account that these data are panel data. Sikkel, Hox, and De Leeuw (2009) warn that response figures for panels may be misleading because the bulk of the nonresponse takes place during the initial recruitment phase; this initial nonresponse should be taken into account when reporting response rates.

In sum, two central problems of Internet surveys are undercoverage (due to limited Internet penetration) and low response rates, while major advantages are its affordability and cost-effectiveness. Mixed-mode designs involving Internet surveys offer an attractive alternative, providing an opportunity to compensate for the weaknesses of Internet surveys yet keeping costs affordable.

However, mixed-mode designs introduce a new problem, that of data integrity. Only when data collected with different modes produce the same results—that is, only when data equivalence is reached—is it allowed to combine these data into one data set. Therefore the main questions concerning all mixed-mode studies are: May data that are collected through different modes be combined in one cross-sectional study? May data collected with different modes at different time points be combined in a longitudinal analysis? May data that are collected through different modes be compared over studies or countries?

In this chapter we focus on Internet surveys as part of a mixed-mode design, and not on mixed-mode research in general. For the latter we refer to Dillman, Smyth, and Christian (2009), De Leeuw, Hox, and Dillman (2008b), De Leeuw (2005), and Roberts (2007). We start with some preliminary notes on data collection and mixed-mode designs. In Section 3.3 we review empirical evidence regarding mode effects and Internet surveys. We then discuss optimal design for mixed-mode situations involving the Internet in Section 3.4, and end with recommendations for the design and analysis of mixed-mode surveys.

3.2 AVAILABLE DATA COLLECTION METHODS

3.2.1 Which Mode to Choose

In survey research there are two basic forms of data collection, self-administered questionnaires and standardized interviews, and these are mainly characterized by the absence or presence of an interviewer. But there are many variations possible. Interviews can be performed face-to-face or over the telephone, and self-administered questionnaires can be handed over by an interviewer during an interview or sent by paper mail or through the Internet. Furthermore, computer-assisted equivalents are available for both face-to-face interviews (computer-assisted personal interviewing, CAPI) and for telephone interviews (computer-assisted telephone interviewing, CATI). There are even self-administered computerized forms that are introduced by an interviewer; prime examples are computer-assisted self-interviewing (CASI), which can be used in a face-to-face situation, and interactive voice response (IVR), which is introduced over the telephone. These interviewer-introduced self-administered surveys, which are a form of mixed-mode surveys, are usually administered when very sensitive questions are being asked; the aim is to reduce social desirability bias.

Besides the presence and absence of an interviewer, data collection methods also differ on two other important dimensions: how the information is presented (visual, aural, or both) and how the respondents convey their answer (spoken, written, or typed); for a more detailed description, see De Leeuw (1992, 2008). These factors not only are of theoretical importance but also have a direct impact on data quality, because they influence the cognitive burden for the respondents, their sense of privacy, and the question–answer process as a whole (cf. Tourangeau, Rips, & Rasinski, 2000). These factors should be taken into account when designing optimal questionnaires for mixed-mode studies; we will come back to this in the section on questionnaire development.

Deciding which data collection mode is best in a certain situation is often complex and depends on many factors, of which the most important are the population under investigation, topic, types of questions to be asked, available time, and funds. When choosing a specific data collection mode, one wants to reduce the total survey error as much as possible, which means taking into account coverage and sampling error, expected nonresponse, and desired data quality. Each data collection method has its advantages and disadvantages (for a detailed overview, see De Leeuw, 2008). By combining different data collections methods in one mixed-mode survey it is possible to compensate for the disadvantages and exploit the advantages of each mode, and survey methodologists have been proposing mixed-mode surveys as the best of all possible modes for decades (Dillman et al., 2009).

There are many forms of mixed-mode surveys, and each serves a specific goal. De Leeuw (2005) presents a detailed typology and discusses the advantages and disadvantages of each design. One can discern four main groups of mixed-mode design.

3.2.1.1 Contacting by Different Modes

The first group of mixed-mode designs focuses on optimizing the *contact* with the respondent. In this form one or more modes are used to contact the respondent; response is stimulated by a different mode. As the actual data collection in these cases is in one mode only, these mixed-mode designs have no negative implication for measurement error or data integrity, but will reduce nonresponse error or coverage error—a win-win situation. Examples are advance notification letters to establish legitimacy or send incentives before telephone interviews and Internet surveys, screening or selecting respondents by telephone while the actual data collection is done through the Internet, and reminders in a mode different from previous contacts. Sir John Sinclair did in fact use this type of mixed-mode design as early as the 1790s, when he decided to send "statistical missionaries" in person to hurry up the overdue written accounts of Scottish ministers.

3.2.1.2 Another Mode for Specific Questions in the Questionnaire

In this type of mixed-mode design, a more private, second data collection method is used to collect data from all respondents during a single data collection period for a specific *subsection* of the questionnaire. The motivations for choosing this design are to reduce social desirability bias for sensitive questions and to reduce overall measurement error. Usually a mix of interview and self-administered forms is used to exploit the strong points of both methods. For instance, within an interview a self-administered form of data collection such as CASI or Audio-CASI is used for sensitive questions to reduce social desirability and enhance privacy, as neither the interviewer nor any other person in the vicinity will know the answers given; all other questions (e.g., complex questions, household composition) are administered by the interviewer, who may provide assistance when necessary. This situation has only positive points and is not a cause for concern regarding data integrity.

3.2.1.3 Different Modes for Different Respondents

A different situation arises when one mode of data collection is used for some respondents of a sample and another mode for others in that same sample in order to collect the *same* data. In other words, different modes are used for different respondents for all questions in one survey. This is usually done in order to reduce coverage and nonresponse errors. For instance, to reduce undercoverage of special groups an Internet survey is implemented together with a mail survey of all sampled units that do not have an Internet connection. Another application of this type of mixed-mode design is to offer multiple data collection methods in a specific sequence during a survey in order to reduce overall nonresponse. For instance, a telephone interview is implemented among the nonrespondents to an Internet survey. A third application is when different modes are used in different regions or countries—for instance, an Internet survey in countries with high Internet penetration and a telephone survey in countries with high telephone coverage, while a face-to-face interview is conducted in countries that have neither. The motivation for this type of mixed-mode design is to respond to cultural differences and variations in survey capabilities in different countries and keep the overall survey costs manageable. In all these situations, data are collected using a different data collection method for discernable (sub)groups of respondents and these data are then combined and analyzed in one data set. Here the question of data integrity does play a role, and differences between subgroups may be confounded with mode differences. For example, do the nonrespondents to an Internet survey really differ in opinions, or is this a (telephone) mode effect? In the former the mixed-mode strategy helps to reduce nonresponse bias, while in the latter the mixed-mode strategy adds bias through differential measurement error.

3.2.1.4 Alternating Modes in a Longitudinal Design

The fourth group of mixed-mode designs involves alternating modes over time in a longitudinal study or a panel. Respondents are surveyed at different time points using different modes. Here practical considerations, such as the availability of a good sampling frame, and costs are the main reasons for this approach. Sometimes addresses are available, but e-mail addresses are not and have to be collected first; sometimes no sampling frame is available and area probability sampling using face-to-face interviews is the only option. This flexibility together with the greater likelihood that an interviewer will gain cooperation in person at the doorstep and the better opportunities for screening make the face-to-face survey a favorite for the baseline study in a panel. To reduce costs a more efficient and less expensive method (e.g., an Internet survey) may be used after the first wave. However, when modes are alternated in a longitudinal design, time and mode effects are confounded, as the change in data collection mode may introduce differences in the measurements, and it is difficult to decide if a change over time is a real change or the result of a change of mode.

In sum, there is no easy solution for the problems mentioned in the last two types of mixed-mode designs. Depending on the survey situation, one has to decide upon the optimal design while carefully appraising the different sources of error. Only after careful consideration can one decide if the expected mode effects are serious enough to avoid mixed-mode designs or if the advantages of mixing modes outweigh the risks.

Using different modes for different parts of a sample or alternating modes in a longitudinal survey can introduce measurement error because people may respond differently to the same questions depending on whether the question is posed through the Internet or with another data collection mode. How serious is this threat? In the following section we provide an overview of empirical mode comparisons with regard to potential mode differences involving Internet surveys.

3.3 A REVIEW OF EMPIRICAL EVIDENCE OF MODE EQUIVALENCE

3.3.1 Threats to Data Integrity

The goal of mixed-mode surveys is to combine data from different sources into one data matrix for analysis. This assumes that data collected through different modes are equivalent, but this assumption is not necessarily true. Data from different sources may differ for the following reasons: (1) because different modes may lead to a different sample composition, (2) because different question formats are employed in different modes, and (3) because the modes themselves lead to different response processes (e.g., De Leeuw, 2005; Dillman & Christian, 2005).

The fact that respondents to different modes may have different background characteristics and therefore provide different answers (point 1) is an advantage, not a disadvantage, of mixed-mode surveys. This is not a threat to our data, but something we aim at and want to achieve. We should remember that one of the main reasons for mixing modes is to overcome coverage and nonresponse errors of single Internet surveys, which means that we explicitly do want to bring in different groups using different modes.

When data from different sources are combined, the danger always exists that one and the same concept is measured using questions that are differently worded or even have a different question format (point 2). As data collection methods have different philosophies of question writing and question format (Dillman, 2008), these different approaches to questionnaire construction may unintentionally lead to nonequivalent questionnaires when an Internet survey is mixed with other data collection methods. A prime example is the way a list of response options is offered. Because of the richness of the visual channel in Internet surveys, a list of response options is visually displayed on the screen (e.g., strongly agree, agree, somewhat agree, neutral, somewhat disagree, disagree, strongly disagree), a procedure akin to mail surveys and interviewer show cards in face-to-face interviews. In telephone surveys branching (unfolding) is used in these cases—for example, asking first the direction of an opinion (e.g., agree, neutral, disagree) and following that up with the intensity (e.g., is this strongly agree, agree, or somewhat agree). These different formats affect the responses, leading to differences between modes that offer the full list of response options visually (Internet, mail) and unfolding in a telephone interview. From past research we know that question format does have an effect on the responses and the response distribution even within a single mode (e.g., Sudman & Bradburn, 1974; Schuman & Presser, 1981; Christian, Dillman, & Smyth, 2008); therefore, question-format effects may be one of the main causes for mode effects in standard mixed-mode designs. To avoid unwanted divergence across modes one should avoid differential questionnaire construction and aim at equivalent questionnaires when employing a mixed-mode design.

The data collection mode itself can influence the data (point 3). Modes vary in terms of (1) interviewer versus self-administered questionnaires and the associated interviewer effects; (2) in the way information is transmitted, the survey question is posed, and the answer is recorded (e.g., aurally versus visually, spoken versus written versus typed); and (3) in general media-related factors, such as knowledge, experience, and social customs related to the medium. These mode characteristics influence the potential for social desirability bias, the difficulty of the task for the respondent, respondent motivation, and the question-answer process in general, which in turn influence data quality. For an overview, see De Leeuw (1992, Chapter 2); Roberts (2007); and Tourangeau et al. (2000, Chapter 10).

3.3.2 Review of Mode Differences for Traditional Data Collection Methods

The influence of data collection method on data quality has been extensively studied for the traditional data collection methods, that is, face-to-face interviews, telephone surveys, and self-administered paper mail questionnaires. These older reviews can provide some insight into media-related effects and potential mode effects involving mixes with Internet surveys. De Leeuw (1992, Chapter 3) performed a meta-analysis of 67 articles and papers reporting mode comparisons. The resulting overview showed consistent but usually small differences between methods, suggesting a dichotomy of survey modes in those with and without an interviewer. Especially with more sensitive questions, self-administered surveys performed better with less social desirability bias in answers and more reporting of sensitive behaviors such as drinking. This is promising for Internet surveys, which are a form of self-administered surveys.

A limited number of studies investigated specific response effects, such as recency and primacy effects. In a visual format, such as a self-administered questionnaire, respondents think in the order in which the response categories are presented and are more likely to choose those presented at the beginning of a list of response alternatives than those at the end (a primacy effect), while in an auditory format, respondents are expected to wait till the interviewer has read the whole question and are more likely to start thinking about the last alternatives read to them (a recency effect). The evidence on this is mixed. Dillman et al. (1995) found inconsistent evidence for primacy effects in mail and recency effects in telephone surveys in a large number of experiments. These inconsistent findings may be due to interaction effects with social desirability. In general, mail surveys produce fewer socially desirable answers than telephone surveys, and when the last response category is also the less socially desirable answer, this may counteract the primacy/recency effects. This may have implications for mixing self-administered modes, such as Internet surveys with interviewer-administered modes.

Finally, in a carefully designed experiment, De Leeuw (1992, Chapter 6) investigated reliability and consistency of answers. Again the main difference was between self-administered and interviewer-administered surveys. In the self-administered mail survey, where the respondent is in control and can read the questions and answer at his or her own pace, more consistent answers were given and less random error was detected in the answers. Again, this is promising for Internet surveys.

3.3.3 Measurement Error in Internet Surveys Compared to Other Data Collection Methods

The above review was limited to comparing paper-and-pencil self-administered questionnaires with face-to-face and telephone interviews; however, the results are of importance for Internet surveys as well. Although Internet surveys are a new form of data collection, one should remember that Internet surveys are a form of self-administered questionnaires and many of the benefits of self-administration should apply, such as absence of interviewer effects, lower social desirability bias, visual presentation, and ability for the respondent to set the pace. On the other hand, there are also differences between paper self-administered questionnaires and computerized forms. Internet surveys may be accessed from any place (e.g., home, office, library, Internet café) at any time, and Internet surveys are more interactive and the medium itself is clearly different from paper and pencil; for instance, the Internet more easily allows for multitasking, scanning the page and quickly skipping from one topic to the next, and satisficing (cf. Krug, 2006), all of which may influence data quality. These considerations have led to a new series of empirical mode comparisons, and we will first review comparisons with paper-and-pencil self-administered forms and then comparisons with either telephone or face-to-face interviews.

3.3.3.1 Self-Administered Questionnaires and the Internet

The importance of the medium of administration for data quality has long been recognized in diagnosing and assessment. When computerized forms of tests were introduced, the American Psychological Association (1986; p. 18) explicitly stated that "the equivalence of scores from computerized versions should be established and documented before using norms of cutting scores obtained from conventional tests." This led to numerous empirical comparisons between computerized and paper-and-pencil versions of well-known tests, which in turn resulted in quantitative summaries and meta-analyses. In general, the mode of administration had no statistically significant effect. In one of the first meta-analyses, Bergstrom (1992) found negligible differences between paper-and-pencil and computerized tests for general aptitude based on 15 studies of adults and high school students. These results were confirmed by Mead and Drasgow (1993) with a notable exception. In a meta-analysis of 29 studies comparing paper and computerized tests for cognitive abilities among young adults and adults, they found that power tests (that is, ability tests without a time limit) were highly equivalent, with a cross-mode correlation of 0.97, but speed tests (tests measuring cognitive processing speed, where simple tasks have to be processed within a time limit) were clearly less equivalent, with a cross-mode correlation of 0.72. Mead and Drasgow (1993) interpret the mode effect for speed tests as an effect of the importance of perceptual and motor skills in responding quickly to time-pressured tests. These overviews go back to comparisons as early as the late 1970s, when far fewer people were acquainted with and were using computers, and we may expect that the present "Nintendo generation" is better trained in the perceptual and motor skills needed for quick and accurate reactions to a computer-offered stimulus. Indeed, later meta-analyses (Kim, 1999; Wang, Jiao, Young, Brooks, & Olson, 2007, 2008) confirm that for high school students computer-assisted and paper achievement tests are equivalent. However, it seems wise to allow ample time when less computer-literate groups, (e.g., the elderly) are studied (De Leeuw, Hox, & Kef, 2003).

Also, for noncognitive instruments, which ask for more subjective information, equivalence has been established. Gwaltney, Shields, and Shiffman (2008) performed a meta-analysis of 65 studies comparing electronic and paper-and-pencil self-reported patient outcome measures on such diverse topics as health status, anxiety, depression, pain, quality of life, and mood. Their results show that computerized and paper-and-pencil measures produce equivalent scores: The mean differences were very small and not significant, and correlations across modes were very high and similar to correlations between repeated administrations of the same paper-and-pencil measurement. Finally, Richman, Kiesler, Weisband, and Drasgow (1999) investigated social desirability distortions; their meta-analysis reports that in the case of computerized versus self-administered paper questionnaires a near zero overall effect was found, both for direct measures of social desirability distortion and for social desirability distortion inferred from other scales. However, a very interesting moderator variable was identified: When respondents were not assured of anonymity, were identified, or were in the close presence of others, they were less willing to reveal personal weaknesses in the computerized form than with paper and pencil. Although the effects were small, this may be of concern when very sensitive data are collected through the Internet, and it underscores the importance of confidentiality assurances in Internet surveys.

For Internet surveys this evidence of test equivalence is promising indeed: After more than three decades of investigation, computerized tests appear to be accepted as being valid and reliable alternatives to traditional methods (Epstein & Klinkenberg, 2001), and online tests can be seen as a special case of computer-assisted testing. Still, there are differences between computerized and Internet administration. Computerized testing is usually done under very controlled conditions, while an Internet survey or online test may be completed from any number of locations at any time and relatively free of controls. Despite these differences, test data collected over the Internet and via paper and pencil appear to be largely equivalent, as Preckel and Thieman (2001) demonstrated for a new intelligence test. No differences were found for reliability and validity for the two versions; the only difference found was in mean score, with online respondents scoring higher than paper-and-pencil respondents, which could be attributed to self-selection. Also, for noncognitive instruments, measurement equivalence of online and paper-and-pencil questionnaires could be established. In a large-scale multinational test in 50 countries, Cole, Bedeian, and Feild (2006) stringently tested equivalence for a leadership test consisting of 20 items. Not only did they find similar reliability coefficients and intercorrelations across modes, but they were also able to establish full equivalence across modes using multigroup confirmatory factor analysis. The only difference found, a slightly higher score in the Internet condition, could be attributed to differences in sample composition. Similar results for a range of personality measures were found by Meade, Michels, and Lautenschlager (2007) and by Ferrando and Lorenzo-Seva (2005). Meade et al. (2007) also reported that while they were able to establish equivalence of measures across modes in a strict experiment where respondents were allocated at random to the Internet or to paper and pencil, the results were more complicated when respondents were given a choice between modes. They comment that although measurement equivalence exists for format (Internet versus paper) when controlling for choice, it may not exist for people allowed to choose and those not allowed to choose, even if respondents (as was the case here) were of the same age and level of education. This could have implications for a well-known form of mixed-mode surveys where respondents are offered a choice of modes. Not only is there evidence that a mode choice does not raise the response rate and may even lower it (see also Dillman et al., 2008), the study by Meade et al. (2007) suggests that it also may offer a potential threat to data integrity.

In sum, the results are promising for mixing Internet and other forms of self-administered questionnaires. Generally, it seems reasonable to assume that respondents use the same psychological processes and metric when responding to Internet and other forms of self-administered questionnaires. However, most studies reviewed are strict migrations, where the exact text of the paper instrument was ported to the computer screen without making substantive changes in the content. When substantial changes in the questionnaire are made or where layout changes substantially, affecting users' perception and ability to respond (e.g., scrolling, drop-down boxes), equivalence is not guaranteed and new studies will be necessary.

3.3.3.2 Interviews and the Internet

There are fewer comparisons with interview surveys, either telephone or face-to-face, and as a consequence there are as yet no comprehensive meta-analyses summarizing mode effects for Internet versus interview surveys. However, one effect is consistently found in the available studies: Internet surveys appear to give rise to less social desirability bias than interviews. In this sense, Internet surveys are indeed more like self-administered questionnaires and share their benefits, as Couper (2008) postulated.

Self-administered questionnaires have been found again and again to lead to less social desirability bias and more openness in answering sensitive questions when compared to interview surveys. This was the case with paper-and-pencil questionnaires and mail surveys (for a meta-analysis, see De Leeuw, 1992) and also with computer-assisted self-administered questionnaires (see, for instance, Tourangeau and Smith, 1996, and Turner et al., 1998).

These results have now been replicated for Internet surveys. In a controlled experiment in Belgium, Heerwegh, Billiet, and Loosveldt (2005) found more socially desirable answers on questions regarding rights for immigrants in a face-to-face interview than in a Web questionnaire. Bronner and Kuijlen (2007), when comparing face-to-face (CAPI), telephone (CATI), and Internet interviewing (which they label CASI@home), also found more reporting of socially undesirable behavior, such as violations of the law, in the Internet condition than in the CAPI or CATI condition. As was the case with Heerwegh et al. (2005), an experimental design was used, and the differences could not be attributed to self-selection or differential respondent characteristics.

In the United States, Link and Mokdad (2005) found more self-reported heavy drinkers in an Internet survey compared to those in a telephone interview. This result remained strong and significant after adjusting for different demographic characteristics of respondents in both modes. Similar results were found in the Netherlands, where less drinking of alcoholic beverages and more ecologically friendly behavior was reported over the phone compared with the Web for the same population (Van Ewijk, 2004).

Krauter, Presser, and Tourangeau (2008) compared CATI, interactive voice response (IVR), and Internet surveys in an experimental setting and confirmed and extended these findings. Internet administration increased reporting of sensitive information among alumni in the United States, such as more yes answers to, and less skipping of, questions asking for undesirable or sensitive information (e.g., dropping a class, GPA). Krauter et al. (2008) also had access to record data and found a higher accuracy in Internet surveys; they report that Internet surveys increased both the level of reporting sensitive information and the accuracy compared to telephone (conventional CATI), with the more private self-administered telephone survey (IVR) in between. Finally, Dillman et al. (forthcoming) compared mail, telephone, IVR, and the Internet and found that more extreme positive answers on satisfaction–dissatisfaction questions were given in the telephone and IVR conditions than when using paper mail or Internet surveys; a careful check showed that this result could not be accounted for by a tendency toward recency over the phone. The less positive answers in the self-administered forms very well could be attributed to more openness and less social desirability bias. Dillman et al. (forthcoming) point out that the visual versus aural communication channel could play a role here too, and warn that mixing modes that depend upon different communication channels (i.e., visual versus aural), may introduce measurement differences that cannot be ignored.

Although the results for social desirability are clear—more openness in Internet than in interview surveys—the pattern is far less clear for other indicators of data quality. Regarding item nonresponse, contradictory findings are reported. Heerwegh and Loosveldt (2008) in a Belgium experiment report more "do not know" answers and more item nonresponse in an Internet survey than in a face-to-face interview of students on attitudes toward immigrants. Van Ewijk (2004) also reports higher item nonresponse for Internet than for telephone interviews in a Dutch experiment using an omnibus questionnaire. Van Ewijk attributes the lower nonresponse in interviews to the fact that it is easier to skip a question in a self-administered questionnaire than to say "do not know" to a real person. However, Fricker, Galesic, Tourangeau, and Yan (2005) report less item nonresponse in an Internet survey than in a telephone interview for a study on attitudes and knowledge toward science. This could be explained by the fact that in the Internet condition respondents were prompted, whereas in the telephone condition "no opinion" was accepted without further probing. To make matters even more complicated, Link and Mokdad (2005) report a very low level of item nonresponse in both Internet and telephone surveys and a slightly higher level in a mail survey on drinking. A similar result is reported by Oosterveld and Willems (2003), with no differences in item nonresponse between Internet and telephone in a survey on finances. In the last two studies the questions asked were of a highly sensitive nature.

Much depends on the nature of the questions and the way the survey is implemented, as Toepoel (2008, Chapter 2) argues in discussing her findings that putting more items on the screen increased item nonresponse; more experimental research is clearly needed here.

It has been argued that Internet surveys may give rise to more satisficing than surveys in which respondents are interviewed (e.g., Krug, 2006; Couper, 2008). This tendency to satisfice may account for more missing data. It may also introduce other response effects. For instance, Heerwegh and Loosveldt (2008) report that Internet respondents differentiate less on rating scales than respondents in a face-to-face interview. Fricker et al. (2005) found similar results when comparing Internet and telephone interviews. However, Smyth, Christian, and Dillman (2008) and Van Ewijk (2004) show that check-all-that-apply questions, which could be seen as encouraging satisficing behavior, perform less well and endorse fewer response options than yes/no questions in *both* Internet surveys and telephone interviews, which suggests a question-form effect instead of a mode effect. Furthermore, Oosterveld and Willems (2003) report more answers to open questions for Internet than CATI when comparing these two conditions. Similar findings are reported by Fricker et al. (2005), who report that Internet respondents performed better on knowledge questions than telephone respondents did and took longer to complete especially the open questions, which points to more thorough cognitive processing and less satisficing for the Internet.

In sum, Internet surveys perform better than both face-to-face and telephone interviews when sensitive questions are asked. Evidence on satisficing behavior is mixed, and there are studies that clearly show that respondents in Internet surveys provide more answers to open questions than in telephone interviews. Finally, some studies report more item nonresponse in Internet surveys, while other report less or no differences at all. Again, how questionnaires were designed and how the actual survey was implemented may be crucial for the quality of answers.

3.4 CONSEQUENCES OF MIXED-MODE DESIGN FOR QUESTIONNAIRE DEVELOPMENT

The empirical mode comparisons cited above show relatively small differences between Internet and other modes of data collection, with the exception of Internet and interview mixes for sensitive questions. This seems reassuring, but usually in experimental mode comparisons extreme care is taken in designing and implementing equivalent questionnaires. In daily survey practice, differences in question wording and question format between specific modes may be the biggest threat to data integrity in mixed-mode surveys, as each survey mode has different conventions in developing questionnaires (Dillman, 2008). Examples are offering a "do not know" category to the response scale in self-administered questionnaires and withholding this in an interviewer-administered mode, using an open question in a telephone interview and a closed question with multiple response categories in an Internet survey, or shortening or changing the structure (e.g., branching or unfolding) of a question with a long list of response categories for telephone use. Implementing standard questionnaires, which are designed separately for individual modes, enhances unwanted measurement error in mixed-mode designs; to avoid this, one should explicitly design a special questionnaire for a mixed-mode survey.

3.4.1 Unwanted Consequences of Independently Designed Questionnaires

What would happen if in a mixed-mode design each mode is developed separately? Advocates of this approach argue that if each mode is optimized separately, this will reduce the total error in the combined data set, as some optimized modes have more error than others (e.g., more item nonresponse in a self-administered questionnaire) and in the combination the overall error is acceptable. The reasoning is that if one mode has strong properties, using these will reduce the error in the data resulting from that mode and thus reduce the total error. This is true only if the very strong assumption holds that all measurement errors associated with the mode are random error, because then we have one method with more random error and another with less. In the case of systematic error or bias (e.g., social desirability, acquiescence), it can be dangerous to optimize each method separately, as the bias may add up and result in increased overall bias for the combined data. As always, the burden of proof is on the researcher to demonstrate that the chosen design indeed results in better quality and that there is no added bias, for instance by embedding a small mode experiment.

3.4.2 Robust Questionnaire Design for Mixed-Mode Surveys: Unified Mode Design

When developing questionnaires for a mixed-mode approach, one should focus on the goal of the mixed-mode design and on the reduction of mode effects by measurement error. It is important to analyze the different modes, recognizing when the media differ and listing the limitations and extra features of each method. When mixing two modes that both use the visual channel—for instance, paper self-administered and Internet surveys—one can design questionnaires using this visual channel and offer longer lists and visual stimuli. When mixing telephone interviews (aural mode) and Internet (visual mode), one cannot use long lists and must find other solutions, such as using an open-ended question or using an unfolding procedure, which can be programmed in both modes.

To provide researchers with general rules in designing questionnaires suitable for modes, Dillman (2007) proposed a unified mode design, or unimode design: designing questions and questionnaires to provide the same stimulus in all survey modes in order to reduce differences in the way respondents answer survey questions in different modes. Dillman (2007, pp. 232–240) outlines several principles to construct unified mode questionnaires. These include making response options the same across modes, incorporating response options in the stem of the question, and using the same descriptive labels for response categories. A good example of a unimode design for the short form of the U.S. census and its complexities is given by Martin et al. (2007), who used the central design principle that all respondents should be presented with the same question and response categories, independent of mode.

Unified mode design is often viewed as aiming at the lowest common denominator. That is not necessarily true; one should see it as an attempt to design robust questionnaires. A good example is check-all-that-apply questions, which are often used in Internet surveys, versus a series of yes/no questions, which is often used in telephone interviews. Smyth et al. (2008) showed that in Internet surveys a series of yes/no questions also performs better than the traditional check-all-that-apply questions. Couper (2008) advises to use check-all-that-apply questions sparingly, but recommends avoiding very long lists of yes/no questions, as this may increase the risk of break-offs. Usually when designing a mixed-mode telephone-Internet survey one would choose a reasonable list of questions to avoid break-offs in telephone and Web; in that case using a uniform yes/no format is no problem and increases the quality in both modes.

3.4.3 Beyond Unified Mode Design: Cognitive Equivalence of Questionnaires

Finally, one can go beyond designs that force different modes to use exactly the same questions. When questions are considered as stimuli that initiate a response process in the respondents, the perspective changes from offered stimulus to perceived stimulus. Using the same stimulus in different modes does not guarantee that the same question–answer process will be initiated, nor that respondents in one mode will perceive the question in the same way as respondents in a second mode. For example, a question in a telephone survey is not necessarily the same perceived stimulus as that same question when it is posed in an Internet survey, since the visual mode may change the meaning of the question and may therefore present a different *perceived* stimulus to the respondent than the aural (telephone) mode (cf. Tourangeau et al., 2000). Thus, in designing questions for a mixed-mode study, one should go a step further and aim at achieving cognitive equivalence of the perceived stimulus, rather than literal uniformity of questions across modes. This may imply that a slightly different question format for each mode is necessary to achieve the needed cognitive equivalence. De Leeuw (2005) labeled this "generalized mode design," while Dillman et al. (2009) use the term "mode-specific design" for the same concept and Couper (2008) emphasizes comparability of data. Whatever the term used, a prerequisite for successful mixed-mode design is that the question designer must understand how differences between modes affect response. A good illustration of this is the work of Wine, Cominole, Heuer, and Riccobono (2006), who used specially designed pop-ups after a "no answer" in an Internet survey, to emulate the probes used in previous telephone interviews.

A study by Christian, Dillman, and Smyth (2005) provides some insight into how and why different question formats across survey modes lead to equivalent results. In a telephone interview that asked, "When did you start attending Washington State University?" only 13% of the respondents reported the month and year, as desired. Instead, most respondents gave comments such as "last spring semester," "fall 2002," or "this is my first semester." These responses were followed up by the interviewer to obtain the desired response format, showing the strength of interviewer-assisted surveys. In the initial Internet survey, where the response had to be provided in open text boxes, only 45% of the respondents answered in the required format (two digits for month and four digits for year). By decreasing the size of the month box relative to the year box, replacing "month" and "year" with the more precise language of symbols (mm/yyyy), and placing those symbols in natural reading order ahead of the appropriate response boxes, the percentage of people responding in the desired way increased from 45% to 95%. These results clearly illustrate how different wording approaches of the question (telephone and Internet survey) can lead to the same result, but through different mechanisms. In the telephone survey, the interviewer served as an intelligent system that could ask for more information and convert the answer to the desired format required by the CATI system. In the Internet survey, the emphasis was on answer space labeling and layout in order to get the respondents to respond in the desired format and avoid error messages. Thus, different wording produced the same results. Using the same wording, "What month and year did you begin the studies?" for both Internet and telephone in this case actually *decreased* the equivalence of the recorded answers.

Just as in comparative research, in an optimal mixed-mode design the burden is on the researcher to demonstrate that these different questions do indeed elicit equivalent responses. This requires that at least some other, correlated questions are kept identical across different modes, which can then be used to test the equivalence of questions in the questionnaire. This is similar to the strategy used to statistically adjust responses in different modes to make them equivalent.

3.5 CONCLUSIONS

3.5.1 Internet Surveys and Mixed Mode

From a total survey error perspective, mixed-mode designs for Internet surveys are very attractive: Mixing modes greatly increases coverage and leads to less nonresponse at affordable costs. But every coin has two sides, and mixing Internet with other modes may lead to problems of data integrity.

A key methodological assumption in all mixed-mode surveys is that data from different modes can be meaningfully combined and compared—in other words, that there is measurement equivalence across modes. For Internet and paper-and-pencil self-administered questionnaires, measurement equivalence has been established in numerous cases, and when differences were found, these could be attributed to differences in sample composition or to self-selection. For Internet versus interview surveys, the situation is less clear. The results summarized in this chapter give confidence in well-designed mixes of visual self-administered modes, such as Internet and paper mail surveys. But mixing data collection modes that depend upon different communication channels (i.e., visual versus aural) may introduce nonignorable differences into the resulting data, and one should be more careful with Internet surveys mixed with interviews. Still, in some well-designed experiments measurement equivalence was established for CATI and Internet surveys (e.g., Oosterveld & Willems, 2003).

One also has to keep in mind that in most empirical comparisons reviewed, the focus was on methodological research, and extreme care was taken in designing the survey and attaining equivalent questionnaires. When different question formats are used in different modes (e.g., two-step unfolding versus full scale) or where layout changes substantially alter the response process (e.g., scrolling), equivalence of measurement is not guaranteed and measurement differences between modes are only to be expected.

3.5.2 Designing for a Mixed-Mode Approach Including Internet Surveys

In the design phase, using a questionnaire design strategy that encourages comparability of questionnaires reduces the impact of mode differences. For instance, the forced-choice yes/no format instead of a check-all-that-apply question format helps respondents to carefully process the questions, as is demonstrated by Smyth, Dillman, Christian, and Stern (2006), who also show that a forced-choice question not only produced more endorsed items than check-all-that-apply questions, it also took respondents longer to answer the forced-choice questions, suggesting less satisficing. Encouraging respondents to process the task carefully, take their time in answering, and allowing for ample time to complete a questionnaire may be crucial issues for quality in Internet surveys, as was also pointed out by Mead and Drasgow (1993) when explaining the lack of equivalence between computerized and paper-and-pencil speed tests.

Other factors also play a role, such as keeping respondents motivated and making the survey a pleasant experience. This is illustrated by the findings of Van Meurs, Van Ossenbruggen, and Nekkers (2009), who developed a system to identify respondents with satisficing response patterns in order to flag dubious or fraudulent respondents in a Dutch online panel. There was no systematic pattern in the demographic profile of panel members who were flagged and those who were not, but the researchers found a systematic pattern related to the questionnaire involved. Questionnaires that were evaluated as less interesting, boring, or too long evoked more dubious responses. Van Meurs et al. (2009) conclude that the most effective way to prevent fraudulent responses is to improve the quality of the questionnaire.

The visual design of Internet surveys is important for the quality of the questionnaire, as Toepoel (2008) shows with her findings that putting more items on a screen not only increased item nonresponse but also led to less positive assessment of the questionnaire itself. For more information on the importance of visual design, see Chapter 7 in this volume. Furthermore, the interactive power of the Internet may be used to replace some of the interviewer's tasks and keep respondents motivated in order to reduce item nonresponse (see Wine et al., 2006) and stimulate responses to open questions (see Chapter 9 in this volume).

When investigating sensitive topics through the Internet, special care should be taken. In general, one should be careful to avoid mixing self-administered modes, such as Internet surveys, with interview modes when sensitive questions are being asked. Mixing Internet with other self-administered forms, such as postal surveys, does not pose problems in this regard. In general, self-administered survey modes, including Internet, give rise to more self-disclosure and less social desirability bias on sensitive topics. But respondent trust is of the utmost importance, and when respondents are not assured of confidentiality or anonymity they are less willing to reveal personal or sensitive information (e.g., Richman et al., 1999). Protecting the confidentiality of the responses is one of the basic ethical rules of the survey industry (see Chapter 6 in this volume), and in Internet surveys with sensitive questions one should make sure to convey this to the respondents. A researcher may follow all the privacy and security guidelines, but if respondents are not aware of this, they may be inhibited when answering sensitive questions. Therefore, researchers should enhance the *perceived* security, especially as potential respondents may be wary of the security of the Web in general. There are several ways the perceived security may be heightened, such as by explicitly stating that answers are confidential, and by implementing a secure Web exchange with encryption during the session and making this clear to the respondent by a well-known icon such as a lock. Establishing trust is most difficult in "cold" Internet surveys, and it may be necessary to use another mode of communication, such as a paper advance letter, to assure the potential respondents of the legitimacy of the survey. When there is an existing relationship with the respondents, for instance in a good organized Internet panel, there is already a basic trust between researcher and respondent to build upon.

3.5.3 Embedded Experiments and Adjustment

3.5.3.1 Measurement Equivalence

Finally, in the analysis stage, researchers need to check equivalence of measurement across modes. This is especially important when different question formats or mode-specific optimization is used.

If the survey contains multi-item scales, multigroup structural equation modeling is a suitable tool to investigate measurement equivalence across modes. Measurement equivalence requires that a confirmative factor model fit the multi-item scale, and that the factor loadings and intercepts can be constrained equally across the groups. Some amount of difference is allowed; see Vandenburg and Lance (2000) for a review and discussion of the issues involved. The problem is that when measurement equivalence is not achieved, it is not clear whether this is the result of a mode effect or of a different sample composition in the two groups.

This can be disentangled to some degree by using subgrouping or propensity score methods. In the propensity score approach, logistic regression is used to predict membership of a specific mode sample, using available background variables. The propensity score is the predicted group membership. It can be used as a covariate, or the inverse of the propensity score can be used as a correction weight. For a review of using propensity scores in surveys, see Lee (2006). If measurement equivalence is achieved after propensity score weighting, we can ignore the difference in mode provided this weighting is used in the subsequent analyses.

If a difference remains, we can attempt to equate the scale scores across modes, as Van Buuren, Eyres, Tennant, and Hopman-Rock (2005) propose. Their method, termed "response conversion," attempts to transform responses obtained on different questions in different surveys onto a common scale. If this can be done successfully, meaningful comparisons can be made using this common scale. The first step in response conversion is the construction of a conversion key using a statistical model. In Van Buuren et al. (2005), the polytomous Rasch model is used, but a confirmatory factor analysis with strong measurement equivalence also would do. A prerequisite for response conversion is that there be sufficient overlap between the different items—in other words, that for some items there must be strong measurement equivalence. For a detailed methodological review, see Van Buuren et al. (2005).

3.5.3.2 ***Embedded Experiments***

Different respondent selection in different modes is a difficult problem, and is hard to solve in daily survey practice. Also, alternating modes in a longitudinal design causes problems by a potential confounding of time and mode effects. A sound approach in all cases is implementing a small mode experiment including randomized assignment of respondents to the different modes in the survey in order to assess and compensate for potential mode effects (De Leeuw, 2005). This will increase the effort and costs, but especially in large national surveys, cross-national studies, and longitudinal surveys this is well worth it, and researchers are advised to allocate a small part of their budget for mode-effect investigations, just as part of the budget is often allocated to studies into nonresponse bias and adjustment.

A small mode comparison embedded into the data collection procedure enables the researcher to estimate potential mode effects, and if necessary to statistically adjust for it, using calibration, propensity score adjustment, or response conversion (e.g., Lee, 2006; Lundstrom & Sarndal, 2002; Van Buuren et al., 2005). For instance, in a longitudinal design a random subsample of respondents can be investigated using the initial data collection mode of the previous wave and the majority of the sample can be surveyed using the main mode of the wave (e.g., a small subsample is interviewed face-to-face, while the intended mode is Internet). If for practical consideration a random subsample is not possible, one could implement a small embedded mode experiment among those with Internet access, where a random half of the subsample is surveyed using the Internet and the remainder using the telephone. Even if in this case the experiment is not performed on a random subsample of the whole population, it will still provide valuable information to extrapolate and assess the risk of mode effects (De Leeuw, 2005).

A good example is the experiment by Jäckle, Roberts, and Lynn (2007), who were able to disentangle the effects of interviewers and use of show cards in telephone and face-to-face interviews, using a subset of the core questions of the European Social Survey. The experiment took place in Budapest and the immediate surrounding area, where telephone penetration was high. Respondents were randomly assigned to three groups: (1) face-to-face interviews with show cards, (2) face-to-face interviews without show cards, and (3) telephone interviews with the same questionnaire as in group 2. After careful analysis, the findings suggest that differences were mainly due to the presence of the interviewer, causing a greater social desirability bias, and that show cards did not appear to affect responses.

3.5.3.3 Adjustment: Disentangling Mode and Selection Effects

Embedding a small randomized mode comparison experiment in a mixed-mode design makes assessing and compensating for mode effects much simpler. Assume that we have a mixed-mode design in which for reasons of efficiency different respondents are self-selected to two different modes. In this design, we embed a small-scale mode experiment where a small number of respondents are randomly assigned to one of these two modes. In this situation, we then effectively have four separate groups in our design. Figure 3.1 illustrates the four groups and the comparisons that can be made.

As Figure 3.1 shows, by embedding a small randomized experiment in the sampling, we can distinguish between the mode effect and the selection effect, and we can examine to what degree propensity score adjustment can correct for the selection bias. More importantly, if the difference in mode is actually a selection effect, we can ignore the apparent mode effect and interpret differences between respondents across modes as reflecting real differences. If the mode effect exists and is not negligible, we can use propensity score adjustment and attempt to equate the model parameters within the same mode

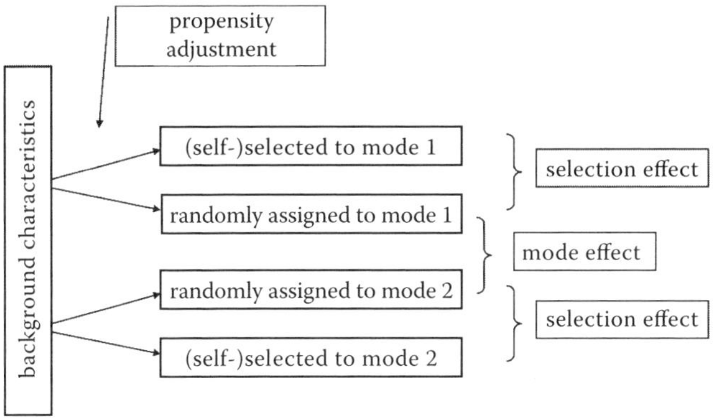

FIGURE 3.1
Combination of (self-)selection and random assignment to modes.

across the randomly assigned and the selected groups. The most principled way to accomplish this would be through structural equation modeling. In practice, however, after the researchers have investigated the various effects depicted in Figure 3.1 thoroughly, they may decide to use a simple dummy variable indicating mode in addition to the propensity adjustment.

In sum, when mixing Internet surveys with other data collection modes, much depends on the characteristics of the mix and the content of the questionnaire. Researchers should clearly evaluate the topic of the questions, the presence/absence of interviewers, and the communication channels (audio versus visual) used. Successful mixed-mode design requires an understanding of how mode differences may affect the answers given. For instance, when sensitive questions are used, the presence of an interviewer may cause social desirability bias associated with mode when CATI or CAPI is mixed with the more anonymous Internet survey. In this case, a mix of paper mail and Internet will be far better. When complex questionnaires are used, the aid of an intelligent system—be it a well-implemented Internet survey or an interviewer in CATI or CAPI—is necessary, and mixes with paper mail surveys may very well introduce respondent error in important routings. Also, the social conventions and customs associated with the mode are important for mixes involving Internet surveys, in particular when special groups (e.g., the elderly) are investigated or when cross-cultural and international surveys are being conducted. Finally, after having chosen the optimal Internet mix, designers must make sure that equivalent questionnaires are implemented, as question-format effects have to be avoided. But even after careful designing, it is still possible that differences between modes will remain. To cope with these, it is useful to collect additional data on possible mode effects, or embed a small-mode experiment. These data are first used to investigate potential mode effects, and may be used later in the analysis phase to correct by statistical means for any mode differences.

REFERENCES

American Psychological Association. (1986). *Guidelines for computer-based tests and interpretations.* Washington, DC: American Psychological Association (APA).

Bergstrom, B. (1992). *Ability measure equivalence of computer adaptive and paper and pencil tests: A research synthesis.* Paper presented at the annual meeting of the American Educational Research Association, San Francisco (as cited by Wang et al., 2007).

Bethlehem, J. G. (2008). Representativity of Web surveys—An illusion? In I. Stoop & M. Wittenberg (Eds.), *Access panels and online research: Panacea or pitfall?* (pp. 19–44). Amsterdam: Aksant/DANS. Retrieved from http://www.jelkebethlehem.nl/surveys/papers/bethlehem01.pdf

Biemer, P. P. & Lyberg, L. E. (2003). *Introduction to survey quality.* New York: John Wiley & Sons.

Blyth, B. (2008a). Mixed-mode: The only "fitness" regime? *International Journal of Market Research, 50*(2), 241–266.

Blyth, B. (2008b). *The implications of variation in national data collection mode access and rate of access change: A European overview.* Paper presented at the 3MC conference, Berlin.

Bronner, F. & Kuijlen, T. (2007). The live or digital interviewer: A comparison between CASI, CAPI, and CATI with respect to differences in response behaviour. *International Journal of Market Research, 49*(2), 167–190.

Christian, L. M., Dillman, D. A., & Smyth, J. D. (2005). *Instructing Web and telephone respondents to report date answers in format desired by the surveyor.* Social and Economic Sciences Research Center Technical Report 05-067. Retrieved November 4, 2009, from http://survey.sesrc.wsu.edu/dillman/papers.htm

Christian, L. M., Dillman, D. A., & Smyth, J. D. (2008). The effects of mode and format on answers to scalar questions in telephone and Web surveys. In J. M. Lepkowski, C. Tucker, J. M. Brick et al. (Eds.), *Advances in telephone survey methodology* (pp. 250–275). New York: John Wiley & Sons.

Cole, M. S., Bedeian, A. G., & Feild, H. S. (2006). The measurement equivalence of Web-based and paper-and-pencil measures of transformational leadership: A multinational test. *Organizational Research Methods, 9*(3), 339–368.

Cook, C., Heath, F., & Thompson, R. L. (2000). A meta-analysis of response rates in Web- or Internet-based surveys. *Educational and Psychological Measurement, 60*(6), 821–836.

Couper, M. P. (2000). Web surveys: A review of issues and approaches. *Public Opinion Quarterly, 64*, 464–494.

Couper, M. P. (2008). *Designing effective Web surveys.* New York: Cambridge University Press.

Couper, M. P. & De Leeuw, E. D. (2003). Nonresponse in cross-cultural and cross-national surveys. In J. A. Harkness, A. J. R. Van de Vijver, & P. Mohler (Eds.), *Cross-cultural survey methods* (pp. 157–177). New York: John Wiley & Sons.

Couper, M. P., Kapteyn, A., Schonlau, M., & Winter, J. (2007). Noncoverage and nonresponse in an Internet survey. *Social Science Research, 36*(1), 131–148.

De Leeuw, E. D. (1992). *Data quality in mail, telephone, and face-to-face surveys*. Amsterdam: TT-Publikaties. Retrieved from http://www.xs4all.nl/~edithl

De Leeuw, E. D. (2005). To mix or not to mix data collection modes in surveys. *Journal of Official Statistics, 21*, 233–255. Retrieved from http://www.jos.nu

De Leeuw, E. D. (2008). Choosing the method of data collection. In E. D. De Leeuw, J. J. Hox, & D. A. Dillman (Eds.), *International handbook of survey methodology* (pp. 113–135). European Association of Methodology Series. New York: Lawrence Erlbaum Associates.

De Leeuw, E. D., Hox, J. J., & Dillman, D. A. (2008a). The cornerstones of survey research. In E. D. De Leeuw, J. J. Hox, & D. A. Dillman (Eds.), *International handbook of survey methodology* (pp. 1–17). European Association of Methodology Series. New York: Lawrence Erlbaum Associates.

De Leeuw, E. D., Hox, J. J., & Dillman, D. A. (2008b). Mixed-mode surveys: When and why. In E. D. De Leeuw, J. J. Hox, & D. A. Dillman (Eds.), *International handbook of survey methodology* (pp. 299–316). European Association of Methodology Series. New York: Lawrence Erlbaum Associates.

De Leeuw, E. D., Hox, J. J., & Kef, S. (2003). Computer-assisted self-interviewing tailored for special populations and topics. *Field Methods, 15*, 223–251.

Dillman, D. A. (2007). *Mail and Internet surveys: The tailored design method* (2nd ed.). New York: John Wiley & Sons.

Dillman, D. A. (2008). The logic and psychology of constructing questionnaires. In E. D. De Leeuw, J. J. Hox, & D. A. Dillman (Eds.), *International handbook of survey methodology* (pp. 161–175). European Association of Methodology Series. New York: Lawrence Erlbaum Associates.

Dillman, D. A., Brown, T. L., Carlson, J., Carpenter, E. H., Lorenz, F. O., Mason, R. et al. (1995). Effects of category order on answers to mail and telephone surveys. *Rural Sociology, 60*, 674–687.

Dillman, D. A. & Christian, L. M. (2005). Survey mode as a source of instability across surveys. *Field Methods, 17*, 30–52.

Dillman, D. A., Phelps, G., Tortora, R., Swift, K., Kohrell, J., Berck, J. et al. (forthcoming). *Response rate and measurement differences in mixed mode surveys using mail, telephone, interactive voice response, and the Internet*. Retrieved from http://survey.sesrc.wsu.edu/dillman/papers.htm (earlier version).

Dillman, D. A., Smyth, J. D., & Christian, L. M. (2009). *Internet, mail, and mixed-mode surveys: The tailored design method* (3rd ed.). New York: John Wiley & Sons.

Dillman, D. A., Smyth, J. D., Christian, L. M., & O'Neill, A. (2008). *Will a mixed-mode (mail/Internet) procedure work for random household surveys of the general public?* Paper presented at the annual conference of the American Association for Public Opinion Research (AAPOR), New Orleans, Louisiana.

Epstein, J. & Klinkenberg, W. D. (2001). From Eliza to Internet: A brief history of computerized assessment. *Computers in Human Behavior, 17*, 295–314.

Ferrando, P. J. & Lorenzo-Seva, U. (2005). IRT-related factor analytic procedures for testing the equivalence of paper-and-pencil and Internet-administered questionnaires. *Psychological Methods, 10*(2), 193–205.

Fricker, S., Galesic, M., Tourangeau, R., & Yan, T. (2005). An experimental comparison of Web and telephone surveys. *Public Opinion Quarterly, 69*(3), 370–392.
Groves, R. M. (1989). *Survey errors and survey costs.* New York: John Wiley & Sons.
Gwaltney, C. J., Shields, A. L., & Shiffman, S. (2008). Equivalence of electronic and paper-and-pencil administration of patient-reported outcome measures: A meta-analytic review. *Value in Health, 11*(2), 322–333.
Hacking, I. (1990). *The taming of chance.* Cambridge, UK: Cambridge University Press.
Heerwegh, D., Billiet, J., & Loosveldt, G. (2005). Opinies op bestelling? Een experimenteel onderzoek naar het effect van vraagverwoording en sociale wenselijkheid op de proportie voor-en tegenstanders van gemeentelijk migrantenstemrecht [Opinions on demand? An experimental investigation of the effect of question wording and social desirability on the proportion of proponents and opponents of municipal suffrage for immigrants]. *Tijdschrift voor Sociologie, 26*(3), 189–208.
Heerwegh, D. & Loosveldt, G. (2008). Face-to-face versus Web surveying in a high-Internet-coverage population: Differences in response quality. *Public Opinion Quarterly, 72*(5), 836–846.
Heiser, W. (1996). *De probabilisering van het wereldbeeld [Chance and our view of the world].* Invited lecture, University of Groningen, symposium in honor of Professor Ivo Molenaar.
Jäckle, A., Roberts, C., & Lynn, P. (2007). *Assessing the effect of data collection mode on measurement.* Paper presented at the ISI conference, Lisbon, Portugal. See also ISER working paper 2006-41. Retrieved June 27, 2009, from http://www.iser.essex.ac.uk/publications/working-papers/iser/2006-41.pdf
Kim, J.-P. (1999). *Meta-analysis of equivalence of computerized and P&P tests on ability measures.* Paper presented at the annual meeting of the Midwestern Educational Research Association, Chicago (retrieved from ERIC).
Krauter, F., Presser, S., & Tourangeau, R. (2008). Social desirability bias in CATI, IVR, and Web surveys: The effect of mode and question sensitivity. *Public Opinion Quarterly, 72*(5), 847–865.
Krug, S. (2006). *Don't make me think: A common sense approach to Web usability: How we really use the Web.* Retrieved April 2009 from http://www.sensible.com/chapter.html
Lee, S. (2006). Propensity score adjustment as a weighting scheme for volunteer panel Web surveys. *Journal of Official Statistics, 22*(2), 329–249. Retrieved from http://www.jos.nu
Link, M. W. & Mokdad, A. H. (2005). Effects of survey mode on self-reports of adult alcohol consumption: A comparison of mail, Web and telephone approaches. *Journal of Studies on Alcohol, 66*, 239–245.
Lozar Manfreda, K., Bosnjak, M., Berzelak, J., Haas, I., & Vehovar, V. (2008). Web surveys versus other survey modes: A meta-analysis comparing response rates. *International Journal of Market Research, 50*(1), 79–104.
Lundstrom, S. & Sarndal, C.-E. (2002). *Estimation in the presence of nonresponse and frame imperfections.* Statistics Sweden.
Martin, E., Childs, J. H., DeMaio, T., Hill, J., Reiser, C., Gerber, E. et al. (2007). *Guidelines for designing questionnaires for administration in different modes.* Washington, DC: U.S. Bureau of the Census. Retrieved July 2009 from http://www.census.gov/srd/mode-guidelines.pdf
Mead, A. D. & Drasgow, F. (1993). Equivalence of computerized and paper-and-pencil cognitive ability tests: A meta-analysis. *Psychological Bulletin, 114*(3), 449–458.

Meade, A. W., Michels, L. C., & Lautenschlager, G. J. (2007). Are Internet and paper-and-pencil personality tests truly comparable? An experimental design measurement invariance study. *Organizational Research Methods, 10*(2), 322–345.

Oosterveld, P. & Willems, P. (2003). Two modalities, one answer? Combining Internet and CATI surveys effectively in market research. In D. S. Fellows (Ed.), *Technovate* (pp. 141–150). Amsterdam: ESOMAR.

Preckel, F. & Thieman, H. (2001). *Testing intellectual giftedness on the Web: Development of a new figural matrices test-online versus paper-and-pencil versions.* Paper presented at the General Online Research conference (GOR '01), Göttingen, Germany. Retrieved April 2009 from www.gor.de

Richman, W. L., Kiesler, S., Weisband, S., & Drasgow, F. (1999). A meta-analytic study of social desirability distortion in computer-administered questionnaires, traditional questionnaires, and interviews. *Journal of Applied Psychology, 84*(5), 754–775.

Roberts, C. (2007). *Mixing modes of data collection in surveys: A methodological review.* ESRC/NCRM Methods Review Paper 008. Retrieved July 2009 from http://eprints.ncrm.ac.uk/418/1/MethodsReviewPaperNCRM-008.pdf

Rookey, B. D., Hanway, S., & Dillman, D. A. (2008). Does a probability-based household panel benefit from assignment to postal response as an alternative to Internet-only? *Public Opinion Quarterly, 72*(5), 962–984.

Schuman, H. & Presser, S. (1981). *Questions and answers in attitude surveys.* New York: Academic Press.

Shih, T.-H. & Fan, X. (2008). Comparing response rates from Web and mail surveys: A meta-analysis. *Field Methods, 20*, 249–271.

Sikkel, D., Hox, J. J., & De Leeuw, E. D (2009). Using auxiliary data for adjustment in longitudinal research. In P. Lynn (Ed.). *Methodology of longitudinal surveys* (pp. 141–155). New York: John Wiley & Sons.

Smyth, J. D., Christian, L. M., & Dillman, D. A. (2008). Does yes or no on the telephone mean the same as check-all-that-apply on the Web? *Public Opinion Quarterly, 72*(1), 103–113.

Smyth, J. D., Dillman, D. A., Christian, L. M., & Stern, M. J. (2006). Comparing check-all and forced-choice question formats in Web surveys. *Public Opinion Quarterly, 70*(1), 66–77.

Sudman, S. & Bradburn, N. M. (1974). *Response effects in surveys: A review and synthesis.* Chicago: Aldine.

Toepoel, V. (2008). *A closer look at Web questionnaire design.* CentER for Economic Research Dissertation Series, no. 220, Tilburg University, the Netherlands.

Tourangeau, R., Rips, L. J., & Rasinski, K. (2000). *The psychology of survey response.* Cambridge, UK: Cambridge University Press.

Tourangeau, R. & Smith, T. W. (1996). Asking sensitive questions: The impact of data collection mode, question format, and question context. *Public Opinion Quarterly, 60*, 275–304.

Turner, C. F., Forsyth, B. H., O'Reilly, J. M., Cooley, P. C., Smith, T. K., Rogers, S. M. et al. (1998). Automated self-interviewing and the survey measurement of sensitive behaviors. In M. P. Couper, R. P. Baker, J. Bethlehem et al. (Eds.), *Computer-assisted survey information collection* (pp. 455–473). New York: John Wiley & Sons.

Van Buuren, S., Eyres, S., Tennant, A., & Hopman-Rock, M. (2005). Improving comparability of existing data by response conversion. *Journal of Official Statistics, 21*, 53–72.

Vandenburg, R. & Lance, C. E. (2000). A review and synthesis of the measurement invariance literature: Suggestions, practices, and recommendations for organizational research. *Organizational Research Methods*, *3*(1), 4–70.
Van Ewijk, R. (2004). Onderzoek via telefoon en Internet: De verschillen [Surveys by means of telephone and Internet: The differences]. *Clou, 14*, 38–40.
Van Meurs, A., Van Ossenbruggen, R., & Nekkers, L. (2009). Rotte appels? Controle op kwaliteit van antwoordgedrag in het Intomart GfK Online Panel [Do rotten apples spoil the whole barrel? Checking the quality of responses in the Intomart GfK Online Panel]. In A. E. Bronner et al. (Eds)., *Ontwikkelingen in het Marktonderzoek, Jaarboek Marktonderzoek Associatie, 34*, 61–81.
Wang, S., Jiao, H., Young, M. J., Brooks, T., & Olson, J. (2007). A meta-analysis of testing mode effects in grade K-12 mathematics tests. *Educational and Psychological Measurement, 67*(2), 219–238.
Wang, S., Jiao, H. Young, M. J., Brooks, T., & Olson, J. (2008). Comparability of computer-based and paper-and-pencil testing in K-12 reading assessments: A meta-analysis of testing mode effects. *Educational and Psychological Measurement, 68*(1), 5–24.
Willems, P., Van Ossenbruggen, R., & Vonk, T. (2006). The effect of panel recruitment and management on research results: A study across 19 online panels. *Proceedings of the ESOMAR World Research Conference, Panel Research 2006, 317*, 79–99. Amsterdam: ESOMAR.
Wine, J. S., Cominole, M. B., Heuer, R. E., & Riccobono, J. A. (2006). *Challenges of designing and implementing multimode instruments.* Paper presented at the Second International Conference on Telephone Survey Methodology, Miami, Florida. Retrieved March 2009 from http://www.rti.org/pubs/TSM2006_Wine_paper.pdf

4

"True" Longitudinal and Probability-Based Internet Panels: Evidence From the Netherlands

Annette C. Scherpenzeel
CentERdata
Tilburg University
Tilburg, the Netherlands

Marcel Das
CentERdata and Tilburg School of Economics and Management
Tilburg University
Tilburg, the Netherlands

4.1 INTRODUCTION

In this chapter we introduce the methodology to set up a panel that combines the new technology of Internet surveys with a "true" longitudinal design. Not many long-running scientific panels in Europe or the United States are Internet panels. Leading scientific panels mostly use face-to-face or telephone interviews to collect data. By contrast, Internet interviewing has become a widespread method for access panels and volunteer panels. These panels should not be confused with true longitudinal and probability-based panels, however. In a true panel, a set of repeated measures is collected at regular intervals (for example, once a year) from the same group of people. Most access panels and other commercial Internet panels collect varying, nonrecurring measures at irregular intervals from a choice of panel members. Thus, the—usually very large—panel is treated as a pool for cross-sectional measures instead of as a longitudinal panel. Furthermore, a true panel demands a probability sample to start with, covering the whole population of interest and thus including people without Internet access and people who do not actively volunteer to answer questions (for more about this aspect, see Chapter 5 in this volume). Finally, it demands a long-term participation by the original sample members.

It is very well possible to combine the scientific standards for a true longitudinal panel with the advantages of Internet interviewing as a method of data collection. We will show how such a panel can be built and maintained, taking a Dutch panel as illustration: the Longitudinal Internet Studies for the Social sciences (LISS) panel administered by CentERdata (Tilburg University, the Netherlands).

The design of the LISS panel includes a core questionnaire that is repeated each year and represents the longitudinal aspect. In addition, the panel can be used for stand-alone questionnaires, allowing for a huge variety of topics to be covered. These questionnaires can be proposed by scientific researchers from the Netherlands and abroad. Some of these proposals concern one-shot surveys, while others have a longitudinal dimension. The LISS panel thus aims to provide a longitudinal survey and an infrastructure for data collection for scientific studies, both based on a probability sample drawn from the Dutch-speaking population.

The remainder of this chapter is organized as follows. Section 4.2 gives a short overview of the field of longitudinal panel surveys. Next, in Section 4.3, we describe new developments in survey research, in particular Internet interviewing. We discuss the consequences of choosing Internet interviewing as a data collection method for a scientific longitudinal panel, instead of the traditional methods used by most other panels. In Section 4.4 we look in detail at the design and setup of the LISS panel. We show that it is possible to combine Internet interviewing with scientific demands in terms of coverage and sample selection. We describe how we combined a longitudinal panel survey with an open facility for data collection for cross-sectional research and short-term panel studies. We also evaluate the first two years of the panel. Finally, Section 4.5 discusses the extent to which the objectives of the panel have been realized so far.

4.2 LONGITUDINAL PANEL SURVEYS

4.2.1 Typology and Examples

Lynn (2009, p. 1) defines a longitudinal survey as follows: "A *longitudinal survey* is one that collects data from the same sample elements on multiple occasions over time." He describes a typology of longitudinal surveys, based on a number of dimensions such as the study topics, the population of interest, the interval between waves, the mode of data collection, and the treatment of new entrants to the population. The variation on these dimensions results in many different types of longitudinal surveys, for example surveys of school-leavers, birth-cohort studies, or epidemiological studies. Within the framework of this typology, the LISS panel is of the type that Lynn calls household panel surveys. This type of survey involves questionnaires with each person in the household at each wave and an extra questionnaire with one person to collect household-level information. The data usually include a wide range of demographic, economic, social, and attitudinal variables and are used for a variety of purposes. The LISS core study, described in Section 4.4.5, aims to collect such repeated measures from the same individuals on a range of topics. Many longitudinal household panel studies in numerous countries have preceded this effort. We mention only a few of the most well known.

Established in 1968, the Panel Study of Income Dynamics (PSID) in the United States is one of the oldest panel surveys. It collects data on economic, health, and social behaviors. Its European equivalent was the much younger European Community Household Panel (ECHP) survey, which monitored developments in income, living conditions, housing, health, and work in the member states of the EU. In 2003 the ECHP was replaced by the European Statistics on Income and Living Conditions (EU-SILC). Probably the oldest and most used European national household panels are the British Household Panel Survey (BHPS) and the German Socio-Economic Panel (GSOEP). The BHPS has now been extended with a large new household panel survey called Understanding Society (initially known as the UK Household Longitudinal Study [UKHLS]), comprising 40,000 British households. The PSID Web site provides an extensive list of panel studies around the world.*

In 2000, Kalton predicted that the use of panel designs would increase even further in the future (Kalton, 2000). We indeed see that new longitudinal surveys are established continually, for example, in Switzerland, Australia, New Zealand, eastern and central European countries, Mexico, South Africa, and several Asian countries. There are also longitudinal surveys that focus on specific topics or target populations; a well-known

* See http://psidonline.isr.umich.edu/Guide/PanelStudies.aspx

example is the University of Michigan's Health and Retirement Study (HRS). Established in 1992, this study surveys more than 22,000 Americans over the age of 50 every two years. The study paints an emerging portrait of an aging generation's physical and mental health, insurance coverage, financial status, family support systems, labor market status, and retirement planning. Modeled on the HRS, a similar study was launched in the United Kingdom in 2002: the English Longitudinal Study of Ageing (ELSA). Two years after that, a parallel study was established in Europe, named the Survey of Health, Ageing, and Retirement in Europe (SHARE).

In the Netherlands, the Socio-Economic Panel (SEP) survey existed from 1984 to 2001. This survey was operated by Statistics Netherlands and followed approximately 5,000 households through time. All household members ages 16 and over were interviewed about their socioeconomic situation, with questions on education, labor market participation, income, assets, and debts. Two waves a year were carried out between 1984 and 1989; between 1990 and 2001 the survey was held annually. Although Statistics Netherlands still conducts an ongoing study of living conditions using a repeated cross-sectional design (the Permanent Study of the Living Situation [POLS]), Statistics Netherlands has not conducted a household panel survey for general purposes since the SEP ended in 2001.

4.2.2 Strengths and Weaknesses

The aim of most longitudinal panel surveys is to collect data about social change, household dynamics, and individual life courses over time (Duncan & Kalton, 1987). In the United States as well as in Europe, researchers have generated large numbers of publications about social change and life course using data from existing household panels (as can be seen on the various panel survey Web sites). Lynn (2009) describes the strengths of longitudinal surveys. First, longitudinal surveys enable special forms of analysis, such as: the analysis of gross change and of unit-level change; the calculation of aggregate measures (for example, 12 monthly measures of expenditure to obtain an estimate of annual expenditure); the calculation of measures of stability or instability; the estimation of the timing and duration of events or circumstances; and the identification of causality. These strengths have frequently been described (e.g., Duncan & Kalton, 1987; Kalton & Citro, 1993; Berthoud & Gershuny, 2000; Lynn, 2009), and they explain the growth of longitudinal surveys in the past decades. Second, the quality of the data that result from longitudinal surveys is often higher. For example, longer histories of events and transitions can be collected (compared to retrospective interviews); the accuracy of data is greater (compared to retrospective recall); it is possible to check and correct inaccurate dating of events; different groups of respondents can be approached in tailored ways and with varying between-waves intervals; and relationships between intentions and behavior can be measured directly, untainted by recall error, as can relationships between expectations and outcomes, and between attitudes and choices. In addition, it can sometimes be more cost effective to carry out repeated surveys with the same sample than to select a new sample for each new study of the same population. This is the case, for example, when an epidemiological survey requires a large-scale population screening to identify a group of respondents with a certain disease.

One of the advantages that Lynn lists is the possibility to detect likely errors in panel data. However, the ability to correct these errors is even more valuable. The ideal strategy in such cases is to go back to the respondents to resolve apparent inconsistencies. One example in which this strategy was successfully applied is the 2001 HRS Asset-Change Reconciliation Callback Project (Hill, 2002). The project staff of the HRS called 1,481 households whose aggregate net worth, or one net worth component, inexplicably changed by a very large amount between two waves. They achieved reconciliation for 1,255 households, and the variance in measured change for the entire sample between the two waves was cut in half.

Another way to correct or prevent errors, which is becoming increasingly common in panel surveys, is dependent interviewing. In this procedure, data from previous waves are available during the interview, so the consistency of answers with data from previous waves can be checked on the fly. In the event of a significant change, the respondent is asked if the answer given is correct. Another form is to present the answer given in the previous wave before the respondent is asked to give the new answer. Recent studies of the effects of both forms of dependent interviewing on the quality of data have been performed by, for example, Hoogendoorn (2004), Jäckle (2008), Jäckle and Lynn (2007), Lynn, Jäckle, Jenkins, and Sala (2006), and Lynn and Sala (2006). A conceptual framework of dependent interviewing, including an overview of current research, has been given by Jäckle (2009). An earlier overview of the state of dependent interviewing in household surveys can be found in Mathiowetz and McGonagle

(2000). Most of these studies show that dependent interviewing—a technique that is possible only in panel surveys—is an effective means of increasing the reliability of survey data.

Longitudinal panel surveys also have a number of weaknesses. All components of the total survey error (Groves et al., 2004) that apply to any survey also apply to longitudinal surveys: coverage error, sampling error, nonresponse error, and measurement error. However, longitudinal panel surveys have some additional problems specific to their design (Laurie, Smith, & Scott, 1999; Lynn, 2009). The first problem is attrition of panel members over time; this source of nonresponse comes on top of the initial nonresponse that panel surveys share with cross-sectional surveys. Attrition can have different causes. The first is a loss of respondents due to panel members who move and cannot be traced. Since the more geographically mobile respondents probably differ from the respondents with a stable address, this is a source of selective attrition (Laurie et al., 1999; Couper & Ofstedal, 2009). A framework for understanding the location problem is given by Couper and Ofstedal (2009). They identify the factors that affect tracking and location propensities, which can guide fieldwork strategies to maintain contact with mobile panel members. In addition, they discuss the role of technological developments such as the growth of the number of databases, often accessible online, and the introduction of telephone number portability. This offers new possibilities of tracking and tracing panel members. For Internet panels, the location problem is somewhat different because Internet connections and e-mail addresses usually move along with the relocation of a household, so contact with the panel is generally not disrupted. However, e-mail addresses are subject to greater turnover than telephone numbers (Couper & Ofstedal, 2009) and thus may require frequent updating.

The second cause of attrition is refusals. At every interview point, respondents have the option of refusing to participate further. As Laurie, Smith, and Scott (1999) and Sikkel and Hoogendoorn (2008) describe, respondents may become bored or lose interest in continued participation (panel fatigue) or simply feel that they have "done enough." Other respondents drop out because of personal or family reasons or because of health problems. As these respondents also tend to have specific characteristics, this type of attrition is another source of bias in the course of a longitudinal panel survey. We will not discuss the extensive literature on selectivity, attrition, and missing data here. The point we want to make is that selective attrition can lead to a weakness in terms of analysis. Compared with estimates from a cross-sectional survey, cross-sectional estimates from a longitudinal survey may be less reliable (Lynn, 2009). The question is, of course, whether it is a relevant aim for a longitudinal panel survey to provide cross-sectional estimates. Moreover, a substantial amount of information may already have been collected on respondents before they drop out of a panel. This makes it easier to reliably model the process of attrition, and hence to correct for the selectivity bias that otherwise would be created by nonignorable attrition. Additional information can also be gleaned from refreshment samples (see, e.g., Hirano, Imbens, Ridder, & Rubin, 2001).

The second problem of longitudinal panel surveys is that panel respondents eventually become experienced respondents, and their response to questions may differ systematically from the response of individuals who are not experienced respondents. This may be good or bad. To the extent that respondents learn how to interpret questions, they may make fewer errors than novice respondents. On the other hand, trained respondents may speed through the survey to reduce the burden of their task. Respondents could, for example, choose strategic answers to avoid follow-up questions (cf. Mathiowetz & Lair, 1994; Meurs, Van Wissen, & Visser, 1989).

Toepoel, Das, and Van Soest (2008, 2009) analyzed whether trained respondents react differently to Web survey design choices than inexperienced respondents. They found little evidence that survey experience influences the question-answering process. Trained respondents tend to take shortcuts in the response process and study the questions less carefully. However, as Lynn (2009) has pointed out, the experience of panel members may not only change how they answer questions but also impact their actual behavior. A recurrent question about monthly expenditure, for example, may make people more aware of how much they spend and thus possibly influence their spending behavior in subsequent months.

In conclusion, longitudinal panel surveys offer some unique possibilities and advantages over single studies, even though they have larger problems of nonresponse and some specific problems of measurement error. The advantages are so widely recognized, however, that many longitudinal panel surveys have been established, and that number continues to grow. The LISS panel is an attempt to provide a source of longitudinal panel data for the Netherlands. The difference is that this panel can make use of recent developments in survey research, whereas most longer-running household panels cannot easily switch from the traditional methods used for years to new technologies. We will now describe some of the new developments in survey research that are relevant for the LISS panel, and next describe how these have been applied in the design of the LISS panel.

4.3 NEW DEVELOPMENTS IN SURVEY RESEARCH

In Section 4.2.1 we described examples of household panels that use a true longitudinal design. The majority of these panels use face-to-face or telephone interviews to collect data. At the same time, the world of survey research is rapidly changing, incorporating new developments and technologies. Scientific surveys using telephone and face-to-face interviews encounter increasing problems of undercoverage and nonresponse bias. Telephone surveys in particular face increasing difficulties as it becomes harder to reach respondents directly, partly because of the increased use of voicemail and cell phones (e.g., Oldendick & Link, 1994; Link & Oldendick, 1999; Berrens, Bohara, Jenkins-Smith, Silva, & Weimer, 2001), and partly because of the vast increase of unlisted telephone numbers (e.g., Piekarski, Kaplan, & Prestegaard, 1999). A decade ago, Kalton already questioned the role of telephone data collection in the future, because of the decreasing response rates to telephone surveys (Kalton, 2000). The diminishing coverage of (landline) telephone interviews in Western countries adds up to the problem of low response rates. Figure 4.1 shows the gradual decrease in fixed telephone lines between 1999 and 2008 for Western European countries, the steep increase in mobile cellular subscriptions in these countries during the same time period, and the increase in Internet users (ITU ICT Eye, 2009). Figure 4.2 shows that the coverage of landline connections in the Netherlands is diminishing faster than this average and that the number of Internet users is higher (ITU ICT Eye, 2009).

These developments have serious effects on survey research methods. In many countries, data collection is moving from telephone and face-to-face surveys to Internet interviewing and the use of mobile devices. In commercial settings, this has led to the use of access panels.

Many different forms of Internet surveys have evolved over time. Couper (2000) provides a taxonomy of eight different types of Internet surveys, distinguishing between probability and non-probability surveys. Two

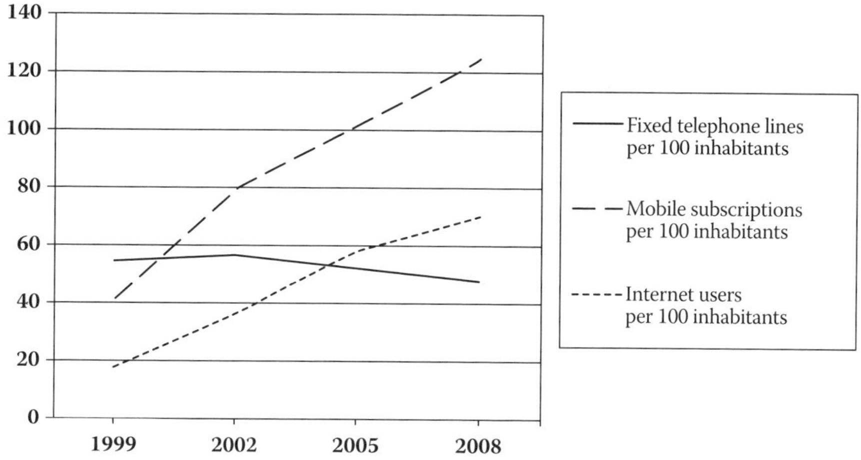

FIGURE 4.1
Development in fixed telephone lines, mobile cellular subscriptions, and Internet users per 100 inhabitants in Western Europe. (Note: The number of Internet users per 100 inhabitants in 2008 averaged over Greece, Italy, Portugal, and Spain is equal to 46. The number averaged over the other Western European countries—Austria, Belgium, Denmark, Finland, France, Germany, Ireland, Luxembourg, the Netherlands, Norway, Sweden, United Kingdom, and Switzerland—is equal to 77.) From ITU ICT Eye, 2009.

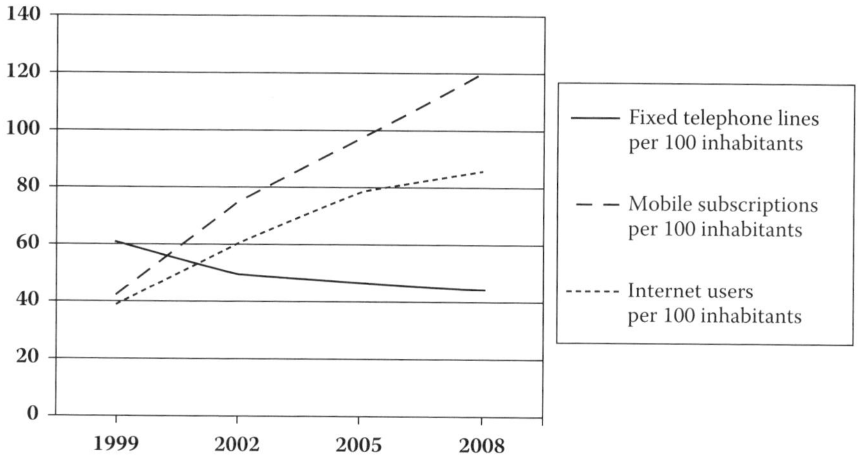

FIGURE 4.2
Developments in fixed telephone lines, mobile cellular subscriptions, and Internet users per 100 inhabitants in the Netherlands. From ITU ICT Eye, 2009.

examples of some of the most prevalent non-probability Internet surveys are self-selected Internet surveys, using open invitations on portals and Web sites with unrestricted access to the survey; and volunteer panels of Internet users, created by appeals on portals and Web sites but with access to the subsequent surveys restricted to panel members by passwords and e-mail invitations. The non-probability Internet surveys suffer from problems of coverage and self-selection bias, as described in Chapter 5 in this volume. The probability Internet surveys in Couper's taxonomy vary from list-based samples of high-Internet-coverage populations (for example, a survey among students) to mixed-mode designs with a choice of completion method. Two of the types of Internet surveys described by Couper are especially relevant for this chapter: prerecruited panels of Internet users and Internet surveys based on a probability sample of the full population. For the first type, panel members are recruited using probability sampling methods such as random-digit-dialing telephone surveys. Following consent to participate, respondents with Internet access are sent an e-mail request to participate in the Internet survey or panel. This design is similar for the second type, which also starts with a probability sample and uses non-Internet approaches to elicit initial cooperation. The difference is that this approach also incorporates respondents without Internet access by providing potential respondents with the necessary equipment in exchange for their participation.

The LISS panel is a typical example of a panel survey based on a probability sample of the general population. Other institutes to have built this type of Internet panel in recent decades are Knowledge Networks and RAND in the United States. Along with CentERdata in the Netherlands, all three institutes provide Internet access to those households in the sample that do not yet have access, in order to solve the problem of noncoverage in Internet surveys. The LISS panel was based on a probability sample of the full population, as this panel should be suitable for scientific research and, as Couper (2000) stated, this is the only approach that allows generalization beyond the current population of Internet users. In Section 4.4, we describe how the sample of the LISS panel was drawn and contacted, and how it fits into Couper's taxonomy.

Strengths and weaknesses of Internet surveys are discussed extensively in Chapter 2 in this volume. One weakness of Internet surveys might be the calculation of response rates. For the non-probability type of Internet survey, response rates cannot even be determined, since the total number of eligible respondents is not known and the population is not defined (see also Chapter 5 in this volume). The probability panel of the general population in Couper's taxonomy (Couper, 2000) often has a rather complex response structure. Hoogendoorn and Daalmans (2009) describe how, in this type of design, nonresponse can occur at various stages in the survey process: first, in the recruitment stage of the Internet panel; second, when panel members do not participate in a particular wave of the survey; and finally, when respondents drop out of the panel after some time. We will describe these stages of nonresponse for the LISS panel in Section 4.4.6 and discuss the consequences.

We have described a typology of longitudinal panel surveys and a typology of Internet surveys. In general, longitudinal household surveys as defined by Lynn (2009) do not use Internet interviewing. The most prevalent Internet panels are access panels based on volunteer sampling (Couper, 2000). The question now is whether it is possible to build a true longitudinal panel, collecting data similar to those in the longitudinal household studies described in Section 4.2, but using Internet interviewing as method of data collection. The next section describes the LISS panel, which is an attempt to combine a true longitudinal design with Internet interviewing.

4.4 THE LISS PANEL

4.4.1 Introduction

In 2006, CentERdata received funding from the Netherlands Organization for Scientific Research for a project entitled *An Advanced Multi-Disciplinary Facility for Measurement and Experimentation in the Social Sciences* (MESS). The grant was used to set up a panel of Dutch (-speaking) households in such a way that the usual coverage and sampling problems in online panels are avoided. The panel was meant to be a facility for testing new, innovative research techniques, freely accessible for academic researchers and focusing on fundamental (longitudinal) research. The project aims at integrating various fields of study, such as economics, social sciences, (bio)medical science, and behavioral science.

The core element of the MESS project is the LISS panel, consisting of 5,000 households representative of the Dutch-speaking population in the

Netherlands. Panel members complete online questionnaires every month (which takes about 30 minutes) and are paid for each completed questionnaire. One member in the household provides the household data and updates this information at regular intervals.

In addition to the online questionnaires, MESS uses new forms of data collection from a wide variety of research fields. For example, studies are prepared using self-administered measurement devices for the collection of biomarkers from the panel members. It also offers possibilities to elicit more and better information from the respondents—for example, measuring preferences or expectations exploiting graphical tools—and to obtain more insight into the respondents' decision processes by collecting data on how long respondents spend on the questions, registering and analyzing mouse movements, and so on.

Half of the interview time available in the panel is reserved for the LISS core study. This core study is the true longitudinal part, repeated yearly and designed to parallel existing household panel studies. It thus follows changes in the life course and living conditions of the panel members and monitors trends in household composition. More details are given in Section 4.4.5. The other half of available interview time per year is reserved for research proposals from the academic world.

To build an Internet panel that fulfills the demands posed by a longitudinal household study and by other academic studies, a number of steps require attention. First, a true probability sample of households has to be drawn from a population register with equal probabilities for each sample unit. Second, all households have to be contacted and recruited using another way than the Internet, to cover the complete sample. Third, as a direct consequence of the first step, the sample also covers the non-Internet population. Households in this subpopulation must be provided with an alternative mode of data collection to be able to participate in the panel. Fourth, the response rates and participation rates must be maximized, since selective nonresponse at the start will significantly affect the representativeness of the panel over time. If applied successfully, these steps should achieve a properly representative panel.

We will now describe the implementation of each of these steps to construct the LISS panel, thus illustrating the feasibility of incorporating new developments in survey research in the design of a scientific household panel study.

4.4.2 Drawing the Probability Sample

The reference population for the LISS panel is the Dutch-speaking population permanently residing in the Netherlands. The sampling and survey units of the LISS panel are independent private households, thus excluding institutions and other forms of collective households. Households in which no adult is capable of understanding the Dutch language are not included in the reference population. The sample frame was the nationwide address frame of Statistics Netherlands. This address frame, consisting of records including an address and a municipality code, was composed by Statistics Netherlands using a random 10% sample from the population registers (Municipal Database) each year. The address frame may include situations in which multiple households reside at a single address, as in student housing. Information about mail delivery was used to identify these multiple-household situations. One address thus could have multiple sampling frame units.

In cooperation with Statistics Netherlands, a simple random sample of 10,150 addresses was drawn from the aforementioned address frame. Since letters addressed to "the inhabitants of this address" are likely to be thrown away unopened, at each address a name was selected from the register to be put on the mailed letter and envelope. Note that the selection of a person within a household was for the purpose of addressing the announcement letter only; the sample unit of the panel is the address, and all members of the households at the addresses in the sample are asked to participate.

For each address in the sample, a telephone number was looked up in a contact database containing landline information only. Landline numbers were found for about 70% of the addresses, as was expected, since the number of households with a landline connection is decreasing rapidly. A Dutch study by KPN and Blauw Research of 750 people between 18 and 65 indicated that one in two people no longer has a landline connection but a cell phone only. The study also showed that 83% of people over 40 years still have a landline connection versus only 65% of people younger than 40 years. The subpopulation of respondents without a known (landline) telephone number in our sample also included households with unlisted numbers and households with no telephone at all, in addition to households with a cell phone only. These households could therefore not be reached by telephone and were contacted face-to-face instead.

The sample from the population registers naturally included individuals and households who did not (yet) have Internet access. At the time of recruiting the LISS panel, in 2007, approximately 15% of the households in the Netherlands did not have access to Internet at home. These participants were provided with a device that offers access to the Internet via a broadband connection, called the simPC. The simPC is a small and simple device using centralized support and maintenance. It can be operated by large buttons for the most frequently used functions, and it has screens that are designed to be readable by elderly people. Sample members with Internet access but without broadband were provided with broadband. The broadband connection facilitates the use of visual displays and video. The computer and the broadband Internet connection were installed for the panel participants. If necessary, they could also get help at home to show them how to operate the simPC and how to complete the questionnaires on-screen.

4.4.3 Recruiting in a Traditional Way

Sampled households were recruited from May to December 2007. Households were contacted in a traditional way: First, an announcement letter was sent in combination with a brochure explaining the nature of the panel study. A copywriting and design agency was hired to create an appealing letter and brochure. The information provided to the respondents at the first contact was tested in several pretests and a pilot study (Scherpenzeel, 2009). Budowski and Scherpenzeel (2005) have shown that the persuasiveness of the text in an announcement letter or an information leaflet can be enhanced by incorporating concepts from social psychology, such as reciprocity, helping, constancy of behavior, and personalization (see also Groves, Cialdini, & Couper, 1992). Some qualitative pretests with varying concepts in the letter showed that the concepts of authority, reciprocity, and helping were perceived as most persuasive with respect to the panel participation request. Consequently, both partners in the project (Tilburg University and Statistics Netherlands) were mentioned, the incentive offered for participating in the panel was emphasized, and it was stated that participation would really help science and contribute to knowledge about society.

In a pilot study, one-half of the sample received a letter informing them about the nature of the panel as well as an explanatory brochure. The other half received a letter that only informed them about the short recruitment interview, with no brochure included. In this condition, interviewers introduced the Internet panel only after the interview had been completed. These two information conditions had no significant effect on the response rates either. The final letter did mention the nature of the panel study, since the experiment did not show an adverse effect of this information on the response, and the researchers considered it fairer to fully inform the respondents. The letter and the brochure referred the reader to the panel Web site for more information. A 10-euro bill was included with the letter because a pilot study had shown that a prepaid 10-euro incentive effectively increased the willingness to participate in the panel (Scherpenzeel, 2009).

Following the letter, respondents were contacted by an interviewer in a mixed-mode design. Those households for which a telephone number was known were contacted by telephone (CATI). The remaining households were visited by an interviewer and thus contacted face-to-face (CAPI). The interviewers were instructed to first try to speak to the person to whom the announcement letter had been addressed. However, if the addressee was not present or not able or willing to be contacted, they could speak to any other adult person living in the same household. Again, the sample unit was at the level of the household or address, not the specific person. When contacting the household, the interviewers referred to the letter and to the enclosed 10-euro bill. If the respondent had neither seen nor read the letter, the interviewer continued to read out the information about the panel and the recruitment from an information screen. This screen also offered links to answers to frequently asked questions.

Once contacted, the interviewer asked the respondents to participate in a 10-minute interview, after which the request to participate in the panel was made. The interview consisted of a few questions about demographics, the presence of a computer and Internet connection in the household, and a series of survey questions about social integration, political interest, leisure activities, survey attitudes, loneliness, and personality. Within one to two weeks after the interview, the respondents with Internet access who consented to participate in the panel received a confirmation by e-mail, as well as a letter with a login code, an information booklet, and a reply card. With this reply card they could formally confirm their willingness to participate. This could also be done directly via the Internet with the login code provided in the letter, after which the respondents in the household

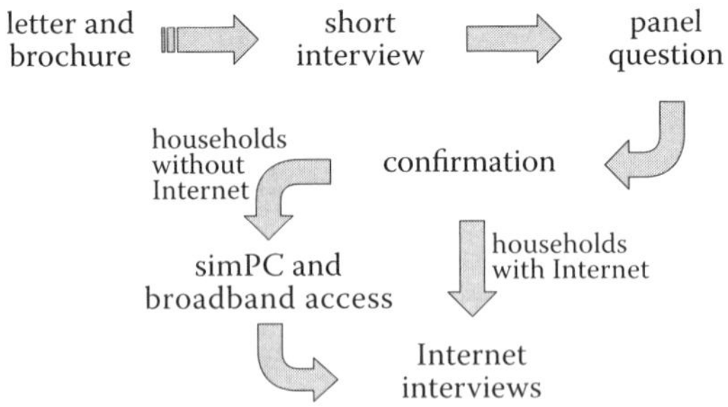

FIGURE 4.3
Overview of the recruitment process for the LISS panel.

could immediately start with the first questionnaire. Respondents without computer and/or Internet had to confirm their willingness to participate by returning the signed reply card, after which CentERdata provided them with the equipment and/or broadband connection necessary to participate. The confirmation procedure ensured the double consent of each respondent. In the confirmation e-mail and letter, respondents were promised an additional 10 euros for logging in or sending back the reply card, to minimize the loss of respondents resulting from the double consent procedure. Figure 4.3 summarizes the recruitment process.

4.4.4 Maximizing the Response Rates

The interviewers who recruited the panel members were instructed to focus on obtaining the cooperation of the selected households, rather than on maximizing the ratio of response to interview time, as they would do for commercial surveys. In the telephone recruiting, the maximum number of contact attempts was 15, at regular intervals, spread over several weeks. If a household was not reached after 15 calls, the address was transferred to face-to-face recruiting. In the face-to-face recruiting, a first series of eight contact attempts was made by the interviewer. A second series of seven attempts was made after a few weeks' pause. If respondents refused the complete interview, the interviewer would propose to ask only one to three central questions. If this was successful, the questions were followed by the request to participate in the panel. This method was extensively used in the nonresponse follow-up stage.

TABLE 4.1

Response in Successive Stages of Recruitment: Percentage of the Total Gross Sample Minus Unusable Addresses

	% of Total Gross Sample
Contact person completed CATI or CAPI recruitment interview or answered central questions	75
Contact person expressed willingness to participate in panel	63
Household registered for panel membership	48
Total gross sample 9,844	

Note: Unusable includes, among other things, nonexistent or uninhabited addresses, companies, long-term infirm or disabled respondents, and respondents with language problems. In total, 306 addresses (3%) of the total gross sample were coded as unusable.

A refusal conversion procedure was designed in cooperation with the fieldwork institute that carried out the recruitment. The procedure was tailored to the type of refusal recorded. If the reason for refusal was, for example, feeling too old to use the Internet, the respondent would be visited at home by an (elderly) interviewer with a demonstration video. If the refusal reason was lack of time, the respondent would receive an Internet link to a shortened interview.

The intensive efforts to contact and motivate respondents to participate resulted in satisfactory response rates. Table 4.1 shows that the response to the short CATI or CAPI interview or to the central questions (the first-stage response) was 75% in total (51% completed interviews, 24% completed central questions). The willingness to participate in the panel among respondents who answered the recruitment interview or the central questions was fairly high: 84% of those participating in the recruitment interview (or 63% of the total gross sample) told the interviewer they were willing to participate in the panel. The pilot study had shown a rather large loss of respondents between the expressed willingness to participate and the actual start in the panel. For this reason, the follow-up procedure in the main recruitment effort was extended and an extra 10-euro incentive after registration was promised. These measures appeared quite successful, as the final panel membership rate was 48% of the total gross sample (see Table 4.1).

After registration, the contact person of a household was asked to complete a household questionnaire, specifying the composition of the

TABLE 4.2

Participating Panel Members

Situation in February 2008	*n*
Household registered as panel member	5,176
Contact person completed household questionnaire	5,005
Eligible people in households	9,831
Actively participating people in households	8,026
Actively participating as percentage of eligible people: 82%	

Note: Eligible people are individuals ages 16 years and over minus those not capable of participating (handicapped, chronically ill, not sufficiently Dutch-speaking, etc.).
Actively participating people are eligible people who have started to complete questionnaires.

household and some demographic information about each member of the household. Table 4.2 shows the number of households registered as panel members and the number of households with a completed household questionnaire in February 2008, when the recruitment stage ended. All individual members ages 16 and over in a household were asked to participate, but they were, of course, not obliged to. Each household in which at least one person participated was included in the panel. The contact person of each household could, in the household questionnaire, indicate which members were not capable or not willing to participate. The third row of Table 4.2 shows the total number of people eligible for individual questionnaires, where eligible is defined as age 16 or over and capable of completing the questionnaires. People who are capable of answering questionnaires but do not want to participate are counted as eligible. The last row of the table shows the actively participating panel members, defined as eligible people who are willing to participate and who have actually started to answer questionnaires. The actively participating panel members make up 82% of the eligible people in the panel.

The high demands on sampling, coverage, and response rates should ultimately lead to a panel that is truly representative of the target population. However, it is likely that the nonresponse, both in the recruitment of the panel and in the monthly questionnaires, is related to respondent characteristics. Chapter 5 in this volume discusses the representativeness of the LISS panel and compares the representativeness to other online panels and traditional surveys. The authors of this chapter conclude that an online panel can fairly approximate a traditional survey when using an appropriate sample design, but the undercoverage of the elderly, non-Internet population is not entirely solved by providing these households with the equipment and an Internet connection to participate. The undercoverage is, in the case of this panel, not present in the gross sample but is due to nonresponse in the recruitment phase.

4.4.5 Core Study and Proposed Questionnaires

As mentioned in Section 4.2.1, the core study conducted in the LISS panel is inspired by various national and international surveys. Most of its themes and issues therefore are not new. However, it covers a broader range of topics and approaches in the social sciences than is usually the case in (panel) survey questionnaires. A traditional interview method, such as a telephone interview or face-to-face interview, is very much restricted by time. Most people do not accept an interviewer in their home for hours, nor answer lengthy questionnaires by telephone. The particular design of the LISS panel allows the use of a much longer core questionnaire than can be used in a traditional panel interview. The panel respondents are contacted each month and asked to complete online questionnaires lasting about 30 minutes in total. They can complete these questionnaires at any time during the month and at their own pace. In addition, respondents can take a break and continue with the questionnaire at some other time. The complete core panel questionnaire is split into shorter modules of about 20 minutes each, which are spread over eight months. Thus, it can be as long as 160 minutes of interviewing in total, summed over the eight monthly modules. Each module contains questions that are all in the same domain of research. The eight thematic modules are

1. Family and Household
2. Economic Situation and Housing
3. Work and Schooling
4. Social Integration and Leisure
5. Health
6. Personality
7. Religion and Ethnicity
8. Politics and Values

Each core module consists of about 100 questions; hence the various domains are covered in more depth than usual. An overview of the underlying concepts of each module and the documentation of all survey items of the core questionnaire are available at http://www.lissdata.nl. The collection of a large number of respondent characteristics in the core questionnaire also provides an efficiency gain, as it bypasses the need to collect background variables at each questionnaire. Furthermore, the characteristics can be used to stratify the sample and tailor questionnaires to the characteristics of a respondent.

The core questionnaire is repeated yearly: The first wave of the entire core questionnaire was carried out between November 2007 and June 2008, the second wave between November 2008 and June 2009. In the second wave of the core questionnaire, we used dependent interviewing in parts of the modules; factual information that respondents gave the year before, for example about occupation, education and income source, was preloaded and displayed on the screen. Respondents could alter the values if necessary. Attitudes and opinions were not preloaded.

An important concern about dependent interviewing is that changes may be underestimated because respondents may be tempted to simply repeat their response of previous waves (see, e.g., U.S. Department of Commerce, 1975; Hill, 1994). However, Hill (1994) showed that the amount of spurious change in occupation codes, obtained with independent interviews, was much higher than the amount of missed true change in these codes as a result of dependent interviewing. Hill (1994) used the 1985 and 1986 Survey of Income and Program Participation (SIPP) waves, in which one panel cohort (1985) was interviewed using independent interviewing and another cohort (1986) using dependent interviewing. The change in occupation codes was, in the dependent interviewing condition, correlated with changes in other characteristics of the job, as it should be. In the independent condition, these correlations were weaker. Moreover, the dependent interviewing measures showed less seam bias than the independent interviewing measures, as another indication of the higher quality of the dependent measures. More generally, as Jäckle (2009) describes on the basis of an overview of many studies, there does not seem to be any evidence to support the concern that dependent interviewing may lead respondents to simply agree with previous information. It was on the basis of these studies that we decided that dependent interviewing would probably improve the quality of the LISS longitudinal data.

On a yearly basis, the eight parts of the core questionnaire use only half of the total interview time available if respondents participate for

30 minutes each month. The other half of available interview time per year is offered as open access data collection to the academic world. Researchers are invited to submit research proposals that, if approved by a scientific board, can be carried out in the panel at no cost. In the next subsection, we evaluate the use of the facility for data collection and the use of the available data in the first two years of the existence of the LISS panel. In addition, we provide an overview of the quality of the panel in terms of longitudinal response rates.

4.4.6 Evaluation of the First Two Years

The first proposed study in the LISS panel was carried out in October 2007 and the first longitudinal core module was collected in November 2007. After two years of data collection, we can now evaluate to what extent the objectives have been met. Is the panel used to answer longitudinal research questions? Is it used at the same time for proposed questionnaires for scientific studies in various disciplines? Do researchers consider the quality of the sample and the response rates good enough to use the panel for their own scientific studies? We will first look at the use of the longitudinal core data. Next, we will briefly focus on the proposed studies that have been carried out in the panel thus far. Finally, we will evaluate the panel response rates over time, the attrition, and the representativeness of the panel.

In February 2009, the LISS data Web site was launched: http://www.lissdata.nl. Several other URLs have been claimed and linked to the Web site as well, including http://www.lissdata.com, http://www.lissdata.org, http://www.messproject.nl, and http://www.messproject.org. The site offers a complete description of the design, sample, and recruitment of the panel. It also presents overviews of response rates, accepted proposed studies, and approval rates of the proposed studies. In addition, it integrates the data-archiving application that was developed based on the Data Documentation Initiative version 3 (DDI 3). There are about 100 data file downloads per month. The most frequently downloaded core modules are Personality, Work and Schooling, and Family and Household. At this moment, we do not know exactly how the downloaded data are used. The number of publications based on the data is still very low, as is common in the first years of a longitudinal panel survey. The second wave of the longitudinal data collection was completed in July 2009, and in general, panel data become useful for longitudinal analysis only after three or more waves. Some researchers have used data from the core questionnaire in combination with data they had collected in a specific, approved study in the LISS panel.

Between the start of the panel and November 2009, more than 50 proposals were submitted for studies in the LISS panel. An overview of the approved studies, which come from a wide range of disciplines, can be found on the LISS Web site.

Many of the approved studies make effective use of the panel design and collect data at several points in time. Although this prolonged data collection delays the appearance of the first publications based on LISS data, it shows that the LISS panel is indeed viewed as a longitudinal panel survey by scientific researchers and also used that way.

The quality of the LISS panel in terms of coverage and sample selection was sufficient to meet the objectives and resulted in wide use of the panel and the core data. However, even when appropriate sampling is used and Internet access is provided whenever needed, there remains a potential source of selectivity in the response rates. Hoogendoorn and Daalmans (2009) note that a key problem with Internet panels based on a probability sample is the low initial response rate to the recruitment interview and the low number of respondents who subsequently agree to participate in the panel. Couper (2000) states that the initial response is often relatively low because the most common techniques used to stimulate response, such as advance letters, personalized signatures, letterhead, and incentives, cannot be implemented in Internet surveys. However, the recruitment strategy of the LISS panel did implement such techniques. As Section 4.4.3 described, a lot of attention and testing was devoted to the design and content of the advance letter, and prepaid incentives were included with the letter. Together with the nonresponse follow-up procedures described in Section 4.4.4, this resulted in a satisfactory initial response rate. Table 4.1 showed that the initial contact rate was 75% in the recruitment phase and the final registration rate was equal to 48%, whereas in the example that Hoogendoorn and Daalmans (2009) describe, these rates were just 60% and 12%, respectively. Nevertheless, the nonresponse in the LISS panel recruitment resulted in selectivity biases that are in many ways similar to those found by Hoogendoorn and Daalmans (2009). In two studies of the representativeness of the LISS panel, De Vos and Knoef (2008) and Van der Laan (2009) found selectivity with respect to household size, age, education, marital status, gender, level of urbanization, and (initially) having a computer and Internet (see also Chapter 5 in this volume). Van der Laan's study (2009) also showed that the response depended on the generations of immigrants present in the household.

In conclusion, the LISS panel does have some biases in sample composition, even though it was based on a proper probability sample and recruited with much attention to coverage and response stimulating procedures. In order to correct these biases, we have drawn a stratified refreshment sample in 2009, oversampling the hard-to-reach groups that had a below-average response in the main recruitment. This sample was stratified on household size, age, and ethnicity. The question remains whether we will succeed to correct for the undercoverage of the elderly and non-Internet population in this way. Elderly respondents appear to be more reluctant than we expected to accept a computer and Internet access free of charge. It may prove necessary to explore the use of supplementary modes for this group in Internet surveys and online panels.

The initial response rates are the first part in the complex response structure of probability panels of the general population (Hoogendoorn & Daalmans, 2009). This complex structure furthermore consists of wave nonresponse and panel attrition. In the remainder of this section we will describe these stages of nonresponse for the LISS panel and discuss the resulting additional selectivity bias.

Between the start of the panel in October 2007 and June 2009, 7% of the households that ever completed the household questionnaire left the panel. Although panel attrition thus remained relatively low in the first two years, De Vos (2009a) examined whether specific groups show especially high or low attrition rates. The probability of attrition is significantly affected by age, the provision of a simPC and broadband Internet connection, and the employment status of the people in the household (i.e., regarding age, the elderly are more likely to drop out; for simPC, households are less likely to drop out; and in terms of employment status, two-earner households are least likely to drop out). However, attrition is much more related to respondents' past response behavior than to household characteristics. Skipping a questionnaire and completing questionnaires irregularly turn out to be the best predictors for future dropout.

Besides attrition, the group of respondents who are still part of the panel but have not completed a questionnaire for several months is equally problematic. Figure 4.4 shows the average participation rates from October

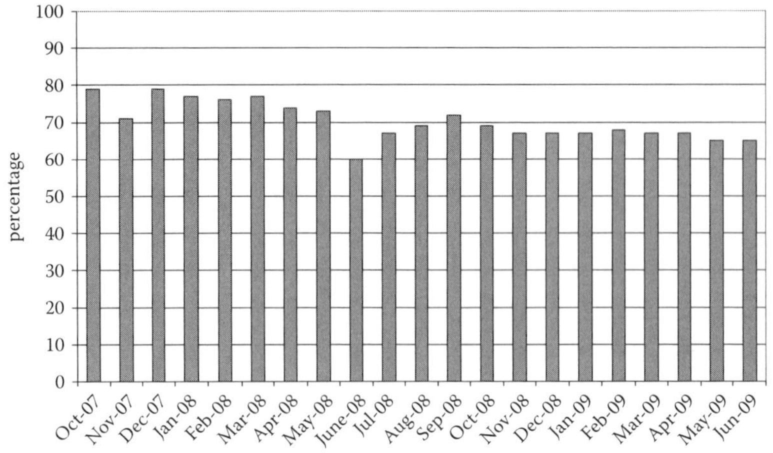

FIGURE 4.4
Response rates of LISS panel members per month. Bars represent the percentage of actively participating people who have completed at least one of the questionnaires in a month. (Note: Actively participating people are eligible individuals who have started to complete questionnaires. See also Table 4.2.)

2007 to June 2009. The bars represent the panel members who completed at least one individual questionnaire that particular month, as a percentage of panel members selected for at least one questionnaire. The monthly response varies between 65% and 79%, decreasing somewhat after the first six months following the start of the panel. A considerable part of the monthly nonresponse is due to the same panel members every month. Panel members who participated before but have not completed a questionnaire for three months or longer are labeled "sleepers." Sleepers made up 22% of the panel members in July 2009.

De Vos (2009b) studied the characteristics of the sleepers. He describes respondent characteristics that increase the likelihood of sleeping. For example, non-Western immigrants have a higher probability of becoming a sleeper than nonimmigrants. However, similar to attrition, previous nonresponse is a better predictor of becoming a sleeper than any of the exogenous explanatory variables included in the analysis. This suggests a need for a general strategy to keep panel members "awake" by regularly attracting their attention and encouraging their participation.

Laurie, Smith, and Scott (1999) identify "panel fatigue" as one of the reasons panel members stop participating. Respondents may become bored or feel overburdened. In the LISS panel, panel members complete online questionnaires every month, for which they receive an incentive of 7.50 euros per 30 minutes of interview time. Each month, there can be several short or one or two longer questionnaires. The brochure we used in the recruitment stage stated that the completion of the questionnaires would take about 30 minutes on average per month. However, the average completion time increased significantly in the second year of the panel, due to the large number of approved studies. Some panel members complain about the burden, but when asked whether they would be willing to complete more questionnaires per month (with concurrent payment), a majority (75%) are willing to do so. When asked about their preferred frequency of completing questionnaires, 74% prefer the monthly rate over a less frequent rate and 18% would even prefer a weekly rate. Finally, only 16% think the questionnaires are often too long. Nevertheless, this 16% represents a group of about 800 panel members, who will be monitored to see whether they have a higher chance of dropping out. At the same time, an attempt will be made to decrease the burden by using dependent interviewing in parts of the longitudinal core questionnaires and by selecting subsamples from the total panel for proposed studies that do not need the full sample size.

4.5 CONCLUSIONS

In the 1980s, a major breakthrough was accomplished by the introduction of remote computer-assisted interviewing in a probability-based panel set up by the University of Amsterdam, which was later continued by Tilburg University. This development stimulated similar initiatives in other countries, such as the Knowledge Networks' Panel and the RAND American Life Panel in the United States. This chapter shows that today it is possible to use Internet interviewing while complying with demands for high quality with respect to coverage, sample composition, and data quality. We have shown that it is possible to correctly apply sampling theory to the construction of an online panel. For the LISS panel, Statistics Netherlands drew a true probability sample of households from a population database. These households were then contacted through a face-to-face interview, asking respondents to join the panel. The research institute provides a computer and Internet connection to those households that otherwise would be unable to participate. Hence, this panel uses online interviewing as just another way of asking questions and not as a sampling frame. It was shown that participants for this online panel can be recruited quite effectively from the probability sample using traditional means of contact such as telephone interviews supplemented with face-to-face contacts for households without a known telephone number. Chapter 5 in this volume shows how this strategy results in a panel that is comparable to a traditional survey on many characteristics, and that it is a true alternative to existing online panels. The complex, multistage response structure of the panel does incur some significant selectivity problems. However, Chapter 5 shows that similar selectivity problems also exist in traditional, face-to-face surveys and are not caused by Internet interviewing, if correct sampling procedures are applied. The exceptions are the oldest age group (70+) and non-Internet households. For these groups, different ways of including them in the panel surveys will be explored. In addition, refreshment samples during the course of the LISS panel will be added regularly. The first refreshment sample will correct the initial selection biases, while further refreshment samples over subsequent years will correct for attrition biases.

We have evaluated the first two years of the panel, in terms of usage of the data collection infrastructure and of available data, and in terms of the longitudinal response rates. The LISS panel has not yet existed for long enough to have generated a significant number of publications that use the longitudinal data. However, the number of proposed questionnaires is quite substantial.

In conclusion, it is our view that this panel offers a new way of collecting household panel data over time. In the LISS panel, a core questionnaire that is comparable to the questionnaires of the well-known household panel studies throughout the world, in terms of content and domains, was implemented. As in the traditional panels, this core questionnaire is repeated every year. Moreover, the core questionnaire of the LISS panel is longer and more extensive than most comparable questionnaires used in traditional panels. The total questionnaire converts into around 160 minutes of interview time, spread over eight consecutive months. Panel members complete one of the eight modules of the core questionnaire every month, starting each year in November and finishing in June of the next year. In addition, the demographics and other general background information on the households are updated each month. The flexibility of online data collection is thus combined with the traditional household samples and panel designs, yielding a uniquely large range of longitudinal data.

REFERENCES

Berrens, R. P., Bohara, A. K., Jenkins-Smith, H., Silva, C., & Weimer, D. L. (2001). *Replacement technology or meaningless data? How close are meaningful Internet surveys?* Working paper, University of New Mexico.

Berthoud, R. & Gershuny, J. (2000). *Seven years in the lives of British families: Evidence on the dynamics of social change from the British Household Panel Survey*. Bristol, UK: Policy Press.

Budowski, M. & Scherpenzeel, A. C. (2005). Encouraging and maintaining participation in household surveys: The case of the Swiss Household Panel. *ZUMA Nachrichten* 29, *56*, 10–36.

Couper, M. P. (2000). Web surveys: A review of issues and approaches. *Public Opinion Quarterly*, *64*(4), 464–494.

Couper, M. P. & Ofstedal, M. B. (2009). Keeping in contact with mobile sample members. In P. Lynn (Ed.), *Methodology of longitudinal surveys* (pp. 183–203). Chichester, UK: John Wiley & Sons.

De Vos, K. (2009a). *Panel attrition in LISS*. Working paper, CentERdata, Tilburg University, the Netherlands.

De Vos, K. (2009b). *Sleepers in LISS*. Working paper, CentERdata, Tilburg University, the Netherlands.

De Vos, K. & Knoef, M. (2008). *The representativeness of the LISS panel*. Paper presented at MESS workshop, Zeist, the Netherlands.

Duncan, G. J. & Kalton, G. (1987). Issues of design and analysis of surveys across time. *International Statistical Review*, *55*, 97–117.

Groves, R. M., Cialdini, R. B., & Couper, M. P. (1992). Understanding the decision to participate in a survey. *Public Opinion Quarterly*, *56*(4), 475–495.

Groves, R. M., Fowler, F. J., Couper, M. P. et al. (2004). *Survey methodology*. New York: John Wiley & Sons.

Hill, D. H. (1994). The relative empirical validity of dependent and independent data collection in a panel survey. *Journal of Official Statistics*, *10*, 359–380.

Hill, D. H. (2002). *Wealth dynamics: Reducing noise in panel data*. Working paper, University of Michigan.

Hirano, K., Imbens, G., Ridder, G., & Rubin, D. (2001). Combining panel data sets with attrition and refreshment samples. *Econometrica*, *69*, 1645–1659.

Hoogendoorn, A. W. (2004). A questionnaire design for dependent interviewing that addresses the problem of cognitive satisficing. *Journal of Official Statistics*, *20*, 219–232.

Hoogendoorn, A. & Daalmans, J. (2009). Nonresponse in the recruitment of an Internet panel based on probability sampling. *Survey Research Methods*, *3*, 59–72.

ITU ICT Eye (2009). *ICT statistics database of the International Telecommunications Union (ITU)*. Retrieved from http://www.itu.int/ITU-D/icteye/Indicators/Indicators.aspx

Jäckle, A. (2008). Dependent interviewing: Effects on respondent burden and efficiency of data collection. *Journal of Official Statistics*, *24*, 411–430.

Jäckle, A. (2009). Dependent interviewing: A framework and application to current research. In P. Lynn (Ed.), *Methodology of longitudinal surveys* (pp. 93–111). Chichester, UK: John Wiley & Sons.

Jäckle, A. & Lynn, P. (2007). Dependent interviewing and seam effects in work history data. *Journal of Official Statistics*, *23*, 529–551.

Kalton, G. (2000). Developments in survey research in the past 25 years. *Survey Methodology, 26*, 3–10.

Kalton, G. & Citro, C. F. (1993). Panel surveys: Adding the fourth dimension. *Survey Methodology, 19*, 205–215.

Laurie, H., Smith, R., & Scott, L. (1999). Strategies for reducing nonresponse in a longitudinal panel survey. *Journal of Official Statistics, 15*, 269–282.

Link, M. W. & Oldendick, R. W. (1999). Call screening: Is it really a problem for survey research? *Public Opinion Quarterly, 63*, 577–589.

Lynn, P. (2009). Methods for longitudinal surveys. In P. Lynn (Ed.), *Methodology of longitudinal surveys* (pp. 1–19). Chichester, UK: John Wiley & Sons.

Lynn, P., Jäckle, A., Jenkins, S. P., & Sala, E. (2006). The effects of dependent interviewing on responses to questions on income sources. *Journal of Official Statistics, 22*, 357–384.

Lynn, P. & Sala, E. (2006). Measuring change in employment characteristics: The effects of dependent interviewing. *International Journal of Public Opinion Research, 18*, 500–509.

Mathiowetz, N. A. & Lair, T. J. (1994). Getting better? Changes or errors in the measurement of functional limitations. *Journal of Economic & Social Measurement, 20*, 237–262.

Mathiowetz, N. A. & McGonagle, K. A. (2000). An assessment of the current state of dependent interviewing in household surveys. *Journal of Official Statistics, 16*, 401–418.

Meurs, H., Van Wissen, L., & Visser, J. (1989). Measurement biases in panel data. *Transportation, 16*, 175–194.

Oldendick, R. W. & Link, M. W. (1994). The answering machine generation: Who are they and what problem do they pose for survey research? *Public Opinion Quarterly, 58*, 264–273.

Piekarski, L., Kaplan, G., & Prestegaard, J. (1999). *Telephony and telephone sampling*. Paper presented at the Annual Conference of the American Association for Public Opinion Research (AAPOR), St. Petersburg, Florida.

Scherpenzeel, A. C. (2009). *Recruiting a probability sample for an online panel: Effects of contact mode, incentives and information*. Working paper, CentERdata, Tilburg University, the Netherlands.

Sikkel, D. & Hoogendoorn, A. (2008). Panel surveys. In E. D. De Leeuw, J. J. Hox, & D. A. Dillman (Eds.), *International handbook of survey methodology* (pp. 479–499). European Association of Methodology Series. New York: Lawrence Erlbaum Associates.

Toepoel, V., Das, M., & Van Soest, A. (2008). Effects of design in Web surveys: Comparing trained and fresh respondents. *Public Opinion Quarterly, 72*, 985–1007.

Toepoel, V., Das, M., & Van Soest, A. (2009). Relating question type to panel conditioning: A comparison between trained and fresh respondents. *Survey Research Methods, 3*, 73–80.

U.S. Department of Commerce, Social and Economic Statistics Administration. (1975). *Comparison of month-to-month changes in industry and occupation codes with respondent's report of change: CPS Job Mobility Study*. Response Research Staff Report 75-5.

Van der Laan, J. (2009). *Representativity of the LISS panel*. Discussion paper 09041. Statistics Netherlands, The Hague/Heerlen, the Netherlands.

5

How Representative Are Online Panels? Problems of Coverage and Selection and Possible Solutions

Annette C. Scherpenzeel
CentERdata
Tilburg University
Tilburg, the Netherlands

Jelke G. Bethlehem
Statistics Netherlands
The Hague, the Netherlands

and

University of Amsterdam
Amsterdam, the Netherlands

5.1 INTRODUCTION

Collecting data using a survey is often a complex, costly, and time-consuming process. Not surprisingly, attempts have been made throughout the history of survey research to improve timeliness and to reduce costs and complexity while maintaining a high level of data quality.

Developments in information technology in the last decades of the previous century have made it possible to use microcomputers for data collection. This led to the introduction of computer-assisted interviewing (CAI). Replacing the paper questionnaire by an electronic one turned out to have many advantages, among which were considerably shorter survey processing times and higher data quality (more on the benefits of CAI can be found in Couper et al., 1998).

The rapid development of the Internet has led to another new type of data collection: computer-assisted Web interviewing (CAWI). Such Internet surveys or online panels are almost always self-administered: Respondents visit a Web site and complete the questionnaire by filling in a form online. At first sight, online data collection seems to have some attractive advantages in terms of costs, timeliness, and ease of use:

- In countries where many people are connected to the Internet, an Internet survey or online panel is a simple means to get access to a large group of potential respondents.
- Questionnaires can be distributed at very low cost. No interviewers are needed, and there are no mailing and printing costs.
- Surveys can be launched very quickly. Little time is lost between the moment the questionnaire is ready and the start of the fieldwork. In addition, the data are quickly available, sometimes almost in real time.
- Respondents can decide when and where they complete the questionnaire.

Thus, Internet surveys and online panels seem to be a fast, cheap, and attractive means of collecting large amounts of data. Not surprisingly, many survey organizations have implemented such surveys and panels. There are numerous examples of both Internet cross-sectional surveys (also called Web surveys) and online panels (also called access panels).

Online data collection is not without methodological problems. These problems can have an impact on the quality of the survey results, such that unweighted estimates may be biased. These problems are at least partly due to incorrect application of the principles of sample survey theory, which have been developed over more than a century. The theory of survey sampling is heavily based on the probability sampling paradigm, which holds that by selecting random samples, probability theory can be applied, making it possible to quantify the accuracy of estimates. This paradigm was first successfully applied in official and academic statistics in the 1940s, and to a much lesser extent also in commercial market research (for a historical account of probability sampling in the Netherlands, see Bethlehem, Stamhuis, & Van Maarseveen, 2008).

At first sight, Internet surveys seem to have much in common with other types of surveys. It is just another mode of data collection—questions are asked not face-to-face or by telephone but over the Internet. What is different for many Internet surveys and online panels, however, is that the principles of probability sampling have not been applied. This can have a major impact on survey results.

Internet surveys and online panels are often claimed to produce representative and therefore generalizable results, based on the application of advanced adjustment weighting procedures (examples of such claims can be found in 21minuten.nl, 2007b, and in De Hond, 2009). The term *representativity* is rather equivocal (Kruskal & Mosteller, 1979a, 1979b, 1979c) and is often used in a very loose sense to convey a vague idea of good quality. A large sample size seems to give some reassurance of validity and reliability. There are serious doubts, however, that a large sample size as a result of self-selection of respondents has the same meaning as a large sample size in a probability-based sample. Similarly, a high response rate in a sample among cooperative panel members is unlikely to have the same impact on the quality of outcomes as a high response rate in a random sample of the population. Therefore, a large sample size or high response rate alone does not suffice to guarantee reliable outcomes.

In this chapter, we describe the most important problems of Internet surveys and online panels, explain how these problems can be overcome, and discuss three types of weighting procedures that can be applied to correct for lack of representativity. As an alternative solution, the LISS panel is described as an example of how sampling theory can be applied to the construction of an online panel and how undercoverage can be diminished. The LISS panel is compared in terms of representativity to another Internet study, to a number of online panels, and to a face-to-face study.

5.2 PROBLEMS IN ONLINE PANELS

Online panels consist of people who have agreed to regularly participate in surveys over the Internet. Such panels are often run by market research organizations. There are various ways to set up online panels. Both probability and non-probability sampling techniques can be used.

Ideally, a panel is constructed using a random sample from a population. To that end, a probability sample is selected from a sampling frame and selected people are invited to participate in a panel. Examples of sampling frames are a population register, an address register, and a telephone directory. Also, random-digit-dialing (RDD) can be applied, although nowadays telephone directories and RDD may not cover the population anymore, because of the vast increase in mobile phone–only households.

However, many Internet surveys and online panels are based on some form of non-probability, self-selection sampling. Major opinion polls in the Netherlands rely on self-selection of respondents. The same is true for the large Dutch 21minuten.nl online survey, which is similar to the German online survey Perspektive Deutschland. A study across 19 online panels of Dutch market research organizations (NOPVO Research) showed that most of them use self-selection, links and banners on Web sites, or snowballing (Van Ossenbruggen, Vonk, & Willems, 2006). This all means that most online research has two fundamental methodological flaws: undercoverage and self-selection. These problems will be described in this section. We refer only to online research that is claimed to represent the general population. The problems we describe might not apply to studies that aim at a special target population.

5.2.1 Undercoverage

Undercoverage occurs when elements in the target population do not appear in the sampling frame. These elements have a zero chance of being selected. Undercoverage can be a serious problem for online surveys. If the target population consists of all people with an Internet connection, there is no problem. However, usually the target population is wider than that. Then undercoverage occurs because many people do not have access to the Internet. As a consequence, survey results apply only to the Internet population and not to the target population as a whole.

Bethlehem (2007) described the situation in the Netherlands with respect to Internet access. In the period from 1998 to 2006 the percentage of people in the Netherlands with Internet access increased from 16% to 85%. A 2008 estimate is 86% (Statistics Netherlands, 2009). The question is whether this Internet population differs from the total population, which includes people with and without Internet access. The answer is affirmative for the Netherlands. Specific groups are substantially underrepresented, including the elderly, those with less education, and the nonnative part of the population. The results described above are similar to the findings of authors in other countries (see, e.g., Couper, 2000; Dillman & Bowker, 2001).

One could argue that this problem may disappear as Internet penetration increases further. However, this is not evident. Bethlehem (2007) showed that the bias due to undercoverage of the estimator for the population mean $\overline{Y}$ of some variable Y is equal to

$$B(\overline{y}_I) = E(\overline{y}_I) - \overline{Y} = \overline{Y}_I - \overline{Y} = \frac{N_{NI}}{N}(\overline{Y}_I - \overline{Y}_{NI}). \tag{1}$$

The estimator $\overline{y}_I$ is the sample mean based on observations from just the Internet population. The means of Y in the Internet population and the non-Internet population are denoted by $\overline{Y}_I$ and $\overline{Y}_{NI}$, respectively. Furthermore, N is the size of the total population and N_{NI} is the size of the non-Internet population.

The magnitude of this bias is determined by two factors. The first factor is the relative size of the population without Internet to the full population (N_{NI}/N). The bias will decrease when a smaller proportion of the population does not have access to Internet. The second factor is the contrast $\overline{Y}_I - \overline{Y}_{NI}$ between the Internet population and the non-Internet population. The more the mean of the target variable differs for these two subpopulations, the larger the bias will be. An increased Internet coverage will reduce the bias because the factor N_{NI}/N is smaller. However, the contrast does not necessarily decrease as Internet coverage grows. It is even possible that the remaining hard-core group of people without Internet access will be more and more deviant. This may cause the contrast to increase. So, taking into account the combined effect of both factors, there is no guarantee that increased Internet coverage will reduce the undercoverage bias.

5.2.2 Self-Selection

Self-selection or non-probability sampling occurs when researchers have no control over the sample selection mechanism. Many online surveys are based on self-selection. The survey questionnaire is simply put on the Web. Respondents are those people who happen to have Internet access, visit the Web site, and decide to participate in the survey. Therefore, selection probabilities are unknown. Horvitz and Thompson (1952) show in their seminal paper that unbiased estimates of population characteristics can be computed only if a real probability sample has been drawn, every element in the population has a nonzero probability of selection, and all these probabilities are known to the researcher. Furthermore, only under these conditions can the accuracy of estimates be computed. Therefore, one result of self-selection is that no unbiased estimates can be computed; another is that the accuracy of estimates cannot be determined.

The effects of self-selection can be illustrated using an example related to the general elections in the Netherlands in 2006. Various organizations made attempts to use opinion polls to predict the outcome of these elections. The results of these polls are summarized in Table 5.1, which compares predicted seats in Parliament with the actual election results.

Peil.nl, De Stemming, and Politieke Barometer are opinion polls carried out by market research agencies. They are all based on samples from online panels. Adjustment weighting has been carried out in an attempt to reduce a possible bias. The polls were conducted one day before the election. The mean absolute difference indicates how large the differences (on average) are between the poll and the election results. Differences are particularly large for the more volatile parties, such as PvdA (social democrats), SP (socialists), and de PVV (right-wing populists).

DPES is the Dutch Parliamentary Study. The fieldwork for DPES was carried out by Statistics Netherlands. The probability sampling principle has been followed here. A true (two-stage) probability sample was drawn. Respondents were interviewed face-to-face (using CAPI). The predictions of this survey are much more reliable than those based on the online opinion polls.

Probability sampling has the additional advantage that it provides protection against certain groups in the population attempting to manipulate the outcomes of the survey. This may play a role in opinion polls. Self-selection does not have this safeguard. An example of this effect could be observed in the voting for the 2005 Book of the Year Award (de NS Publieksprijs), a high-profile literary prize. The winning book was determined by means of a poll on a Web site. People could vote for one of the nominated books or mention another book of their choice. More than 90,000 people participated in the survey. The winner turned out to be the new interconfessional Bible translation launched by the Netherlands and Flanders Bible Societies. This book was not nominated, but nevertheless an overwhelming majority (72%) voted for it. This was due to a campaign launched by (among others) Bible societies, a Christian broadcaster, and a Christian newspaper. Although this was all completely within the rules of the contest, the group of voters was clearly not representative for the Dutch population.

Participation in a self-selection based survey requires in the first place that respondents be aware of the existence of a survey. They have to visit

TABLE 5.1

Dutch Parliamentary Elections 2006: Outcomes and the Results of Various Opinion Surveys (Weighted)

	Election Result	Dutch Parliamentary Election Study 2006	Peil.nl	De Stemming	Politieke Barometer
Sample Size		**2600**	**2500**	**2000**	**1000**
Sampling Type		**Probability Selection**	**Self-Selection**	**Self-Selection**	**Self-Selection**
Seats in Parliament					
CDA (Christian Democrats)	41	41	42	41	41
PvdA (Social Democrats)	33	32	38	31	37
VVD (Liberals)	22	22	22	21	23
SP (Socialists)	25	26	23	32	23
GL (Green Party)	7	7	8	5	7
D66 (Liberal Democrats)	3	3	2	1	3
ChristenUnie (Christian)	6	6	6	8	6
SGP (Christian)	2	2	2	1	2
PvdD (Animal party)	2	2	1	2	2
PVV (Conservatives)	9	8	5	6	4
Other parties	0	1	1	2	2
Mean Absolute Difference		0.36	1.45	2.00	1.27

the Web site or accidentally come across an invitation to participate in a survey or join in a panel. In the second place, they have to make the decision to fill in the questionnaire on the Internet. All this means that each element k in a population (of size N) has an unknown probability ρ_k of participating in the survey. The responding elements can be denoted by a series $R_1, R_2, \ldots, R_N$ of N indicators, where the kth indicator R_k assumes the value 1 if element k participates, and otherwise it assumes the value 0, for $k = 1, 2, \ldots, N$. The expected value $\rho_k = E(R_k)$ is called the *response propensity* of element k.

The random variables $R_1, R_2, \ldots, R_N$ are independent. This sample selection process is a form of Poisson sampling. However, in standard applications of Poisson sampling the selection probabilities are known, whereas they are unknown in a self-selection survey.

Bethlehem (2008a) shows that the bias of the sample mean $\bar{y}$, as an estimator of the population mean $\bar{Y}$, is approximately equal to

$$B(\bar{y}) = E(\bar{y}) - \bar{Y} \approx \frac{R_{\rho Y} S_\rho S_Y}{\bar{\rho}} \tag{2}$$

in which $R_{\rho Y}$ is the value of correlation between the target variable and the response propensities, S_ρ is the standard deviation of the response propensities, and S_Y is the standard deviation of the target variable. The bias of the sample mean is determined by two factors:

- The average response propensity. The less likely people are to participate in the survey, the lower the average response propensity will be, and thus the larger the bias will be.
- The relationship between the target variable and response behavior. The higher the correlation between the values of the target variable and the response propensities, the higher the bias will be.

Three situations can be distinguished in which this bias vanishes:

- All response propensities are equal. This is the case in which the self-selection process can be compared with a simple random sample.
- All values of the target variable are equal. This situation is very unlikely to occur. If this were the case, no survey would be necessary. One observation would be sufficient.

- There is no relationship between target variable and response behavior. It means the likelihood for participation does not depend on the value of the target variable.

Given the mean response propensity $\bar{\rho}$, there is a maximum value the standard S_ρ cannot exceed:

$$S_\rho \leq \sqrt{\bar{\rho}(1-\bar{\rho})} \tag{3}$$

This implies that in the worst case (S_ρ assumes its maximum value and the correlation $R_{\rho Y}$ is equal to either +1 or –1) the absolute value of the bias will be equal to

$$\left|B_{\max}(\bar{y})\right| = S_Y \sqrt{\frac{1}{\bar{\rho}} - 1} \tag{4}$$

Bethlehem (1988) showed that formula (4) also applies in the situation in which a probability sample has been drawn, and subsequently nonresponse occurs during the fieldwork. Consequently, formula (4) provides a means to compare potential biases in various survey designs. For example, regular surveys of Statistics Netherlands are all based on probability sampling. Their response rates are around 70%. Thus, the absolute maximum bias is equal to $0.65 \times S_Y$. One of the largest Internet surveys in the Netherlands until now was 21minuten.nl. This yearly survey is set up to supply answers to questions about important problems in Dutch society. Several newspapers and television stations paid attention to it, making people aware they could visit the 21minuten.nl Web site and fill in the questionnaire. In addition, an advertisement on television called for participation in the study, and the Web site showed some Dutch politicians and celebrities. Perhaps stimulated by this media attention, about 170,000 people completed the Internet questionnaire within a period of six weeks in 2006. That is a very large sample size, but it was constructed by self-selection of the respondents. The target population of this survey was not defined, as everyone could participate. If the target population consisted of all Dutch people 18 and over, the average response propensity would be equal to 170,000/12,800,000 = 0.0133. Hence, the absolute maximum bias would be equal to $8.61 \times S_Y$. It can be concluded that the bias of this Internet survey theoretically could be 13 times larger than the bias of a smaller probability-based survey. Indeed, as remarked earlier, a large sample size is no guarantee of a representative sample.

5.3 CAN WE CORRECT THE BIAS? WEIGHTING ADJUSTMENT

The previous section showed that online data collection may suffer from serious methodological defects, which can result in unreliable outcomes. A possible way to repair these defects is the application of advanced adjustment weighting procedures. Weighting adjustment is a family of techniques that attempt to improve the quality of survey estimates by making use of auxiliary information. Auxiliary information is defined here as a set of variables that have been measured in the survey and for which information on their population distribution is available. By comparing the population distribution of an auxiliary variable with its sample distribution, it can be assessed whether or not the sample is representative for the population (with respect to this variable). An example of such an analysis is described in the next section.

Note that for a probability-based sample in which nonresponse has occurred, it is also possible to use the distribution of the auxiliary variables in the complete sample instead of their population distribution. Such information can sometimes be retrieved from the sampling frame. This situation does not apply to self-selection-based samples, as there is no sampling frame.

To correct for a lack of representativity, adjustment weights can be computed. Weights are assigned to records of all respondents. Estimates of population characteristics can now be obtained by using weighted values instead of the unweighted values. Weighting adjustment is often used to correct surveys that are affected by nonresponse (see, e.g., Bethlehem, 2002). Weighting adjustment can also be applied to reduce the bias of Internet survey estimates.

There are several adjustment weighting techniques. We will describe three of them: poststratification, the reference survey approach, and propensity weighting. The basic poststratification method divides the population into a number of nonoverlapping strata using available qualitative auxiliary variables. All sampled people in a specific stratum are assigned a weight that is obtained by dividing the population percentage in that stratum by the corresponding sample percentage. This makes the weighted sample representative with respect to these auxiliary variables. The hope is that the sample also becomes representative with respect to the target variables of the survey. It can be shown that the bias of estimates is reduced if:

- The response propensities are similar within strata.
- The values of the target variable are similar within strata.
- There is no correlation between response behavior and the target variable within strata.

These conditions can be realized if there is a strong relationship between the target variable and the stratification variables. Then the variation in the values of the target variable manifests itself between strata but not within strata. In other words, the strata are homogeneous with respect to the target variable. Also, if the strata are homogeneous with respect to the response propensities, the bias will be reduced. In nonresponse correction terminology, this situation comes down to missing at random (MAR).

In conclusion, we can say that application of adjustment weighting will successfully reduce the bias of the estimator if proper auxiliary variables can be found. Such variables should satisfy three conditions:

- They have to be measured in the survey.
- Their population distribution must be known.
- They must produce very homogeneous strata.

Unfortunately, such variables are not very often available, or there is only a weak correlation.

If proper auxiliary variables are not available, conducting a reference survey may be considered. This reference survey is based on a small probability sample, where data collection takes place with a mode different from the Web (e.g., CAPI, personal interviewing with laptops, or CATI, computer-assisted telephone interviewing). The reference survey approach has been applied by several market research organizations (see, e.g., Börsch-Supan et al., 2004; Duffy, Smith, Terhanian, & Bremer, 2005).

Under the assumption of no nonresponse, or ignorable nonresponse, this reference survey will produce unbiased estimates of the population distribution of the auxiliary variables. Therefore, adjustment can be computed using estimated population proportions. Bethlehem (2008b) shows that the reference survey approach does indeed have the potential to reduce the bias of estimates, provided homogeneous strata can be constructed. An interesting aspect of the reference survey approach is that any variable can be used for adjustment weighting as long as it is measured in both the reference and the Internet surveys. For example, some market research organizations divide the population into "mentality groups." People in the same group have more or less the same level of motivation and interest to participate in such surveys. Effective weighting variables approach the MAR situation as much as possible. This implies that within weighting strata there is no relationship between participating in a Internet survey and the target variables of the survey.

Using a reference survey approach has the important disadvantage that it substantially reduces the precision of estimators. Bethlehem (2008b) shows that the variance of estimators is to a large extent determined by the small sample size of the reference survey. So the large number of observations in the Internet survey does not help to produce precise estimates. One could say that the reference survey approach reduces the bias of estimates at the cost of a higher variance. In other words, the effective sample size is smaller than without weighting.

Another weighting method is propensity weighting. It also is often used by market research organizations to correct for a possible bias in their online surveys (see, e.g., Börsch-Supan et al., 2004; Duffy et al., 2005). The original idea behind propensity weighting goes back to Rosenbaum and Rubin (1983, 1984). The market research agency Harris Interactive was among the first to apply propensity score weighting (Terhanian, Smith, Bremer, & Thomas, 2001).

Propensity scores are obtained by modeling a variable that indicates whether or not someone participates in the survey. Usually a logistic regression model is used where the indicator variable is the dependent variable and attitudinal variables are the explanatory variables. These attitudinal variables are assumed to explain why someone participates or not. Fitting the logistic regression model comes down to estimating the probability (propensity score) of participating, given the values of the explanatory variables.

The propensity score $\rho(X)$ is the conditional probability that a person with observed characteristic X participates. Once propensity scores have been estimated, they are used to stratify the population. Each stratum consists of elements with (approximately) the same propensity scores.

If indeed all elements within a stratum have the same response propensity, there will be no bias if just the elements in the Internet population are used for estimation purposes. Cochran (1968) claims that five strata are usually sufficient to remove a large part of the bias.

To be able to apply propensity score weighting, two conditions have to be fulfilled. The first condition is that proper auxiliary variables must be available. These are variables that are capable of explaining whether or not someone is willing to participate in the Internet survey. Some frequently used auxiliary variables measure general attitudes and behavior. They are sometimes referred to as psychographic variables, in contrast to demographic variables; the term *webographic* may be used when the variables are specifically related to participation in Internet surveys. Schonlau et al. (2004) mention as examples "Do you often feel alone?" and "On how many separate occasions did you watch news programs on TV during the past 30 days?"

The second condition for this type of adjustment weighting is that the population distribution of the auxiliary, webographic variables must be available. This is generally not the case. A possible solution to this problem is to carry out an additional reference survey. To allow for unbiased estimation of the population distribution, the reference survey must be based on a true probability sample from the entire target population.

Such a reference survey can be small in terms of the number of questions asked. It can be limited to the webographic questions. Preferably, the sample size of the reference survey should be large, to allow for precise estimation. A small sample size results in large standard errors of estimates.

Schonlau et al. (2004) describe the reference survey of Harris Interactive. This is a CATI survey, using random-digit-dialing. This reference survey is used to adjust several Internet surveys. Schonlau, Fricker, and Elliott (2003) stress that the success of this approach depends on two assumptions: (1) the webographic variables are capable of explaining the difference between the Internet survey respondents and the other people in the target population, and (2) the reference survey does not suffer from nonignorable nonresponse. In practical situations it will not be easy to satisfy these conditions. Research by Schonlau, Van Soest, and Kapteyn (2007) seems to suggest that use of these webographic variables in propensity weighting may work, but not always.

It should be noted that from a theoretical point of view, propensity weighting should be sufficient to remove the bias. However, in practice the propensity score variable will often be combined with other (demographic) variables in a more extended weighting procedure (see, e.g., Schonlau et al., 2004).

How successful are weighting procedures in repairing the self-selection and undercoverage defects of Internet surveys and online panels? In some studies weighted online panel data were compared to traditionally obtained survey results. The results were diverse, but in several cases the weighting adjustments did not eliminate all differences between the online panel data and the traditional survey data (Vehovar, Batagelj, & Lozar Manfreda, 1999; Taylor, 2000; Duffy et al., 2005; Malhotra & Krosnick, 2007). Table 5.1 shows that the poll results from various online panels differ substantially from the election results even after adjustment weighting. In studies comparing respondents with and without Internet access, Taylor (2000) and Couper, Kapteyn, Schonlau, and Winter (2007) showed that differences in relevant research variables persist after applying weighting adjustments. In a more recent study, Loosveldt and Sonck (2008) evaluated the effects of poststratification weights and of propensity score adjustment, applied to data from a self-administered online access panel survey and compared to data from a face-to-face interview with a probability-based sample of the general population. The two weighting techniques did not make the online panel respondents comparable with the randomly selected people regarding their work participation, satisfaction, political interest, and various attitudes.

In summary, weighting adjustment can sometimes improve survey results, but it is no cure-all. Possible bias will be reduced only when the auxiliary variables explain response behavior and are in addition strongly related to the research variables. Furthermore, one should note that using a small reference survey for weighting purposes leads to larger variances of estimates. It diminishes the advantages of the large Internet survey sample.

5.4 A BETTER ONLINE PANEL?

The previous sections noted that self-selected, non-probability-based Internet surveys and online panels should be used with caution, even when weighting adjustments are made. This raises the question of whether it is possible to create an online panel that is not affected by undercoverage and self-selection.

The LISS panel is the result of such an attempt. This online panel has been constructed by selecting a random sample of households from the population register of the Netherlands. Selected households were approached by means of CAPI or CATI. So sample selection is based on true probability sampling instead of self-selection. Moreover, cooperative households without Internet access were provided with equipment giving them access to the Internet.

The details of the sampling design, the recruitment procedure, and the response rates of the LISS panel are described in Chapter 4 in this volume. The question to be answered in this chapter is whether application of a proper sampling design with complete coverage and traditional recruitment can help to create a panel that more closely resembles the population, and which therefore produces more reliable estimates. To this end, the LISS panel will be compared with the population, traditional surveys, self-selection panels, and self-selection surveys.

For all comparisons, we selected those demographic characteristics in which two studies about the representativity of the LISS panel, by De Vos and Knoef (2008) and Van der Laan (2009), found the largest biases:

- Percentage of elderly (ages 70 and up)
- Percentage of single-person households
- Percentage of immigrants with a foreign, non-Western background

In addition, we looked at a few webographic variables that, as we described above, are known to be biased in online panels:

- Percentage of voters in the last general elections (2006). Note that this is reported voting behavior and not necessarily true voting behavior.
- Percentage of voters for the Socialist Party (SP). These people are typically overrepresented in online surveys.
- Percentage of voters for the Christian Democratic Party (CDA). These people are typically underrepresented in online surveys.
- Percentage of people having access to the Internet. These people are obviously overrepresented in online surveys.

5.4.1 Comparing the LISS Panel With the Population

It has already been mentioned that many definitions of representativity exist (see Kruskal & Mosteller, 1979a, 1979b, 1979c). Representativity is defined here as representativity with respect to specific variables. For example, a panel is representative with respect to age if the age distribution in the panel is equal to the age distribution in the population.

De Vos and Knoef (2008) compare the composition of the LISS panel with that of the population based on demographic variables. They find differences by household size, age, education, marital status, gender, and level of urbanization. The elderly are underrepresented, especially elderly women. In addition, single-person households are underrepresented. This may have to do with the sample framework and/or with specific characteristics of single-person households. For example, there will be a connection between the underrepresentation of elderly and single-person households. This is confirmed by the comparison of the household type distribution in the LISS panel with the Dutch population. The degree of underrepresentation is large among elderly single people. Couples younger than 65 without children and couples with two children are overrepresented.

The comparison by De Vos and Knoef of the education levels for several age groups in the LISS panel and in the Dutch population shows that people with postsecondary education are somewhat overrepresented in all age groups.

Finally, people with a non-Western background and especially with a first generation non-Western background are somewhat underrepresented. This may come as no surprise as the LISS panel includes only households where the adults have mastered the Dutch language sufficiently to complete the surveys. When looking more specifically at countries of origin, it appears that especially people with a Turkish or Moroccan background are underrepresented. However, people from the Netherlands Antilles are not underrepresented at all. This may indicate that language probably plays a role in the recruitment process.

In another study of the representativity of the LISS panel, Van der Laan (2009) investigates a set of variables that was known from the population register for both respondents and nonrespondents. Looking at the overall response in the recruitment of the panel, he found differences between different types of households. In particular, the response for single-person households was lower than for other types of households. Furthermore, the response depends on the average age of the household members, the presence of household members with a first or second generation foreign background, number of people in the household, possession of a landline, number of minors in the household, and status of the neighborhood. In

TABLE 5.2

Comparing the LISS Panel With the Population (%)

Group	LISS Panel	Population	Bias
Age ≥ 70	7	13	–6
Living alone	15	20	–5
Non-Western background	4	7	–3
Did not vote in election	13	20	–7
Voted SP in election	17	17	0
Voted CDA in election	25	26	–1
Has Internet access	93	85	8

addition to the study of the response in the recruitment of the panel, Van der Laan also investigated the effect of giving access to Internet to people without computer or Internet access at the time of the recruitment. Results showed that the representativity of the panel, especially the representativity of households with older members, was improved by this strategy (for a complete description, see Van der Laan, 2009).

In conclusion, the LISS panel does have some biases in sample composition, even though it was based on a proper probability sample and recruited with much attention to coverage and response rates. De Vos and Knoef's comparison with population statistics and Van der Laan's estimate of response probabilities by register characteristics both show biases in the same variables. In Table 5.2 we summarize the biases by concentrating on the categories we selected above as the basis of comparison with other studies. The estimations are based on 8,089 LISS panel members 18 years and older (the same age criterion applies to all following tables).* Bias is calculated simply as the difference between the percentage found in the LISS panel and the population percentage.

In addition to the underrepresentation of the elderly, single-person households, and people with a non-Western background, Table 5.2 shows there also is an overrepresentation of voters in the panel. This does not come as a surprise, as the literature shows there is often a positive correlation between voting and responding in a survey. Apparently, there is little bias with respect to voting for the political parties SP and CDA. As could be expected, Internet access is overrepresented in the LISS panel, although it still is less than 100%. The population proportion of people having

* The age range in the studies differed. To keep the tables comparable, the same lower age limit was applied to all research data and population data.

Internet access in the Netherlands is not known exactly, but the figure of 85%, resulting from the face-to-face surveys of Statistics Netherlands (2007), is generally used as an estimate.

Almost all surveys and panels have some underrepresentation of certain groups. Therefore, the question is whether the LISS panel is closer to traditional non-Internet studies than Internet studies using self-selected, non-probability-based samples. For that purpose, we compared the LISS panel with a major traditional national survey in the Netherlands, with a very large Internet survey, and with a comprehensive evaluation study across 19 commercial market research panels. This comparison is not meant to judge the other online studies and panels; rather, it is intended to evaluate whether it is worth it to make a large investment in probability sampling and recruitment, as was done for the LISS panel.

5.4.2 Comparing the LISS Panel With a Traditional Survey

We first compared the LISS panel with a major traditional national survey in the Netherlands, the Dutch Parliamentary Electoral Study (DPES) conducted in 2006. Sample selection and fieldwork were carried out by Statistics Netherlands (Aarts, Van der Kolk, & Rosema, 2007). A true (two-stage) probability sample was selected. Data were collected by means of CAPI. The response rate was relatively high: about 70%, resulting in 2,806 completed questionnaires. We used the publicly available data of the DPES 2006 to calculate the percentages in our categories of comparison (DPES, 2006). The results are summarized in Table 5.3. The appendix shows the percentages on which the bias estimations in Tables 5.3 to 5.5 are based.

Compared to the DPES 2006, the LISS panel is more biased in the oldest age category and in the category of those with Internet access. Note that the DPES data are one year older than the LISS panel data, and figures for Internet access rise strongly each year. The DPES and the LISS panel have a similar bias in single-person households and in people with a foreign, non-Western background.

The number of people who say they did not vote is usually much lower in surveys than the number of actual nonvoters in elections. This is also the case in the LISS panel and in the DPES. However, the percentage of nonvoters in the LISS panel is closer to the election results than the percentage in the DPES. Note that the LISS panel respondents completed the

TABLE 5.3

Comparing the LISS Panel With the DPES

Group	LISS Panel Bias	DPES Bias
Age ≥ 70	–6	1
Living alone	–5	–4
Non-Western background	–3	–2
Did not vote in election	–7	–13
Voted SP in election	0	1
Voted CDA in election	–1	1
Has Internet access	8	–2

Note: Bias defined as the difference between the observed percentage and the population percentage.

questionnaire in December 2007, one year after the election. In contrast, DPES respondents were asked about their voting behavior just after the elections of November 2006. The relation between voting and survey participation might be stronger in the case of the DPES because of the subject of this survey; the LISS panel covers a much broader range of topics. The percentage of SP and CDA voters are approximately equally biased.

In conclusion, the LISS panel is quite close to a traditional face-to-face survey, except for the coverage of the elderly and non-Internet population.

5.4.3 Comparing the LISS Panel With an Online Survey

The second comparison is with the Dutch 21minuten.nl online survey, which is fully based on self-selection of respondents, as described in Section 5.2.2. In 2007, it solicited the opinion of Dutch citizens on the subject of democracy and government. Table 5.4 shows the results of a comparison of the LISS panel and the unweighted 21minuten.nl respondents of 2007 (B. Verhoeven, personal communication, 2009).

In the analysis of the poll results and the published report (21minuten.nl, 2007a) the sample was weighted based on population data from Statistics Netherlands and two reference studies (21minuten.nl, 2007b). According to 21minuten.nl, the weighted results are representative of the opinions of the Dutch population ages 15 to 69 years (21minuten.nl, 2007b). The 4,000 respondents ages 70 and older who filled in the 21minuten.nl questionnaire were studied as a separate group for the general report (21minuten.nl, 2007a).

TABLE 5.4

Comparing the LISS Panel With 21minuten.nl

Group	LISS Panel Bias	21minuten Bias
Age ≥ 70	−6	−9
Living alone	−5	3
Non-Western background	−3	−5
Did not vote in election	−7	−14
Voted SP in election	0	2
Voted CDA in election	−1	−13
Has Internet access	8	15

Note: Bias defined as the difference between the observed percentage and the population percentage.

Table 5.4 shows that the unweighted version of 21minuten.nl has a stronger underrepresentation of respondents 70 or older than the LISS panel. However, the study did not target this group; it was meant to be representative for the 15-to-69-year-old group. Remarkably, 21minuten.nl actually has an overrepresentation of single-person households, in contrast to the LISS panel and the DPES underrepresentation. People with a non-Western background and nonvoters are better represented in the LISS panel than in 21minuten.nl. We expected to find an overrepresentation of Socialist Party voters, as Bethlehem (2008b) showed that this category of voters often tends to participate more than others in self-selection-based Internet surveys. However, we find only a very slight bias in the 21minuten.nl survey. In contrast, the Christian Democratic Party voters are strongly underrepresented in the unweighted 21minuten.nl study while almost completely accurately represented in the LISS panel. The percentage that has Internet access is, by definition, 100% in the 21minuten.nl study.

To conclude, the LISS panel better represents the elderly, non-Internet-users, people with a non-Western background, and Christian Democratic Party voters than the unweighted 21minuten.nl Internet survey. Other groups, such as Socialist Party voters and single-person households, were just as well or better represented in the 21minuten.nl survey.

5.4.4 Comparing the LISS Panel With Samples From 19 Online Panels

In 2006, Van Ossenbruggen et al. (2006) carried out an evaluation study across 19 online panels of Dutch market research organizations, called

Nederlands Online Panel Vergelijkings Onderzoek (Dutch Online Panel Comparison Study [NOPVO]). The study comprised two parts (Vonk, Van Ossenbruggen, & Willems, 2008). First, an inventory of all online panels in the Netherlands based on ESOMAR's 25 questions was made.* All participating panels provided information about recruitment of their panel members, incentives, panel size, response rates, and so forth. An overview of this information is available on the Web site of the Dutch Market Research Association (MOA). The second part was an empirical study for which samples of the same gross sample size (1,000 panel members) were drawn from the 19 panels, and the same survey was conducted in each of these samples. The agencies that administer these panels use different methods to recruit panelists, but the main recruitment is done online, through links on Web sites and snowball methods among participating panelists (Van Ossenbruggen et al., 2006). The agencies were asked to provide a sample that would generate a representative net sample for age, gender, education, and region. In total, 18,999 people from the different panels were selected and invited to participate; 9,514 people responded. For our comparison, we use some data from the empirical study (T. Vonk, personal communication, 2009). A description of the sampling, response, data collection, and outcomes can be found in Vonk et al. (2008). Our comparison is restricted to the bias in the demographic and webographic categories we identified before, averaged over all 19 samples. We use the averaged bias across all 19 samples because we think it gives a more general standard of comparison than the bias of a single online panel or a small selection of panels. Table 5.5 presents the results.

Since the NOPVO samples were restricted to the age range of 18 to 65, no comparison can be made for the elderly (70 and over). The NOPVO panel samples are, on average, better than the LISS panel with regard to the representation of single-person households. The underrepresentation of people with a non-Western background and nonvoters is similar to the 21minuten.nl study (see Table 5.4) and thus stronger than in the LISS panel. With respect to voting behavior and party choice, we have used the results of the questions about intention to vote at the next elections instead

* The European Society for Opinion and Marketing Research (ESOMAR) is a world body of market research professionals and organizations. In 2005, ESOMAR published a set of 25 questions about research methodology that all online sample providers should be able to answer. A revised set of questions (now numbering 26) can be found on the ESOMAR Web site: http://www.esomar.org/uploads/pdf/professional-standards/26questions.pdf

TABLE 5.5

Comparing the LISS Panel With NOPVO

Group	LISS Panel Bias	NOPVO Bias
Age ≥ 70	–6	Not included
Living alone	–5	–1
Non-Western background	–3	–5
Did not vote in election	–7	–12
Voted SP in election	0	1
Voted CDA in election	–1	–17
Has Internet access	8	15

Note: Bias defined as the difference between the (average) observed percentage and the population percentage.

of the reported voting in the elections of 2003. Since these elections were held three years before the study, we considered the voting intentions in 2006 a better comparison to the results of the LISS panel, the DPES, and the 21minuten.nl study, all of which were carried out after the elections of 2006. Socialist Party voters are well represented in the NOPVO samples, but Christian Democratic Party voters are very much underrepresented. Like in the 21minuten.nl study, this underrepresentation might be partly due to the age limit of the study and partly to the sampling strategy of some of the panels. The percentage that has Internet access is, by definition, 100% in the samples from the online panels.

In summary, existing online access panels in the Netherlands on average differ more from the population than the new LISS panel on four of the six characteristics tested.

5.5 CONCLUSIONS

The world of survey research is moving from face-to-face and telephone interviews to Internet interviewing. For many online surveys, the principles of sample survey theory that have been developed more than a century ago are not applied. These principles indicate that probability sampling must be applied, where each member of the population must have a nonzero probability of being selected. Furthermore, these probabilities must be known. Only then can unbiased estimates be constructed, and only then can the accuracy of estimates be quantified.

Sampling methods used in online surveys not only exclude the non-Internet population but in addition often rely on self-selected samples. Therefore, they do not fulfill the scientific standards of survey sampling, probability, and representativeness described in this chapter.

A possible way to reduce the bias caused by undercoverage and self-selection may be weighting adjustment. We have described three frequently used weighting techniques: poststratification, the reference survey approach, and propensity weighting. Adjustment weighting can reduce the bias only if proper auxiliary information is available. In practice, the auxiliary variables are often not sufficiently strongly related to the research variables of interest. In addition, weighting on the basis of a small reference survey diminishes the advantages of the large Internet survey sample.

We have shown that another solution is to correctly apply sampling theory to the construction of an online panel. In fact, the problems of undercoverage and self-selection are not an intrinsic characteristic of online interviewing. For a new panel, a true probability sample of households was drawn from a population register by Statistics Netherlands and contacted by means of household face-to-face interviews, asking respondents to join the panel. The institute provides a computer and Internet connection to those households that could not otherwise participate (about 15% of households do not have Internet access). Hence, this panel uses online interviewing as just another way of asking questions and not as a sampling frame.

The question, then, is whether this strategy has resulted in an online panel that is a good alternative to the traditional panel survey methods and to existing online panels. We have compared the composition of the new panel to a traditional face-to-face survey, to a large Internet survey, and to samples from 19 online panels. When comparing the unweighted data, the new panel was close to the traditional survey and better than the Internet survey and online panels on five of the seven characteristics we tested. The exceptions were found in the oldest age group (70 and older) and in the non-Internet households, two characteristics that are significantly correlated.* Although the elderly and the non-Internet group were far better covered in the new panel than in the other online studies,

* In the LISS panel recruitment data, the correlation between Internet access and age is –.38. The percentage of people younger than 70 having Internet access in the household is 90%, while the percentage for those 70 and older is 48%. The recruitment data were collected by telephone or in face-to-face interviews and include people who were not willing to become a member of the online panel.

they were clearly better represented in the traditional face-to-face survey. On the other hand, Socialist Party voters were well represented in all studies, and single-person households were in fact better represented in the online studies based on self-selected samples than in both the probability-based panel and the traditional face-to-face survey. It might be that online self-selection sampling reaches those single people who are not easily reached with other recruitment methods. The result cannot be explained by the exclusion of the elderly (over 65) in the two non-probability-based online studies. If we select only panel members younger than 66 from the LISS panel, the percentage of single-person households decreases from 15% to 14%, still much lower than in the online samples based on self-selection, and closer to the face-to-face DPES data.

In conclusion, an online panel can come quite close to a traditional survey when a correct sample design is used, but the undercoverage of the elderly and the non-Internet population is not entirely solved by providing these households with equipment and an Internet connection in order to participate. The undercoverage is, in the case of this panel, not present in the gross sample but is caused by nonresponse: The oldest respondents were more reluctant to accept the equipment offered to them and more unwilling to participate in the online panel. It has to be noted also that this type of panel demands a larger financial investment than a regular, non-probability-based Internet panel.

As a general conclusion, we could state that with the use of modern techniques of interviewing, the difficult-to-reach groups and problems of representativity shift: People with a non-Western background generally remain an underrepresented group in most surveys, but the elderly, who are often rather willing to participate in traditional surveys, are the most difficult group to reach in Internet surveys. Young, working singles are, on the other hand, perhaps easier to reach by new rather than by traditional modes. Consequently, the use of supplementary modes to study special groups could be considered. For large scientific studies, we see a trend evolving toward mixed-mode studies and multimode studies. For example, large, traditional European studies such as the European Value Study and the European Social Survey are currently investigating these possibilities. We have to explore how Internet surveys and online panels can also profit from the new possibilities of combining different modes for different groups.

Perhaps the optimal future design of surveys of the general population is a combination of the advantages of Internet interviewing with the principles of classic probability theory, as was done in the LISS panel, and supplementary modes for specific groups in the sample.

REFERENCES

Aarts, K., Van der Kolk, H., & Rosema, M. (2007). *Een verdeeld electoraat: De Tweede Kamerverkiezingen van 2006* [A divided electorate: The parliamentary elections of 2006]. Utrecht, the Netherlands: Het Spectrum.

Bethlehem, J. G. (1988). Reduction of nonresponse bias through regression estimation. *Journal of Official Statistics, 4*(3), 251–260.

Bethlehem, J. G. (2002). Weighting nonresponse adjustments based on auxiliary information. In R. M. Groves, D. A. Dillman, J. L. Eltinge, & R. J. A. Little (Eds.), *Survey nonresponse* (pp. 275–288). New York: John Wiley & Sons.

Bethlehem, J. G. (2007). *Reducing the bias of Web survey based estimates.* Discussion paper 07001. The Hague/Heerlen, the Netherlands: Statistics Netherlands.

Bethlehem, J. G. (2008a). *How reliable are self-selection Web surveys?* Discussion paper 08014. The Hague/Heerlen, the Netherlands: Statistics Netherlands.

Bethlehem, J. G. (2008b). Representativity of Web surveys—an illusion? In I. Stoop & M. Wittenberg (Eds.), *Access panels and online research: Panacea or pitfall? Proceedings of the DANS symposium* (pp. 19–44). Amsterdam: Aksant.

Bethlehem, J. G., Stamhuis, I. H., & Van Maarseveen, J. G. S. J. (2008). Complete enumerations or sampling? The historical debate about sampling for surveys. In I. H. Stamhuis, P. M. M. Klep, & J. G. S. J. Van Maarseveen (Eds.), *The statistical mind in modern society: The Netherlands 1850–1940: Volume II. Statistics and scientific work.* Amsterdam: Aksant.

Börsch-Supan, A., Elsner, D., Fassbender, H., Kiefer, R., McFadden, D., & Winter, J. (2004). *Correcting the participation bias in an online survey.* Report. University of Munich, Germany.

Cochran, W. G. (1968). The effectiveness of adjustment by subclassification in removing bias in observational studies. *Biometrics, 24*, 209–213.

Couper, M. P. (2000). Web surveys: A review of issues and approaches. *Public Opinion Quarterly, 64*(4), 464–494.

Couper, M. P., Baker, R. P., Bethlehem, J. G., Clark, C. Z. F., Martin, J., Nicholls, W. L. et al. (1998). *Computer assisted survey information collection.* New York: John Wiley & Sons.

Couper, M. P., Kapteyn, A., Schonlau, M., & Winter, J. (2007). Noncoverage and nonresponse in an Internet survey. *Social Science Research, 36*, 131–148.

De Hond, M. (2009). *Verschillen tussen de drie peilingen in week 39-2009 [Differences between the three polls in week 39-2009].* Retrieved from http://maurice.ooip.nl/wp-content/uploads/2009/09/Verschillen-tussen-de-drie-peilingen-sep-20091.pdf

De Vos, K. & Knoef, M. (2008). *The representativeness of the LISS panel.* Paper presented at MESS workshop, Zeist, the Netherlands.
Dillman, D. A. & Bowker, D. (2001). The Web questionnaire challenge to survey methodologists. In U.-D. Reips & M. Bosnjak (Eds.), *Dimensions of Internet science* (pp. 159–178). Lengerich, Germany: Pabst Science Publishers.
DPES (2006). Dutch Parliamentary Election Study 2006 [data file]. Retrieved from DANS EASY electronic archiving system, Data Archiving and Networked Services (DANS), http://www.dans.knaw.nl
Duffy, B., Smith, K., Terhanian, G., & Bremer, J. (2005). Comparing data from online and face-to-face surveys. *International Journal of Market Research, 47*, 615–639.
Horvitz, D. G. & Thompson, D. J. (1952). A generalization of sampling without replacement from a finite universe. *Journal of the American Statistical Association, 47*, 663–685.
Kruskal, W. & Mosteller, F. (1979a). Representative sampling I: Non-scientific literature. *International Statistical Review, 47*, 13–24.
Kruskal, W. & Mosteller, F. (1979b). Representative sampling II: Scientific literature excluding statistics. *International Statistical Review, 47*, 111–127.
Kruskal, W. & Mosteller, F. (1979c). Representative sampling III: The current statistical literature. *International Statistical Review, 47*, 245–265.
Loosveldt, G. & Sonck, N. (2008). An evaluation of the weighting procedures for an online access panel survey. *Survey Research Methods, 2*, 93–105.
Malhotra, N. & Krosnick, J. A. (2007). The effect of survey mode and sampling on inferences about political attitudes and behavior: Comparing the 2000 and 2004 ANES to Internet surveys with non-probability samples. *Political Analysis, 15*, 286–323.
Rosenbaum, P. R. & Rubin, D. B. (1983). The central role of the propensity score in observational studies for causal effects. *Biometrika, 70*, 41–55.
Rosenbaum, P. R. & Rubin. D. B. (1984). Reducing bias in observational studies using subclassification on the propensity score. *Journal of the American Statistical Association, 79*, 516–524.
Schonlau, M., Fricker, R. D., & Elliott, M. N. (2003). *Conducting research surveys via e-mail and the Web.* Santa Monica, CA: RAND Corporation.
Schonlau, M., Van Soest, A., & Kapteyn, A. (2007). Are "webographic" or attitudinal questions useful for adjusting estimates from Web surveys using propensity scoring? *Survey Research Methods, 1*(3), 155–163.
Schonlau, M., Zapert, K., Payne Simon, L., Haynes Sanstad, K., Marcus, S., Adams, J. et al. (2004). A comparison between responses from a propensity-weighted Web survey and an identical RDD survey. *Social Science Computer Review, 22*, 128–138.
Statistics Netherlands. (2007, 2009). *ICT gebruik van personen naar persoonskenmerken [ICT use of people by demographics].* Retrieved from http://statline.nl
Taylor, H. (2000). Does Internet research work? Comparing online survey results with telephone surveys. *International Journal of Market Research, 42*(1), 51–63.
Terhanian, G., Smith, R., Bremer, J., & Thomas, R. K. (2001). Exploiting analytical advances: Minimizing the biases associated with Internet-based surveys of non-random samples. *ARF/ESOMAR: Worldwide Online Measurement, 248*, 247–272.
21minuten.nl. (2007a). *Report 21minuten.nl Editie 2007.* Retrieved from http://www.21minuten.nl/21minuten/images/21minuten_2007_rapport.pdf
21minuten.nl. (2007b). *Report representativiteit.* Retrieved from http://www.21minuten.nl/21minuten/images/21minuten_2007_representativiteit.pdf
Van der Laan, J. (2009). *Representativity of the LISS panel.* Discussion paper 09041. The Hague/Heerlen, the Netherlands: Statistics Netherlands.

Van Ossenbruggen, R., Vonk, T., & Willems, P. (2006). *Results, Dutch online panel comparison study (NOPVO)*. Retrieved from http://www.nopvo.nl.

Vehovar, V., Batagelj, Z., & Lozar Manfreda, K. (1999). Web surveys: Can the weighting solve the problem? *Proceedings of the Survey Research Methods Section, American Statistical Association*, 962–967.

Vonk, T., Van Ossenbruggen, R., & Willems, P. (2008). A comparison study across 19 online panels (NOPVO 2006). In I. Stoop & M. Wittenberg (Eds.), *Access panels and online research: Panacea or pitfall? Proceedings of the DANS symposium* (pp. 53–78). Amsterdam: Aksant.

APPENDIX: COMPARISONS OF PERCENTAGES IN DPES, 21MINUTEN.NL, NOPVO, AND THE DUTCH POPULATION

All tables show data for people 18 years or older living in private households. Since the age range in the studies differed, this selection was applied to all data and population data to keep the tables comparable. Bias is calculated as the difference between the percentage observed in the study and the population percentage.

TABLE 5.A1

Percentages (Unweighted) in Dutch Parliamentary Electoral Study (DPES) and Population

Group	DPES	Population 2006	Bias
Age ≥ 70	13	12	1
Living alone	16	20	–4
Non-Western background	5	7	–2
Did not vote in election	7	20	–13
Voted SP in election	18	17	1
Voted CDA in election	27	26	1
Has Internet access	83	85	–2

TABLE 5.A2

Percentages (Unweighted) in 21minuten.nl and Population

Group	21minuten	Population 2007	Bias
Age ≥ 70	4	13	–9
Living alone	23	20	3
Non-Western background	2	7	–5
Did not vote in election	6	20	–14
Voted SP in election	19	17	2
Voted CDA in election	13	26	–13
Has Internet access	100	85	15

TABLE 5.A3

Percentages (Unweighted) in Dutch Online Panel Comparison Study (NOPVO) and Population

Group	NOPVO	Population 2006	Bias
Age ≥ 70	Not included	12	
Living alone	19	20	−1
Non-Western background	2	7	−5
Intends not to vote in election	8	20	−12
Intends to vote SP in election	18	17	1
Intends to vote CDA in election	9	26	−17
Has Internet access	100	85	15

6

Ethical Considerations in Internet Surveys[1]

Eleanor Singer
Survey Research Center
University of Michigan
Ann Arbor, Michigan

Mick P. Couper
Survey Research Center
University of Michigan
Ann Arbor, Michigan

6.1 INTRODUCTION

Surveys done via the Internet pose ethical issues similar to those posed by all surveys. In addition, they present some unique concerns because of the way information is collected from respondents. As a result, a number of professional organizations have already developed codes of ethics and ethical guidelines dealing with Internet research (Lozar Manfreda & Vehovar, 2008; Association of Internet Researchers, 2002; ESOMAR, 2008; Marketing Research Association, 2000). In this chapter, we begin by reviewing general ethical principles applicable to all surveys, including those done on the Internet, with special reference to how Internet administration affects their implementation. We then discuss issues specific to Internet surveys, concluding with the report of an experiment designed to address one of these issues.

6.2 BASIC ETHICAL PRINCIPLES: CONFIDENTIALITY AND INFORMED CONSENT

The ethical, as distinct from the legal, principles for protecting the rights of respondents and other subjects of social and behavioral as well as biomedical research are rooted in the Helsinki Declaration and the Belmont Report. The Helsinki Declaration (and the earlier Declaration of Geneva, adopted by the General Assembly of the World Medical Association in 1948), originally adopted by the World Medical Assembly in 1964, was a direct response to gross violations of subjects' rights by biomedical scientists during the Nazi era, and defined the ethical responsibilities of physicians to their patients as well as to the subjects of biomedical research. The Belmont Report, issued in the United States in 1979, was the work of the National Commission for the Protection of Human Subjects of Biomedical and Behavioral Research, created under the National Research Act of 1974, and was a response primarily to the violations of subjects' rights in the Tuskegee Study (Tuskegee Syphilis Study Ad Hoc Advisory Panel, 1973).

As professionals, survey researchers have relationships not only with participants or respondents but also with three other important groups: clients or sponsors, the public, and other researchers. The codes of ethics of professional organizations define the norms of these relationships and, in some cases, have created mechanisms for dealing with norm violations. The World Association for Public Opinion Research (WAPOR) has such a code (http://www.unl.edu/wapor/ethics.html), as does the American Association for Public Opinion Research (AAPOR) (http://www.aapor.org). And the World Organization for Market Research (ESOMAR), as well as market research organizations in the United States and other countries, have developed similar codes for their members, many of whom are survey researchers.

In addition to codes of ethics, which are enforced by the professional organizations themselves, many governments have adopted regulations for the protection of human subjects of research which carry the force of law. Many of these can be traced to the Belmont Report, which lays out three basic ethical principles: beneficence, justice, and autonomy. The principle of beneficence gives rise to the requirement to minimize harm and maximize benefit for the individual subject; the principle of justice requires that the burdens of research should not be shared unequally among groups of subjects, with some primarily bearing the burdens of research and others reaping the benefits; and the principle of autonomy underlies the requirement for obtaining informed consent from subjects for their research participation. In social surveys, the potential for harm generally arises from possible breaches of confidentiality, though psychological distress as a result of being asked certain types of questions or being asked to recall certain life events is also recognized as a potential harm. Thus, the two preeminent ethical issues for survey researchers are obtaining informed consent and maintaining the confidentiality of responses, and these are considered in detail in what follows. In social surveys the issue of justice is primarily linked to methodological concerns about sample representativeness and generalizability of results, and we do not consider these in the present chapter.*

6.2.1 Protecting the Confidentiality of Responses

Although known breaches of confidentiality in survey research are exceedingly rare (but see Seastrom, 2008), such breaches are the most likely source of harm to survey respondents. This is because disclosure of certain kinds of information about the respondent, along with respondent identifiers, may result in damage to reputation, loss of employment or other status, and even criminal liability. In fact, such disclosure might conceivably result in physical harm if, for example, a parent learns about a child's illegal behavior through the child's survey responses and decides to inflict physical punishment. On the other hand, surveys, unlike biomedical research, are unlikely to expose the respondent *directly* to physical harm. Nor, we would argue, is psychological harm a likely consequence of responding to a survey, even if respondents are temporarily disturbed by the content of the questions they are asked.

Aside from potentially harming respondents, breaches of confidentiality are also harmful to the survey enterprise itself, because people who are concerned about invasions of privacy or breaches of confidentiality are less likely to answer survey questionnaires, at least when these are fielded

* In biomedical research justice was a pressing ethical issue, since indigent patients in hospital wards were more readily available as subjects but rarely benefited from the fruits of the research. In Internet surveys there is increasing concern about results based on volunteer members of opt-in panels (see Couper, 2000), but this is not an ethical issue with respect to respondents.

by the U.S. Census Bureau (National Research Council, 1979; Singer, Mathiowetz, & Couper, 1993; Singer, Van Hoewyk, & Neugebauer, 2003; Hillygus, Nie, Prewitt, & Pals, 2006).

Confidentiality breaches can occur for a variety of reasons, the most common being simple carelessness—failure to remove direct identifiers from a data file, failing to lock cabinets containing respondent identifiers, and so on. Confidentiality may also be breached as a result of law enforcement activities (e.g., subpoenas for data); in the United States, surveys collecting sensitive information are encouraged to obtain a certificate of confidentiality, and similar protections may be available in other countries.* Finally, confidentiality may be breached as a result of statistical disclosure—that is, identification of the respondent through matching of a data file from which direct identifiers have been removed with one containing such identifiers, along with many of the other variables that exist in the original data file (see, e.g., National Research Council, 2006, Chapter 4; Zayatz, 2007). Internet surveys do not differ from surveys administered by other modes with respect to these risks of confidentiality breaches. Confidentiality in panel surveys, however, is more difficult to protect than confidentiality in cross-sectional surveys, because there is a great deal more information available about the respondent. Such information increases the possibility of reidentification even if all direct identifiers have been removed from the data file.

There are, in addition, some threats to confidentiality that may appear to be unique to Internet surveys, though even these turn out, on closer inspection, to have analogues in other types of surveys. For example, identified data are vulnerable to hackers while being transmitted to a secure server, but this is also true of data transmitted by interviewers unless the data are encrypted first; and phone interviews are similarly vulnerable. Once transmitted, Internet survey data must be stored on secure servers, but this is equally true of survey data collected by any other method.

* To protect against potential subpoena of individual records for law enforcement purposes or civil litigation, U.S. researchers studying sensitive topics, whether federally funded or not, may apply for certificates of confidentiality from the U.S. Department of Health and Human Services. The National Institute of Justice (in the U.S. Department of Justice) also makes confidentiality certificates available for criminal justice research supported by agencies of the Justice Department. Such certificates, which remain in effect for the duration of a study, protect researchers in most circumstances from being compelled to disclose names or other identifying characteristics of survey respondents in federal, state, or local proceedings (42 CFR 2a.7, Effect of Confidentiality Certificate).

Various methods can be used to protect the confidentiality of Internet survey data during survey completion. Basic protections include reducing the amount of metadata included in the transmission of responses to the Web server. For example, transmitting a question label (e.g., "smoke marijuana") and verbal response (e.g., "yes") provides more information to those intercepting the transmission than an uninformative label (e.g., "Q27") and response (e.g., "1"). Some responses are in recognizable forms and can be vulnerable to sniffer programs searching the Internet for transmissions of this type. If identifiers (such as names, addresses, e-mail addresses, or telephone numbers, for example) are collected, using some form of encryption is advisable. For most surveys, using Secure Sockets Layer (SSL) or Transport Layer Security (TLS) should be sufficient. Higher levels of security, such as digital signatures or 128-bit encryption, may be considered when the survey is collecting both highly sensitive data and identifying information. But these run the risk of making it harder for respondents to access and complete the survey. Survey researchers should carefully consider the need to collect identifying data in the survey itself and balance this against the security requirements needed to protect the confidentiality of the respondents.

Another potential security risk can come from respondents (or others) inadvertently entering someone else's ID, potentially gaining access to data already provided. Access controls (such as an ID and password) reduce this risk. The ID should be sufficiently long that consecutive numbers are not used. For example, the (2006) Canadian census required entry of a 15-digit ID to access the online version. The Canadian census went one step further to prevent unauthorized access to census responses. If one wished to suspend and resume completion of the online form, one was required to create a unique password to regain access to the partially completed form. This further minimized the risk of another person gaining access to someone else's stored responses by entering the incorrect ID. As soon as a survey has been completed, the data should be removed from the Web server and further access by the respondent prohibited.

Another source of security concerns may be those using public terminals (e.g., at a library or Internet café) to complete Internet surveys. Here it is important to clear cache (the temporary memory used to store Web pages to reduce bandwidth usage and server load) at the end of a session so that subsequent users cannot access these pages. Similarly, if cookies are used to control the process of survey completion, using transient cookies that expire at the end of the session provides greater security than persistent cookies that remain on the computer (see Thiele & Kaczmirek, 2010). This helps ensure that someone else cannot revisit the pages submitted by the respondent.

Thus far we've been focusing on identifiable surveys, where respondents' identities can be linked to the responses they provide. Internet surveys, particularly those using non-probability sampling and selection methods (see Couper, 2000), can be conducted anonymously, where no personally identifiable information is collected. However, such surveys often use cookies to prevent multiple completions by the same respondent, and often collect IP addresses as part of the general server log. Such IP addresses identify a machine, not a user, but still have the potential to be linked to other information from that machine. So even in anonymous surveys, caution must be exercised.

In general, we believe that the risks of confidentiality breaches in Internet surveys are no worse than in other modes of survey data collection, and that appropriate levels of security and careful design will minimize such risks. However, of greater concern may be the *perceived* lack of security of Internet transactions in general, and the potential this may have to deter people from participating in Internet surveys or being less candid when they do so. With frequent stories in the press about security breaches and identity theft associated with the Internet, it is important for survey researchers to reassure respondents that all necessary measures have been taken to mitigate the risk of disclosure. Informing them of such risks is an element of informed consent, which we turn to next.

6.2.2 Obtaining Informed Consent

6.2.2.1 General Requirements for Informed Consent

The second crucial ethical element of Internet surveys, as in other surveys, is informed consent. Informed consent implies that two requirements have been met: First, research participants have been informed about the essential elements of the research and have understood the information, and second, they have given their consent to participate. In many surveys, participation itself is taken as an adequate indication of consent; Internet surveys make it even easier to meet this requirement by allowing respondents to check a box indicating consent. In principle, Internet surveys can provide for electronic respondent signatures on consent documents; requesting such signatures, however, means that potential respondents who object to providing a signature may refuse to participate for that reason alone (Singer, 1978, 2003). Since signed consent forms do more to protect the research organization than the participant, we argue that signed consent forms should rarely, if ever, be required.

The first requirement, however—adequately informing potential participants about the research—is crucial to obtaining informed consent, and is often neglected. Below are listed the essential elements of informed consent required for federally funded research in the United States under Subpart A, 45 Code of Federal Regulations (CFR) 46, otherwise known as the Common Rule.* These elements include descriptions of the purposes of the research, benefits and potential harm from participation, terms of confidentiality of the data, and a statement that participation is voluntary. Other elements, unique to Internet surveys, are not listed; we consider these in Section 6.2.2.2, below.

1. A statement that the study involves research, explanation of the purposes of the research and the expected duration of the subject's participation, a description of the procedures, and identification of any procedures that are experimental.
2. A description of any foreseeable risks or discomfort.
3. A description of any benefits to the subject or others that may reasonably be expected.
4. A disclosure of appropriate alternative procedures or courses of treatment.

---

* Canada and Australia have guidelines for research on human subjects that are similar to those in the United States. In Canada, all research involving human subjects must be reviewed by Research Ethics Boards (http://www.pre.ethics.gc.ca/english/policystatement/section1.cfm#1A); in Australia, such review boards are known as Human Research Ethics Committees (http://www.health.gov.au/nhmrc/issues/researchethics.htm). Regulations in the European Union tend to stress the importance of privacy and confidentiality protections rather than informed consent. Recognizing the continued growth of international research, the Office for Human Research Protections (OHRP) in the United States has developed an International Compilation of Human Subject Research Protections. The compilation lists the laws, regulations, and guidelines of more than 50 countries where research funded or supported by the Department of Health and Human Services is conducted. The compilation provides direct Web links to each country's key organizations and laws whenever available. The compilation can be accessed on the OHRP Web site: http://www.hhs.gov/ohrp/international/index.html#NatlPol

5. A statement describing the extent, if any, to which confidentiality of records identifying the subject will be maintained.
6. For research involving more than minimal risk, an explanation of whether and what kind of compensation or treatment is available if injury occurs.
7. An explanation of whom to contact with further questions about the research, subjects' rights, and research-related injury.
8. A statement that participation is voluntary and the subject may discontinue participation at any time without penalty or loss of benefits.

Many of the elements of informed consent are self-explanatory, but some, such as the description of the purposes of the research, are not. It is often difficult to anticipate all the purposes for which the information collected on a survey can or should be used. Furthermore, there may be reasons to avoid a clear statement of even the immediate purpose in order to avoid biasing respondents' answers. On the other hand, not providing an explanation of the reasons for the survey invites respondents to invent their own, which may also lead to bias, and it defeats one of the main purposes of the informed consent process, namely, giving research participants control over their participation. Thus, we believe that at least a general statement regarding the purpose of the survey is always appropriate when obtaining informed consent.

People often think the purpose of informed consent is to protect human subjects of research, including respondents, from harm. As a result, the argument is sometimes advanced that if there is no risk of harm, there is no need to obtain informed consent. In fact, the real purpose of obtaining consent is to give respondents and other research subjects meaningful control over information about themselves, even if the question of harm does not arise. For example, informing potential respondents of the voluntary nature of their participation in an interview is essential to ethical survey practice, even if this leads some of them to refuse to participate.

So far we have been talking about the kinds of information that should be provided to potential respondents in advance of their participation. Another issue, however, is whether or not participants comprehend the information provided. This problem exists for surveys of all types, not just Internet surveys, and in fact Internet surveys are in an especially advantageous position to facilitate such comprehension. Hyperlinks can provide explanations or elaborations of terms and concepts in the informed consent statement, for example, or potential respondents can be asked questions whose answers indicate whether they understand crucial aspects of the research. If they do not, further explanations could be provided. Obviously, the complexity of the explanation and the elaborateness of the consent process should be tailored to the complexity and risks of the research, keeping in mind that the process is designed to safeguard autonomy as well as to protect people against knowingly exposing themselves to harm.

6.2.2.2 Special Issues of Informed Consent in Internet Surveys

Recruitment and selection issues. An issue of specific relevance to Internet surveys relates to the acquisition and use of e-mail addresses for invitations to surveys or enrollment in online panels. Because of concerns about unwanted e-mail solicitations, spam, phishing scams, and the like, users appear to be particularly protective of their e-mail addresses. For example, the code of ethics of the Council of American Survey Research Organizations (CASRO, 2008) includes the following: "Research Organizations (ROs) are required to verify that individuals contacted for research by e-mail have a reasonable expectation that they will receive e-mail contact for research." The code goes on to note that "ROs are prohibited from using any subterfuge in obtaining e-mail addresses of potential respondents, such as collecting the data from public domains, or doing so without individuals' awareness or under the guise of some other activity." The ESOMAR code (http://www.esomar.org) has similar provisions. We view this as an extension of informed consent, informing sample participants about how and why their contact information was obtained.

Observational research. Observational research using the Internet—for example, observation of chat room behavior, with or without recording of participants' actual comments (e.g., Kraut et al., 2004; Whitehead, 2007; Walther, 2002; Frankel & Siang, 1999)—is analogous to observational research in general and raises similar ethical questions. Chief among these is whether respondents have a reasonable expectation of privacy with respect to their behavior. If they do, then questions of informed consent and protection against risk of harm arise; if they do not, such questions would appear to be moot. However, because observational research generally does not make use of Internet surveys, we do not further consider the ethical issues raised by such research in the present chapter.

Surveying minors and other special populations. In the United States, the Regulations for the Protection of Human Subjects mandate special protections for children, prisoners, and other vulnerable populations (see Subparts B, C, and D of 45 CFR 46). In particular, parental consent is required for research with children, defined as anyone under 18 years of age.* The Children's Online Privacy Protection Act (COPPA) regulates the collection of personal information online from those less than 13 years old (see http://www.coppa.org). Because of the difficulty of ascertaining the true age of participants, this requirement raises problems for surveys conducted via the Internet, though as a practical matter this problem exists for telephone surveys as well (Walther, 2002). In both types of surveys, the researcher (or interviewer) is dependent on the accurate and truthful reporting of age by the participant in order to screen out underage respondents, although Kraut et al. (2004) suggest that special precautions can be taken, such as requesting the respondent to enter data that only an adult would have (e.g., information from a driver's license). The problem is less severe when the intent is to recruit a sample of children or adolescents. Here, presumably, the researcher starts with a list of households or parents, who are approached in order to obtain consent for sending the survey instrument to their children. Although practical and technical difficulties may arise, these are no different, in principle, from those in other surveys of children or adolescents.

Identifying duplicate and fraudulent responses. A related problem to that of identifying minors arises with respect to "unduplicating" multiple responses from the same respondent. This is a particular problem in anonymous Internet surveys with no authentication control, but it may also occur in online opt-in panels where people may sign up under different aliases. Inadvertent multiple responses, if they are identical, are in principle easy to eliminate, but deliberate falsifications may be more difficult to detect, and if they are numerous relative to legitimate responses (as might occur if respondents are motivated by an incentive or by the topic of the research), they might in fact bias the outcome. Both IP addresses and cookies are used to detect "ballot stuffing" or multiple submissions from the same machine, but neither approach is foolproof. Similarly, methods are being developed to identify fraudulent responses in Internet panels (see Downes-Le Guin,

* The age of consent varies by country; in the Netherlands, for example, parental consent is required for people under 16 years of age (http://dutchdpa.nl/indexen/en_ind_wetten_wbp_wbp.shtml).

Mechling, & Baker, 2006). While this is a challenge for data quality in Internet surveys, we do not see this as an issue of informed consent.

Tracking and spyware. Tools to track user behavior are widely employed on the Internet, whether to measure the size of online audiences, to improve the design of Web sites, or to deliver targeted advertising. These vary greatly in the type and amount of information collected and the intrusiveness of the approach. For example, basic Web site analytics or user metrics gathered on the Web server can include such information as the number of page visits, unique visits by IP address, time spent on each page, search terms entered, and so on. Aside from basic characteristics of a user's machine (e.g., browser type, IP address, what plug-ins are installed), no additional information is collected about the user. Commercial Web sites make extensive use of cookies to gather additional information about user behavior across sessions (and sometimes across sites). Cookies are small text files stored on a user's computer. They are associated with a specific domain and can only be accessed or modified by that domain. These are used to remember a user's preferences, access a profile, remember previous searches, and so on. Third-party cookies typically operate less obtrusively, often associated with objects delivered within the context of the larger Web page but not directly requested by the user (Abraham, Meierhoefer, & Lipsman, 2007). They typically provide information to advertisers about general browsing behavior to facilitate the delivery of relevant advertising and to measure the effect of such advertising (e.g., click-through behavior). Generally, cookies can be deleted by users, or browsers can be set to not accept cookies or to prompt before accepting them.

Further along the continuum, spyware is covert software installed on a user's machine to collect information about users without their knowledge. Klang (2004) identifies three features of such software that pose ethical concerns for survey respondents:

1. The installation occurs without the explicit consent or knowledge of the user.
2. The software collects (or aids collection) of personal data about the user.
3. The software employs the user's Internet connection to send information to the information collector.

At the extreme, spyware can be used to record all keystrokes on a computer, such as the entry of passwords or other personally identifiable information.

Of concern to survey researchers is respondent understanding of the different ways information may be collected about their browser, their browsing behavior, or their entire set of activities on a computer. Concerns about spyware and media stories about identity theft resulting from such spyware may raise respondent concerns about privacy, either directly or indirectly affecting people's willingness to participate in surveys and provide honest and accurate answers. For example, some Internet survey software requires cookies to pass a unique respondent ID from page to page, and a respondent who has blocked cookies will be unable to advance through the survey.* While some types of tracking software directly benefit the user, the use of these tools is often not apparent and is done without the user's explicit consent or understanding of purpose. There is a danger that all forms of unobtrusive measurement may be viewed in the same negative light.

Several studies have explored public opinion about such tracking of individuals' online activities, which has become a central concern in the area of online privacy in recent years. Corning and Singer (2003) reviewed the public opinion literature available at the time. They found that roughly 60% to 80% of Internet users in the United States were familiar with the tracking function of cookies. In one study, six in ten agreed that "when I go to a Web site it collects information about me even if I don't register" (Turow, 2003), while eight in ten in a Pew 2000 survey thought it was "very" or "somewhat" common "for Internet companies to keep track of the Web pages you go to" (Fox, 2000). Knowledge of the term *cookies* was more limited: Just 40% of Internet users in *Business Week*'s 2000 Harris survey claimed to know what a cookie was (*Business Week*, March 20, 2000), as did 43% in the Pew survey (Fox, 2000).

Most studies Corning and Singer reviewed showed that respondents dislike Internet tracking. In the Pew study, 54% thought Internet tracking was "harmful, because it invades your privacy," while only 27% found it "helpful, because the company can provide you with information that matches your interests" (Fox & Lewis, 2001). Similarly, the 2003 Annenberg study found that only 23% of Internet users agreed that "I like to give information to Web sites because I get offers for products and services I personally like" (Turow, 2003). *Business Week*'s Harris survey in 2000 asked a series of questions about the ways in which companies

* The LISS panel software uses transient cookies to keep track of the session ID during survey completion.

manipulate and profit from information. Respondents seemed most tolerant of tracking that was not linked to personally identifiable information (28% reported being "not very comfortable" and 35% "not at all comfortable" with this practice), but they registered strong discomfort with other Internet practices, particularly businesses' sale of information to other groups (19% "not very comfortable" and 74% "not at all comfortable") and the creation of comprehensive personal profiles (13% and 82%, respectively).

In a more recent Pew survey (Fox, 2005), 43% of Internet users in the United States reported having had a spyware, adware, or other type of tracking program on their home computer. About half (49%) agreed that "software programs like spyware are a serious threat to my online security," while 78% said it would be a serious problem if a program they installed or Web site they visited transmitted information about their Internet habits back to a central source; 57% said it would be a serious problem if such programs or sites collected the information but did not transmit it to a third party. In response to these concerns about privacy, 43% of Internet users reported that they stopped visiting certain Web sites, while 34% stopped downloading software. However, 78% of the Pew respondents reported not reading user agreements, privacy statements, or other disclaimers before downloading or installing programs.

There have also been attempts to measure the behavior of Internet users. For example, a 2007 study by comScore (Abraham et al., 2007) found that 31% of users deleted first-party cookies and 27% deleted third-party cookies over the course of a month. However, these data are based on 400,000 monitored home computers, where the panelists have agreed to install software on their computers to record their Internet behavior.* In a survey among 500 of the comScore panelists, 15% reported that cookies detract from their user experience, while 13% said they improve the experience, and 43% said they both improve and detract from the experience. About half the respondents (49%) reported removing all cookies, with a further 23% selectively deleting cookies and 23% deleting third-party but not first-party cookies, leaving only 4.2% who reported not intentionally deleting cookies. When asked, 30% indicated that they understood the

* On one hand, this may underestimate such behavior, as these panelists appear willing to have their Internet activities tracked; on the other hand, it may overestimate such behavior, because such panelists know they are being watched.

difference between first- and third-party cookies. In a study by Jupiter Research in March 2005, 39% of Internet users surveyed acknowledged deleting cookies. Finally, in an analysis of selected Web sites, WebTrends reported that third-party cookie denial has risen from 2.8% in January 2004 to 12.4% in April 2005 (Regan, 2005).

In summary—as in the case of offline consumer privacy—these and other survey findings convey a mixture of concern and ignorance (see Corning & Singer, 2003):

- Much as in the offline world, online users feel that there are few institutional or legal measures to help protect the privacy of their online activities.
- A majority of Internet users and the general public support the passage of new laws on how information can be collected and used on the Internet.
- Respondents are conflicted about whether various major institutions—advertisers, government, banks and credit card companies, and makers of privacy protection software—pose a threat to their privacy or will help protect it. There is general consensus that advertisers are likely to release rather than protect personal information, but respondents are fundamentally uncertain as to whether they should trust or distrust most other institutions involved in privacy issues.
- The lack of legal and institutional protection has not spurred Internet users to implement protective measures of their own. A relatively small proportion of Internet users overall say their browsers are set to reject cookies, though larger proportions have erased cookies at least once.
- The majority of Internet users report not reading user agreements and disclaimers before downloading or installing software.
- One fifth to one third of Internet users claim to resort to "guerilla tactics" such as providing false information or using a secondary e-mail address when registering at Web sites. Larger proportions simply refuse to give information they consider too personal or avoid visiting Web sites they believe to be disreputable.

In response to rising concerns about tracking software, the Federal Trade Commission recently proposed a set of principles to guide the regulation of online behavioral advertising (FTC, 2007). One such principle, related to informed consent, is "Every Web site where data is collected for behavioral advertising should provide a clear, concise, consumer-friendly, and prominent statement that (1) data about consumers' activities online is being collected at the site for use in providing advertising about products and services tailored to individual consumers' interests, and (2) consumers can choose whether or not to have their information collected for such purpose. The Web site should also provide consumers with a clear, easy-to-use, and accessible method for exercising this option." The Council for Marketing and Opinion Research (CMOR) is opposing such restrictions because of the concern that they would be applied broadly to all types of tracking (including cookies) and all types of online activity (including survey research). Whatever the outcome of this legislative process, it is important to understand how respondents view the use of tracking software and how they can be informed of the uses of such software in surveys without jeopardizing their participation. We return to this issue later in the context of our experiment on paradata.

Additional elements of informed consent in Internet surveys: Collection of paradata. Paradata—the data captured by computerized systems during the process of data collection (see Couper & Lyberg, 2005)—are increasingly being used in surveys, especially those conducted online (see Chapter 13 in this volume). Online survey paradata are generally of two types. The first type consists of characteristics of a respondent's browser captured from the server logs when they visit the survey Web page. These are called Web metrics or server-side paradata. The second type is information collected about the respondent's behavior on each Web page of the survey. The latter is typically collected by embedding JavaScript code in the hypertext markup language (HTML) code delivering the survey questions and capturing the answers on the respondent's browser (i.e., the client). These are called client-side paradata and are the focus of our interest here. Client-side paradata have been used to examine response latencies (e.g., time to first click), order of responding, changing of answers, mouse movements, and other respondent behaviors—see Baker and Couper (2007); Couper, Singer, Tourangeau and Conrad (2006); Heerwegh (2003); Stern (2008); Stieger (2004); and Yan and Tourangeau (2008) for examples.

Unlike active agents, with JavaScript no software or cookies are stored on the respondent's computer. JavaScript is part of the code on the active

Web page. It lasts only as long as that page is open. JavaScript is used in most commercial Web sites to provide a variety of interactive tools for the user, extending the basic functions of HTML, which was designed for the static presentation of text and images. JavaScript is increasingly being used to deliver more dynamic or interactive Internet surveys to respondents (e.g., Couper, 2007; Couper, 2008, Chapter 3). While users can disable JavaScript on their browsers, rendering the collection of paradata or the delivery of the enhanced tools inactive, in practice very few survey respondents do so (e.g., Kaczmirek & Thiele, 2006).*

Typically, the collection of paradata has not been shared with respondents, on the grounds that this information is used only to modify and improve the questionnaire and that explaining paradata to respondents is difficult. But as the practice has increasingly come to be used in making substantive interpretations of the responses, ethical questions are being raised about the need to inform respondents about the practice and to give them an opportunity to refuse to participate in this phase of the data collection. In other words, as the focus of attention in the use of paradata shifts from the instrument or data collection process to the respondent, principles of informed consent become relevant. According to the ESOMAR code, one of the standard elements of privacy statements requires a "clear statement of any invisible processing related to the survey that is taking place. Most Internet surveys can detect information about the respondent without respondent knowledge. Browser type, user name and computer identification are amongst the list of detectable information. Statements should say clearly what information is being captured and used during the interview (e.g., to deliver a page optimized to suit the browser) and whether any of this information is being handled as part of the survey or administrative records" (ESOMAR, 2008, p. 10).

Given these requirements, and the possibility that the distinctions between active agents and paradata may be blurred in the mind of both respondents and those regulating Internet activities, we need to find the best ways of informing respondents about the use of paradata without jeopardizing their participation in our surveys. The study reported in this chapter is a first attempt to gauge the effects of different ways of informing respondents about the collection and use of paradata in online surveys.

* Only 0.5% of LISS panel members do not have JavaScript enabled (A. Scherpenzeel, personal communication, December 2008).

6.3 OBTAINING CONSENT FOR THE COLLECTION OF PARADATA: REPORT OF AN EXPERIMENT

6.3.1 Introduction

So far, we have been talking about some of the ethical requirements for doing Internet surveys. We would be remiss, however, if we did not also discuss some of the consequences of giving respondents information about the survey that might well influence their decision to participate or refuse. What do we know about the consequences of giving respondents such information?

Not surprisingly, the effects are likely to depend on the kind of information communicated, often in interaction with other aspects of the survey. For example, we know that concerns about privacy and confidentiality impede responses to surveys. An early experiment by the Census Bureau (National Research Council, 1979) demonstrated that varying the length of time for which confidentiality of responses to the decennial census was assured had a significant inverse relationship to refusal rates—the longer the period for which confidentiality was promised, the lower the refusal rate. Refusal to answer the most sensitive questions on the survey, concerning income, was similarly affected. However, a subsequent experiment by Singer, Hippler, and Schwarz (1992) demonstrated that in a survey whose content was essentially innocuous, appending a long and legalistic assurance of confidentiality actually reduced the response rate to the survey, and also led to increased perceptions of the survey's sensitivity. A meta-analysis of many experiments (Singer, Von Thurn, & Miller, 1995) showed an interaction effect between the strength of the confidentiality assurance and the content of the survey: Stronger assurances improved response rate or quality if the survey contained sensitive content, but not otherwise. In another early survey, specifically designed to investigate the effect of informed consent requirements on survey response, Singer (1978) found that neither variations in information about the survey's sensitive content nor variations in the assurance of confidentiality had a significant impact on response rates; the only variable significantly affecting likelihood of response was a request for a signature to document consent. However, even the amount of information offered in the longer description of survey content was kept quite short and general.

More recent experiments that involve telling potential respondents to an Internet survey about the risk of disclosing their personal information to others, as well as the harm such disclosure might cause, suggest that information about risk (i.e., probability) alone does not affect stated willingness to participate, whereas the perceived sensitivity of the survey topic does have such an effect (Couper, Singer, Conrad, & Groves, 2008). However, telling respondents about both risk and harm is found to have significant effects, in the expected direction. These effects are stronger for sensitive topics (e.g., in the United States, money and sex) than for those not considered sensitive (e.g., leisure activities and work; Couper, Singer, Conrad, & Groves, 2010).

Thus, it is by no means clear that telling respondents about the collection of paradata will automatically reduce their willingness to participate in the survey. On the contrary, we would expect this information to interact with the content of the survey: Respondents to surveys with sensitive content might be more reluctant to agree to the collection of paradata. Furthermore, we would expect certain personal characteristics of respondents to influence their reaction to a request for collecting paradata. For example, respondents who are less sensitive to privacy concerns are likely to be more willing to agree to the collection of paradata than respondents who are more sensitive to such concerns.

Below, we describe the paradata experiment in detail.

6.3.2 Methods

6.3.2.1 Sample

The data come from an experiment embedded in a survey administered to members of the LISS panel (see Chapter 4 in this volume for details of the panel). The panel is a probability-based online panel designed to represent the adult population of the Netherlands. The panel is developed and maintained by CentERdata at Tilburg University.

In July 2008, a series of questions on general privacy concerns was administered to panel members. This survey was sent to 8,606 panel members, with 5,767 responding, for a response rate of 67%. The survey containing the vignette experiment was fielded in August 2008 among adults (ages 18+) in the panel. Altogether 8,561 panel members were invited to the survey, and 5,895 completed it, for a survey response rate of 69%. We restrict our analyses to the 5,198 panel members who completed both surveys.* This yields approximately 325 respondents per cell of the 16-cell design.

6.3.2.2 Experimental Manipulations

Because paradata are currently being collected in the LISS panel, we could not query respondents directly about their willingness to have such information collected. Rather, we developed a series of hypothetical descriptions, an approach we have used successfully in experiments in which we inform respondents about the potential risks and harms of statistical disclosure (Couper et al., 2008; Singer & Couper, 2008). Respondents were randomized to one of four descriptions about the collection of paradata. The first is a control condition, in which paradata are not mentioned at all; the second is a condition in which respondents are given a simple description of what paradata are collected, which we regard as equivalent to the condition in which we mention the risk of disclosure; the third is a condition in which we describe not only what paradata are collected but also what might be done with this information, which we regard as equivalent to the condition in which we mention both the risk and the potential harm of statistical disclosure; the fourth is a condition in which we give respondents a simple description of what paradata are collected and offer them a hyperlink to further information on the Internet, which contains the statement about potential harm given to respondents in condition 3. We added this fourth condition for two reasons: first, because the Internet is uniquely suited to providing information in this way, and second, because offering this information to respondents might give them a sense of greater control and make them more willing to agree to the collection of the paradata. Specifically, the four conditions were as follows:

1. No mention of paradata.
2. A simple description of what is collected: "In addition to your responses to the survey, we collect other data including keystrokes, time stamps, and characteristics of your browser. Like your answers themselves, this information is confidential."

* We find no significant association between privacy and confidentiality concerns expressed in the July survey and response to the August survey.

3. A simple description plus explicit mention of what will be done with the paradata: "In addition to your responses to the survey, we collect other data including keystrokes, time stamps, and characteristics of your browser. Among other things, this makes it possible to see whether people change their answers, measure how long they take to answer, and keep the answers from questions they answered before they quit the survey. Like your answers themselves, this information is confidential."
4. A simple description with a hyperlink to the additional information about uses: "In addition to your responses to the survey, we collect other data including keystrokes, time stamps, and characteristics of your browser. (Click here for more information.) Like your answers themselves, this information is confidential." The hyperlink contained the additional information presented in condition 3, above.

In addition to varying the description of the paradata, we varied the topic of the survey ("risk behaviors such as sexual activity, drug use, and alcohol use" versus "sport, recreation, and leisure time") to test whether willingness to provide paradata would vary with the sensitivity of the topic. Finally, we also varied the sponsorship of the hypothetical survey, with half the vignettes describing a survey invitation from a government health agency and the other half describing an invitation from a market research company. Our expectation here is that willingness to permit the collection of paradata may vary with trust in the sponsor.

Crossing these three factors yields a 4 × 2 × 2 design, with respondents randomly assigned to receive one of the 16 vignettes. The vignette was followed by a question on their willingness to participate (WTP) in the survey described, on a scale ranging from 0 ("definitely would not take part in the survey") to 10 ("definitely would take part"). For those who were exposed to one of the three descriptions of paradata and who expressed some willingness to participate (6–10 on the scale), we asked the following question: "In addition, would you be willing to permit use of the browser, keystroke, and time stamp data?" ("yes/no").

We formulated the following specific hypotheses about respondents' willingness to participate in the survey and to permit use of their paradata:

1. We expected WTP to be highest in the control condition, and higher in the condition that gives a simple description of paradata

only rather than in the condition that also describes how paradata might be used. Because of the degree of control offered by the hyperlink, we also expected WTP in that condition to be higher than in condition 3.
2. Because of the greater perceived social utility (i.e., greater benefit) of research by the government than by market research companies, we expected WTP to be higher when the survey was said to be sponsored by the government than when it was said to be sponsored by a market research company.
3. Because of the varying sensitivity of the information asked about, we expected WTP to be higher on surveys about leisure time and sports than on surveys about risk behaviors.
4. On the basis of our earlier research (Couper et al., 2008a, 2000b), we expected an interaction between the sensitivity of the survey and information about paradata collection on WTP.
5. We expected people who reported more concerns about privacy to be less likely to be willing to participate in the surveys described, and also less likely to permit the collection of paradata about them.

We also expected willingness to permit use of the paradata to be lower in every condition than willingness to participate in the survey in that condition. This expectation is based in part on conversational logic (Schwarz, 1996), and in part on earlier research involving requests for signed consent forms among those willing to participate in surveys (Singer, 1978, 2003). We first describe the results of the data collection effort, then discuss the analyses addressing these hypotheses.

6.3.2.3 Questionnaire and Measures

In addition to the paradata vignettes, the August survey measured a variety of respondent background characteristics. We focus on three key demographics found to be useful in our earlier informed consent studies (Couper et al., 2008, 2010), namely, gender, age, and education. From the general privacy-related attitudes asked about in the July survey, we created several measures, again based on our earlier work. These are:

1. A single privacy item: "In general, how worried are you about your personal privacy?" ranging from 1 = "not at all worried" to 4 = "extremely worried."
2. A single confidentiality item: "Different private and public organizations have personal information about us. How concerned are you about whether or not they keep this information confidential?" ranging from 1 = "not concerned at all" to 4 = "very concerned."
3. An index of privacy concerns based on the following items: "Please indicate whether or not you ever feel your privacy is violated by the following: (a) Banks and credit card companies when they ask about finances; (b) The government when it collects tax returns; (c) The government when it conducts surveys of the population; (d) Computers that store a lot of information about you; or (e) People who ask questions on public opinion surveys." The number of "yes" responses was summed for an index ranging from 0 to 5.
4. A trust in confidentiality index, based on the following items: "How much do you trust each of the following to keep the information they collect from you confidential: (a) Public opinion research companies? (b) Market research companies? (c) Government agencies, like the Central Bureau of Statistics?" Responses ranged from 1 = "not at all" to 4 = "a lot," and the mean response to the three items is used.

A final item ("Do you feel that different government agencies can get information about you if they try to?") yielded insufficient variation (96.4% of respondents said "yes"), so it is not used in further analyses.

We also extracted two items from the initial profile surveys completed by all panel members. One was a series of questions on various Internet activities they engage in. We created a count of four of these activities (purchasing items via the Internet, downloading software, downloading music or films, and Internet banking) likely to involve the use of cookies, JavaScript, or other active content. The other item was a single indicator of whether the respondent was provided a simPC, indicating that the panel member did not have a computer—with the minimum technical standards required for the LISS panel and also often no Internet access—prior to joining the LISS panel (see Chapter 4 in this volume).

6.3.2.4 Analysis and Results

Our dependent variable of interest is WTP in the hypothetical survey. We examine both the mean WTP on the 11-point scale, using a general linear model, and the percentage who say they are willing (a score of 6 or higher on the scale), using a logistic model. The overall mean for respondents is 5.41, with 59.5% saying they would be willing to participate in the hypothetical survey described in the vignette.

In testing the hypotheses, we examined models containing only the three experimental factors, as well as models controlling for the background, behavioral, and attitude measures described above. As our primary focus is not on these variables, we do not present the full models here. In general, males have significantly higher levels of WTP ($p = .0042$ in the linear model and $p = .046$ in the logistic model). Education is significantly associated with WTP ($p < .0001$ in both models), but the effect is curvilinear, with those in the lowest (primary school) and highest (university degree) education categories exhibiting lower levels of WTP than those with a high school or college education. Age shows a significant ($p < .001$) negative association with WTP. The Internet activity index is not associated with WTP, and those with a simPC have a significantly higher mean WTP ($p = .012$), but this variable is not significant ($p = .14$) in the logistic model.

Turning to the first hypothesis, we expected WTP to be highest in the control condition and lowest in the condition that describes how paradata might be used. We find a significant main effect ($p < .0001$) of the paradata disclosure manipulation, whether including only the three experimental variables in the model or controlling for the background, behavioral, and attitude measures, and whether examining mean WTP or the percentage willing to do so. Table 6.1 shows the predicted values for the three experimental manipulations, both in terms of mean WTP and the percentage willing, from the full model controlling for the variables above.

As can be seen, mean stated WTP is lower for all three paradata conditions than the control condition. However, providing additional information on the uses of paradata appears to help, especially when using a hyperlink. In percentage terms, while 65% expressed willingness to participate (a score of 6–10 on the scale) in the hypothetical survey with

TABLE 6.1

Adjusted Means, Odds Ratios, and Predicted Percentage Willing to Participate for Experimental Manipulations, From Full Model

Manipulation	Mean WTP (and std. err)	OR (and 95% CI)	Predicted % Willing
Paradata Description			
No mention	5.88 (0.12)	—	65.4%
Simple description	5.14 (0.12)	0.66 (0.56, 0.78)	55.5%
Explicit description	5.36 (0.12)	0.72 (0.61, 0.84)	57.4%
Simple description + link	5.39 (0.12)	0.79 (0.67, 0.93)	59.8%
Survey Sponsor			
Market research company	5.31 (0.09)	0.83 (0.74, 0.93)	57.3%
Government health agency	5.58 (0.09)	—	61.8%
Survey Topic			
Risk behaviors	5.06 (0.09)	0.70 (0.63, 0.78)	55.2%
Sport, recreation, and leisure time	5.83 (0.09)	—	63.8%

no mention of paradata, this dropped to 56%, 57%, and 60%, respectively, for the three paradata conditions.*

Turning to the second hypothesis, we find a significant ($p < .0001$) main effect of survey sponsorship, with those seeing the government sponsor being more willing to participate in the hypothetical survey than those seeing the market research sponsor. The relevant means and percentages are presented in Table 6.1. We find no interaction of sponsorship with the paradata manipulation; in other words, the sponsorship of the survey does not affect whether people would be more or less willing to participate given different paradata descriptions.

Our third hypothesis—that WTP would vary with the sensitivity of the topic—also finds support. As shown in Table 6.1, those seeing the description of the survey on sensitive topics (sex, drugs, and alcohol use) are significantly ($p < .0001$) less willing to participate than those exposed to the less sensitive survey. The fourth hypothesis posits an interaction between topic sensitivity and the paradata manipulation. However, the interaction term is not significant ($p = .85$ in the full linear model and $p = .90$ in the full logistic model). That is, topic sensitivity and the paradata disclosure manipulation have independent effects on WTP, so the fourth hypothesis is not supported.

* Using predicted proportions from the logistic regression model with all other variables set at their mean.

In our fifth hypothesis, we expected those who were more concerned about privacy and confidentiality to be less willing to participate in the survey described, and also less likely to permit the collection of paradata about them. All of the privacy and confidentiality attitude measures we included in the July survey are related to stated willingness to participate in the expected direction. However, while all are significant in bivariate analyses, they do not all reach statistical significance in the full multivariate models, in part because of the correlations (ranging from 0.16 to 0.63) among them. In the full linear model, the confidentiality item ($p = .012$), the privacy index ($p = .0033$), and the trust in confidentiality index ($p < .0001$) are all significant, while in the logistic model, only the confidentiality item ($p = .0065$) and the trust in confidentiality index ($p = .0002$) reach significance. We find no significant interactions between the privacy and confidentiality measures and the paradata manipulation on WTP. In other words, the effect of the paradata disclosure manipulation does not vary systematically between those with varying levels of concern about privacy and confidentiality.

The second part of the hypothesis is based on the follow-up question asked only of those who said they would participate in the survey, among those in one of the three conditions describing paradata. Table 6.2 presents the overall percentages agreeing to the use of paradata in these three groups, both as a percentage of those agreeing to do the survey and as a percentage of the full group exposed to that condition.

We can see from Table 6.2 that only about a third of those who said they were willing to do the survey described in the vignette were also willing to allow capture and use of their paradata. This translates to about one in five of all respondents agreeing to both the survey *and* the paradata. Those shown the detailed description of the uses of paradata are significantly

TABLE 6.2

Percentage Agreeing to the Use of Paradata, Among Those Agreeing to Do Survey, and Among All Respondents

	Among Those Agreeing to Do Survey		Among All Respondents	
Paradata Description	**Percent**	**(*n*)**	**Percent**	**(*n*)**
Simple description	35.0	(703)	19.4	(1267)
Explicit description	29.6	(794)	17.0	(1383)
Simple description + link	35.8	(771)	21.5	(1284)

($\chi^2(2) = 7.96$, $p = .019$) less willing to allow their use. However, only 22.2% of those in the condition with the hyperlink clicked on the link. Among those that did so, 35.1% agreed to the use of the paradata, while 36.0% of those who did not click on the link agreed to such use (the difference is not significant, $\chi^2(2) = 3.66$, $p = .83$).

Returning to the fifth hypothesis, we ran a logistic regression among those in the three paradata description conditions who agreed to participate in the survey, predicting whether they permitted use of the paradata or not. Conditional on agreeing to participate in the hypothetical survey, only two variables from the full models reach statistical significance. The first is the paradata manipulation ($p = .017$) reflecting the differences seen in Table 6.2. The other is the single confidentiality item ($p = .0020$), with greater concern about confidentiality associated with lower willingness to allow use of the paradata. We thus find support for the hypothesis for one of the general measures of privacy and confidentiality concerns, but not the others.

6.4 CONCLUSIONS

By their very nature, Internet surveys, like other online activities, produce paradata. Such data have uses—for example, recovering from system failure or monitoring and improving system performance—that have no implications for informed consent requirements. But as paradata use expands beyond methodological to substantive domains, such as evaluating attitude intensity through response latencies or assessing the cognitive performance of individual respondents, issues of informed consent become more salient. For surveys where the paradata are being captured with the explicit intent to study the behavior of individual respondents and link such data to their substantive responses, we would argue that respondents should be informed about the collection of these data.

Under these circumstances, the results of our experiment suggest that there may be a potential conflict between research considerations and obligations to respondents, because informing them appears to reduce both their willingness to participate in the research and, more substantially, their willingness to permit use of the paradata collected. This potential conflict is heightened by more general respondent concerns about the unobtrusive measurement of online behavior (e.g., through spyware or active agents), which is often done with malicious intent.

However, the information value of the present experiment is limited by at least three considerations. First is the way willingness to participate is measured. Even in the condition without mention of paradata, expressed willingness to participate in the hypothetical study described is only 65.5%. The reduction in WTP caused by different ways of describing paradata uses ranges from 6 to 10 percentage points, though it would be hazardous to project a decline in actual response rates from these data. When asked explicitly about something (1) of which they have little knowledge and (2) which engenders associations with broader intrusions into online activities, it is not surprising that substantial numbers of respondents are disinclined to permit use of the paradata as described in our vignettes. Furthermore, it is not clear that informing respondents about the collection of paradata also requires asking explicit consent for their use. Researchers do not, for example, tell respondents about the kinds of questions they will be asked and, in addition, ask for permission to analyze their answers.

The utility of the present experiment is further limited by the specific experimental conditions chosen, which were not informed by qualitative research or pretests with potential respondents. In designing those conditions, we had no empirical evidence to draw on about particular concerns respondents may have about paradata and their uses, or about how best to alleviate those concerns. Different descriptions might well have produced very different results.

Finally, we note that this experiment was conducted in a particular country with very specific norms about survey participation as well as concerns about confidentiality.

To overcome these limitations, we need qualitative work and pretesting to understand respondents' concerns and to find the best ways of alleviating them, and we need experiments involving actual surveys rather than hypothetical vignettes about surveys, carried out in a variety of cultural settings.

As already noted, paradata have uses without any implications for informing respondents. Even the use of paradata for research purposes is very unlikely to expose respondents to risks over and above those created by their participation in the research itself. Nevertheless, because informed consent has less to do with protecting respondents from risk of harm than it does with ensuring their right to make informed, voluntary decisions, we need much more research such as that described above in order to meet ethical as well as scientific research goals.

[1] Acknowledgments: This work was supported in part by the U.S. National Institutes of Health (NICHD grant P01 HD045753-01). We are also grateful to the CentERdata staff at Tilburg University for implementing this study on the LISS panel, and to the editors for their valuable feedback on earlier drafts of the chapter.

REFERENCES

Abraham, M., Meierhoefer, C., & Lipsman, A. (2007). *The impact of cookie deletion on the accuracy of site-server and ad-server metrics: An empirical comScore study.* Reston, VA: comScore.

Association of Internet Researchers. (2002). *Ethical decision-making and Internet research: Recommendations from the AoIR Ethics Working Committee.* Milwaukee, WI: AoIR. Retrieved from www.aoir.org/reports/ethics.pdf

Baker, R. P. & Couper, M. P. (2007). *The impact of screen size and background color on response in Web surveys.* Paper presented at the General Online Research conference (GOR '07), Leipzig, Germany.

Corning, A. & Singer, E. (2003). *Survey of U.S. privacy attitudes.* Report prepared for the Computer Science and Telecommunications Board, Division on Engineering and Physical Sciences, National Academy of Sciences.

Council of American Survey Research Organizations (CASRO). (2008). *Code of standards and ethics for survey research.* Port Jefferson, NY: CASRO.

Couper, M. P. (2000). Web surveys: A review of issues and approaches. *Public Opinion Quarterly, 64*(4), 464–494.

Couper, M. P. (2007). Whither the Web: Web 2.0 and the changing world of Web surveys. In M. Trotman, T. Burrell, L. Gerrard et al. (Eds.), *The challenges of a changing world: Proceedings of the fifth international conference of the Association for Survey Computing* (pp. 7–16). Berkeley, UK: ASC.

Couper, M. P. (2008). *Designing effective Web surveys.* New York: Cambridge University Press.

Couper, M. P. & Lyberg, L. E. (2005). The use of paradata in survey research. In *Proceedings of the 55th Session of the International Statistical Institute* [CD]. Sydney, Australia: ISI.

Couper, M. P., Singer, E., Conrad, F. G., & Groves, R. M. (2008). Risk of disclosure, perceptions of risk, and concerns about privacy and confidentiality as factors in survey participation. *Journal of Official Statistics, 24*(2), 255–275.

Couper, M., Singer, E., Conrad, F. G., & Groves, R. M. (2010). An experimental study of disclosure risk, disclosure harm, incentives, and survey participation. *Journal of Official Statistics*, 26(2), in press.

Couper, M. P., Singer, E., Tourangeau, R., & Conrad, F. G. (2006). Evaluating the effectiveness of visual analog scales: A Web experiment. *Social Science Computer Review, 24*(2), 227–245.

Downes-Le Guin, T., Mechling, J., & Baker, R. P. (2006). Great results from ambiguous sources: Cleaning Web panel data. In *Proceedings of ESOMAR World Research Conference, Panel Research* [CD] (pp. 285–293). Barcelona, Spain: ESOMAR.

ESOMAR (2008). *Conducting market and opinion research using the Web.* Amsterdam: ESOMAR. Retrieved from http://www.esomar.org/index.php/codes-guidelines.html

Federal Trade Commission (FTC). (2007). *Online behavioral advertising: Moving the discussion forward to possible self-regulatory principles.* Retrieved from http://www.ftc.gov/os/2007/12/P859900stmt.pdf

Fox, S. (2000). *Trust and privacy online: Why Americans want to rewrite the rules.* The Pew Internet and American Life Project. Retrieved from http://www.pewinternet.org

Fox, S. (2005). *Spyware: The threat of unwanted software programs is changing the way people use the Internet.* The Pew Internet and American Life Project. Retrieved from http://www.pewinternet.org

Fox, S. & Lewis, O. (2001). *Fear of online crime: Americans support FBI interception of criminal suspects' e-mail and new laws to protect online privacy.* The Pew Internet and American Life Project. Retrieved from http://www.pewinternet.org

Frankel, M. S. & Siang, S. (1999). *Ethical and legal aspects of human subjects research on the Internet: A report of a workshop June 10–11.* Washington, DC: American Association for the Advancement of Science.

Heerwegh, D. (2003). Explaining response latencies and changing answers using client-side paradata from a Web survey. *Social Science Computer Review, 21*(3), 360–373.

Hillygus, D. S., Nie, N. H., Prewitt, K., & Pals, H. (2006). *The hard count.* New York: Russell Sage.

Jupiter Research. (2005). *Accurate Web site visitor measurement crippled by cookie blocking and deletion.* New York: Jupitermedia Corporation. Retrieved from http://www.jupitermedia.com/corporate/press.html

Kaczmirek, L. & Thiele, O. (2006). *Flash, JavaScript, or PHP? Comparing the availability of technical equipment among university applicants.* Paper presented at the General Online Research conference (GOR '06), Bielefeld, Germany.

Klang, M. (2004). Spyware—the ethics of covert action. *Ethics and Information Technology, 6*, 193–202.

Kraut, R. M., Olson, J., Banaji, M., Bruckman, A., Cohen, J., & Couper, M. (2004). Psychological research online: Report of Board of Scientific Affairs' Advisory Group on the Conduct of Research on the Internet. *American Psychologist, 59*(2), 106–117.

Lozar Manfreda, K. & Vehovar, V. (2008). Web surveys. In E. D. De Leeuw, J. J. Hox, & D. A. Dillman (Eds.), *International handbook of survey methodology* (pp. 264–284). European Association of Methodology Series. New York: Lawrence Erlbaum Associates.

Marketing Research Association. (2000). *Use of the Internet for conducting opinion and marketing research: Ethical guidelines.* Glastonbury, CT: Marketing Research Association. Retrieved from http://www.imro.org/pdf/Internet%20guidelines%20for%20web.pdf

National Commission for the Protection of Human Subjects of Biomedical and Behavioral Research. (1979). *The Belmont Report: Ethical principles and guidelines for the protection of human subjects of research.* Washington, DC: U.S. Government Printing Office.

National Research Council. (1979). *Privacy and confidentiality as factors in survey response.* Washington, DC: National Academy Press.

National Research Council. (2006). *Expanding access to research data: Reconciling risks and opportunities.* Washington, DC: National Academy Press.

Regan, K. (2005). Web analytics industry confronts cookie-deletion trend. *E-Commerce Times*. Retrieved from http://www.ecommercetimes.com/story/43284.html

Schwarz, N. (1996). *Cognition and communication: Judgmental biases, research methods, and the logic of conversation*. Mahwah, NJ: Lawrence Erlbaum Associates.

Seastrom, M. (2008). *The impact of privacy breaches on survey participation in a national longitudinal survey*. Paper presented at the Joint Statistical Meetings, Denver, Colorado.

Singer, E. (1978). Informed consent: Consequences for response rate and response quality in social surveys. *American Sociological Review, 43*(2), 144–162.

Singer, E. (2003). Exploring the meaning of consent: Participation in research and beliefs about risks and benefits. *Journal of Official Statistics, 19*(3), 273–285.

Singer, E. & Couper, M. P. (2008). Do incentives exert undue influence on survey participation? Experimental evidence. *Journal of Empirical Research on Human Research Ethics, 3*(3), 49–56.

Singer, E., Hippler, H.-J., & Schwarz, N. (1992). Confidentiality assurances in surveys: Reassurance or threat? *International Journal of Public Opinion Research, 4*, 256–268.

Singer, E., Mathiowetz, N., & Couper, M. P. (1993). The role of privacy and confidentiality as factors in response to the 1990 census. *Public Opinion Quarterly, 57*, 465–482.

Singer, E., Van Hoewyk, J., & Neugebauer, R. (2003). Attitudes and behavior: The impact of privacy and confidentiality concerns on participation in the 2000 census. *Public Opinion Quarterly, 67*, 368–384.

Singer, E., Von Thurn, D. R., & Miller, E. R. (1995). Confidentiality assurances and response. *Public Opinion Quarterly, 59*, 66–77.

Stern, M. J. (2008). The use of client-side paradata in analyzing the effects of visual layout on changing responses in Web surveys. *Field Methods, 20*(4), 377–398.

Stieger, S. (2004). *What the h . . . are they doing? What are respondents doing while filling in an online questionnaire*. Paper presented at the General Online Research conference (GOR '04), Duisburg, Germany.

Thiele, O. & Kaczmirek, L. (2010). Security and data protection: Collection, storage, and feedback in Web research. In S. D. Gosling & J. A. Johnson (Eds.), *Advanced methods for behavioral research on the Web*. (pp. 235–253). Washington, DC: American Psychological Association.

Turow, J. (2003). *Americans and online privacy: The system is broken*. Philadelphia, PA: Annenberg Public Policy Center of the University of Pennsylvania. Retrieved from http://www.asc.upenn.edu/usr/jturow/internet-privacy-report/36-page-turow-version-9.pdf

Tuskegee Syphilis Study Ad Hoc Advisory Panel (1973). *Final report of the Tuskegee Syphilis Study Ad Hoc Advisory Panel*. Washington, DC: Department of Health, Education, and Welfare.

Walther, J. B. (2002). Research ethics in Internet-enabled research: Human subjects issues and methodological myopia. *Ethics and Information Technology, 4*, 205–216.

Whitehead, L. C. (2007). Methodological and ethical issues in Internet-mediated research in the field of health: An integrated review of the literature. *Social Science and Medicine, 65*(4), 782–791.

Yan, T. & Tourangeau, R. (2008). Fast times and easy questions: The effects of age, experience and question complexity on Web survey response times. *Applied Cognitive Psychology, 22*(1), 51–68.

Zayatz, L. (2007). *Disclosure avoidance practices and research at the U.S. Census Bureau: An update*. Paper presented at the workshop on Ensuring Data Access and Confidentiality Protection for Highly Sensitive Data, University of Michigan, Ann Arbor.

Part II

Advanced Methods and Applications

7

How Visual Design Affects the Interpretability of Survey Questions

Vera Toepoel
Department of Leisure Studies
Tilburg University
Tilburg, the Netherlands

Don A. Dillman
Social and Economic Sciences Research Center
and Department of Sociology
Washington State University
Pullman, Washington

7.1 INTRODUCTION

It has been little more than a decade since systematic research was begun on how visual layout of questions in surveys influences respondent answers. This work has been motivated and sustained, in part, by the development of Internet survey methods and the desire to relate research findings to those collected through interviews. One of the difficulties faced by surveyors in the early 21st century is that most individual survey modes face specific problems such as inadequate coverage and poor response rates, making it increasingly necessary to consider the mixing of survey modes so that some data are collected by one mode and other data by a different mode (De Leeuw, 2005; Dillman, Smyth, & Christian, 2009). In addition, research has shown that different visual layouts produce different answers for all types of survey questions, from scalar to open-ended (Jenkins & Dillman, 1997; Christian & Dillman, 2004). Two important research questions that have emerged concern the extent to which formats need to be controlled between visual modes and which visual formats translate most effectively to aural modes. These developments make it imperative that we develop a better understanding of how visual design of questions affects the quality and interpretability of survey data.

Although each mode has its own limitations, design plays a much larger role in Internet surveys compared to other modes of administration. More tools are available, such as pictures, sound, video, drop-down boxes, slider scales, automatic fill-ins, feedback, and information links. However, every tool can introduce its own specific errors; for example, adding pictures may cause a different interpretation of the verbal language of the question (Couper, Conrad, & Tourangeau, 2007; Couper, Tourangeau, & Kenyon, 2004). Furthermore, Internet surveyors often do not know exactly how a questionnaire appears on individual respondents' screens. The intentions of the survey researcher for the questionnaire are mediated through hardware, software, and user preferences (Dillman et al., 2009). It is quite likely that the questionnaire seen by the respondent will not be exactly as the researcher intended it to appear because of different operating systems, Web browsers, and screen configurations, although this can be controlled to some extent by the use of cascading style sheet (CSS) construction of Internet surveys (see Chapter 2 in this volume). In addition, the lack of a high-speed connection in many households may prevent some design features of Internet surveys from being displayed as intended by the Web programmer. The fact that one respondent might see something quite different from that seen by another respondent presents a significant methodological concern, as described in this chapter. Although Internet questionnaires may draw on the principles of visual design in paper questionnaires, they also have new elements (e.g., the use of keyboard and mouse) that require independent testing.

This chapter first discusses the theoretical background of processing visual information (Section 7.2). Then a literature review is provided on effects of visual layout in survey questions (Section 7.3). We also identify research issues in need of investigation (Section 7.4). The chapter ends with thirteen dos and don'ts with regard to visual design in survey questions (Section 7.5).

7.2 HOW VISUAL INFORMATION IS PROCESSED

Respondents are cooperative communicators and will process survey questions by drawing on all information provided by the survey researcher

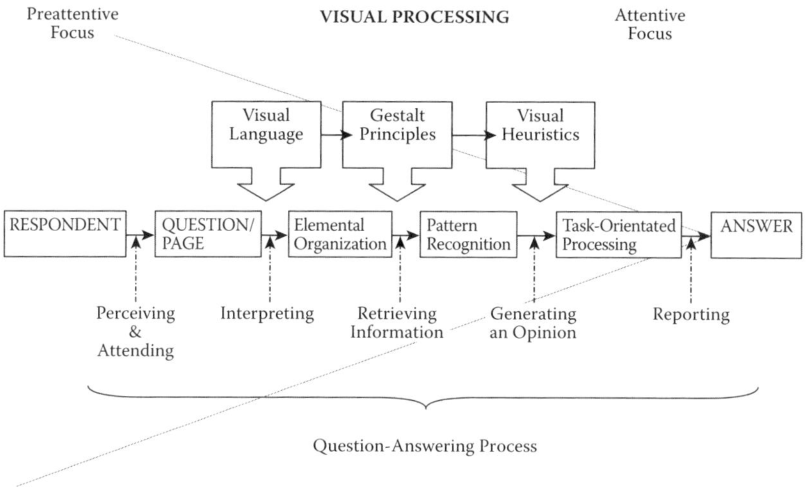

FIGURE 7.1
A schematic view of elements and tasks involved in visual processing of survey questions, as envisioned by the authors.

(Schwarz, 1996). They find specific cues in the verbal language (words) in the questionnaire, as well as in the visual (nonverbal) language. Visual language includes graphical, numerical, and symbolic languages that convey meaning in addition to the verbal language (Christian & Dillman, 2004). For a description of these languages, see Dillman (2007, p. 496). The visual layout of a question is an important source of information that respondents use when deciding which answer to select (Christian, 2003). Since respondents extract meaning from how the information is shaped, spaced, and shaded, researchers need to pay close attention to how visual information is arranged on a page. Figure 7.1 shows one way of describing how respondents process visual information to arrive at an answer to a survey question. It represents our attempt to integrate the seminal work of Palmer (1999), Hoffman (2004), and Ware (2004) and apply it to the development of survey redesigns as described elsewhere (Dillman, Gertseva, & Mahon-Haft, 2005; Dillman et al., 2009).

The act of reading and responding to a question (the question-answering process) contains at least four steps: comprehending the question, retrieving information, generating an opinion or a representation of the relevant behavior, and reporting it (Tourangeau, 1987). Mistakes can be made because of problems at any one of these steps, resulting in measurement error. Redline and Dillman (2002) specify a fifth step for visual surveys, perceiving and attending, which must occur prior to the four steps mentioned above. According to them, respondents must first perceive the information presented visually and give it their attention before going through the sequence of activities involved in responding to a question. Although words are probably the most important feature of survey questions that respondents use to interpret the precise intent of the survey question (see, e.g., Toepoel & Dillman, 2008; Tourangeau, Couper, & Conrad, 2007), graphical layout, numbers, and symbols may prevent words from being seen or understood as intended by the surveyor (Redline & Dillman, 2002).

Respondents process visual information in a sequential manner (Figure 7.1). Preattentive processing occurs when respondents glance at a page and immediately recognize general features essential to making sense of the scene. During preattentive processing respondents selectively pick up on certain symbols, shapes, or other features of a page, which subconsciously attract attention (Ware, 2004). Attributes that are processed preattentively are number in a group, enclosure, size of elements, line orientation, additional elements, contrast, curvature, subtracted elements, and shape (see Dillman, 2007, p. 467, for a visualization of these attributes). Attentive processing refers to giving attention to a small visual field, usually within a visual span of about eight characters (also known as the foveal view), and bringing those few elements into the visual working memory, where they are better recalled later (Dillman, 2007). After glancing at a questionnaire (preattentive processing), a respondent should be able to attend to the details of the questionnaire (attentive processing) unambiguously, if visual language is applied in a consistent matter.

Visual processing of a questionnaire page involves three levels of processing (Dillman, 2007, pp. 466–470). First, eyes preattentively organize the entire page into basic regions according to shared visual properties such as color and texture, a process that is called elemental organization. Visual language is apparent in every question in an Internet survey; the size of the answer space, labels on answer categories, signals, the placement of instructions, symbols, spacing between response options, ordering of response options, color, numbers, pictures, and visibility in general all provide specific visual cues. Verbal and nonverbal cues can independently and jointly influence answers to questions. For example, Redline, Dillman, Carley-Baxter, and Creecy (2005) provide evidence that the visual and verbal complexity of information in a questionnaire affects what respondents read, the order in which they read it, and ultimately their comprehension of the information. Considerable research shows that independent and combined effects of visual manipulations affect respondents' answer choices (Christian & Dillman, 2004; Dillman & Christian, 2002; Jenkins & Dillman, 1997; Redline & Dillman, 2002; Toepoel, Das, & Van Soest, 2006, 2008, 2009; Tourangeau, Couper, & Conrad, 2004, 2007).

The second level is pattern recognition, in which figures are grouped together to be better understood and to speed up processing. Visual elements that share visual qualities, such as color, shape, size, and so on, are perceived as belonging to each other. This midlevel processing is explained by grouping principles drawn from Gestalt psychology:

- Proximity: objects that are closer together will be seen as a group.
- Similarity: objects with the same shape, size, contrast, etc. will be seen as a group.
- Connectedness: elements connected by other elements will be seen as a group.
- Continuity: elements that continue smoothly across a field will be seen as a group.
- Common region: elements within the same common region will be seen as a group.
- Closure: elements forming a closed figure will be seen as a group.
- Pragnänz: elements that are simpler and of the same shape are easier to perceive and remember.

By developing consistency among elements, surveyors send cues that are clear and strong, while inconsistency sends cues that are ambiguous and weak. The effects of these concepts are summarized in Dillman (2007, pp. 466–493, and additional journal articles referenced there).

Third, when the basic visual elements are perceived as aligned in a meaningful way, the respondent can then focus attentively and get on with the response task. Tourangeau et al. (2004) expand beyond the Gestalt psychology principles, arguing that respondents follow simple heuristics in interpreting the visual features of questions:

- Middle means typical: respondents will see the middle item as the most typical.
- Left and top means first: the leftmost or top item will be seen as the "first" in conceptual sense.

- Near means related: items that are physically near each other are expected to be related conceptually.
- Up means good: the top item will be seen as the most desirable.
- Like means close: visually similar options will be seen as closer conceptually.

Each heuristic assigns a cultural association to a visual cue. Thus, their research goes a step beyond simply understanding how individuals respond cognitively, as described by the Gestalt psychology laws of perception and vision science findings described by Palmer (1999), Hoffman (2004) and Ware (2004). We return to understanding the relative importance of these heuristics later in this chapter.

7.3 RESEARCH ON HOW VISUAL LAYOUT INFLUENCES ANSWERS

The origins of research on visual layout go back to observations made by Smith (1995), who was one of the first to demonstrate that in addition to question wording, elements such as response format, context, and nonverbal aspects including physical layout and visual presentation can noticeably influence answers. This section provides a summary of research findings on visual design in question-and-answer formats that has utilized the aforementioned concepts and perspectives on how people process and respond to the visual aspects of questions.

7.3.1 Larger Answer Spaces Elicit More Information

Smith (1995) has argued that allowing more space, which is one of the graphical concepts described in Section 7.2 as conveying meaning for recording open-ended questions, may produce results closer to actual verbatim. He demonstrated that allowing more space for recording open-ended answers produced longer recorded responses. Christian and Dillman (2004) tested the idea that size of the answering space sets an expectation for what the surveyor interprets the response task to be. They found that providing larger answer spaces for open-ended questions increased both the number of words and the number of themes offered by respondents. Smyth, Dillman, Christian, and McBride (2009) have shown for Internet questionnaires similar effects, as well as greater size of space leading to elaboration in answers that aids coding of responses. Stern, Dillman, and Smyth (2007) confirm in their analysis of personal characteristics that some demographic groups are more likely to provide longer responses than others. Respondents ages 60 years and over, those with less than a college degree, and women all provided responses that were longer than those by other adults in a general public sample.

In another experiment Christian and Dillman (2004) tested the effects of adding lines in open-ended answer spaces. When only a few lines are added to the open-ended question, it is expected that this results in shorter answers compared to no lines, just as the size of the answer boxes also conveyed the researcher's expectations for the size of the answers. They found no evidence, however, that the version of the question without lines provided more substantive answers to the question, even though more respondents wrote something in the answer space.

7.3.2 Connections Among Answer Spaces, Labels, and Symbols Affect Answers

Respondents draw information from answer categories to decide whether and how to report answers. Research has found that the task communicated to the respondent by an answer space may appear to contradict the task communicated by question wording, resulting in associated errors. For example, Couper, Traugott, and Lamias (2001) found that respondents receiving a short-entry box version were much more likely to leave the box blank (52%) than those receiving a long-entry box version (18%). Furthermore, respondents were more likely to type in an explicit "don't know/not applicable" answer in the long-entry box version than in the short-entry box version. In addition, in the long-entry box version respondents were significantly more likely to enter an invalid response than in the short-entry box version, providing more information than was required. For example, instead of simply providing a number, respondents entered "about 3", "between 4 and 5," and similar answers. Thus, the lack of correspondence between the size of the space and the desire for one- or two-digit answers led to undesired word answers rather than the preferred numerical answers.

In addition, Christian, Dillman, and Smyth (2007) found that a successive series of visual language manipulations more than doubled, from 45% to 96%, respondents' use of the desired format (two digits for the month and four digits for the year) for reporting dates. Specifically, this research showed successive improvements from the application of a series of Gestalt psychology and graphical design concepts, including size, proximity, similarity, and location. Making the month box smaller by half than the year box modestly improved the reporting of two digits in the month box and four in the year box. Changing the location of the symbols (from following the boxes to before each box) also improved compliance a bit. In addition, connecting boxes using the Gestalt proximity concept (items seen together will be treated the same) improved compliance (that is, reporting digits in both boxes rather than characters—e.g., "August"—in one box and numbers in the other). Most dramatically, changing from words ("month/year") to symbols with embedded numeracy ("mm/yyyy") doubled compliance.

In a paper experiment, Christian and Dillman (2004) tested an arrow as a symbol that is culturally defined to focus one's attention in the direction the arrow is pointing. They placed the arrow within the foveal view of six to eight characters, to draw attention toward a subordinate question. The adding of the symbol significantly increased the percentage of eligible respondents answering the subordinate question.

The importance of these three experiments is that they show that respondents are guided in various ways by connections between answering spaces and graphical design elements as well as symbols, as discussed in Section 7.2. These connections are critical in helping respondents decide among a variety of response behaviors for reporting information in blank spaces. Some of this guidance comes from question wording, while symbols and the size of spaces play additive roles.

7.3.3 Effects of Spatial Separation and Lack of Visual Linearity on Choosing Scalar Categories

When respondents are asked to indicate answers to a scalar question, they are usually being asked to utilize an implied continuum that is linear in nature. Graphical and symbolic language can be used to provide a reminder to respondents of how scalar questions are to be used. Because these languages cannot be provided in aural modes, it was reasoned that incorporating into the stem of a question all directions for placing an

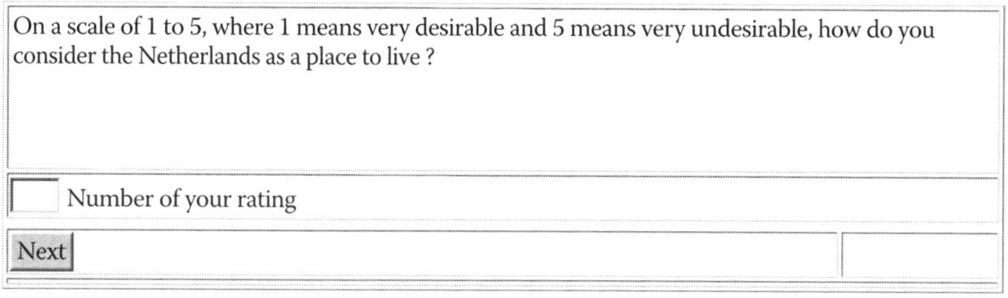
On a scale of 1 to 5, where 1 means very desirable and 5 means very undesirable, how do you consider the Netherlands as a place to live ?
Number of your rating
Next

FIGURE 7.2
Ordinal scale without graphical layout: number box.

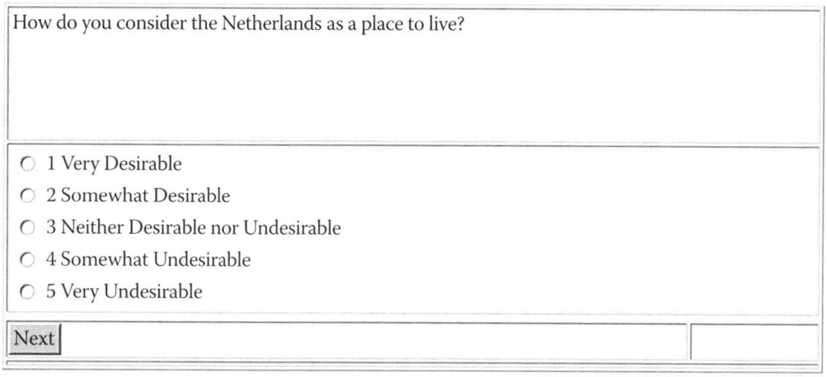

FIGURE 7.3
Ordinal scale with graphical layout.

answer in an answer box might make it possible to provide equivalent stimuli across visual and aural survey modes, thus producing equivalent answers. In an experiment, Christian and Dillman (2004) assigned respondents to read either a question (as shown in Figure 7.2) in which the location of the meaning of numbered categories was separated from the answer space, or an alternative linear layout (Figure 7.3) that identified all categories by number and a label. Respondents who were asked to provide their answers in a number box located a few spaces below the question wording provided much more negative answers than did respondents who were asked to utilize the numbered scale choices. Further investigation of these mail respondents indicated that nearly 10% of the respondents had erased their original answer, most of which were reversals of 1 and 5, or 2 and 4. This suggested that the detail of the question wording had not been carried mentally to the answer space. A replication of this experiment in Internet surveys produced similar results and also showed through paradata that respondents took considerably longer to answer the questions that used a box (Christian, Parsons, & Dillman, 2009). An additional test by Stern et al. (2007) in a general public paper survey supported these findings and confirmed the differences across demographic groups. A separately located number box runs contrary to the law of proximity (closer objects are seen together) and requires respondents to remember the specifics of a scale and transfer that from one visual location (the stem of the question) to another (the answer spaces). An additional factor that may have contributed to this failure to transfer visual information effectively from one location to another on the page is the heuristic identified by Tourangeau et al. (2004) that people tend to associate more positive answer categories with higher numbers.

The meaning of a scale may also become confused when the graphical layout is nonlinear. Nonlinear layouts such as double- or triple-banked responses are sometimes used to save space or reduce the need for scrolling. Figures 7.4 and 7.5 show an ordinal scale in multiple columns, which could be due to line breaks on small screens. The law of prägnanz

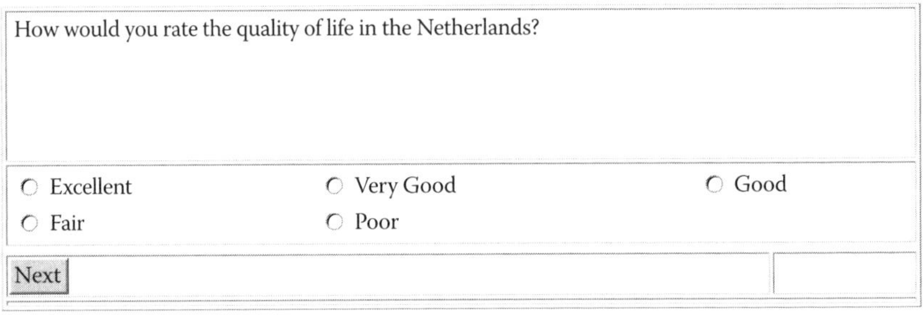

FIGURE 7.4
Ordinal scale in multiple columns: horizontally oriented.

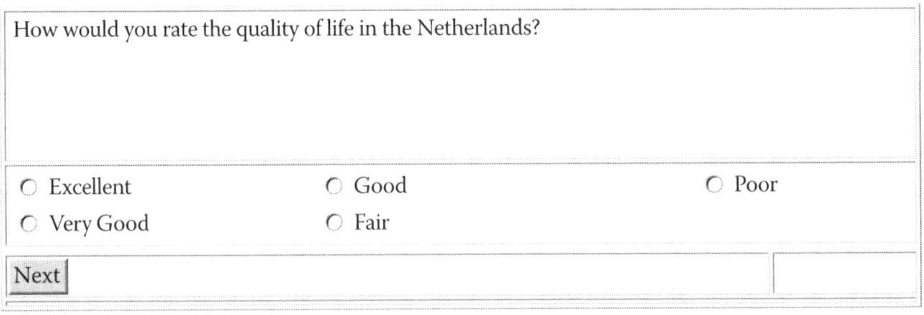

FIGURE 7.5
Ordinal scale in multiple columns: vertically oriented.

(Gestalt psychology) states that simpler elements are easier to perceive and remember. Graphically speaking, a linear layout facilitates the process of identifying where a respondent best fits on a continuum. Christian and Dillman (2004) showed that a linear format produced different answers than a horizontally oriented multiple-banked format in which the first three options were displayed horizontally and the remaining two options were on the next line, placed under the first two scalar points. That continued from left to right, as shown in Figure 7.4. Toepoel et al. (2006) replicated these findings for horizontal layouts and also found differences in a vertically orientated multiple-banked format, as shown in Figure 7.5. While Christian and Dillman (2004) found that respondents were significantly more likely to select responses from the top line in a nonlinear version, Toepoel et al. (2006) found that respondents were more eager to specifically select the second answer on the top line. Their results also suggest that options that require less movement of the mouse might be more easily chosen than answers requiring more hand and eye movements.

These experiments suggest that answers to scalar questions are negatively affected by requiring people to overcome spatial distances while carrying important information in their heads, and that a nonlinear layout of scales also has negative influences on answers. The desired format for scalar questions is to use a labeled and linear representation of the scale for people to mark their answers.

7.3.4 Unnecessary Pictures Influence Answers

Gratuitously adding pictures may increase respondents' enjoyment in answering a survey. Although a picture may be added only as a stylistic element, respondents may see it as relevant to the task of interpreting a question, so the content of the image may change the interpretation of the accompanying question for a respondent. Question text and accompanying pictures may be processed in parallel, and interference effects can occur if the verbal and visual languages are inconsistent with each other. Couper et al. (2007) found that when exposed to a picture of a fit woman, respondents consistently rate their own health lower than when exposed to a picture of a sick woman. In addition, Couper, Tourangeau, and Kenyon (2004) showed that presenting a picture of a high-frequency instance enhances the retrieval of such instances and increases the total number of instances reported. For example, respondents who got an intimate restaurant picture reported they went out to eat less often compared to respondents who received a picture of a fast-food restaurant. The effects of the pictures were also apparent in follow-up questions. Respondents who got the intimate restaurant picture were significantly more likely to say they enjoyed their last meal very much than those receiving a fast-food picture. They also reported spending a significantly higher amount of money. Pictures can suggest either a broader or narrower scope than the text of the question conveys, especially with relatively broad, poorly defined questions. Thus, it seems important to avoid adding pictures to Internet questionnaires simply to increase interest, as the deleterious side effects may be substantial.

7.3.5 Partial Visibility of Drop-Down Menus Affects Answers

Respondents are more likely to notice and use information that is visible than information that is hidden or outside the foveal view of six to eight characters of type. The visibility principle states that options that are visible to the respondents are more likely to be selected than options that are not visible until the respondent takes some action to display them (Couper, Tourangeau, & Conrad, 2004).

Drop-down boxes are often used because they take up less space on a screen. These elements require added effort from respondents, however, because people have to click and scroll to see all of the response options. Displaying some of the options initially (before the respondent clicks to see the others, as shown in Figure 7.6) reduces the required efforts. Couper, Tourangeau, and Conrad (2004) explored three response formats

FIGURE 7.6
Drop-down menu with 3 of 10 options initially displayed.

to check the visibility principle: a series of radio buttons, a drop-down box with none of the options initially displayed until the respondent clicks on the box, and a scrollable drop-down box with some of the options initially visible, requiring the respondent to scroll to see the remainder of the options. They find evidence that visible response options are endorsed more frequently. In addition, drop-down boxes increased a primacy effect (more use of one of the first response options), since they require more action by the respondent before a response option is selected from the lower part of the response options list. Although they find evidence of response order effects, they found stronger evidence that visible response options are chosen more often, suggesting that visibility may be a more powerful effect than primacy in Internet surveys.

Although for most questions a drop-down box with a truncated view of categories is undesirable, some question types might still use the advantage of drop-down boxes and save space on a screen without the threats of measurement error (primacy and visibility). Drop-down boxes may be useful when the respondents must search a long list of response options for a well-known target answer, such as country of residence.

7.3.6 Ignoring the "Middle Means Typical" Heuristic Affects Answers

As discussed earlier in this chapter, it has been proposed that respondents apply various interpretive heuristics in assigning meaning to visual cues in a questionnaire. One of the heuristics proposed by Tourangeau et al. (2004) is the "middle means typical" heuristic. It suggests that respondents see the visual midpoint of a scale as representing the typical or middle response.

Smith (1995) demonstrated that respondents were seriously confused by a seemingly simple misalignment of response categories relating to giving money for the environment. Figure 7.7 shows an example of misalignment of response categories. Tourangeau et al. (2004) examined what happens when the answer categories for an item are unevenly spaced and as a result the conceptual midpoint for an item does not coincide with the visual midpoint. When a response option was displaced toward the visual midpoint, it was selected more often. It may seem to represent a less extreme statement when placed toward the visual midpoint.

Tourangeau et al. (2004) also demonstrated that when nonsubstantive options ("don't know" and "no opinion") were not visually separated

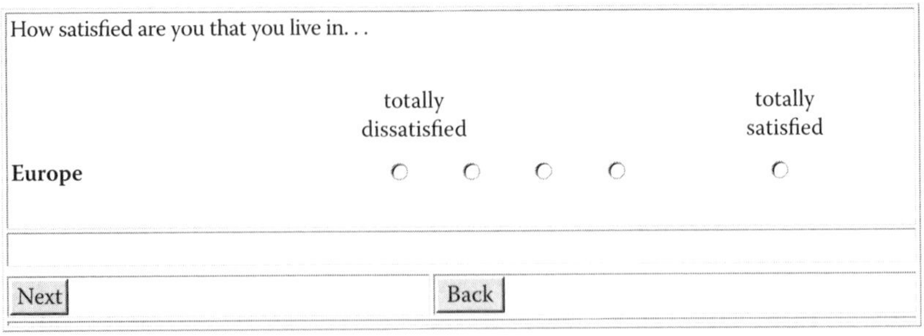
How satisfied are you that you live in. . .
totally dissatisfied
totally satisfied
Europe
Next
Back

FIGURE 7.7
Middle means typical: uneven spacing of response options (polar point).

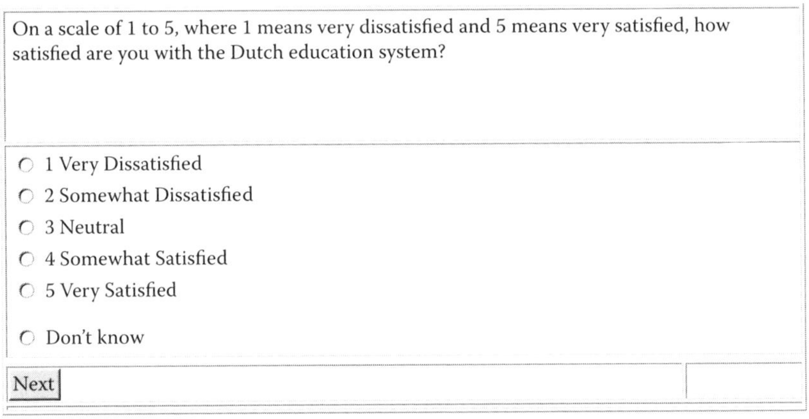
On a scale of 1 to 5, where 1 means very dissatisfied and 5 means very satisfied, how satisfied are you with the Dutch education system?
1 Very Dissatisfied
2 Somewhat Dissatisfied
3 Neutral
4 Somewhat Satisfied
5 Very Satisfied
Don't know
Next

FIGURE 7.8
Visual separation of nonsubstantive "don't know" option.

from the scale points, respondents tended to the visual midpoint of the scale as a reference point and were more likely to select answers from the conceptual end of the scale with the nonsubstantive answer option. Their results suggest that respondents assign meaning of each response option partly based on its relative position within the array of response options. As the middle or neutral option appears to move to one side of the visual midpoint, the meaning respondents assigned to it may shift as well. The authors used a divider line or space to separate the nonsubstantive options from the substantive responses. Figure 7.8 shows the visual separation of the "don't know" option by means of extra space.

Christian and Dillman (2004) found an effect of equal versus unequal spacing between response categories for nominal scale questions as well. When one category was more widely separated from the remaining three categories, respondents were more likely to choose that response category. It was concluded that unequal spacing can increase the visual prominence of the isolated category. Subsequent research by Christian et al. (2009) has shown that varying the distance between categories in a symmetrical fashion—that is, providing varied distances between adjacent categories on both sides of the midpoint—did not change respondent answers.

Besides spacing, the shape of a scale influences respondents' answers. Smith (1995) found that responses were noticeably shifted because of a different presentation of a 10-point scale. Instead of equally shaped answer boxes, a pyramid was used for Dutch respondents, with the bottom boxes wider than those in the middle and top. Respondents were attracted to the lower boxes because they were wider and probably were seen as indicating where more people were. Therefore, more Dutch respondents chose one of the lower boxes compared to respondents from other countries who were presented with equal-sized answer boxes. Schwarz, Grayson, and Knauper (1998) extended this research by comparing an onion, pyramid, and stacked boxes scale and found that respondents rated their academic performance less favorably (chose the bottom boxes more often) when the 10-point scale was presented in the form of a pyramid.

It is now clear that changing spacing may influence how people choose response categories. Changing the midpoint of a scale toward one or another extreme or using disproportionate box sizes influences the location people choose on scales. However, keeping the midpoint constant while varying the distance between it and outlying categories may not influence the choice of answers. Thus, not all visual changes have behavioral effects. The "middle means typical" heuristic provides an explanation of the divergence between the Tourangeau et al. (2004) and Christian et al. (2009) findings.

7.3.7 Ignoring the "Left and Top" Heuristic Affects Answers

Ordinal scale questions follow an order starting at one pole, proceeding through intermediate options, and ending at the other pole. The "left and top means first" heuristic states that respondents see response options in a logical order, with the first item also the first in a conceptual sense. Here, Tourangeau et al. (2004) found that respondents answer questions most quickly when items followed a logical progression in line with the heuristic. A rearrangement of response options also affected the distribution of responses. Respondents might overlook the unconventional order and select an option based on the order they expected.

Tourangeau et al. (2004) also tested whether respondents who were confronted with an unfamiliar item used the "left and top means first" heuristic to infer the item's characteristics from its position within a series of similar items. Their results supported the use of visual heuristics by showing that responses to items were clearly affected by the context in which they appeared (where the context was determined by the physical position of the target item within the series). Their results show that respondents assimilate the target item into nearby items but also contrast it with items close by. Bradlow and Fitzsimons (2001) found that when items are not labeled or clustered, respondents based their responses on the previous item to a greater degree, regardless of whether the items were intrinsically related.

7.3.8 Ignoring "Near Means Related" May Affect Answers

The third heuristic introduced by Tourangeau et al. (2004) suggests that items physically near one another are defined by respondents as related. Underlying this heuristic are the Gestalt grouping principles of proximity (placing objects closely together will cause them to be perceived as a group), similarity (objects sharing the same visual properties will be grouped together), and common region (elements within a single closed region will be grouped together), all of which suggest that placing items near each other (e.g., grouping items on one page) affects the answering process. Thus, it can be inferred that items are more likely to be seen as related if grouped on one screen, reflecting a natural assumption that blocks of questions bear on related issues, much as they would during ordinary conversations (Schwarz & Sudman, 1996; Sudman, Bradburn, & Schwarz, 1996).

Couper et al. (2001) and Toepoel et al. (2009) found that correlations are consistently higher among items appearing together on a screen than among items separated across several screens, but the effect they found was small and differences between pairs of correlations were insignificant. Tourangeau et al. (2004) found significant differences between correlations, however. They concluded that respondents seemed to use the proximity of the items as a cue to their meaning, perhaps at the expense of reading each item carefully. Respondents who got eight items on a single screen showed less differentiation than those who got them on two screens or on eight separate screens. In addition, the relation of reverse-worded items to overall scores was weaker when the eight items were presented on a single screen, indicating that respondents were less likely to notice the reverse wording when the items appeared in a single grid. Another drawback of grouping items on a screen is the fact that item nonresponse tends to be higher in multiple-item-per-screen designs (Lozar Manfreda, Batagelj, & Vehovar, 2002; Smith, 1995; Toepoel et al., 2009) and that respondents evaluate more items per screen worse (Toepoel et al., 2009). Couper et al. (2001), Lozar Manfreda et al. (2002), Toepoel et al. (2009), and Tourangeau et al. (2004) all find evidence that a multiple-item-per-screen design took less time to complete than a one-item-per-screen design.

7.3.9 Ignoring "Up Means Good" May Affect Answers

The fourth visual heuristic from Tourangeau et al. (2004) states that people expect categories to appear from positive to negative—that is, the first response option in a list is the most desirable. While in English-speaking countries decremental scales are used more frequently (see, e.g., the "up means good heuristic"), in Dutch-speaking countries, for example, incremental scales are used most (Hofmans et al., 2007). Therefore, differences between cultures can be expected with regard to scale orientation and visual heuristics such as "up means good." Orientation effects can occur because of the position of a response option, but they also can be due to a change in perceived intensity of the verbal label resulting from the positioning of this label on the scale. The perceived intensity of a verbal label at position *x* may differ from that of the same verbal label placed at position *y*. Both the meaning of the verbal label and its position on the scale can therefore influence the appraisal made by respondents (Hofmans et al., 2007). There are two types of orientation effects: primacy and recency effects. A primacy effect occurs when options in the beginning of a response list are more easily selected, while recency effects occur when options near the end of a response list are chosen more often, independent of the meaning of the response option (Krosnick & Alwin, 1987). Satisficing occurs when respondents are more likely to choose items earlier in a list because they find the first position that they can reasonably agree with and consider it a satisfactory answer, rather than processing each response option separately (for a detailed description of satisficing, see Krosnick & Alwin, 1987; Krosnick, Narayan, & Smith, 1996; Tourangeau,

Rips, & Rasinski, 2000). By changing the position of a response option in a scale, these effects can noticeably affect answers.

Research on orientation effects in rating scales yield inconsistent results. While in some studies respondents altered their responses when the orientation of a scale is changed, in other studies responses remained unaffected (as discussed in Weng & Cheng, 2000). For example, Christian et al. (2009) have shown that a consistent placement of all categories from negative to positive does not produce different answers than does placing all of them from positive to negative. However, Toepoel et al. (2006, 2008) have found differences in a decremental scale compared to an incremental scale. Switching directions within a survey will produce different answers, as Israel (2007) has shown by changing the direction of the test item from that used for three items that preceded it on the same page. This issue appears not to be entirely settled, and further research is warranted to find out if some questions, cultures, or populations are more or less affected by orientation effects.

7.3.10 Ignoring "Like Means Close" Heuristic May Affect Answers

This heuristic (as mentioned in Tourangeau et al., 2004) is based on the law of similarity (Gestalt psychology), which states that people see similar objects as forming a single figure. The law of prägnanz states that elements with simplicity, regularity, and symmetry are easier to perceive and remember, indicating that similar objects lead to less cognitive processing. For example, when the endpoints in a scale are perceptually more distinct, respondents will see them as differing more from each other conceptually. Schwarz, Knauper, Hippler, Noelle-Neumann, & Clark (1991) demonstrated this by adding numbers ranging from –5 to +5 or 0 to 11 to verbal labels. This resulted in lower scores for the 0 to 11 version compared to the –5 to 5 format; respondents hesitated to assign a negative score to themselves (scale label effect; see Tourangeau et al., 2000, p. 248). The ends of the scale seemed further apart conceptually to the respondents when the numerical labels differed in both sign and value than when they differed only in value.

The principle that dimensions are seen as differing more sharply when they vary along two dimensions than when they differ only in a single dimension applies also to the shading of response options (see Figure 7.9). Tourangeau et al. (2007) demonstrated that when the verbal and numerical

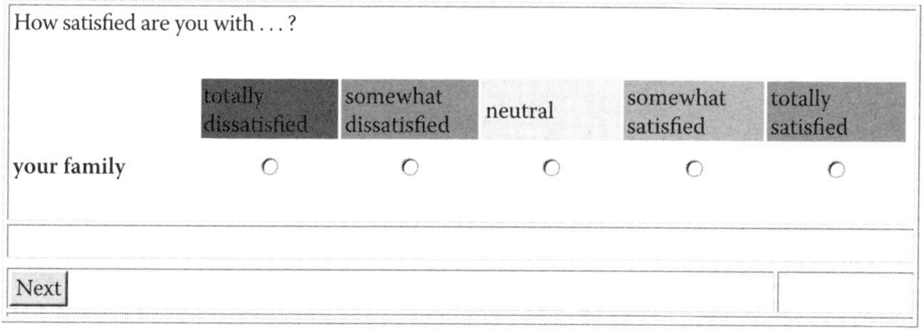

FIGURE 7.9
Like means close: different colors for the endpoints of the scale (fully labeled). (From left to right, the colors are red, light red, light gray, light green, and green.)

labeling of scale points provided minimal interpretive help to respondents, the shading of the response options had a noticeable effect on answers to the questions when different colors for the endpoints of the scale are used. Respondents more easily selected an option with a blue color than an option with a red or yellow color. The researchers provided additional evidence on the impact of (negative) numerical labels: The effects of the numerical labels were consistently larger than the effects of the shading of response options. This suggests a hierarchy of features that respondents attend to, with verbal labels taking precedence over numerical labels and numerical labels taking precedence over purely visual cues such as color.

7.4 NEEDED RESEARCH ON WHICH VISUAL LAYOUT CONSIDERATIONS ARE MOST IMPORTANT

In just over a decade we have gone from virtually nothing having been written about how vision and visual language concepts might affect survey responses to the availability of dozens of papers on how visual manipulations affect respondent answers. In the earlier research, studies often manipulated a number of concepts simultaneously and reported the overall result. An example is the work by Redline and Dillman (2002) demonstrating that the simultaneous manipulation of symbols, size of font, brightness of font, and placement of wording could reduce certain branching errors in the U.S. decennial census by nearly one third, from 20% to 13%. However, the design of this experiment did not allow the relative importance of individual manipulations to be assessed.

Subsequent studies, many of which have been summarized in Section 7.3, have focused on individual effects of specific uses of graphical, symbolic, and numerical language to communicate the survey designer's intent. These studies confirm the potential of many different design factors, such as boldness of words, use of arrows (a symbol), association of blank spaces with word directions, amount of space allowed for answers, and the grouping of related information, to influence answers. Many other questions about individual effects have not been answered but are likely to be in the coming years.

It is apparent from this research that many different kinds of visual layout effects are likely to occur in surveys that require respondents to read and answer questions, whether by Internet or on paper. It also appears that the effects are quite similar across these modes. That is, to date there is little evidence that visual effects differ significantly between those that occur on paper versus the Internet except for the unique features of construction (for example, explicit branching instructions that must be used on paper but are not necessary for the Internet, and drop-down menus used on the Internet but impossible to use on paper).

It seems important to continue assessing the relative importance of visual factors in influencing people's answers to surveys and whether the use of some design features will cancel out the use of others. It is possible that some effects that appear in the literature may be amplified when combined with other features of construction, whereas others may disappear. In order to develop effective guidelines for the construction of Internet questionnaires, it is important to learn which visual effects are most important and which least important.

Toepoel and Dillman (2008) made a start with their attempt to find out whether there exists a hierarchy of features, as suggested by Tourangeau et al. (2007), with verbal and numerical language taking precedence over visual language. They conducted experiments on the five visual heuristics to find out if the effects of visual layout can be diminished through greater use of verbal and numerical language. They demonstrated for a 5-point rating scale that respondents use the "middle means typical" heuristic only for a polar point scale. When the numbers 1 to 5 were added to the polar point format and with fully labeled scales, the effect of spacing between response options (see Figure 7.7) disappeared.

Toepoel and Dillman (2008) also found evidence that respondents use the "near means related" heuristic only in a polar point format. When multiple items were presented on a single screen, interitem correlations were higher with a polar point scale compared to when items were presented on a single screen. The effect got smaller when the numbers 1 to 5 were added to the polar point scale, while in a fully labeled scale there was no evidence that presenting items on a single screen increased correlations between items. These results explain the differences in results found in the literature (see Section 7.3.8): Tourangeau et al. (2004) used a polar point format and found significant differences between one-item-per-screen and multiple-items-per-screen formats, while Toepoel et al. (2009) used a fully labeled scale and found no significant differences.

Toepoel and Dillman (2008) also found evidence that respondents use the "like means close" heuristic; they used color (shadings of red for negative answers and shadings of green for positive answers; see Figure 7.9) and numbers that differed in both sign and value (–2 to 2) to test whether different endpoints affected answers. Again, the effect of color was apparent only in the polar point format and not in a fully labeled format. The adding of numbers that differed in both sign and value was apparent in both the polar point and fully labeled formats, suggesting that respondents change their interpretation of verbal labels when negative signs are used (scale label effect; see Tourangeau et al., 2000, p. 248). The experiments on the "left and top means first" heuristic (reordering response options illogically) and "up means good" heuristic (starting with the negative end of the scale) showed no significant results. The latter may be due to the fact that a Dutch panel was used for this research. In Dutch-speaking countries an incremental scale is used more often (Hofmans et al., 2007); this might interact with the results. Another explanation may be the use of a horizontal format instead of a vertical arrangement of response options. Toepoel (2008) suggests that placing response options horizontally reduces the effect of visual language. Overall, these experiments show that only if verbal and numerical language are ambiguous (e.g., polar point scale without numbers) is visual language apparent.

Toepoel and Couper (2009) also studied the hierarchy of features, in this case the use of pictures. Their results show that the effect of verbal instructions is more powerful than the effect of pictures, supporting the conjecture that verbal language reduces the effect of visual language. Their study included an experimental condition in which the verbal language counteracted the visual language; respondents got a picture of a high-frequency event (e.g., grocery shopping) with the verbal instruction not to include this high-frequency event. Their results suggest that respondents ignore the picture when confronted with a verbal instruction.

These two studies provide evidence that verbal language takes precedence over nonverbal language, as originally proposed by Tourangeau et al. (2007). The results suggest that by using verbal language effectively, the effects of visual language can be reduced. Further research should be conducted on the relative importance of visual effects to develop effective guidelines for the construction of Internet questionnaires. Researchers need to know when visual layout effects are important and when they are not; ways to reduce these effects also need to be found. It is important that surveys include information on how the survey questions were presented visually (e.g., screenshots) in order to get a full understanding of the reliability and validity of the collected data.

7.5 CONCLUSIONS

Based upon our summary of recent research on how visual displays and question formats affect answers, we suggest consideration of the following practical guidelines for effective question writing.

1. The size of the answer box should match the size of the desired answer.
2. Use visualness (connections among answer spaces, labels, and symbols) to help respondents interpret a question.
3. Make sure every answer option receives the same visual emphasis.
4. Place ordinal scales consistently in a decremental or incremental order.
5. Present ordinal scales with radio buttons, in a linear format, with even spacing of response options, so that the graphical language conveying the scale is clear to respondents.
6. Make sure that the visual midpoint of a scale coincides with the conceptual midpoint.
7. If multiple items are presented on each screen, be aware that correlations might be higher between items, especially when polar point scales are used.

8. Use fully labeled scales. If this is not desirable (for example, because of a mixed-mode survey involving the telephone), add numbers to polar point scales, starting with 1.
9. Use a logical order of response options (e.g., a progression) and be aware that respondents extract meaning from that order.
10. Preferably, present nominal answer options randomly, to avoid order effects.
11. Use instructions right in front of the answer options (within the foveal view) and make sure respondents do not have to make an extra effort to remember them for use elsewhere on the screen.
12. Avoid using gratuitous visual language (such as pictures, numbers, and colors) unnecessary for the correct interpretation of questions.
13. When comparing results from different studies, make sure respondents get the same (visual) stimulus.

Researchers using surveys should keep in mind that many different question elements may account for variance in how survey questions are answered, including (size of) answer space, spacing, ordering, color, numbers, pictures, labels, symbols/signs, instructions, and visibility.

A great deal has been learned during the past decade about how the meaning of questions is influenced by visual language—numbers, symbols, and graphics—in addition to the specific verbal language used to ask questions. While the research shows clearly that some visual layouts should be avoided, other visual effects seem relatively weak, and some undesirable visual effects may be neutralized by other visual elements used in the questionnaire construction. Thus, the current situation may be described as one of the glass being both half full and half empty. More research is needed in order to fully understand the relative importance of specific visual and word cues relative to others. It is important that such research be undertaken during the coming decade as we advance toward a full-fledged theory of visual layout and design as it applies to the creation of high-quality questionnaires.

REFERENCES

Bradlow, E. T. & Fitzsimons, G. J. (2001). Subscale distance and item clustering effects in self-administered surveys: A new metric. *Journal of Marketing Research*, *38*, 254–261.

Christian, L. M. (2003). *The influence of visual layout on scalar questions in Web surveys.* Unpublished master's thesis. Retrieved from http://www.sesrc.wsu.edu/dillman/papers.htm

Christian, L. M. & Dillman, D. A. (2004). The influence of graphical and symbolic language manipulations on responses to self-administered questions. *Public Opinion Quarterly, 68*(1), 57–80.

Christian, L. M., Dillman, D. A., & Smyth, J. D. (2007). Helping respondents get it right the first time: The influence of words, symbols, and graphics in Web surveys. *Public Opinion Quarterly, 71*(1), 113–125.

Christian, L. M., Parsons, N. L., & Dillman, D. A. (2009). Designing scalar questions for Web surveys. *Sociological Methods and Research, 37,* 393–425.

Couper, M. P., Conrad, F. G., & Tourangeau, R. (2007). Visual context effects in Web surveys. *Public Opinion Quarterly, 71*, 623–634.

Couper, M. P., Tourangeau, R., Conrad, F. G., & Crawford, S. D. (2004). What they see is what we get: Response options for Web surveys. *Social Science Computer Review, 22*, 111–127.

Couper, M. P., Tourangeau, R., & Kenyon, K. (2004). Picture this! Exploring visual effects in Web surveys. *Public Opinion Quarterly, 68*, 255–266.

Couper, M. P., Traugott, M. W., & Lamias, M. J. (2001). Web survey design and administration. *Public Opinion Quarterly, 65*, 230–253.

De Leeuw, E. D. (2005). To mix or not to mix data collection modes in surveys. *Journal of Official Statistics, 21*, 233–255.

Dillman, D. A. (2007). *Mail and Internet surveys: The tailored design method.* Hoboken, NJ: John Wiley & Sons.

Dillman, D. A. & Christian, L. M. (2002). *The influence of words, symbols, numbers, and graphics on answers to self-administered questionnaires: Results from 18 experimental comparisons.* Retrieved from http://survey.sesrc.wsu.edu/dillman/papers.htm

Dillman, D. A., Gertseva, A., & Mahon-Haft, T. (2005). Achieving usability in establishment surveys through the application of visual design principles. *Journal of Official Statistics, 21*, 183–214.

Dillman, D. A., Smyth, J. D., & Christian, L. M. (2009). *Internet, mail, and mixed-mode surveys: The tailored design method.* Hoboken, NJ: John Wiley & Sons.

Hoffman, D. D. (2004). *Visual intelligence.* New York: Norton.

Hofmans, J., Theuns, P., Baekelandt, S., Mairesse, O., Schillewaert, N., & Cools, W. (2007). Bias and changes in perceived intensity of verbal qualifiers effected by scale orientation. *Survey Research Methods, 1*, 97–108.

Israel, G. (2007). *Effects of answer space size on responses to open-ended questions in mail surveys.* Paper presented at the annual Joint Statistical Meeting of the American Statistical Association (ASA), Salt Lake City, Utah.

Jenkins, C. R. & Dillman, D. A. (1997). Towards a theory of self-administered questionnaire design. In L. Lyberg, P. Biemer, M. Collins et al. (Eds.), *Survey measurement and process quality* (pp. 165–196). New York: John Wiley & Sons.

Krosnick, J. A. & Alwin, D. F. (1987). An evaluation of a cognitive theory of response-order effects in survey measurement. *Public Opinion Quarterly, 51*, 201–219.

Krosnick, J. A., Narayan, S., & Smith, W. R. (1996). Satisficing in surveys: Initial evidence. *New Directions for Program Evaluation, 70*, 29–44.

Lozar Manfreda, K., Batagelj, Z., & Vehovar, V. (2002). Design of Web survey questionnaires: Three basic experiments. *Journal of Computer-Mediated Communication, 7*(3). Retrieved from http://www.ascusc.org/jcmc/vol7/issue3/vehovar.html

Palmer, S. E. (1999). *Vision science: Photons to phenomenology.* London: Bradford Books.

Redline, C. D. & Dillman, D. A. (2002). The influence of alternative visual designs on respondents' performance with branching instructions in self-administered questionnaires. In R. M. Groves, D. A. Dillman, J. Eltinge, & R. Little (Eds.), *Survey nonresponse* (pp. 179–193). New York: John Wiley & Sons.

Redline, C. D., Dillman, D. A., Carley-Baxter, L., & Creecy, R. (2005). Factors that influence reading and comprehension of branching instructions in self-administered questionnaires. *Algemeines Statistisches Archiv, 89*, 21–38.

Schwarz, N. (1996). *Cognition and communication: Judgmental biases, research methods, and the logic of conversation.* New York: Lawrence Erlbaum Associates.

Schwarz, N., Grayson, C. E., & Knauper, B. (1998). Formal features of rating scales and the interpretation of question meaning. *International Journal of Public Opinion Research, 10*, 177–183.

Schwarz, N., Knauper, B., Hippler, H.-J., Noelle-Neumann, E., & Clark, L. (1991). Rating scales: Numeric values may change the meaning of scale labels. *Public Opinion Quarterly, 55*, 570–582.

Schwarz, N. & Sudman, S. (1996). *Answering questions.* San Francisco: Jossey-Bass.

Smith, T. W. (1995). Little things matter: A sampler of how differences in questionnaire format can affect survey responses. *Proceedings of the American Statistical Association, Survey Research Methods Section* (pp. 1046–1051).

Smyth, J., Dillman, D. A., Christian, L. M., & McBride, M. (2009). Open-ended questions in Web surveys: Can increasing the size of answer boxes and providing extra verbal instructions improve response quality? *Public Opinion Quarterly, 73*, 325–337.

Stern, M. J., Dillman, D. A., & Smyth, J. D. (2007). Visual design, order effects, and respondent characteristics in a self-administered survey. *Survey Research Methods, 1*, 121–138.

Sudman, S., Bradburn, N. M., & Schwarz, N. (1996). *Thinking about answers.* San Francisco: Jossey-Bass.

Toepoel, V. (2008). *A closer look at Web questionnaire design.* Doctoral dissertation. CentER for Economic Research Dissertation Series No. 220. Tilburg University, the Netherlands. Retrieved from http://center.uvt.nl/gs/thesis/toepoel.html

Toepoel, V. & Couper, M. P. (2009). *Can verbal instructions counteract visual context effects in Web surveys?* Paper presented at the MESS workshop, Santpoort, the Netherlands.

Toepoel, V., Das, M., & Van Soest, A. (2006). *Design of Web questionnaires: The effect of layout in rating scales.* CentER Discussion Paper 2006-30, CentER, Tilburg University, the Netherlands.

Toepoel, V., Das, M., & Van Soest, A. (2008). The effects of design in Web surveys: Comparing trained and fresh respondents. *Public Opinion Quarterly, 72*, 985–1007.

Toepoel, V., Das, M., & Van Soest, A. (2009). Design of Web questionnaires: The effect of number of items per screen. *Field Methods, 21*, 200–213.

Toepoel, V. & Dillman, D. A. (2008). *Words, numbers, and visual heuristics in Web surveys: Is there a hierarchy of importance?* CentER Discussion Paper 2008-92. CentER, Tilburg University, the Netherlands.

Tourangeau, R. (1987). Attitude measurement: A cognitive perspective. In H. J. Hippler, N. Schwarz, & S. Sudman (Eds.), *Social information processing and survey methodology* (pp. 149–162). New York: Springer Verlag.

Tourangeau, R., Couper, M. P., & Conrad, F. (2004). Spacing, position, and order: Interpretive heuristics for visual features of survey questions. *Public Opinion Quarterly, 68*, 368–393.

Tourangeau, R., Couper, M. P., & Conrad, F. (2007). Color, labels, and interpretive heuristics for response scales. *Public Opinion Quarterly, 71*, 91–112.

Tourangeau, R., Rips, L. J., & Rasinski, K. (2000). *The psychology of survey response.* Cambridge, UK: Cambridge University Press.

Ware, C. (2004). *Information visualization: Perception for design.* San Francisco: Morgan Kaufmann.

Weng, L.-J. & Cheng, C. P. (2000). Effects of response order on Likert-type scales. *Educational and Psychological Measurement, 60*, 908–924.

8

Attention and Usability in Internet Surveys: Effects of Visual Feedback in Grid Questions[1]

Lars Kaczmirek
GESIS—Leibniz Institute for the Social Sciences
Mannheim, Germany

8.1 INTRODUCTION

Visual design is an integral part of constructing a self-administered questionnaire. Several guidelines have been proposed to help design or redesign surveys with a focus on visual design principles (e.g., Chapter 7 in this volume; Dillman, Gertseva, & Mahon-Haft, 2005). Survey researchers have learned to benefit from areas such as cognitive psychology and usability concepts, which helped to improve survey methodology and data quality. This chapter shows how concepts drawn from usability can be applied and tested in survey research. Specifically, the research reported here applied the concept of feedback to the response process and tested the impact of different types of feedback on data quality. The hypothesis is that tailoring visual feedback to the answering process in a set of grid questions using rating scales can improve data quality in Internet surveys.

The work reported here connects the methodology of survey design with principles from usability. The potential of usability for survey methodology is most apparent in Internet surveys. Previous work analyzed existing sets of principles in usability and explained their meaning and relevance in the context of surveys (Kaczmirek, 2009). The sets were taken from Norman (1988), Nielsen (1993), Couper (1994), Shneiderman (1998), and the ISO 9241-110 (2006).

All sets specifically include one or more demands that stress the importance of feedback to achieve higher usability. These demands are explicitly stated in the heuristics' titles, such as "offer informative feedback" (Shneiderman, 1998) and "informative feedback" (Couper, 1994), or are provided in the explanation of titles such as "make things visible" (Norman, 1988), "visibility of system status" (Nielsen, 1993), and ultimately "self-descriptiveness" (ISO 9241-110, 2006). For survey researchers, this means that feedback should aid respondents in completing the survey. In the question-answering process respondents should have no doubt about the current status of their task, the task being to answer a question. Survey researchers have developed several design patterns to utilize or test the advantages of feedback. Examples for interactive feedback include automatic calculation and display of sums in tally questions (Conrad, Couper, Tourangeau, & Galesic, 2005), self-adjusting display of corresponding percentages in visual analog scales (Couper, Tourangeau, & Conrad, 2006), and validation of answers (Peytchev & Crawford, 2005). In the broader context of self-descriptiveness, Christian, Dillman, and Smyth (2007) have shown how labels should be designed and placed to minimize input errors when asking about dates.

This chapter is organized as follows. Section 8.2 describes which feedback techniques are currently used to help select an answer and summarizes the literature and research. Section 8.3 outlines the hypotheses, design, and implementation of the conducted study. The results are presented in Section 8.4. Section 8.5 provides a discussion of the results and reviews the strengths and weaknesses of different feedback types.

8.2 BACKGROUND

This chapter concentrates on interactive visual feedback that can be provided in rating scales before and after an answer is selected. When considering the similarities between choosing an answer and selecting an option in computer programs, many computer programs apparently have employed such feedback: Whenever a user clicks on an option in a menu, the option is highlighted with a change in the background color of the option. This is done so that users know what they are going to select if they click. A much more subtle form of feedback is already implemented in the standard Web forms of many browsers: When respondents hover over an answer element with their mouse pointer, the feedback is a small visual change of the button. However, such a small change may go unnoticed. In contrast, the study described in this chapter used several highly visible feedback techniques. Apart from providing feedback before a selection is made, it is also possible to give feedback after a respondent has clicked on an answer. The current standard in Web forms is to display a small dot in the radio button to acknowledge the mouse click. Again, this is a very small change in the visual field of respondents.

When reviewing these two types of feedback, the answer process can be decomposed into preselection (before the click) and postselection (after the click) phases. Standard Web forms provide feedback in both phases. However, when considering that the main task is to provide an answer, the question arises whether these existing visual changes are too subtle and whether respondents would benefit from improved feedback techniques. Apart from that, the task of answering single questions or items must also be understood in its relation to the overarching task of moving from one item to the next. In grid questions with several items to be answered, the possibility for feedback can be extended to feedback emphasizing the specific answer category and feedback emphasizing the whole item. Therefore, to study effects of feedback it is necessary to consider both preselection feedback and postselection feedback and to test specific implementations such as feedback that emphasizes the specific answer category or the whole item (Figure 8.1).

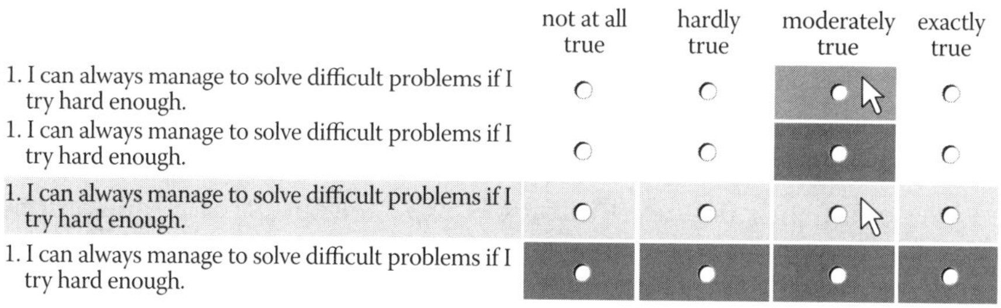

FIGURE 8.1
Different types of feedback for the same item (translated). The first illustrates preselection feedback emphasizing the answer category by highlighting the table cell in a light orange color identical to the logo color in the survey with a mouse-over event (Prebox). The second illustrates postselection feedback emphasizing the answer category by darkening the table cell with gray after a click was made (Postbox). The third and fourth illustrate preselection and postselection feedback emphasizing the item (Prerow and Postrow).

Theoretically, feedback should have several advantages in terms of leading attention, a higher focus on the task, and less disorientation. Nevertheless, usability must prove its worth within the criteria of data quality in survey research. The criteria used in this work are three outcome variables: nondifferentiation (also known as straight-lining), amount of changes in answers, and item nonresponse.

For nondifferentiation, Krosnick formalized the "conditions that foster satisficing" (1991, p. 220). Nondifferentiation is expected to increase as a function of increased task difficulty (respondent burden), reduced respondent motivation, and reduced respondent ability. Because feedback is expected to positively influence task difficulty and respondent motivation, data quality should benefit in terms of less nondifferentiation. Respondent ability is not considered to be influenced by feedback. Nondifferentiation is a response behavior describing respondents' tendency to choose the same answer category regardless of the question. For this concept, the answer category chosen most often by each respondent is central. For example, a respondent who selects the answer "moderately true" 8 times out of 10 items shows a higher degree of nondifferentiation than a respondent who selects "disagree" 7 times out of the same 10 items.

For corrections in answers, Draisma and Dijkstra (2004) argue that changes in answers are an indicator of uncertainty or weak attitudes. Here, feedback is supposed to help clarify respondents' thoughts so that they feel less need to change their answers.

Item nonresponse is one of the most widely used indicators for data quality in the literature on survey design (e.g., Bosnjak, 2002; Peytchev, 2007; Couper, 2008; Toepoel, 2008; Dillman, Smyth, & Christian, 2009; Kaczmirek, 2009). It is well known that a loss in motivation or increased respondent burden can cause respondents to abandon the survey or start to overlook items. Because feedback is expected to increase motivation, reduce task difficulty by keeping up attention, and help the respondent stay focused on the task, item nonresponse should be reduced as well.

So far, the potential benefits of survey usability have been outlined. In the following, the empirical evidence with respect to interactive feedback in the answering process is summarized.

All research on this topic so far has been done with grid questions. The reason for this might be that grid questions are more promising than other types of questions when researchers are developing new ways of improving questionnaires. Much research has gone into optimizing grid questions because they are commonly used in survey design but still show some problems, such as increased break-off rates. These aspects make grid questions ideal for testing different interaction designs. As Couper wrote: "Grids require careful design. If designed correctly, they can facilitate the task of survey completion. If poorly designed, they can confuse or even overwhelm respondents, leading to satisficing behaviors such as non-differentiation, item missing data, and breakoffs" (2008, p. 194).

Despite the huge variety of button designs in grids, there has been little research on feedback in grid questions or how the change in the appearance of buttons affects respondents. Galesic, Tourangeau, Couper, and Conrad (2007) used dynamic elements to provide feedback after an answer was clicked (postselection feedback). After respondents clicked on an answer, the row background color changed from white to gray, or in a different condition the font color changed from black to gray. Overall, the versions with change (that is, additional feedback) had significantly less missing item data compared to the control condition. Similarly, Kaczmirek (2007, 2009) reported a significant positive effect of feedback after an answer was clicked, operationalized as a change in the row color, resulting in fewer missing items. Respondents also stated that they were more satisfied with the questionnaire. However, visual feedback before an answer was clicked (preselection feedback), operationalized as a visual cross that followed the mouse pointer, interfered with the task of survey completion, and led to even fewer complete answers than the control condition without any dynamic visual feedback. In a second experiment Kaczmirek (2007, 2009) found a positive effect of a combined pre- and postselection feedback that emphasized the answer category.

Summarizing, there is empirical evidence for a beneficial effect of feedback on data quality. However, the specific kind of feedback that optimally should be administered remains unclear. Therefore, the study reported in this chapter was conducted to differentiate between different forms of feedback (preselection feedback, postselection feedback, feedback emphasizing the item, and feedback emphasizing the answer category) with respect to the three quality criteria (nonresponse, changes in answers, and nondifferentiation).

8.3 HYPOTHESES, DESIGN, AND IMPLEMENTATION

8.3.1 Hypotheses

The hypotheses are presented with respect to each quality criterion, that is, in the same way the analyses are presented in the results section. When developing the hypotheses, it is important to distinguish between the two possible feedback implementations of coloring the table cell and the item row. Visually changing the color of a table cell is not a weaker form of feedback compared to visually changing the item row. Instead, these two types of feedback emphasize different parts of the grid (i.e., the answer or the item) and thus direct the attention of respondents to different aspects of the questions. This makes these types of feedback conceptually different and leads to different effects on the criteria variables.

For item nonresponse, there are at least two reasons why an item is left unanswered. First, respondents might overlook that they did not answer that item. Second, respondents might accidentally slip one item down when moving from the item to the answer and thus seemingly skip that item. The first behavior can be reduced by visually emphasizing the items that have already been answered. The missing item is visualized so that respondents can easily see which answers they still have to provide (i.e., which are still missing) because answering more items reduces the amount of unshaded items (postselection feedback conditions Postbox and Postrow). The second behavior can be reduced with a visually stronger connection between item text and answer categories before an answer is selected (feedback condition Prerow).

For respondents who change their answers, the underlying cognitive process is the status of the task. If it is perceived as completed (i.e., the respondent is satisfied with the answer), then no further change is made. This means that feedback that stresses task completion and therefore indicates that the task is finished reduces the amount of changes in answers (postselection feedback conditions Postbox and Postrow).

For nondifferentiation, the underlying cognitive process is the comparison to any previously given answers. Here, visually emphasizing the answer categories that were selected and the answer that is to be selected makes it easier for respondents to take previous answers into account and to differentiate the current item from previous answers. This could be achieved with feedback emphasizing the answer category (feedback conditions Prebox and Postbox).

From the above, the following hypotheses were derived to be tested in this study:

> H1. Missing items are reduced by postselection feedback emphasizing the item or the answer category and by preselection feedback emphasizing the item (conditions Postbox, Postrow, and Prerow compared to no feedback).
>
> H2. Changes in answers are reduced by postselection feedback (conditions Postbox and Postrow compared to no feedback).
>
> H3. Nondifferentiation is reduced by feedback emphasizing the answer category (conditions Prebox and Postbox compared to no feedback).

8.3.2 Experimental Manipulations

The randomized experiment consisted of nine conditions. The conditions were derived from a two-factorial design with three levels each. The first factor varied preselection feedback (highlight), the second factor postselection feedback (grayout). Both factors implemented three conditions: no additional feedback, visual feedback on the answer category, and visual feedback on the item row. Preselection feedback was provided per item before an answer was selected, that is, before the mouse click—while the mouse pointer hovered over a potential answer, the table cell (feedback emphasizing the answer category, Prebox) or the row (feedback emphasizing the item, Prerow) was shaded in a light orange color. Postselection feedback was provided after an answer was selected—either the table cell (Postbox) or the row (Postrow) was shaded in a dark gray color.

Conceptually, the condition with no additional feedback is identical to current standard implementations in Internet surveys. Table 8.1 summarizes the experimental conditions and shows the number of respondents in each condition.*

8.3.3 Sample and Questionnaire

The fieldwork was carried out by CentERdata (Tilburg University, the Netherlands). Respondents were members of the LISS panel, which employs a probability-based sampling procedure. In this panel, Internet

* Apart from this experiment, the full study included a tenth condition. It was different from all other conditions in that it used no precolored shading of every second item, and responses were valid only with direct hits on a radio button. Because this condition is not comparable with the feedback conditions and is not addressing interactive feedback, it is not reported here.

TABLE 8.1

Factorial Design of the Experiment

	Factor 2, Postselection Feedback		
Factor 1, Preselection Feedback	**Postnone**	**Postbox**	**Postrow**
Prenone	254 (256)	236 (239)	240 (242)
Prebox	250 (252)	253 (254)	253 (255)
Prerow	249 (250)	260 (261)	248 (250)

Note: The table shows the number of respondents per condition after data cleaning with the raw numbers in parentheses, $N = 2{,}243$. All conditions were implemented with a fixed standard alternate shading of every second item. Valid answers could be provided by clicking on the table cell. The box conditions emphasized the answer category. The row conditions emphasized the item.

surveys are used as the mode for data collection and panel members who do not have an Internet connection or a computer at home are provided with a so-called simPC, an easy-to-handle computer, and a high-speed Internet connection (see Chapter 4 in this volume). E-mail invitations were sent to 3,500 household members. The response rate was 71.5%. Nonrespondents received two reminders. The optimal sample size for the design was calculated a priori assuming a small effect size and aiming at a power of .95 (β-error of .05) and an α-error of .05 according to Cohen (1992) with the program G*Power (Faul, Erdfelder, Lang, & Buchner, 2007). Sixteen respondents were excluded from data analysis because the respondents' computers did not meet the technical requirements for the survey (e.g., JavaScript disabled, $n = 15$) or an unreasonable amount of switches in answers occurred ($n = 1$, who switched answers 822 times within 10 items), leaving 2,243 respondents for data analysis. Among these, 1,096 respondents were 55 years of age or older and 327 respondents used a simPC. The mean age was 51.6, ranging from 16 to 95 ($SD = 15.9$), and 53% of the respondents were female.

The questionnaire consisted of three pages and was administered in Dutch. An introduction screen was followed by two pages, each of which had 10 items in a grid layout. Grid A contained the Dutch adaptation of the General Self-Efficacy Scale by Schwarzer and Jerusalem (1995) with a four-point scale. Grid B contained 10 items on personality with a five-point fully labeled answer scale (see the appendix for details). The two pages were randomly administered in the sequence AB or BA. The questionnaire was chosen to include common scales that had not previously been presented to respondents of the LISS panel.

8.4 RESULTS

The questionnaire was fielded in August 2008 and respondents were randomly assigned to one of the experimental conditions.* To test the effects of the different feedback conditions on data quality, the following procedure was used. Three indicators of data quality—item nonresponse, changes in answers, and nondifferentiation—were analyzed separately with a set of three models to identify the best-fitting model for each dependent variable and to test the existence of interaction effects and effects of respondents' characteristics. The first model included only the main effects. In a second model the interaction terms were added. A third model added the variables age, education, and use of simPC. Each model was tested for its explanatory advantage against the previous model. This procedure led to a preferred model for each quality indicator. To take account of the different distributions of the dependent variables, appropriate methods for analysis were employed, such as logistic regression, general linear model (GLM) assuming a Poisson distribution of the dependent variable, and general linear model assuming a Gaussian distribution of the dependent variable. The next sections describe the analyses in detail.

8.4.1 Item Nonresponse

Following a typology of nonrespondents by Bosnjak and Tuten (2001), the analysis separates lurkers from respondents. A lurker is a respondent who refrains from answering a substantial number of questions while viewing some or all pages. For example, this is the case when someone is mainly interested in looking at the questions without real intent to participate in the survey. Table 8.2 shows the number of missing answers for both grid questions and respondent type. There were no respondents who only answered six, five, four, or two items on one grid. Thus, respondents were defined as lurkers if they had only answered three or fewer items and were classified as partial responders if only one, two, or three items were not answered. With only 15 respondents defined as lurkers on either Grid A or Grid B, there was no effect of the experimental conditions on the probability of respondents becoming a lurker. It is important to distinguish between these two respondent

* The data used in this research are available in the LISS panel data archive (http://www.lissdata.nl).

TABLE 8.2

Distribution of Missing Answers (Item Missing) for Both Grid Questions

Number of Items Missing	Grid A	Percent	Grid B	Percent
0 (complete responder)	2,109	94.03	1,982	88.36
1 (partial responder)	115	5.13	230	10.25
2 (partial responder)	5	0.22	17	0.76
3 (partial responder)	2	0.09	2	0.09
7 (lurker)	0	0	1	0.04
9 (lurker)	1	0.04	2	0.09
10 (lurker)	11	0.49	9	0.40

Note: $n = 2{,}243$, including 15 lurkers (0.7%), 334 partial responders (14.9%), and 1,894 complete responders (84.4%).

types because lurkers are conceptually different from partial nonresponders, and the reasons that lead to such behavior differ (Bosnjak, 2002; Bosnjak & Tuten, 2001). For example, lurkers might not have a real intent to participate, whereas partial nonresponse might be a result of respondent fatigue.

For the analysis of partial response a binary variable was computed to indicate whether at least one answer was missing under the condition that at least seven answers were provided (dichotomized partial response variable). This was feasible because combining the amount of missing items into a 0/1-variable affected only 24 respondents (approximately 1%). The following analysis predicted the effect of the experimental conditions on the occurrence of missing items with a logistic regression. In order to identify the best logistic regression model, a main-effects model with the main treatment dummy variables only (Model 1, main-effects model), a main-effects model including all interactive terms (Model 2, interactive model), and a third model including the respondent characteristics of age, education, and use of simPC (Model 3, extended main-effects model) are used. Model 1 is specified as $\text{logit}(\pi) = \alpha + \beta_1$ Prebox + β_2 Prerow + β_3 Postbox + β_4 Postrow; the other models are specified accordingly with additional explanatory variables.

All effects were compared to the condition without any visual feedback. *Pre* and *Post* refer to the preselection and postselection feedback conditions with either shading the table cell (*Box*) or the row (*Row*). Model 1 was significant, $n = 2{,}228$, $\chi^2(4) = 19.36$, $p < .001$. Table 8.3 shows a significant negative impact on missing items for highlighting the table cell (Prebox) and a significant positive impact of coloring the row after a click (Postrow). The effect can be illustrated by calculating the change in percentage of complete answers that were obtained from the raw data: Prebox resulted in a 2.6 percentage point loss of complete answers for both grids, whereas Postrow increased the amount of complete answers by 3.9 percentage points. The other two conditions (Prerow and Postbox) had no effect on item nonresponse. To check for interaction effects, Model 2 includes the interaction terms and is specified as logit(π) = Model 1 + β_5 PreboxXPostbox + β_6 PreboxXPostrow + β_7 PrerowXPostbox + β_8 PrerowXPostrow.

None of the interaction terms was significant (Table 8.3). A likelihood ratio test used to compare the added value of Model 2 to Model 1 showed a preference for Model 1, $\chi^2(4) = 1.35$, $p = .85$. Therefore, Model 3 was constructed on the basis of Model 1 and added respondents' characteristics as follows: logit(π) = Model 1 + β_5 Age + β_6 Education + β_7 simPC. The results show that older respondents have a significantly higher probability of leaving items unanswered. In contrast, higher education has a significant positive effect on fully completing the questionnaire. The use of a simPC seems to have a negative effect, although this is not significant, $p = .087$. Prebox and Postrow remain significant, with odds ratios similar to those of Model 1. A likelihood ratio test to compare the added value of Model 3 to Model 1 shows a preference for Model 3, $\chi^2(3) = 28.11$, $p < .001$. The same conclusions can be drawn with the corresponding general linear models to predict the number of items missing.

Summarizing, preselection shading of the table cell under the mouse pointer increased item nonresponse, whereas postselection shading of the row decreased item nonresponse. In addition, higher age was associated with higher item nonresponse, whereas respondents with higher education provided more complete answers. No interaction effects were found, and the main effects remained regardless of the inclusion of the additional respondent characteristics of age, education, and use of simPC. For hypothesis H1 this means that feedback leading to fewer missing items was confirmed for Postrow but not for Postbox or Prerow. These findings can be interpreted as a result of the visual changes that make missing items more prominent and thus make it easier for respondents to identify and answer all items.

8.4.2 Changes in Answers

The number of corrections respondents make to their initial answer is another indicator of data quality. Respondents were confronted with

TABLE 8.3

Logistic Regression Predicting the Occurrence of Item Nonresponse

	Model 1			Model 2			Model 3		
Variable	**OR**	**95% CI**	*p*	**OR**	**95% CI**	*p*	**OR**	**95% CI**	*p*
Prebox (1)	1.57	[1.18, 2.09]	<.01	1.34	[0.85, 2.13]	.21	1.58	[1.19, 2.11]	<.01
Prerow (2)	1.06	[0.78, 1.43]	.71	0.91	[0.56, 1.48]	.70	1.08	[0.79, 1.46]	.64
Postbox (3)	0.94	[0.72, 1.24]	.67	0.81	[0.49, 1.35]	.42	0.95	[0.72, 1.25]	.72
Postrow (4)	0.68	[0.51, 0.91]	.01	0.55	[0.31, 0.95]	.03	0.68	[0.50, 0.91]	.01
preXpos 1x3				1.18	[0.60, 2.31]	.62			
preXpos 1x4				1.43	[0.70, 2.94]	.33			
preXpos 2x3				.130	[0.64, 2.64]	.46			
preXpos 2x4				1.26	[0.58, 2.73]	.56			
Age							1.01	[1.00, 1.02]	<.01
Education							0.90	[0.83, 0.97]	<.01
simPC							1.32	[0.96, 1.82]	.09

Note: n = 2,228; OR = odds ratio; CI = confidence interval; Prebox = Preselection feedback emphasizing the answer; Prerow = Preselection feedback emphasizing the item; Postbox = Postselection feedback emphasizing the answer; Postrow = Postselection feedback emphasizing the item.

visual feedback techniques to which they had not been exposed in the LISS panel before.

Changing answers was a common behavior among respondents in the Internet survey: 23% changed their initial answer at least once in the grid with the self-efficacy scale, and 26% changed their answer in the grid with the personality items. Switching an answer could be observed among 41% of all respondents when considering all 20 items. This high frequency of changes in answers during the response process was also observable in the no-feedback condition. This might be an indication that respondents use initial responses in an Internet survey as part of the ongoing decision process, whereas in other survey modes a response is usually provided much later in the response process. It is much easier to change an answer in an Internet survey than to change a check mark on paper or to ask an interviewer to change the last answer.

Because 20% of the respondents had changed their answer more than once, a GLM approach could take advantage of the variance in counts of changed answers, which ranged from 0 to 19. Thus, the analysis was conducted for the aforementioned models with a GLM approach. Here, a Poisson distribution for the dependent variable of changed answers is more appropriate than a normal (Gaussian) distribution. The reason is the data distribution, which shows a peak in the beginning with a tail to the right: Most respondents (60%) did not change their initial answers, followed by 20% who changed one answer, and a diminishing proportion for higher amounts of changes. Because item nonresponse was not missing at random, only respondents who answered all 20 items were entered into the analysis to avoid false conclusions and side effects from missing answer behavior on switching answer behavior.

In the main-effects model (Model 1, n = 1,894), the condition Prebox significantly increased the number of changes in answers (B = 0.21, CI 95% [0.09, 0.33], $p = .001$), whereas the condition Prerow significantly decreased the amount of changes (B = −0.14, CI 95% [−0.26, −0.01], $p = .036$).

Adding the interactive terms and the variables age, education, and use of simPC contributed to the explanatory power of the model. Therefore, the preferred model was the extended interactive model, which includes the main effects, interactive terms, and the additional variables. Here, similar to the main-effects model, the condition Prebox significantly

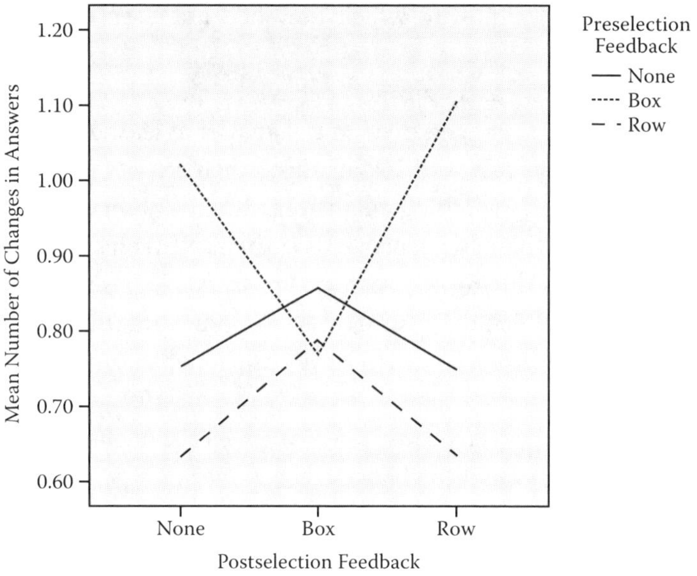

FIGURE 8.2
Changes in answers for respondents who answered all questions.

increased the amount of changes (B = 0.29, CI 95% [0.08, 0.50], $p = .006$). Age was significantly associated with fewer changes (B = −0.015, CI 95% [−0.02, −0.01], $p < .001$).

The results are illustrated in Figure 8.2, which shows the mean number of changes in each condition separated by pre- and postselection feedback for respondents who answered all items. Obvious is the significant interaction effect of the condition Prebox-Postbox (B = −0.46, CI 95% [−0.76, −0.16], $p < .003$). The condition Prerow (preselection feedback emphasizing the item, bottom line in Figure 8.2) seems superior to no preselection feedback. Similar to the findings on item nonresponse, the condition Prebox (preselection feedback emphasizing the answer) leads to decreased data quality. The exception here is the interaction effect, that is, when the table cell is shaded both before and after an answer was selected (dotted V-shaped line). In Figure 8.2 Prerow feedback shows the least number of changes in a combination with either no postselection feedback or Postrow feedback (left and right data points in the bottom line, respectively). For the hypothesis H2 this means that feedback leading to fewer changes was not confirmed as hypothesized in the conditions Postbox and Postrow, but turned out to be present in the condition Prerow.

Concluding, preselection feedback emphasizing the row seems to work best. In addition, it is possible to add the same type of postselection feedback (Postrow) without increasing the frequency of changes in answers. Although these findings are not in line with the hypothesis, an explanation for the findings might be that preselection feedback emphasizing the item helps respondents to focus and think more profoundly about their answers before selecting an answer category. This would then lead to fewer changes. However, emphasizing the answer category alone has the contrary effect and might distract respondents from the item text and lead to premature answer clicks.

8.4.3 Satisficing and Nondifferentiation

On one hand, in the construction of scales high item correlations are often perceived as a quality indicator of the scale (e.g., Cronbach's α). On the other hand, when testing for visual design effects or survey usability, higher item correlations are interpreted as an indicator of satisficing. For example, the visual design of grid questions may increase respondent burden or reduce respondent motivation. According to the satisficing model (Krosnick, 1991), this would result in a behavior that Krosnick has termed "nondifferentiation." Nondifferentiation can be calculated by identifying the highest count of identical answers a respondent selects in a list of items (here Grid A and Grid B). This count is then divided by the number of available items (Tourangeau, Couper, & Conrad, 2004). For Grid A, with 10 items and four response categories, nondifferentiation can range from 0.3 to 1; for Grid B, with five response categories, the range is from 0.2 to 1 (respondents who answered all items must at least select the same response category three times or two times, respectively).

The data were analyzed separately for both pages with a GLM including only respondents who answered all items on the respective page. Again, this was necessary because the missing data were not missing at random and thus otherwise could influence the conclusions from the analysis. A plot of the data distributions provided no reasons not to use the standard Gaussian distribution in the GLM.

The items on the two grids differ considerably in terms of their mean nondifferentiation value. This can be understood mainly as a result of the self-efficacy scale being well constructed (Grid A, Cronbach's $\alpha = .86$, mean nondifferentiation = .66, n = 2,109), whereas the personality items

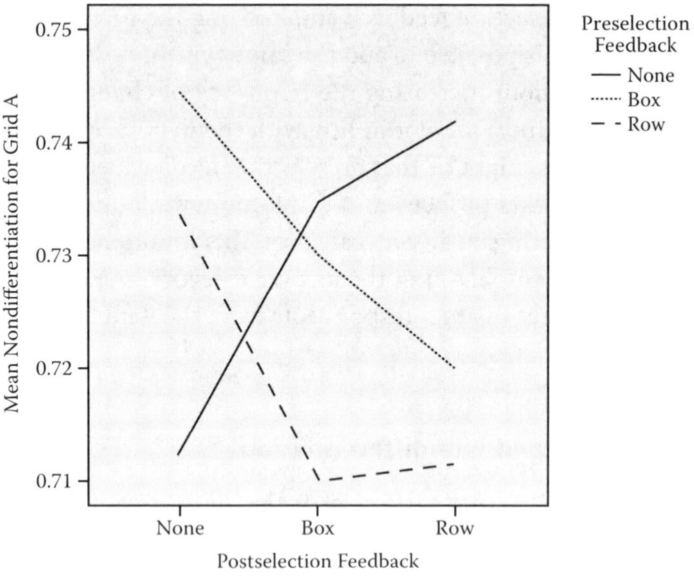

FIGURE 8.3
Nondifferentiation in Grid A (n = 2,109). Nondifferentiation in Grid A can range from 0.3 to 1. The number multiplied by 10 is an average of how often the same answer category was selected among the 10 items, regardless of which specific answer it was.

were not chosen according to a specific construct (Grid B, Cronbach's α = .54, mean nondifferentiation = .34, n = 1,982).

For Grid A—the self-efficacy scale—the preferred model is the main-effects model including the interactive terms (Model 2). The extended model with age, education, and use of simPC (Model 3) shows no significant effects. In the preferred interactive model (Model 2), the condition Prebox significantly increases nondifferentiation (B = 0.031, CI 95% [0.001, 0.061], p = .04). An increase is also visible for the condition Postrow (B = 0.029, CI 95% [0.001, 0.059], p = .06). However, these findings need to be interpreted taking all interaction effects, which are Prebox-Postbox (p = .08), Prebox-Postrow (p = .01), Prerow-Postbox (p = .04), and Prerow-Postrow (p = .02) into account. Figure 8.3 illustrates these results. The point in the lower left is the standard condition without any feedback. It serves as the baseline when comparing the differences in nondifferentiation. The significant increase for the condition Prebox is clearly visible as the dotted upper line, which is always above the baseline. The nearly significant effect of the condition Postrow is illustrated by the two mean values on the right, which show that Postrow feedback does not work well under Prenone or Prebox feedback. This leaves the best conditions, shown at the bottom of the figure, which are no feedback at all and postselection feedback when combined with Prerow feedback. The analysis for Grid B yields no significant results of any main effects or interactive terms in any of the three specified models. For the hypothesis H3 this means that feedback leading to less nondifferentiation was not confirmed for the condition Postbox. Moreover, and in contradiction to hypothesis H3, the condition Prebox showed a higher degree of nondifferentiation.

Summarizing, feedback shows no positive effects on nondifferentiation. However, the combinations Prerow-Postrow and Prerow-Postbox feedback are equal to the no feedback condition. Nevertheless, it is important to note that again Prebox feedback leads to poorer data quality. Finally, some caution seems in order when interpreting these findings on nondifferentiation because the effects do not hold for both grids.

8.5 CONCLUSIONS

The goal of this research was to test whether assumptions about feedback that were deduced from usability concepts also hold true for survey research. An experiment was conducted to reach a decision about the best possible implementation of visual feedback in grid questions. A summary of the results is illustrated in Table 8.4. The overall conclusion drawn from the findings described above and the summary in Table 8.4 is that a combined pre- and postselection feedback that emphasizes the item and not the answer category is superior in terms of the data quality indicators compared to no feedback or other feedback conditions.

First, postselection feedback emphasizing the item row (Postrow) reduces the number of missing items and the number of changed answers, a result that is in line with the assumed positive effect of the implemented feedback techniques. Second, although not predicted, highlighting the item row before an answer is selected shows a positive effect in terms of fewer changes in answers. Third, contradicting the assumptions of a positive feedback effect, preselection feedback highlighting the answer category (Prebox) does not help to reduce nondifferentiation. Worse still, this feedback seems to interfere with the answer process instead of supporting

TABLE 8.4

Effects of Feedback on Data Quality Indicators

Preselection Feedback	None	None	None	Box	Box	Box	Row	Row	Row
Postselection Feedback	None	Box	Row	None	Box	Row	None	Box	Row
Item Nonresponse	9.6	7.9	5.7**	12.2**	12.9	9.8	7.7	8.6	**5.6**
Changes in Answers	37.6	42.9	37.4	51.0***	38.4	55.3	**31.6***	39.4	**31.8**
Nondifferentiation A	64.6	66.0	67.8*	68.9*	66.3	64.7	67.0	63.0	**63.5**
Nondifferentiation B	34.6	34.2	33.7	34.5	33.9	34.1	**33.2**	35.1	**33.2**

Note: The numbers show the mean percentages for 10 items. It can be read as follows: For the condition with no feedback (first data column) a respondent shows on average 0.96 missing items, 3.76 changes in answers, 6.46 answers in the same answer category in Grid A and 3.46 same answers in Grid B on a single screen with 10 items. Bold font highlights the conditions with the lowest percentages. Values for item nonresponse were calculated without lurkers ($n = 2{,}228$), values for changes in answers and nondifferentiation for respondents who answered all items ($n = 1{,}894$).

* $p < .05$

** $p < .01$

*** $p < .001$

it, which results in a negative impact on all three criteria: more missing items, more changes in answers, and more nondifferentiation.

For the specific hypotheses, this means that feedback leading to fewer missing items (H1) is confirmed for Postrow but not for Postbox or Prerow. Feedback leading to fewer changes (H2) was not confirmed as hypothesized, although it becomes relevant for Prerow, which was not included in the original hypothesis. Feedback leading to less nondifferentiation (H3) is not confirmed for Postbox. Moreover, and in contradiction to H3, Prebox leads to more nondifferentiation.

There are two practical implications from this. The combined effect of emphasizing an item (Row) both before *and* after an answer is selected shows more benefits than any other feedback combinations. Moreover, specific feedback implementations should be tested because they can even have negative effects on data quality. This interpretation is also corroborated when considering that missing items as a part of nonresponse are the most important threat to data quality.

Previous research by Galesic et al. (2007) and Kaczmirek (2009), who found fewer missing items as a result of feedback after an answer was provided, was largely confirmed. However, the negative effect of emphasizing the answer categories contradicts earlier findings by Kaczmirek (2009). This earlier study differed in the following ways from the study reported here because it only operationalized the conditions Prebox-Postbox and compared that to a no-feedback condition. Therefore, it was by design unable to detect interaction effects or compare those effects to other forms of feedback.

One explanation for the negative impact of preselection feedback emphasizing the answer category by highlighting the table cell could be that respondents who would otherwise think about the right answer start to focus on and play with the optical changes that appear while moving the mouse over the answer categories. This would then interfere with the cognitive process of retrieving an answer and instead lead to a behavior where respondents focus on the visual pattern they are about to produce. Because respondents would then invest less cognitive effort in understanding the item and retrieving the answer, this would result in more satisficing and thus nondifferentiation. This interpretation is also supported by higher item nonresponse and an increased number of changes. Both are an indication that respondents are distracted from their task.

On the contrary, emphasizing the item by highlighting the item row does not lead to visually distracting changes while choosing an answer, but serves to reduce the effort needed to keep track of the connection between answer categories and the item. Hence, fewer respondents need to correct their answers because they focus more on the task of completing that specific item.

The negative effects of feedback emphasizing the answer categories also raise questions as to the potential drawbacks or benefits of graphical answer buttons instead of radio buttons. Many survey software products allow for exchanging the standard radio buttons with bigger graphics that change their appearance when the mouse hovers over them. As survey researchers, we hope that the specific implementations in survey software do not come with negative effects. Future research needs to consider these aspects.

A limitation of this study is that the findings had to be based on a single operationalization of each feedback type. This affected choices in color, saturation, and the fact that feedback was always administered in colored rectangles. Although these choices were constant across conditions, they could have affected the outcome. Professional graphic design might prove even more successful when it comes to specific implementations, such as rounded edges for rectangles or 3-D design.

The study has high internal validity due to the complete experimental design and randomized assignment of respondents to conditions. Regarding external validity, the study has advantages in terms of a probability-based sample of the population of the Netherlands irrespective of Internet penetration, a benefit many experimental Internet studies lack. Thus, it might be reasonable to extend these findings to the general population with the limitation that respondents were part of a panel and might have received a high initial incentive and receive continued compensation for their participation (see Chapter 4 in this volume). With respect to an overlap in tests and effect sizes, the approach used in analyzing the data was to first identify the most appropriate models so that inflation in the number of tests was minimized. An optimal sample size was chosen according to Cohen's classification (1992) to allow a power of .95 with an α of .05. Thus, the study was able to identify which feedback had a significant positive or negative effect on the outcome variables and which feedback might be seen as irrelevant.

The results extended findings from previous research by unveiling the different effects of various feedback types on data quality and provided an explanation of the process by which feedback is expected to influence respondent behavior. Beyond data quality, good feedback is part of a successful human–survey interaction in that it is always better to prevent errors such as missed items before the survey instrument needs to raise attention to it by means of error messages. Applications in survey design could shade items before and after the answer is selected to increase data quality. For feedback before an answer is selected, researchers should avoid highlighting the table cell. Here, the operationalization used in this experiment provided clear evidence of undesired negative effects. Future research should fine-tune specific implementations of feedback to identify advantages or disadvantages of graphical buttons compared to radio buttons. This research has clearly shown that "design has a specific function—that of facilitating the task. It is not a goal in itself" (Couper, 2008, p. 134). Being a participant in a survey should be interesting and effective and should yield valid answers. Human–survey interaction design plays a crucial role in making this happen.

[1] Acknowledgments: The data collection was funded by the MESS project and collected by means of the LISS panel. I thank Annette Scherpenzeel, Vera Toepoel, and Maurice Martens for their work in collecting the data and programming the questionnaire. I thank Sarah Heinz and Timo Lenzner for comments on an earlier version of this chapter.

REFERENCES

Bosnjak, M. (2002). *(Non)response bei Web-befragungen [(Non)response in Web surveys].* Aachen: Shaker.

Bosnjak, M. & Tuten, T. L. (2001). Classifying response behaviors in Web-based surveys. *Journal of Computer-Mediated Communication, 6*(3). Retrieved from http://jcmc.indiana.edu/vol6/issue3/boznjak.html

Christian, L. M., Dillman, D. A., & Smyth, J. D. (2007). Helping respondents get it right the first time: The influence of words, symbols, and graphics in Web surveys. *Public Opinion Quarterly*, 71(1), 113–125.

Cohen, J. (1992). A power primer. *Psychological Bulletin, 112*(1), 155–159.

Conrad, F. G., Couper, M. P., Tourangeau, R., & Galesic, M. (2005). *Interactive feedback can improve the quality of responses in Web surveys.* Paper presented at the conference of the American Association for Public Opinion Research (AAPOR), Miami Beach, Florida.

Couper, M. P. (1994). Discussion: What can CAI learn from HCI? In *Proceedings of the seminar on new directions in statistical methodology* (pp. 363–377). Washington, DC: Statistical Policy Office, Office of Management and Budget.

Couper, M. P. (2008). *Designing effective Web surveys*. New York: Cambridge University Press.

Couper, M. P., Tourangeau, R., & Conrad, F. G. (2006). Evaluating the effectiveness of visual analog scales. *Social Science Computer Review, 24*(2), 227–245.

Dillman, D. A., Gertseva, A., & Mahon-Haft, T. (2005). Achieving usability in establishment surveys through the application of visual design principles. *Journal of Official Statistics, 21*, 183–214.

Dillman, D. A., Smyth, J. D., & Christian, L. M. (2009). *Internet, mail, and mixed-mode surveys: The tailored design method*. Hoboken, NJ: John Wiley & Sons.

Draisma, S. & Dijkstra, W. (2004). Response latency and (para)linguistic expressions as indicators of response error. In S. Presser et al. (Eds.), *Methods for testing and evaluating survey questionnaires* (pp. 131–147). New York: John Wiley & Sons.

Faul, F., Erdfelder, E., Lang, A.-G., & Buchner, A. (2007). G*Power 3: A flexible statistical power analysis program for the social, behavioral, and biomedical sciences. *Behavior Research Methods, 39*, 175–191.

Galesic, M., Tourangeau, R., Couper, M. P., & Conrad, F. G. (2007). *Using change to improve navigation in grid questions*. Presentation at the General Online Research conference (GOR '07), Leipzig, Germany.

ISO 9241-110 *[Ergonomics of human-system interaction—part 110: Dialogue principles]* (International Standard). (2006). Geneva, Switzerland: ISO Copyright Office.

Kaczmirek, L. (2007). *Cognition, attention and usability in online surveys*. Workshop on Social Research and the Internet: Advances in Applied Methods and New Research Strategies. Mannheim, Germany.

Kaczmirek, L. (2009). *Human-survey interaction: Usability and nonresponse in online surveys*. Cologne: Herbert von Halem Verlag.

Krosnick, J. A. (1991). Response strategies for coping with the cognitive demands of attitude measures in surveys. *Applied Cognitive Psychology, 5*, 213–236.

Nielsen, J. (1993). *Usability engineering*. New York: Academic Press.

Norman, D. A. (1988). *The psychology of everyday things*. New York: Basic Books.

Peytchev, A. (2007). *Participation decisions and measurement error in Web surveys*. Unpublished doctoral dissertation, University of Michigan.

Peytchev, A. & Crawford, S. (2005). A typology of real-time validations in Web-based surveys. *Social Science Computer Review, 23*(2), 235–249.

Schwarzer, R. & Jerusalem, M. (1995). Generalized self-efficacy scale. In J. Weinman, S. Wright, & M. Johnston (Eds.), *Measures in health psychology: A user's portfolio. Causal and control beliefs* (pp. 35–37). Windsor, UK: NFER-NELSON.

Shneiderman, B. (1998). *Designing the user interface: Strategies for effective human-computer interaction* (3rd ed.). Boston: Addison-Wesley.

Toepoel, V. (2008). *A closer look at Web questionnaire design*. Doctoral dissertation. CentER for Economic Research Dissertation Series No. 220. Tilburg University, the Netherlands.

Tourangeau, R., Couper, M. P., & Conrad, F. G. (2004). Spacing, position, and order: Interpretive heuristics for visual features of survey questions. *Public Opinion Quarterly, 68*(3), 368–393.

APPENDIX

The questionnaire consisted of three pages and was conducted in Dutch. An introduction screen was followed by two pages with several items in a grid layout. The two pages with questions were administered in a randomized order. The instruction on the introduction page read (translation from the Dutch original): "On the following screens, there are phrases describing people's behaviors. Please use the answer scale on the following pages to describe how accurately each statement describes you. Describe yourself as you generally are now, not as you wish to be in the future. Describe yourself as you honestly see yourself, in relation to other people you know of the same sex as you are, and about your age. Please read each statement carefully, and then click on the radio button that corresponds to the number on the scale."

Grid A used the Dutch adaptation of the General Self-Efficacy Scale from Schwarzer and Jerusalem (1995). The items used a 4-point fully labeled answer scale (not at all true, hardly true, moderately true, exactly true). The items were

1. I can always manage to solve difficult problems if I try hard enough.
2. If someone opposes me, I can find the means and ways to get what I want.
3. It is easy for me to stick to my aims and accomplish my goals.
4. I am confident that I could deal efficiently with unexpected events.
5. Thanks to my resourcefulness, I know how to handle unforeseen situations.
6. I can solve most problems if I invest the necessary effort.
7. I can remain calm when facing difficulties because I can rely on my coping abilities.
8. When I am confronted with a problem, I can usually find several solutions.
9. If I am in trouble, I can usually think of a solution.
10. I can usually handle whatever comes my way.

Grid B used a personality inventory with a five-point fully labeled answer scale (very inaccurate, moderately inaccurate, neither inaccurate nor accurate, moderately accurate, very accurate). The items were

1. Wait for others to lead the way.
2. Think of others first.
3. Love order and regularity.
4. Get caught up in my problems.
5. Love to read challenging material.
6. Am skilled in handling social situations.
7. Love to help others.
8. Like to tidy up.
9. Grumble about things.
10. Love to think up new ways of doing things.

9

Using Interactive Features to Motivate and Probe Responses to Open-Ended Questions

Marije Oudejans
CentERdata
Tilburg University
Tilburg, the Netherlands

Leah Melani Christian
Pew Research Center for the People and the Press
Washington, DC

9.1 INTRODUCTION

Internet surveys are self-administered in that respondents initiate and control many aspects of the survey experience. However, they also share many features with interviewer-administered surveys. The interactivity of the Internet can be used to provide respondents with customized feedback as they complete the survey, similar to the way interviewers provide feedback in telephone and personal interview surveys. Interactive features can be programmed to ask respondents specific follow-up questions, request that people provide a response, provide links to definitions or examples, calculate totals, or play a video showing an interviewer. Thus, these interactive design features have the potential to improve the quality of responses by motivating respondents, providing clarification, and reviewing responses submitted. This dynamic nature of Internet surveys allows for surveyors to integrate some of the benefits of interviewer-administered surveys with the increased respondent control and privacy of self-administered surveys.

The interactivity of Internet surveys offers new opportunities for providing feedback to respondents that may be used to help motivate them to answer open-ended questions and provide accurate and complete responses. Motivation is especially important for questions that require more effort and thought, such as open-ended ones. Although early studies have suggested that responses to open-ended questions may be better in Internet than paper surveys, item nonresponse can be a significant problem with these types of questions in self-administered surveys (Holland & Christian, 2009). Motivating respondents is still a concern in self-administered surveys, particularly Internet surveys where respondents can easily decide to quit and abandon the survey.

In this chapter, we use the interactivity of the Web to adapt two specific interviewer strategies for encouraging quality responses to open-ended questions: motivational statements and follow-up probes. First we discuss previous research on improving responses to open-ended questions and introduce hypotheses about how we expect these features to influence responses. Then we discuss the results of experiments testing the independent and combined effects of including motivational statements and follow-up probes on responses to open-ended questions in Internet surveys. The experimental comparisons were embedded in CentERdata's LISS panel, a longitudinal Internet panel of households in the Netherlands.

9.2 THEORETICAL BACKGROUND AND HYPOTHESES

9.2.1 The Interactivity of the Internet

Internet surveys can integrate a number of interactive features that have the potential to better engage respondents than is possible in self-administered paper surveys (Couper, 2005). The flexibility of computer programming and the ability to offer a variety of tailored features creates a more interactive experience for the survey respondent that more closely resembles interviewer-administered surveys but allows respondents to maintain more control over how they complete the survey. The interactivity of the Internet may be used to help improve the quality of responses by motivating respondents to complete the survey, providing help or clarification, reviewing responses submitted, and enhancing the overall respondent experience (Couper, 2008).

Internet surveys provide the opportunity to clarify information for respondents to help them answer the question (Conrad & Schober, 2005). Internet surveys can use hyperlinks to provide additional definitions, examples, or other information to respondents when they click on the link. Conrad, Couper, Tourangeau, and Peytchev (2006) found that, in general, a low percentage of respondents use the hyperlinked definitions when they are available, and the more steps required to access the feature (e.g., clicking twice, clicking and scrolling, etc.), the less the hyperlinked definitions get used. This perhaps suggests that most Internet users may not be willing to put forth the extra effort involved with using this particular interactive feature (Conrad, Couper, & Tourangeau, 2003).

Error messages are another interactive feature commonly used in Internet surveys. As respondents navigate through the survey, their responses on each page are submitted and are often evaluated to ensure the responses meet any designated criteria (Conrad et al., 2003). Error messages can then be programmed to inform respondents that a question has not been answered or that the response is not in an acceptable format. Respondents may get frustrated if they receive several error messages, particularly if corrections are required for them to proceed to the next question, and they may abandon the survey (Best & Krueger, 2004). Thus, many Internet surveyors do not use error messages to require a response before the respondent can move to the next question but instead use them as soft reminders to request an answer from respondents.

In addition to error messages, Internet surveys can be programmed to provide specific follow-up questions to respondents based on their answers to previous questions or other information the researcher may already have about the respondent. For example, different questions can be asked of those who attended a particular event than of those who did not. Similarly, questions or response items can be modified to reflect an earlier response (e.g., hotels listed for the city that the respondent chose or activities that the respondents said they participated in). The flexibility of Internet surveys, where questions can be varied for different respondents without requiring them to execute the skip instructions themselves, is one of the strengths of this mode compared with paper self-administered surveys. This type of filtering or branching can be applied to a variety of different topics and for many reasons, which gives surveyors the ability to tailor their surveys to particular respondents within the population.

9.2.2 Open-Ended Questions

Open-ended questions are very important tools because they allow researchers to collect detailed information about a particular topic from a large sample of respondents and people's responses are not constrained by a given set of answer categories. Schuman and Presser (1979) presumed there were two main advantages of open-ended questions. First, respondents are asked to provide a response in their own words, and often a more specific and detailed picture of what the respondent really thinks about the question topic is obtained. Second, they are particularly useful for explorative research when the researcher is unable to construct an appropriate set of answer categories or wants to get respondents' top-of-the-head answers without influencing them by providing a particular set of response options. Open-ended questions are important tools for identifying what respondents are thinking about selected topics, ensuring that a set of closed-ended categories includes all the relevant options, and asking follow-ups to important closed-ended questions to gain further insight into why respondents provided a particular answer.

However, open-ended questions are more burdensome because they take longer to answer and require respondents to formulate their own responses rather than simply select from a list of potential responses. Most survey respondents are willing to answer open-ended questions and provide high-quality answers when there is an interviewer present to motivate them and probe for further information or clarification. But researchers often have limited the use of open-ended questions in self-administered surveys because of the extra time and effort they require for respondents, the higher rates of item nonresponse, and the difficulty of getting high-quality responses without an interviewer present. However, the respondents who do provide a response to open-ended questions can answer at their own pace and take as much time as they want, so they can provide more complete responses (Fricker, Galesic, Tourangeau, & Yan, 2005). Thus it is important to pay particular attention to designing open-ended questions in self-administered surveys so they elicit high-quality responses from nearly all respondents (Dillman, Smyth, & Christian, 2009).

Internet surveys have increased interest in open-ended questions, as some studies have shown that they can produce comparable and sometimes even higher-quality responses than paper surveys. More people respond to the open-ended questions, and respondents provide longer, more thoughtful answers by Internet or e-mail than by paper (Schaefer & Dillman, 1998; Ramirez, Sharp, & Foster, 2000; Smyth, Dillman, Christian, & McBride, 2009). In addition, enhanced visual design, interactive features, and other aspects of Internet surveys may be utilized to motivate respondents and improve the quality of answers respondents provide. We discuss previous research on two specific features, motivational statements and follow-up probes, that have been shown to modestly improve responses to open-ended questions.

9.2.3 Motivational Statements

Interviewers can play an important role in motivating respondents (Groves et al., 2005). They can help motivate respondents to answer open-ended questions by explaining how important their responses are and reinforcing that they are doing a good job of responding. Interviewer feedback (for example, short comments such as "okay" or "that is interesting" and more detailed statements that ask respondents to elaborate on their answers) increased the amount of information respondents reported to open-ended questions in face-to-face interviews (Cannell, Miller, & Oksenberg, 1981). Adding instructions to the questions also increased the amount of information reported and improved the quality of the answers (as measured by more precise dates and greater external validity). In self-administered surveys, where the respondent rather than a live interviewer controls the delivery of the survey, motivational statements or instructions may be incorporated to encourage people to respond to individual questions and to provide complete and thoughtful answers.

These types of motivating statements can be particularly important for open-ended questions to help reinforce that respondents should spend more time answering the question. Smyth et al. (2009) found that including an introduction with the initial open-ended question emphasizing how important the responses were for the research improved the answers provided. The motivational instruction increased the number of themes reported and the number of respondents providing descriptive elaboration as well as the length of responses. In addition, mean response times were longer for those who received the motivational statement, suggesting they may have spent more time developing a response to the question (Smyth et al., 2009). These results lead to our first hypothesis so we can test whether the same results occur in the Dutch LISS panel:

> H1. A motivational statement will encourage more people to respond to the initial question and to provide longer responses with more themes and elaboration.

9.2.4 Follow-Up Probes

Very little research has examined how the interactive nature of Internet surveys can be used to ask follow-up probes after people's initial responses to open-ended questions. Internet surveys provide a unique opportunity to ask follow-up probes in a self-administered setting, similar to how interviewers probe responses in interviewer-administered surveys. In telephone and face-to-face surveys, interviewers ask follow-up probes both to motivate respondents and to help ensure complete and accurate responses.

Probing can be used to encourage answers from respondents who may not provide a response, thereby reducing item nonresponse. Although all respondents can benefit from probing, it can be especially useful when people are willing to provide at least some response. Follow-up probes can ask for more information or for the respondents to elaborate on their answer; these types of probes help to improve responses from those who provide only a short response or one that was given without much thought. Probes are also important in helping clarify the question and respondents' answers (Groves et al., 2005). Overall, probing is helpful to both the respondent and the researcher: Respondents have an opportunity to ensure that their responses are understood, and researchers can obtain more accurate or more complete responses than were initially given (Billiet & Loosveldt, 1988).

Follow-up probes can be more general and asked of virtually any respondent who answers the question—for example, "Do you want to add anything else?" or "Are there any other reasons why you like living here?" More specific and tailored follow-up probes can also be asked based on people's responses to the initial question, such as "Why do you like this program?" In addition, specific probes requesting a response can be asked of those who did not provide an answer to the initial question, similar to how error messages in Internet surveys ask nonrespondents to provide an answer.

To help ensure quality responses, it is important that probing does not lead respondents by giving any indication of a "correct" answer or other cues that might bias people's answers (Cannell et al., 1981). This nondirective probing avoids biases while still giving respondents an opportunity to provide an answer or add to their responses. It is also important to consider that any instruction given in a probe can influence how respondents behave later in the survey (Cannell et al., 1981). Thus, probing should be used carefully because feedback provided at one point in a survey can influence responses for the remainder of a survey (Miller & Cannell, 1982).

The only study we are aware of that explored the use of interactive probing in Internet surveys reported the results of an experiment embedded in a survey of university students where half of the respondents were asked a follow-up probe after two initial open-ended questions (Holland & Christian, 2009). After the initial response was submitted, the respondent's initial answer to the question was shown along with a follow-up probe asking for additional countries or issues depending on the nature of the initial question. The probe was the same regardless of whether respondents provided an initial response or not, and the probe did not ask for additional descriptive information or elaboration but instead asked for additional themes (Holland & Christian, 2009). The study found that probing can improve the quality of responses to open-ended questions for the small percentage of respondents who responded to the probe, but overall the effects are quite small. Responses to the first question showed no differences in mean number of words, a slight difference in the mean number of themes, and slight differences in the percentage elaborating for the version without the probe compared to the version with the probe. Respondents also elaborated more on their answers to the second question when probed, but there were no differences between the two conditions in mean number of words or mean number of themes mentioned. These findings lead to the following hypothesis:

> H2. A follow-up probe will encourage more people to provide longer responses with more themes and elaboration.

Holland and Christian (2009) also found that people who were more interested in the question topic were more likely to respond to the initial question and the follow-up probe and provided answers that were longer with more themes. Because this study as well as the Smyth et al. (2009) study surveyed university students in the United States, the use of a general population sample of the Dutch people allows us to analyze demographic differences. Similar to the Holland and Christian (2009) study, we are able to see what effect interest in the questionnaire has on who responds and the length of the responses provided. Based on the findings about interest from this study and because some studies have found that education can be related to whether people respond, we hypothesize that:

> H3. Interest in the questionnaire and demographic characteristics (especially education) will influence who responds and the length of respondents' answers.

Our current research design also allows us to extend the previous studies by testing the combined influence of motivational statements and follow-up probes on responses to open-ended questions. This leads to our fourth hypothesis:

> H4. A motivational statement provided with the follow-up probe will encourage more people to respond to the probe and to provide longer responses with more themes and elaboration than a probe alone or a motivational statement alone.

The Holland and Christian (2009) experiment demonstrated that the probe did not encourage respondents to answer who did not provide an initial response, but Smyth et al. (2009) found that adding motivational and clarifying instructions did reduce item nonresponse. Our experiment allows us to examine whether a combination of a follow-up probe and a motivational statement that is tailored specifically to those who did not respond will encourage them to provide a response:

> H5. A motivational statement with the follow-up probe will encourage nonrespondents to provide an answer.

9.3 METHODS

9.3.1 Experimental Comparisons

We tested four different experimental treatments using four questions at different points in the survey (see Table 9.1). The first open-ended question, "Why are you (satisfied/dissatisfied) with the way things are going in the Netherlands today?" was asked of all respondents, but the question varied based on whether respondents had chosen "satisfied" or "dissatisfied" in the preceding closed-ended question. The question "What are the most important problems facing the Netherlands today?" was also asked of all respondents. The other two open-ended questions were asked of a subset of respondents. The 80% of respondents who rated the Netherlands as an excellent or good place to live were asked the question "Why do you like living in the Netherlands?" Similarly, only those who thought a Dutch identity existed (96% of overall respondents) were asked about the essential aspects of the Dutch identity.

Respondents to the Internet survey were randomly assigned to one of the four versions of the open-ended questions (see Figure 9.1 through Figure 9.5 for examples of the experimental versions that have been translated into English). The control version simply displayed the open-ended question and a scrollable text box; no motivating statement was included with the question, and respondents were not branched to a follow-up probe (see Figure 9.2). In the second version, the open-ended question included the motivational statement "This question is very important to our survey," but, as in the control version, respondents were not asked a follow-up probe (see Figure 9.3). This statement was chosen because it is similar to the one that was effective in the Smyth et al. (2009) study. The comparison of the control version to the version with the motivational statement makes it possible to test our first hypothesis, that adding a motivational statement to the question will increase the number of people who respond to the initial question and the length of responses.

In the third version respondents were asked the open-ended question without a motivating statement, but after they submitted their initial response, they were branched to a follow-up probe. This page displayed the respondent's answer to the initial open-ended question and a follow-up probe (e.g., "Is there anything else you would like to add?") with a text box for their response to the probe (see Figure 9.4). Analyzing the effect of the follow-up probe will tell us whether our second hypothesis is true: that the addition of a follow-up probe encourages longer answers with more themes and elaboration. Respondents to the fourth version were also asked the initial open-ended question (without a motivational statement) and then branched to a follow-up probe with a motivational statement (see Figure 9.5). This version allows us to test the combined effects of these treatments to see whether the fourth hypothesis can be confirmed: that more people are likely to respond and provide longer answers when a follow-up probe with a motivational statement is offered.

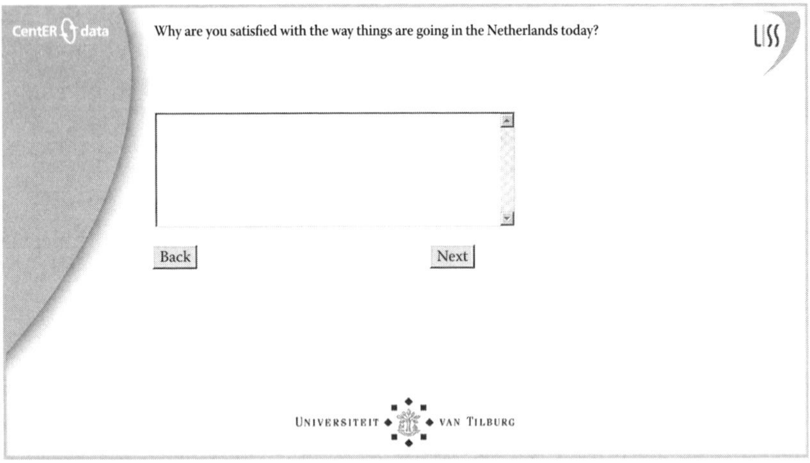

FIGURE 9.1
Control.

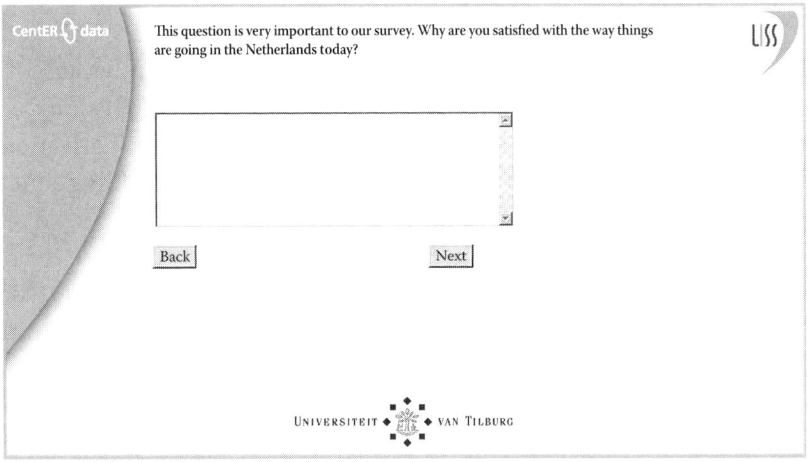

FIGURE 9.2
Motivational statement.

A pilot experiment where these open-ended questions were asked showed that not all people who do not want to or are not able to answer the questions skip the questions altogether. There are some respondents who provide an answer such as "don't know," "won't say," "no idea," or another nonsubstantive answer containing just a few characters (e.g., "??" or "..."). Therefore, people who did not answer the initial open-ended question, who provided one of 11 text answers explaining that they did not want to

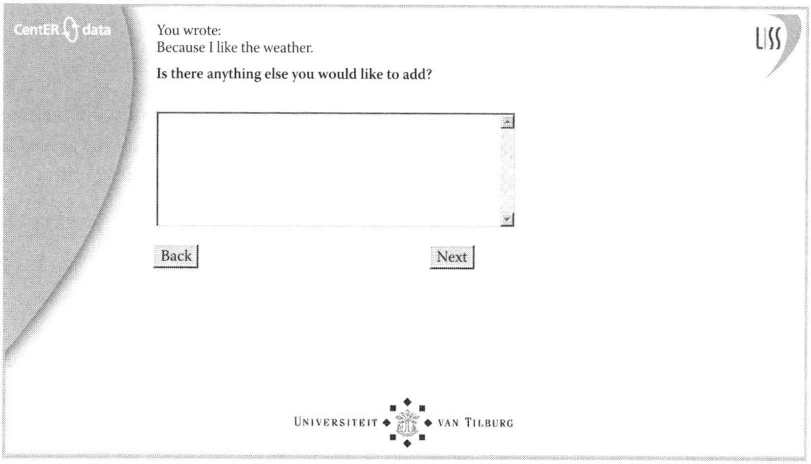

FIGURE 9.3
Follow-up probe.

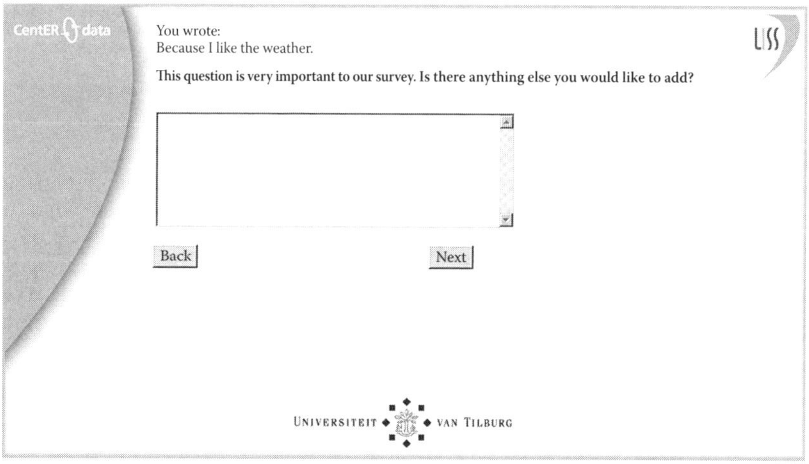

FIGURE 9.4
Follow-up probe and motivational statement.

answer, or whose answers were less than four characters were routed to the nonrespondent version. This version allows us to test our fifth hypothesis: whether nonrespondents can be motivated to provide an answer by a follow-up probe with a motivational statement that encourages them to provide a response.

Figure 9.1 through Figure 9.5 display the questions in the exact way as they were used in the experiment, but question and answer texts as well

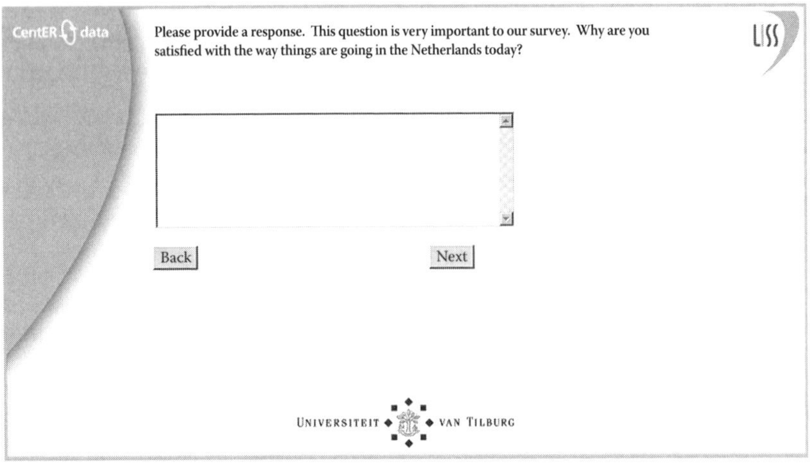

FIGURE 9.5
Nonrespondent version.

as the navigation buttons are translated into English for the convenience of the reader.

9.3.2 Data Collection and Analysis

The experimental comparisons were embedded in an Internet survey conducted as part of the Dutch CentERdata LISS panel. This LISS panel consists of about 5,000 households. The reference population for the LISS panel is the Dutch-speaking population permanently residing in the Netherlands. The sample frame is the nationwide address frame from Statistics Netherlands where the sampling units are independent, private households (thereby excluding nursing homes, institutions, and other forms of collective households). The households in the sample frame were approached by mail, telephone, or a personal visit. Households without a computer or Internet access were provided an Internet connection and a personal computer if they chose to take part in the panel. Since the summer of 2007, panel members have been asked to complete Internet questionnaires every month, up to 30 minutes of interview time. The surveys cover a wide variety of topics, and scientific researchers can submit proposals for questions they would like to have included in the panel.

The questionnaire for this experiment was fielded in August 2008; 68% (2,928 of the 4,268 panel members sampled) completed the questionnaire, and the median response time was 11 minutes. Twenty-five respondents did not complete the entire questionnaire and thus were removed from analysis; there were no significant differences in abandonment for the four different versions, although many did occur on the open-ended questions. Exact sample sizes for each version are shown in Table 9.1. Each respondent was randomly assigned to one of the four versions (as shown in Figures 9.1 to 9.4); every version of the questionnaire was completed by at least 700 respondents.

The follow-up probe used for the first open-ended question asked: "Is there anything else you would like to add?" This probe is vague as to whether more themes or elaboration should be provided. The follow-up probe for the other three questions asked: "Are there any other problems you would like to mention?", "Are there any other reasons why you like living in the Netherlands?", and "Are there any other things you think are typically Dutch?" requesting that respondents add additional themes.

We report the response rate for each question, which is the number of respondents who gave a valid response divided by the total number who received that question. Answers such as "don't really know" or "I will not answer this question" were coded as nonresponse (unfortunately, not all of these respondents were branched to the fifth nonrespondent version because only 11 variations of "don't know" or "won't say" types of responses were programmed to route people to the nonrespondent version). It is important to note that most people in the panel are accustomed to providing a response to each question, so item nonresponse rates tend to be low (in this experiment between 2% and 8%). We return to the implications of this later in the chapter. We also counted the number of words in the response to both the initial question and the follow-up probe for the versions with a probe (outliers at two standard deviations from the mean were excluded for analysis). The number of words has been used as a general measure of response quality in other studies evaluating responses to open-ended questions. Although it does not evaluate the substantive quality of responses to the researchers, it can provide a measure of how much time and effort respondents spent in providing an answer.

To evaluate other measures of response quality, a random sample of about 10% of responses were selected and coded for additional detail (300 random responses for each question—this results in a number of about 100 responses for the control version for each question because we had to leave out the respondents who received a follow-up probe). For each response, one of the authors coded the number of themes or independent topics mentioned and whether respondents elaborated on their answers by providing additional explanation or giving examples of what they meant. An answer can include a fair amount of words but contain only a small number of themes. Consider the following response to the question "Why are you dissatisfied with the way things are going in the Netherlands today?":

> I think that people in the Netherlands show a lack of respect and do not understand each other. Everybody is too focused on themselves and their own performance. The weaker people in this society (not just the financially weaker ones) struggle to survive. Those who cannot keep up with the pace of life nowadays do not count anymore. Nobody is interested in the reasons behind this.

This response was counted as including one theme (selfishness of people in Dutch society). The respondent did elaborate on the answer by explaining what was meant and why the respondent feels dissatisfied. Other responses might include fewer words but more themes, as in this response to the question "What do you think are essential aspects of the Dutch identity?":

> Complaining about small things, lack of sympathy for other cultures, narrow-minded, rudeness, internationally oriented, lack of individuality, often too tolerant, very zealous.

This response was counted as including eight different themes. The respondent did not elaborate but just mentioned the themes without clarifying anything or providing examples.

A research assistant trained in coding answers also coded a subset of the responses, and the coders agreed about 75% of the time on the number of themes and whether respondents provided elaboration. The coders agreed on the quality of the answer when they counted the same number of themes mentioned by a respondent and when they both thought a respondent did or did not elaborate on his or her answer.

Chi-square tests are shown for comparisons of response rates and elaboration across experimental treatments. A mixed between-subjects analysis of variance was conducted to assess the impact of adding a motivational statement to the question and a follow-up probe on the number of words used, across the four questions in the survey. *T*-tests are shown for comparisons of mean number of topics because we took a random sample for each question to count the number of topics people mentioned rather than looking at the total sample of respondents across all four questions. Multivariate regression models were employed to analyze the effect of the experimental treatments on whether or not someone responded (logistic regression) and the average number of words provided (linear regression). The models isolate the effect of each treatment while controlling for other demographic variables.

9.4 RESULTS

9.4.1 What Is the Effect of a Motivational Statement With the Initial Question?

Comparing the control version that did not have the motivational statement (Figure 9.1) to the version that included the motivational statement with the initial question (Figure 9.2), we find that response rates are 1 to 4 percentage points higher for three of the four questions when respondents received the motivational statement (see Table 9.1, columns a and b). However, the difference is significant only for the first question, about why people are satisfied or dissatisfied with the way things are going (98% vs. 94%; χ^2 (1, n = 1,451) = 10.53, $p < .01$). A multivariate logistic regression confirms these results, controlling for other social and demographic characteristics. The motivational statement does not have a significant effect on response in the overall model where the dependent variable is whether or not someone responded to all four open-ended questions (see Table 9.2). The effect of the motivational statement is significant only in the model for the first open-ended question; those who received the motivational statement are more likely to respond (receiving the motivational statement increases the odds of responding by a factor of 2.42).

Looking at various measures of response quality, responses are significantly longer, on average, for all four questions when respondents received the motivational statement. There is a significant but small interaction effect on the length of responses between the question and whether there was a motivational statement included in the question (Wilks $\lambda = .99$, $F(3, 1604) = 8.20$, $p < .01$, partial $\eta^2 = 0.02$). The difference between the motivational statement condition and the control condition is slightly larger (five words) for the first open-ended question than for subsequent questions.

The mean number of topics is slightly higher for two of the four questions when respondents received the motivational statement, but the difference is significant only for the first question (1.8 vs. 1.4 topics, t (396) = –2.32, $p < .05$). There is no consistent pattern for whether respondents elaborated on a topic mentioned in their responses; the only significant difference is for the first question where respondents to the control version are actually more likely to elaborate on their response (28% vs. 17%, $\chi^2(1, n = 398) = 4.80$, $p < .05$). Overall, the number of words declines as respondents progressed through the survey regardless of which version they received. However, the number of topics mentioned and the percentage elaborating on their response differ for the four questions but do not show a significant decline throughout the survey.

The multivariate analysis also shows that the effect of the motivational statement decreases as respondents progressed through the survey (see Table 9.3). Respondents provide five more words to the first open-ended question but only about one more word to the last one.

Our first hypothesis was only partially confirmed: A motivational statement does encourage more people to respond, but not for all the open-ended questions that were included in the survey. Furthermore, we do see an increase in the number of words used when a motivational statement is included in the question, as stated in the first hypothesis, but the effect on the number of topics that are mentioned and whether respondents elaborate or not is not convincing.

9.4.2 What Is the Effect of a Follow-Up Probe?

Comparing the control version that did not include a follow-up probe (Figure 9.1) to the version with a follow-up probe (Figure 9.3), we find a small but significant interaction effect between the question and the follow-up probe on the length of responses (Wilks $\lambda = .99$, $F(3, 1604) = 6.61$, $p < .01$, partial $\eta^2 = 0.01$). There is a larger difference in mean number of words used when looking at the first two questions (difference of two to three words) than later on in the survey with the third and fourth questions (one-word difference).

Similarly, the mean number of topics is also greater for the respondents who received the version with the probe. Again, the effect is modest, with

TABLE 9.1

Percent Responding and Measures of Response Quality for Each Question by Treatment

	a. Control (No Probe or Motivation)				b. Motivational Statement With Initial Question				c. Follow-Up Probe				d. Follow-Up Probe With Motivational Statement			
	Q2	Q5	Q11	Q16	Q2	Q5	Q11	Q16	Q2	Q5	Q11	Q16	Q2	Q5	Q11	Q16
n	744	744	590	711	707	707	557	676	759	759	610	721	718	718	565	690
% responding initially	94	95	95	88	98	95	97	89	95	94	93	86	95	96	93	87
n[1]	—	—	—	—	—	—	—	—	730	732	582	657	690	704	536	625
% responding probe	—	—	—	—	—	—	—	—	28	39	35	30	46	42	41	33
n[1]	686	707	547	625	670	652	515	603	679	675	531	609	649	643	486	568
Mean number of words[2]	19	14	11	10	24	15	13	11	21	17	12	11	25	18	14	11
Analysis of Randomly Selected Subset of Total Responses (About 10%)																
n[1]	108	92	97	106	290	289	295	278	300	300	300	300	300	300	300	300
Mean number of topics[2]	1.4	2.1	1.8	2.7	1.8	1.9	2.0	2.4	1.9	2.7	2.3	3.1	2.0	2.5	2.5	3.2
n[1]	108	92	97	106	290	289	295	278	300	300	300	300	300	300	300	300
% elaborating[2]	28	20	14	25	17	25	19	18	30	27	22	16	34	35	26	20

Q2: Why are you (dis)satisfied with the way things are going in the Netherlands today? (first open-ended question)
Q5: What do you think are the most important problems facing the Netherlands today? (second open-ended question)
Q11: What do you like about living in the Netherlands? (third open-ended question)
Q16: What would you say are the essential aspects of the Dutch identity? What do you think is considered typically Dutch? (fourth open-ended question)
a. Control condition: Only the initial question was presented.
b. Experimental condition: Every initial question was preceded by the statement "This question is very important to our survey."
c. Experimental condition: The initial question was followed by a probe.
d. Experimental condition: The initial question was followed by the probe that also included the same motivational statement as condition b.
[1] *N*s are based only on those who responded (and for mean number of topics and % elaboration for only a subset of respondents).
[2] Mean number of words and topics and % elaborating based on responses to both initial question and follow-up probe for versions c and d.

TABLE 9.2

Logistic Regression Predicting Whether People Respond

	Responded to All Four Questions[1]		Q2 Reasons Why (Dis) Satisfied With Way Things Are Going		Q5 Most Important Problems in the Netherlands		Q11 Things People Like About Living in the Netherlands		Q16 Essential Aspects of the Dutch Identity	
	Odds Ratio	***SE***	**Odds Ratio**	***SE***	**Odds Ratio**	***SE***	**Odds Ratio**	***SE***	**Odds Ratio**	***SE***
Motivational statement	1.16	.186	2.42 **	.726	1.03	.249	1.33	.430	1.13	.202
Follow-up probe	0.83	.126	1.11	.265	0.86	.196	0.59 **	.155	0.85	.144
Follow-up probe w/motivation	0.96	.151	1.29	.325	1.35	.351	0.61 *	.166	0.82	.140
Gender (female = 1)	0.95	.108	0.71 *	.138	1.21	.211	1.25	.243	0.89	.112
Higher education	2.05 **	.287	1.54 *	.349	1.54 *	.345	1.04	.232	2.22 **	.370
Primary education	0.79	.142	1.08	.361	0.88	.254	1.11	.398	0.68 **	.128
Age	1.00	.011	1.00	.016	0.98	.012	1.02	.025	0.98 **	.009
Employed	0.73 **	.087	0.85	.169	0.67 **	.124	0.65 **	.137	0.68 **	.088

Married	0.98		.123	1.26		.264	1.18		.227	1.30		.277	0.96		.131
No. of years Internet use	1.02		.015	0.98		.021	1.02		.022	1.03		.026	1.03		.016
Satisfied with the Netherlands	1.15		.160	0.27	**	.078	2.91	**	.644	0.91		.220	1.09		.158
Headed in right direction	0.84		.106	0.81		.165	0.54	**	.122	1.17		.254	1.08		.161
Years living in the Netherlands	1.01		.010	1.01		.015	1.02	**	.011	0.98		.023	1.02	**	.009
Dutch identity exists	1.28		.195	1.23		.345	1.31		.334	1.08		.289	1.68	**	.318
Questionnaire was interesting	2.41	**	.271	3.79	**	.797	1.56	**	.271	3.11	**	.639	2.47	**	.307
N		2134			2793			2793			2214			2762	
LR χ^2		141.33			131.19			56.88			59.9			132.27	
p		.000			.000			.000			.000			.000	
Adj R^2		.065			.126			.049			.064			.067	

Note: * $p < .10$
** $p < .05$

[1] Based on those who were asked all four questions

TABLE 9.3

Regression Predicting the Number of Words Respondents Provide

	Mean No. of Words for People Who Answered All Four Questions			Mean No. of Words for People Who Were Asked All Four Questions			Q2 Reasons Why (Dis)Satisfied With Way Things Are Going			Q5 Most Important Problems in the Netherlands			Q11 Things People Like About Living in the Netherlands			Q16 Essential Aspects of the Dutch Identity		
	SE		b	*SE*		b	*SE*		b	*SE*		b	*SE*		b	*SE*		b
Motivational statement	1.93	**	.589	2.72	**	.498	5.13	**	.887	2.09	**	.765	2.09	**	.574	1.23	**	.511
Follow-up probe	1.92	**	.594	2.09	**	.489	2.95	**	.885	3.31	**	.756	1.74	**	.571	0.94	*	.508
Follow-up probe w/ motivation	2.72	**	.601	3.28	**	.497	6.56	**	.895	4.90	**	.765	3.02	**	.584	0.69		.515
Gender (female = 1)	1.41	**	.437	1.37	**	.361	2.48	**	.643	1.64	**	.554	2.11	**	.421	1.28	**	.370
Higher education	1.33	**	.489	1.20	*	.404	1.15		.733	2.56	**	.634	1.17	**	.477	2.29	**	.419
Primary education	−0.89		.795	0.08		.630	−0.93		1.125	−2.29	**	.976	−0.37		.738	0.93		.675
Age	−0.02		.044	−0.05		.035	−0.13	**	.057	−0.01		.049	−0.02		.041	0.01		.033
Employed	−0.28		.455	−0.10		.377	0.42		.675	−0.86		.578	−0.90	**	.437	−0.67	*	.387

Married	−1.02	**	.494	−0.64		.398	−0.93		.711	−0.64		.616	−1.23		.468	−0.44		.417
No. of years Internet use	0.06		.051	0.07	*	.043	0.18	**	.071	0.06		.061	−0.01		.050	0.05		.040
Satisfied with the Netherlands	−0.69		.533	−0.72	*	.438	−1.72	**	.756	0.88		.656	−0.78		.510	0.00		.436
Headed in right direction	−1.17	**	.485	−1.21	**	.402	−2.08	**	.766	−3.87	**	.662	0.37		.469	−0.42		.437
Years living in the Netherlands	0.06		.041	0.09	**	.033	0.18	**	.053	0.10	**	.046	0.07	*	.039	0.04		.031
Dutch identity exists	0.55		.551	0.26		.454	0.81		.848	−0.16		.730	0.42		.542	1.00	**	.471
Questionnaire was interesting	3.10	**	.438	3.17	**	.363	5.36	**	.648	5.03	**	.555	3.33	**	.421	2.68	**	.376
	9.34		1.134	8.64		.939	12.57		1.609	6.86		1.370	6.85		1.098	4.81		.923
N		1393			2105			2528			2472			1944			2174	
F		8.88			14.84			14.19			16.73			10.9			9.39	
p		.000			.000			.000			.000			.000			.000	
R^2		.088			.0963			.078			.093			.078			.061	

Note: * $p < .10$
** $p < .05$

those receiving the probe providing less than one additional topic in their response. The effect is significant for the first question (1.9 vs. 1.4 topics, $t\,(262) = -3.56, p < .01$), the second question (2.7 vs. 2.1 topics, $t\,(390) = -2.93, p < .01$), and the third question (2.3 vs. 1.8 topics, $t\,(395) = -2.57, p < .01$). There are no significant differences in elaboration, although slightly more respondents elaborate on their responses when provided with the probe for three of the questions. As with the control version and the version with a motivational statement, the number of words declines as respondents progress through the survey, but the number of topics mentioned and the percentage elaborating on their response do not.

The follow-up probe significantly influences the number of words people provide, even controlling for other social and demographic characteristics, but again the increase is very small. On average, those who received the probe provide about two more words per question than those who did not (see Table 9.3). Similar to the bivariate analysis, the effect of the follow-up probe is higher for the first two open-ended questions (about three words each) but drops below two words for the third question and is less than one word more for the last question.

Because the treatment does not occur until after respondents submit their initial answer, the follow-up probe is not expected to impact responses to the initial question. There might be a carryover effect, where asking a follow-up probe after the first question affects whether people provide a response to subsequent open-ended questions. In this study, the follow-up probe does not have a significant effect on whether someone responded to all four open-ended questions, even controlling for other social and demographic characteristics in the logistic regression (see Table 9.2). The effect of the follow-up probe is significant only for the third open-ended question (receiving the follow-up probe decreases the odds of responding by a factor of .59).

As we predicted with our second hypothesis, the number of words used and the number of topics mentioned increase when a follow-up probe is added to the question. However, we did not find an effect on whether respondents elaborate on their answers.

9.4.3 What Is the Effect of a Motivational Statement With the Follow-Up Probe?

To explore the effect of the motivational statement "This question is very important to our survey" with the follow-up probe, we can compare this version (Figure 9.4) to the control version (Figure 9.1) and to the one with only a follow-up probe (Figure 9.3). Compared with the control version, the mean number of words is higher for all four questions when respondents received the motivational statement with the follow-up probe (see Table 9.1, columns c and d). However, we did not find a significant interaction effect between question, motivational statement, and follow-up probe on the length of responses in the analysis of variance. The mean number of topics is slightly larger for respondents to the version with the probe and motivation (significant only at the .10 level for the second question) than for those who received the control version (first question: 2.0 vs. 1.4 topics, t (285) = −4.13, $p < .01$; second question: 2.5 vs. 2.1 topics, t (390) = −1.96, $p < .1$; third question: 2.5 vs. 1.8 topics, t (198) = −3.86, $p < .01$; fourth question: 3.2 vs. 2.7 topics, t (284) = −2.25, $p < .05$). Again, the effect is modest, with those receiving the probe providing less than one additional topic in their response. More respondents elaborate on their response when provided with the probe and motivational statement; the difference is significant for the second (35% vs. 20%, $\chi^2(1, n = 392) = 7.09$, $p < .01$) and third questions (26% vs. 14%; $\chi^2(1, n = 397) = 4.88$, $p < .05$).

There is only one significant difference in the response rate between the two probe versions, where slightly more people who received the motivational statement responded initially to the second open-ended question (96% vs. 94%; $\chi^2(1, n = 1{,}477) = 3.96$, $p < .05$). Including the motivational statement with the follow-up probe significantly increases the percentage responding to the probe for the first and third open-ended questions and improves it slightly for the other two questions. The effect of the motivational statement with the probe is largest for the first open-ended question (46% vs. 28%; $\chi^2(1, n = 1{,}420) = 50.20$, $p < .01$), but the response rate is still 6 points higher for the third open-ended question (41% vs. 35%; $\chi^2(1, n = 1{,}118) = 4.53$, $p < .05$).

The follow-up probe with motivation also increased the mean number of words (by one to four words) than a follow-up probe alone. The analysis of variance did not show significant interaction effects between question, motivational statement, and follow-up probe on the number of words used to answer the question, but t-tests do show significant differences for the first three questions. The difference is greatest for the first open-ended question (25 vs. 21; t (1259) = −4.36, $p < 0.01$) but differed only by one word for the second question (18 vs. 17; t (1279) = −2.16, $p < 0.05$), two words for the third question (14 vs. 12; t (1015) = −2.49, $p < 0.05$), and not at all for the fourth question. As discussed earlier, the length of respondents' answers decreased as they moved through the survey. There are no significant differences in the mean number of topics. The percentage elaborating is slightly higher for those who receive the probe with motivation, but only the difference for the second open-ended question is significant (35% vs. 27%; $\chi^2(1, n = 600) = 4.12$; $p < .05$).

The linear regression model confirms that the follow-up probe significantly influences the number of words people provide, even controlling for other social and demographic characteristics. Those who received the probe with motivation provide about two to three more words on average than those who did not, and the effect is significant for the first three open-ended questions (see Table 9.3). The effect of the follow-up probe is higher than the effect of the motivational statement or probe alone, but—like with the other effects discussed—it does seem to decrease for later questions (from about six more words to five and then three).

Lastly, including a motivational statement with the follow-up probe (see Figure 9.4) seems to have more impact on the quality of responses than including it with the initial question (see Figure 9.2). The response rate is somewhat higher for three of the questions when the motivational statement is included with the initial question, but significantly so only for the third open-ended question (97% vs. 93%; $\chi^2(1, n = 1{,}122) = 6.50$; $p < .05$). Although the average number of words is slightly higher for three of the four questions when the motivational statement was included with the probe rather than with the initial question (see Table 9.1, columns b and d), only the three-word difference (18 vs. 15) for the second question is statistically significant ($t\,(1242) = -3.77$; $p < .01$). The mean number of topics mentioned is higher (but by less than one topic) for all four open-ended questions when the motivational statement is included with the follow-up probe rather than with the initial question (first question: 2.0 vs. 1.8 topics, $t\,(588) = -2.01$, $p < .05$; second question: 2.5 vs. 1.9 topics, $t\,(551) = -5.15$, $p < .01$; third question: 2.5 vs. 2.0 topics, $t\,(573) = -3.53$, $p < .01$; fourth question: 3.2 vs. 2.4 topics, $t\,(528) = -4.17$, $p < .01$). Providing the motivational statement with the follow-up probe has a significant effect on the percentage of respondents elaborating on their answers for three out of four questions, when compared to including the motivational statement with the initial question (first question: 34% vs. 17%; $\chi^2(1, n = 590) = 20.04$; $p < .01$; second question: 35% vs. 25%; $\chi^2(1, n = 589) = 6.17$; $p < .05$; third question:

26% vs. 19%; $\chi^2(1, n = 595) = 4.22$; $p < .05$). The percentage elaborating is 7 to 17 points higher when respondents receive the motivational statement with the follow-up probe rather than with the initial question.

As expected, there are no significant differences in people responding to the initial question when they receive the probe with a motivational statement compared with the control version (see Table 9.1, columns a and d). The logistic regression shows that the follow-up probe with motivation does not have a significant impact on whether someone responded to all four open-ended questions, controlling for other social and demographic characteristics (see Table 9.2). Receiving the probe with motivation decreased the odds of responding to the third question by a factor of .61 ($p < .100$).

According to the fourth hypothesis, we expect more people to respond to the question when a follow-up probe with a motivational statement is presented to the respondent rather than a follow-up probe or motivational statement alone. Adding a motivational statement to the follow-up probe does increase the percentage responding initially, compared with a follow-up probe alone. On the other hand, for some of the questions more people respond to the question when the motivational statement is included with the initial question instead of with the follow-up probe. Furthermore, when a motivational statement is included with the follow-up probe, we see increases in the length of responses as well as the number of topics mentioned and the number of respondents who elaborate on their responses, compared with not providing a motivational statement or including it with the initial question (confirming the second part of the fourth hypothesis).

9.4.4 Can Motivation Encourage Nonrespondents to Answer Open-Ended Questions?

Looking at whether people who did not respond to the initial question (ranging from 2% to 8% for each question) provided a response after receiving the nonrespondent version allows us to test the effect of this treatment on people who are less motivated to respond to open-ended questions. The nonrespondent version requested that people provide an answer, said the question is important to the survey, and repeated the initial question (see Figure 9.5). Strikingly, between 62% and 78% of those who did not respond to the initial question provided a response to the nonrespondent version; however, the quality of those responses was

TABLE 9.4

How Does a Follow-Up Probe With Motivational Statement Influence Nonrespondents?

	Q2	Q5	Q11	Q16
n	106 (4%)	70 (2%)	88 (4%)	217 (8%)
% responding to probe	76%	63%	78%	62%
Mean number of words	8	3	8	3
Mean number of topics	0.9	0.8	1.1	1.0
% elaborating after probe	12	7	13	1

Note: Based on those who did not respond to the initial question.

fairly low (see Table 9.4). The mean number of words ranges from three to eight, respondents provide only about one topic on average in their response, and very few respondents elaborate on that topic. These results confirm our fifth hypothesis: The follow-up probe including the motivational statement does encourage nonrespondents to provide an answer.

9.4.5 What Other Factors Influence Whether People Respond and the Quality of Responses They Provide?

The regression models show that one of the largest predictors of response and response quality is whether people thought the questionnaire was interesting. Saying the subject of the questionnaire was interesting increased the odds of responding by a factor of 2.4 (ranging from 1.6 to 3.8 for an individual question). Similarly, those who thought the questionnaire was interesting provided three more words on average (ranging from three to five more words for an individual question). The effect of questionnaire interest did vary for the individual questions, but the effect was stable as respondents progressed through the survey and it was the strongest predictor in our models.

Education was also a significant predictor of response and the number of words used. Having completed college or university increased the odds of responding to all four questions by a factor of 2 and resulted in slightly longer responses (only about one more word on average). Females were not more likely to respond on average but provided about one more word per question than males. Being employed slightly decreased the odds of responding to all four questions. Other factors, such as satisfaction with the Netherlands, whether the country is headed in the right direction, and whether a Dutch identity exists, had significant impacts on questions that addressed these themes. In the overall model, those who said the Netherlands was headed in the right direction provided fewer words in their response. These results show that the third hypothesis is true: Interest in the questionnaire and education do influence who responds and the length of the responses.

9.5 CONCLUSIONS

Overall, we demonstrate how the interactive nature of the Internet allows for features commonly used in surveys, motivational statements and follow-up probes, to be incorporated into Internet surveys. Although research in this area is only beginning, our results and those from other studies suggest that motivational statements and follow-up probes can improve response rates and the quality of answers provided to open-ended questions in Internet surveys, although the effects are rather modest. This study finds that the combined use of a follow-up probe with a motivational statement had a somewhat larger impact on response rates and quality and can be effective in eliciting response from those who do not provide a response initially (although the quality of these responses from initial nonrespondents is often very low).

The influence of these features seems to be greatest the first time they are used and more modest when incorporated on subsequent questions. Several factors could be influencing this finding. The question topics in our and other studies varied, the same motivational statement was used across all four questions, and the follow-up probes were also similar. However, the finding that the effect is largest the first time the feature is used could mean that the effect is different when respondents receive the treatment early versus later in the questionnaire and/or that the effect decreases after repeated use of the feature. Future studies should try to disentangle these effects, but for now researchers should use caution when including motivational statements or follow-up probes multiple times in a survey because the effect seems to be largest the first time they are employed. Future research should also test different motivational statements, vary the motivational statement used in the survey, and experiment with other types of follow-up probes to see if they have smaller or larger impacts on responses.

The findings from this study are especially important because of the difficulty in getting quality responses to open-ended questions in self-administered surveys. Maximizing response quality and encouraging response, even among those who are less motivated, is essential for the results to be accurate and representative. In general, our research shows that the quality of responses provided to open-ended questions tends to decline as respondents progress through the survey, regardless of whether motivational statements or follow-up probes are included. Thus, researchers should employ a variety of design strategies to improve the quality of responses to open-ended questions in Internet surveys, but these types of questions should be reserved for a few key topics where high-quality answers in the respondents' own words are necessary.

In our study, education is a significant factor in whether people responded to the open-ended questions: Those who had completed college or university education were more likely to respond and provide longer responses than those with lower education levels. Perhaps even more important, interest in the subject of the questionnaire had the largest impact on whether people responded and the length of the responses, and in most cases the effect of questionnaire interest was even stronger than the effect of the experimental comparisons tested here. These findings are similar to those reported by Holland and Christian (2009), where more people who were very interested in the subject of the question provided a response and their responses were of higher quality.

Interest is an important factor in Internet surveys, as it is easy for respondents to quit and abandon the survey. More studies are demonstrating the importance of interest in understanding whether people respond to survey requests and individual questions. Further research is needed to understand how Internet surveys can be designed to improve participation among those who are interested but also to analyze how responses can be improved among those who are less interested so that responses to open-ended questions can be more representative.

One of the most promising capabilities of Internet surveys is the ability to integrate interactive features into the survey that can engage respondents and help them stay motivated to complete the survey and provide quality responses. Although there are some limitations to how flexible these features can be compared with live interviewers, new Internet technologies allow for a more continuous and dynamic interaction between the respondent and the survey instrument. As technology continues to evolve (and people's bandwidths increase), there will be even greater possibilities for increasing interaction with survey respondents and combining the benefits of self-administered and interviewer-administered surveys in a multimedia platform.

REFERENCES

Best, S. J. & Krueger, B. S. (2004). *Internet data collection*. Thousand Oaks, CA: Sage Publications.

Billiet, J. & Loosveldt, G. (1988). Improvement of the quality of responses to factual survey questions by interviewer training. *Public Opinion Quarterly, 52*, 190–211.

Cannell, C. F., Miller, P. V., & Oksenberg, L. (1981). Research on interviewing techniques. *Sociological Methodology, 12*, 389–437.

Conrad, F. G., Couper, M. P., & Tourangeau, R. (2003). *Interactive features in Web surveys.* Paper presented at Joint Meetings of the American Statistical Association (ASA), San Francisco, CA.

Conrad, F. G., Couper, M. P., Tourangeau, R., & Peytchev, A. (2006). Use and non-use of clarification features in Web surveys. *Journal of Official Statistics, 22*, 245–269.

Conrad, F. G. & Schober, M. F. (2005). Promoting uniform question understanding in today's and tomorrow's surveys. *Journal of Official Statistics, 21*, 215–231.

Couper, M. P. (2005). Technology trends in survey data collection. *Social Science Computer Review, 23*(4), 486–501.

Couper, M. P. (2008). *Designing effective Web surveys.* New York: Cambridge University Press.

Dillman, D. A., Smyth, J. D., & Christian, L. M. (2009). *Internet, mail, and mixed-mode surveys: The tailored design method.* Hoboken, NJ: John Wiley & Sons.

Fricker, S., Galesic, M., Tourangeau, R., & Yan, T. (2005). An experimental comparison of Web and telephone surveys. *Public Opinion Quarterly, 69*, 370–392.

Groves, R., Fowler, F. J. Jr., Couper, M. P. Lepkowski, J. M., Singer, E., & Tourangeau, R. (2005). *Survey methodology*. New York: John Wiley & Sons.

Holland, J. L. & Christian, L. M. (2009). The influence of topic interest and interactive probing on responses to open-ended questions in Web surveys. *Social Science Computer Review, 27*, 196–212.

Miller, P. V. & Cannell, C. F. (1982). A study of experimental techniques for telephone interviewing. *Public Opinion Quarterly, 46*, 250–269.

Ramirez, C., Sharp, K., & Foster, L. (2000). *Mode effects in an Internet-paper survey of employees.* Paper presented at the annual conference of the American Association for Public Opinion Research (AAPOR), Portland, Oregon.

Schaefer, D. & Dillman, D. A. (1998). Development of a standard e-mail methodology: Results of an experiment. *Public Opinion Quarterly, 62*, 378–397.

Schuman, H. & Presser, S. (1979). The open and closed question. *American Sociological Review*, *44*, 692–712.

Smyth, J. D., Dillman, D. A., Christian, L. M., & McBride, M. (2009). Open-ended questions in Web surveys: Can increasing the size of answer boxes and providing extra verbal instructions improve response quality? *Public Opinion Quarterly*, *73*, 325–337.

10

Measuring Attitudes Toward Controversial Issues in Internet Surveys: Order Effects of Open and Closed Questioning[1]

Peter Ester
Rotterdam University
Rotterdam, the Netherlands

Henk Vinken
Pyrrhula BV, Social Research Network
Tilburg, the Netherlands

10.1 INTRODUCTION

The accurate representation of the latent by the manifest is the essence of social survey research. The reliable and valid measurement of cognitions, affections, intentions, and reported behavior is what professional survey research is all about (Blalock, 1979; Carmines & Zeller, 1979). The classic problem in survey methodology, however, is how to make sure that our measures really tap a genuine correspondence between the manifest and the latent, between overt response and underlying motivation (Russ-Eft, 1980). In other words: "Is the measurement procedure isomorphic to reality?" (Kerlinger, 1964, p. 417). Or more simply, how do we know that we measure what we want to measure? This question is particularly relevant for psychological and sociological constructs that cannot be directly observed. There is not much sense in asking respondents directly whether they are ethnocentric, politically alienated, cognitively sophisticated, or empathic.

We need measurement instruments, often complex ones, to assess such multidimensional attitudinal and personality concepts. Survey research aims at making the latent manifest, at making the unobservable observable (Babbie, 1973). When the latent construct is pretty straightforward, such as a soda preference or one's favorite singer-songwriter, the measurement instrument can be rather straightforward too. This especially holds when the process of making the latent manifest is not related to social desirability and does not pose any psychological cost or threat to the respondent.

Establishing an accurate correspondence between the latent and the manifest is much more complicated in case of psychologically or socially sensitive topics (Lee, 1993; Lensvelt-Mulders, 2008; Peeters, 2005; Renzetti & Lee, 1993). Questions are considered sensitive "when they are about private, stressful or sacred issues, and when answering them tends to generate emotional responses, or potential fear of stigmatization on the part of the person or his/her social group" (Lensvelt-Mulders, 2008, p. 478). Asking respondents about illicit drug use, drinking habits, cheating, tax fraud, or involvement in crime commonly results in underreporting of such behaviors. On such topics, priming trustful self-disclosure is a major matter (Rasinski, Willis, Baldwin, Yeh, & Lee, 1999). Response bias will be stronger in a face-to-face interview situation, as the presence of the interviewer in a nonanonymous interview context will increase the probability of social desirability. The absence of an interviewer effect is one of the greatest advantages of Internet surveys over other survey modes (Lozar Manfreda & Vehovar, 2008). This advantage is particularly significant in studying the public's attitudes toward socially sensitive issues. And knowing people's attitudes toward sensitive issues matters. In a consensus-based representative democracy it is crucial to know how populations really feel about sensitive social topics such as abortion, euthanasia, marijuana use, or positive discrimination (Dekker & Ester, 1989). Policy support on those topics depends on social acceptance by the public, which in turn is rooted in deeper (more latent) cognitions, affections, intentions, and dispositions. A serious misunderstanding of the public opinion climate and public policy support may generate public reactance (Brehm & Brehm, 1981). In studying attitudes toward sensitive issues, survey researchers have to meet the challenge of how to measure latent beliefs and affects in a reliable and valid way (Lensvelt-Mulders, 2008; Lensvelt-Mulders, Hox, Van der Heijden, & Maas, 2005; Renzetti & Lee, 1993; Tourangeau & Smith, 1998;

Sieber & Stanley, 1988). This challenge is particularly demanding regarding a specific subclass of sensitive topics: socially controversial issues. Such issues signify pressing social questions that are highly debated and on which the public is strongly divided. These issues can be related to intergroup clashes on fundamental social, political, or religious values, to basic ethical controversies in a society, or to distributive policy programs for various social and ethnic minority groups. Examples of such social issues are tolerance of sexual minorities, genetic manipulation, medical experimentation, social adaptation of religious subcultures, the role and impact of Islam, opening the borders to immigrants, or the war on terrorism.

It is vital for politicians and policy makers to know the public opinion climate on such controversial issues. How divided is the public, and among and between which social groups is dissensus peaking? It is an important role of professional social survey researchers to give an accurate picture of public attitudes toward socially controversial issues and their main determinants. A wrong understanding by political actors of the public opinion climate on such issues may lead to social policies that lack overall public support and may intensify social antagonism (Dekker & Ester, 1989). In this chapter we report an experiment we conducted with the LISS panel on measuring attitudes toward controversial issues with a specific emphasis on order effects of open-ended and closed questions.

10.2 BACKGROUND

Measuring and monitoring beliefs about controversial issues is not an innocent exercise, as it has wider societal and political relevance and can greatly impact the debate on such issues. Here the issue of validity is obviously important, not least in terms of mode effects. Self-administered Internet surveys have some major validity advantages over other survey modes in studying attitudes toward controversial issues. The anonymous interview setting, the absence of interviewer error, and the privacy of the response situation lead to more self-disclosure and less social desirability bias (Weisband & Kiesler, 1996). There are fewer barriers to expressing one's basic beliefs about issues that divide the public and are widely debated. Moreover, the use of the computer in Internet surveys yield a higher level of self-control and self-efficacy, which are important features in thinking about how to respond to controversial issues. In this sense Internet surveys have major benefits over other data collection modes in surveying attitudes toward controversial issues (Couper, 2000; Dillman, 2007). Anonymity and privacy decrease the psychological costs of really saying what one thinks about topics that are highly controversial. The interview context and the use of the computer lead to quite direct answers as well and do not prompt response bias toward strongly nuanced or balanced middle-of-the-road responses. But there is more to it. The way we measure attitudes toward controversial issues is also related to the use of open-ended or closed questions. In the Dutch CentERdata Millennium Survey that we conducted in 1999, substantial differences between open-ended and closed questions were observed concerning attitudes toward future developments in Dutch society (Ester & Vinken, 2001). The answers to the closed questions pictured a rather stable, optimistic public opinion climate. Yet the answers to the open-ended questions were considerably different: Large shares of respondents extensively commented on future trends, displaying explicit and unfiltered fears for the future. Many of those fears related to foreigners and the impact of Islam, topics that turned out to be very sensitive and controversial. The following years in the Netherlands (and elsewhere in Europe) were politically highly turbulent. Much of the turmoil was directly related to the fear-evoking—and at that time strongly controversial—issues already tapped by the open-ended questions in our survey. Thus, a substantial difference between answers to open-ended and closed questions was observed. It appears that the combination of Internet interviewing and open-ended questioning is especially suited for tapping beliefs on controversial issues. It permits the respondent to phrase his or her thoughts, hopes, fears, trust, despair, confidence, and anger in a self-controlled and anonymous way (Ester & Vinken, 2001). The interview context enables the respondent to enter the debate on controversial issues on his or her own terms. As a result, this combination of Internet interviewing and open-ended questions may be one of the best survey tools for making the latent manifest when studying the public's attitudes toward controversial topics. The advantages and disadvantages of the use of open-ended vis-à-vis closed questions is, of course, a much discussed issue in survey research. In fact, it is as old as survey methodology itself (Converse, 1984; Schuman & Presser, 1981). And the discussion still continues (Schuman, 2006; Langer & Cohen, 2006). Our position in this debate is—as indicated above—that the use of open-ended questions in Internet surveys is a promising method to tap deeper motivations and feelings, especially with respect to sensitive issues. In this sense, using such questions may evoke richer responses (Schaefer & Dillman, 1998; Kwak & Radler, 2002; Schwarz, 1996). The disadvantages of open-ended questions include higher response burdens on the respondent, the cost aspect of coding answers to open-ended questions, and selective response rates according to strength of attitudes (Bosnjak, 2001a, 2001b; Knapp & Heidingsfelder, 2001; Lozar Manfreda & Vehovar, 2008). The final issue to be discussed with respect to the validity of measurements of attitudes toward controversial topics is question-order effects. Should such questions be posed at the beginning of the questionnaire or at the end? Should they be preceded or followed by more general or more specific questions on such topics? The issue of order effects has been intensively discussed and studied in survey research and generally shows that preceding questions can indeed influence answers to later questions (McFarland, 1981; Moore, 2002; Schuman & Presser, 1981; Sudman, Bradburn, & Schwarz, 1996; Schwarz, Knäuper, Oyserman, & Stich, 2008; Tourangeau, Rips, & Rasinski, 2000). By applying a cognitive information-processing approach, Schwarz and his colleagues argue that preceding questions do affect inferences made by respondents on later questions and can create a benchmark against which a topic is evaluated. Strack, Martin, and Schwarz (1988) give a clarifying example. In a study among students they included two questions: (1) "How satisfied are you with your life?" and (2) "How often do you have a date?" Given this order, it turned out that the two answers were not statistically related, and so one would conclude that overall life satisfaction has nothing to do with dating success. But reversing the question order led to a strong relationship: The more often students had dates, the higher their satisfaction with life. Here one would conclude that dating success is markedly associated with life satisfaction. It is a prime example of a question-order effect (cf. Schwarz, 2001). This example illustrates that respondents tend to answer to more general questions based on a more specific answer that was given to a preceding question. Respondents' judgments of an attitude object depend on the way this object is represented and the availability of an evaluation standard. Both representations (topic and standard) can be influenced by context information available when respondents are prompted to make an evaluation. Information retrieved by earlier questions is one of the sources that may influence such evaluations (Schwarz et al., 2008, pp. 28–31). The answer to a second question is based on the information activated by a preceding question. Placing general or abstract questions before more specific ones or vice versa can yield rather different results. In the literature on survey question-order effects, two types of question-order effects are distinguished: consistency effects and contrast effects (Schuman & Presser, 1981). *Consistency effects*—some authors speak of assimilation effects—imply that responses to a later question are brought closer to the responses to an earlier question. *Contrast effects* refer to the phenomenon of responses becoming more different as a result of question order (Schuman & Presser, 1981, pp. 27–28). A general rule is that if a question refers to the same attitude object or topic as a preceding question, this will result in greater judgmental similarity. Such a consistency effect implies that the answer to a preceding question guides the answer to a subsequent and similar question in the same direction. In fact, respondents' answers to more general questions are influenced by their answers on more specific (related) preceding questions (Schuman, 1992). Attribution takes place in which attitudes toward sequentially ordered objects or topics generate assimilation. For example, a survey first asks about attitudes toward freedom of speech and next about freedom of speech for anti-Islam organizations. A consistency or assimilation effect points at the likelihood that, for example, a positive attitude toward freedom of speech in general also prompts a positive attitude toward such rights for anti-Islam groups. No groups are excluded from this general rule of freedom of speech. The first judgment is included in the second one. If the first question had been omitted, the answer to the second question probably would have been less positive: A smaller share of respondents would have favored freedom of speech rights for such groups. A contrast effect occurs when, for example, a positive attitude toward freedom of speech is followed by a negative attitude toward freedom of speech for anti-Islam organizations. This example also nicely illustrates the working of context effects: Asking the question about granting freedom of speech rights to anti-Islam groups first will lead to a less positive attitude toward a general rule of freedom of speech in a subsequent question. The underlying psychological process is a cognitive priming in which information retrieved (consciously or unconsciously) by a previous question is used in thinking of an answer to a related next question (Strack, 1992). It activates judgmental schemata that became available through answering a previous question.

In this chapter we are particularly interested in the way these context effects influence attitudes toward controversial issues in Internet surveys. The key issue is that changing the order of substantively related questions also changes the information these questions bring to mind (Schwarz et al., 2008). Modifying the order of questions implies a difference in the cognitive cues provided by prior items, which in turn affect responses to subsequent items. The key research question, in summary, is whether we can assess the effects of presenting open-ended and closed questions on controversial topics in varying orders, and if so, how large are these effects?

10.3 DESIGN AND IMPLEMENTATION

In October 2008 about 1,580 LISS panel members were presented with a questionnaire on future expectations (see Chapter 4 in this volume for more on the LISS panel). Somewhat more than 1,050 respondents completed the questionnaire (a response rate of 67%). This 2008 questionnaire consisted of a selection of questions from the CentERdata Millennium Survey mentioned above (see Ester & Vinken, 2001). The central theme of the 2008 survey, as explained to the respondents, was about their future expectations for the next 25 years. A key division was made between expectations about the future of Dutch society and those about their own personal future. Central issues dealt with affection toward the future (optimism/pessimism), the extension of their expectations (how far ahead they look into the future), and control mechanisms as regards the future (e.g., adapting to circumstances versus changing those circumstances in order to fulfill one's dreams). Another stream of questions dealt with societal issues or problems that Dutch society may face. A 21-item question, for instance, tapped optimism on specific societal trends, such as the environment, (un)employment, migration, and so on. Respondents indicated whether they thought the trends would decrease, remain stable, or increase. See the appendix for the exact wording of the questions used here.

In the original order of the questionnaire, respondents were first asked to indicate their affection toward the future (see question Q1 in the appendix), followed by an open-ended question on the reasons for this optimism or pessimism (Q2). These questions were then repeated for the respondent's personal future in the next 25 years (not listed in the appendix). After these questions they were asked to rate 21 societal issues and problems more precisely to indicate whether they thought these phenomena would decrease, stay the same, or increase in the Netherlands in the next 25 years (Q3 in the appendix). In an experimental design of this survey we changed the order and first asked for the societal issue rating (Q3) before asking for affection and the motivation of this affection (Q1 and Q2).

In order to examine in more detail whether there are order effects and what these effects entail substantively, we need to code open-ended questions. In this survey, for instance, if we knew what reasons respondents gave for their optimism, we could quantitatively check whether the prevalence of these reasons varied across the two questionnaires: the original order and the changed order. The more precise question, then, is whether affection toward the future and the reasons given for a specific future affection were different in the original format, without any prompting from a long list of all kinds of societal issues or problems, as compared to the changed-order format, in which this list was provided and evaluated first.

For several weeks two coders separately worked with a total of six open-ended questions in the 2008 questionnaire (not all used in this chapter). For the coding process they used the original list of 21 items (Q3 in the appendix). If the answer did not fit these categories, they (independently) created a new category. In some cases answers were lengthy and covered more than one issue. In that case the coders could choose to pick the first issue raised or to use the issue to which the bulk of the answer pointed regardless of its position; the coders reported that they mostly chose the second option, focusing on the general tendency in the long answers and creating a new coding category if necessary. After the answers to each question were coded, the codings were compared between the two coders and a match ratio was calculated. The average overlap in coding across the six open-ended questions was 83%. The mismatches were subsequently discussed between the coders and when necessary with the authors of this chapter. After the discussion a final code was chosen (not necessarily the coding of one of the two coders).

In line with the central theme of the questionnaire (future expectations), the codes covered general trends and dispositions, but also sometimes some very specific phenomena. General trends and dispositions, for instance, might refer to "individualization," "freedom," or "respect," but also to "all is well, stable, good" or "things will always get worse." Specific phenomena were also mentioned, such as "traffic jams," "tensions between religions," and "environmental degradation."

Below we address one key open-ended question: reasons people have for being optimistic or pessimistic about the future of the Netherlands in the next 25 years. The respondents were given as much room as they needed to elaborate on the reasons for their optimism or pessimism. In general, most people took the opportunity to comment extensively on their affection regarding the future of Dutch society. The general overlap between the coders on this question was somewhat lower than average: 75%. Probably this was due to the fact that this open-ended question was the first in the sequence of six. For this one, the coding process was more elaborate than it was for the other open-ended questions. It consisted of three phases in which the coders first worked separately, then compared differences in coding categories and compiled a new full coding list, and then again worked separately with this new list before discussing and integrating their matching and nonmatching codings. After the coding process a file was saved that includes the original codings per coder as well as the final agreed-upon coding. The two coders also wrote a short reflection on the coding process. Their impression was that the respondents were predominantly worried about economic issues, especially about pension problems. Issues related to the integration of immigrants in Dutch society, climate change, or radicalism and terrorism seemed to be underrated, the coders noted to their surprise.

10.4 RESULTS

Half of the sample answered the questionnaire in the original order: They were first asked to rate their degree of optimism/pessimism about the future of the Netherlands in the next 25 years, and then to elaborate on the reasons for this optimism/pessimism, before rating trends for the Netherlands in the next 25 years based on a long list of societal issues and problems. About 32% of these Dutch respondents reported being optimistic or very optimistic. When the respondents first rated several societal issues offered to them in a closed question, the proportion of optimists declined to almost 25%. On average, respondents in both groups were not optimistic but also not pessimistic; most of them were neutral.

The reasons for the degree of optimism and pessimism were quite diverse: About 28 different categories of reasons could be identified, some of which were mentioned by just one respondent (i.e., "discrimination"). A large share of the respondents, however, could not express any well-defined reason for their level of optimism or pessimism. They (again) gave a neutral answer, said they did not know what to answer, or responded that they had no particular reason. In Tables 10.1 to 10.4 such answers are summarized under the heading of "no substantive answer." Relatively large groups were generally positive about the way Dutch society was or would be developing: "We're doing great in the Netherlands"; "Isn't everything going well at the moment? We hope this will continue"; "We have a strong country, even though there is a financial crisis. I believe things are not that bad here"; "All is well organized here"; "Up until now everything only improved. I think all the 'doom thinking' is caused by the media"; "I trust the Dutch spirit, including the trade-oriented spirit and the political spirit and the Dutch population." Besides these generic optimists there were those who stressed future economic disparities: "Because poverty rises, at this moment too, and I see no change in the coming years, at most a worsening"; "Large difference between rich and poor"; "Disparity rich-poor will increase, as will discrimination, and I see a growing impact of Islam and the loss of Christian civilization"; "Everything only gets more expensive. Incomes hardly rise. Finding a job becomes more difficult with getting older"; "Listen to the news reports. Among others: the banking crisis"; "There is a financial crisis now. One will have learned from mistakes and work toward an improved economy. At least, I hope so"; "I think the luxury in which we lived was too much. Several holidays, wasting things, there was no limit." Another group of respondents emphasized an unspecified or generic form of pessimism about the future of Dutch society: "Degradation of the moral, mentality"; "It is all about façade, the fundament of politics and deceit"; "Society changes and especially hardens"; "I think the Netherlands pauperizes in several domains"; "Society becomes, in my view, more egoistic, violent, intolerant, and disrespectful"; "All pretty promises are a beautiful façade"; "Because I think things can only get worse; if we look at the present government, things already get much worse." Only small numbers of respondents specifically mentioned ethnic and/or religious tensions as reasons for their optimism or (mostly) their pessimism: "Because a large share of the Dutch population sees we have to reduce immigration and to send as many as possible

TABLE 10.1

Self-Mentioned Issues

	Economic Disparities	Ethnic, Religious Tensions	Generic Optimism	Generic Pessimism	Other Issues	No Substantive Answer	*n*	%
Original order	17	3	21	14	8	37	512	48
Changed order	11	4	18	13	8	46	545	52
n	147	38	205	144	86	437	1057	
%	14	4	19	14	8	41		100

Note: Cramer's V: .117 ($p = .013$).

TABLE 10.2

Optimism Original Order: Before Evaluating 21 Societal Issues

Reasons (Right) Versus Optimism (Below) in %	Economic Disparities	Ethnic, Religious Tensions	Generic Optimism	Generic Pessimism	Other Issues	No Substantive Answer	*n*	%
1. Very optimistic	0	0	6	0	0	1	7	2
2. Optimistic	25	6	84	12	18	6	138	30
3. Neutral	44	41	9	27	43	92	219	47
4. Pessimistic	29	53	1	59	40	1	96	21
5. Very pessimistic	2	0	0	1	0	0	3	1
n	87	17	108	73	40	138	463	
%	19	4	23	16	9	30		100

Note: η (optimism dependent): .656; Cramer's V: .454 ($p = .000$); F-value (ANOVA average): 68.957 ($p = .000$).

TABLE 10.3

Optimism Changed Order: After Evaluating 21 Societal Issues

Reasons (Right) Versus Optimism (Below) in %	Economic Disparities	Ethnic, Religious Tensions	Generic Optimism	Generic Pessimism	Other Issues	No Substantive Answer	*n*	%
1. Very optimistic	0	0	0	0	2	0	1	0
2. Optimistic	20	10	79	7	24	5	116	24
3. Neutral	27	19	21	31	22	91	244	50
4. Pessimistic	50	62	0	58	50	4	115	24
5. Very pessimistic	3	10	0	4	2	1	9	2
n	60	21	97	71	46	190	485	
%	12	4	20	15	10	39		100

Note: η (optimism dependent): .630; Cramer's *V*: .466 ($p = .000$); *F*-value (ANOVA average): 63.091 ($p = .000$).

TABLE 10.4

Average Optimism

Means	Economic Disparities	Ethnic, Religious Tensions	Generic Optimism	Generic Pessimism	Other Issues	No Substantive Answer	All
Original order	3.09	3.47	2.06	3.49	3.23	2.94	2.89
Changed order	3.37	3.71	2.21	3.59	3.26	3.01	3.03
η	.171	.171	.178	.070	.021	.096	.092
F-value	4.377	1.084	6.622	.693	.039	3.018	8.021
p	.038	.305	.011	.407	.845	.083	.005

back to their own country"; "Although I am not against foreigners, I think these people will disrupt the peace in the Netherlands"; "It is an uncertain world in which we live. We have become a refuge for foreigners, which means we will be in a minority"; "Because of the intolerance that keeps increasing as too many people are allowed to enter our country."

We first examine whether different societal issues were mentioned depending on the position of the open-ended question: before (original order) or after (experimental order) a 21-item list of these issues. This is not the case, as Table 10.1 indicates. The proportions of respondents mentioning economic disparities and of the generic optimists declined somewhat, but these shifts were not very strong. What is striking is the increase in the number of people who provided no substantive answer. In the originally ordered questionnaire the latter group represented 37% of the subsample; in the changed-order questionnaire that was 46%. After digesting a long list of problems, a fair share of respondents apparently were less apt to name a substantively specified future issue, such as economic, ethnic, or religious problems, that might affect the future of Dutch society. Having seen the list seemed to neutralize the ability to identify one focal future problem. This is in line with theory (e.g., Schwarz et al., 2008). Theory expects respondents to have more difficulty in mentioning specific problems in an answer to a generally phrased question (like the open-ended question) if they first have seen a highly specific question, such as the detailed 21-item list presented here, compared to the reverse situation. They will interpret the general question as referring only to concepts that have not been mentioned before. The list of issues reduces their opportunity to mention issues in general.

Except—unsurprisingly—for the generic optimists, all respondents who gave substantive reasons were on average pessimistic about the future of the Netherlands. Clearly this pessimism deepened when respondents were presented with the list of 21 societal issues and problems first, that is, before they were asked for their level of optimism/pessimism and the reasons for that. This is also to be expected: Respondents were likely to report more pessimism after having seen the full list of societal problems. Comparing Tables 10.2 and 10.3, one can discern that pessimism rose among those stressing economic disparities and those who focused on ethnic and religious tensions; pessimism also rose among those who were generically pessimistic and even those who were generically optimistic. It rose significantly overall, as Table 10.4 shows, as well as among those who emphasized economic disparities and those who displayed general optimism. Presenting respondents with a long list of potential future problems therefore seemed to increase pessimism about the future both among respondents in general and among specific groups of respondents (groups who focused on economic issues, and people who displayed an optimistic disposition). Yet there are reasons to be modest about drawing strong conclusions. Presenting problems first does seem to influence affection levels related to the future (such as the level of optimism) of respondents, but when checking associational measures (see, e.g., the Cramer's *V* and η), we cannot make very bold assessments. All η's are well below 0.25, indicating that changing the order in the questionnaire—that is, first triggering respondents by presenting them with an extensive list of societal problems—did contribute (far) less than 5% to the explanation of the observed changes in affection toward the future.

The weak associational measures are reasons to doubt the effects of changing questionnaire order. The previously mentioned rising share of respondents without a substantive answer adds to this doubt, as does the increasing share of respondents who were neutral instead of optimistic or pessimistic. Instead of giving respondents reasons to be optimistic or pessimistic or giving them ideas about what problems might be the most significant issues for the future, presenting a list of future problems made them less affectionately outspoken and less issue-focused when assessing their own affection toward the future.

There are several other ways to address questionnaire order effects in our study. We can attempt to trace the overlap in the self-mentioned societal issues that served to underpin people's optimism or pessimism versus the issues offered to the respondents from the 21-item list mentioned above. Does it matter if respondents first saw and evaluated this long list of problems? Table 10.5 to Table 10.7 provide the empirical answers for a selection of issues from the 21-item list: unemployment, poverty, tension between religions, economic growth, criminality, and tension between ethnic groups. These items were selected from the long list because most of them, except perhaps economic growth, had a substantial share of respondents who thought these phenomena would be on the rise in the future of the Netherlands, thus enabling us to perform more detailed analyses. In Tables 10.5 and 10.6 one can discern self-mentioned issues in the columns and the selection of the offered issues on the lines. Table 10.5 mentions the issue overlap before respondents saw the 21-item list (original order), Table 10.6 after they were presented with this list.

TABLE 10.5

Original Order: Before Evaluating 21 Societal Issues

Self-Mentioned (Right) Versus Offered Issues (Below) (% 3 = Increase)	Economic Disparities	Ethnic, Religious Tensions	Generic Optimism	Generic Pessimism	Other Issues	No Substantive Answer	*n*	%	Cramer's *V*
Unemployment	21	4	15	19	7	33	206	41	.137 (.044)
Poverty	19	5	13	19	8	35	274	55	.196 (.000)
Tension between religions	20	5	15	18	8	34	282	58	.192 (.000)
Economic growth	17	0	32	9	5	37	129	26	.224 (.000)
Criminality	20	4	14	19	9	35	303	61	.199 (.000)
Tension between ethnic groups	20	5	14	19	8	34	298	61	.198 (.000)

Note: Original format offered issues 1 = decrease, 2 = stable, 3 = increase, 4 = never thought about (missing); *p*-value in parentheses.

TABLE 10.6

Changed Order: After Evaluating 21 Societal Issues

Self-Mentioned (Right) Versus Offered Issues (Below) (% 3 = Increase)	Economic Disparities	Ethnic, Religious Tensions	Generic Optimism	Generic Pessimism	Other Issues	No Substantive Answer	*n*	%	Cramer's *V*
Unemployment	17	6	14	17	6	41	218	41	.165 (.001)
Poverty	13	3	14	17	9	45	339	63	.158 (.003)
Tension between religions	12	5	13	17	7	47	325	61	.184 (.000)
Economic growth	2	4	26	8	14	46	104	20	.201 (.000)
Criminality	13	5	15	16	7	44	364	68	.154 (.005)
Tension between ethnic groups	12	5	15	16	8	44	372	70	.178 (.000)

Note: Original format offered issues 1 = decrease, 2 = stable, 3 = increase, 4 = never thought about (missing); *p*-value in parentheses.

TABLE 10.7

Average Trend Perception in Six Selected Offered Issues

Self-Mentioned (Right) Versus Offered Issues (Below) (Mean)		**Economic Disparities**	**Ethnic, Religious Tensions**	**Generic Optimism**	**Generic Pessimism**	**Other Issues**	**No Substantive Answer**	**All**
Unemployment	Original order	2.36	2.47	2.04	2.40	2.21	2.21	2.24
	Changed order	2.47	2.32	2.08	2.36	1.91	2.17	2.19
	η	.070	.108	.026	.031	.191	.031	.028
	p	.401	.532	.719	.715	.084	.535	.375
Poverty	Original order	2.50	2.76	2.14	2.61	2.50	2.44	2.43
	Changed order	2.68	2.25	2.31	2.76	2.57	2.53	2.53
	η	.139	.356	.117	.123	.050	.065	.075
	p	.095	.031	.095	.144	.658	.184	.015
Tension between religions	Original order	2.55	2.76	2.21	2.71	2.46	2.48	2.48
	Changed order	2.57	2.70	2.24	2.76	2.35	2.57	2.52
	η	.010	.058	.020	.050	.078	.067	.033
	p	.902	.732	.778	.555	.476	.174	.297

Economic growth	Original order	1.87	1.29	2.27	1.62	1.84	1.95	1.93
	Changed order	1.39	1.95	1.96	1.60	2.00	1.88	1.81
	η	.321	.490	.210	.016	.101	.050	.075
	p	.000	.002	.003	.850	.365	.313	.016
Criminality	Original order	2.64	2.53	2.31	2.75	2.60	2.58	2.56
	Changed order	2.75	2.86	2.51	2.80	2.44	2.63	2.64
	η	.096	.292	.161	.055	.117	.047	.071
	p	.248	.075	.022	.513	.285	.337	.024
Tension between ethnic groups	Original order	2.60	2.82	2.30	2.80	2.54	2.56	2.55
	Changed order	2.72	2.90	2.47	2.86	2.49	2.63	2.64
	η	.101	.092	.131	.072	.035	.060	.074
	p	.225	.587	.065	.397	.755	.223	.019

Note: Average of offered issues 1 = decrease, 2 = stable, 3 = increase, 4 = never thought about (missing).

Looking at Table 10.5, we can note that about a fifth of the respondents who spontaneously mentioned economic disparities as a reason for their optimism/pessimism, before evaluating the long list, thought that all the issues selected here would increase in importance in the future, including economic growth. Those who first mentioned ethnic and religious tensions themselves hardly saw increasing problems. The generic optimists most clearly focused on economic growth among the issues offered (and selected for analysis here). The generic pessimists were much like those who stressed economic disparities except that a far less substantial group supported the expectation that economic growth was likely to occur in the future. The strongest support for all the trends mentioned was from those who did not express any substantive answer concerning their optimism or pessimism—about a third of them thought these issues would be on the rise. Taking account of the associational measures (especially by zooming in on Cramer's *V*s of 0.20 or higher), we can conclude that only in regard to economic growth is there a relationship with prior problem identifications (given as a reason for future affections). Generic optimists and respondents with a neutral stance (with no substantive answer) were more likely to support the notion of economic growth. What is striking is that the group who spontaneously came up with the ethnic and religious tensions problem when asked why they were optimistic or pessimistic was the least likely to predict an increase in these very same tensions.

Table 10.6 shows that first presenting the long list of societal problems, including the six selected here, was not very likely to change the results, as can be seen clearly in Table 10.5. A somewhat lower number of those who chose economic disparities thought the issues would be on the rise, and a very similar (and very low) proportion of people who stressed ethnic and religious tensions identified various upward trends there; similarly, a rather high proportion of generic optimists selected economic growth as a likely trend, and there was also almost no change among the generic pessimists. The exception is, again, the rising proportions of the respondents who gave no substantive reason for their optimism or pessimism. The share changes from a third to almost half of these respondents who thought the selected problems would be increasing in the next 25 years in the Netherlands. When taking account of the Cramer's *V*s we can again conclude that only as regards economic growth was there a connection with the reasons people gave for their optimism and pessimism. Like in the original questionnaire, the generic optimists and neutral respondents stood out in their belief that economic growth was imminent in the Dutch future.

Yet another way of looking at the overlap is offered in Table 10.7. Of the 42 possible effects of the change in question order on the mean trend perception (ranging from decrease to increase), there is only a disappointing total of nine effects that are significant ($p < 0.05$). Of these nine effects, there are only three with an η of 0.25 or higher. The first conclusion is therefore that the effect of changing the order of questions—more specifically, of first asking for reasons for optimism or pessimism before presenting a list of problems, versus first presenting this list and then asking for these reasons—is very modest. Looking at the three significant and substantial effects, we can furthermore conclude that the results do not seem to display much logic. Respondents who first spontaneously saw ethnic and religious tensions as a reason for their optimism or (more often) pessimism were more likely to then rate poverty and economic growth as significant when confronted with the list of issues; when they saw the list first, they displayed a less extreme answer pattern, downgrading the likelihood of poverty and becoming more positive about the likelihood of economic growth. We must keep in mind that two of the three significant and substantial effects were found among a rather small group who emphasized ethnic and religious tensions to begin with. In other words, the effects can just as well be considered coincidental. The other effect was seen among the group who mentioned economic disparities as a reason for their optimism or pessimism. When confronted with the list of issues after having given reasons for their optimism or pessimism, this group was likely to think that economic growth would be modest, if not stable. They were far less positive about the likelihood of economic growth when they saw the list first.

10.5 CONCLUSIONS

Times have changed. Beginning in late October 2008 the reality of the worldwide banking crisis and predictions of an imminent crisis in the "real economy" dominated the media, public discussions, and policy debates. The sharp tone about foreigners and Islam and the explicit and unfiltered fear for the future of Dutch society found in the answers to open-ended questions in 1999 persisted among only a small proportion of the Dutch population in late 2008. Instead, nine years after the survey, relatively large shares of the Dutch worried about the economy. The survey contexts in 1999 and 2008 were similar: an Internet survey, exactly the same questions, posed in a similar closed and open-ended format. The subject of multiculturalism seemed to have become less socially sensitive or controversial; the social and political turmoil of the early 2000s might well have taken the issue off the list of controversial topics. As a result, respondents no longer needed to debate the issue in an anonymous setting such as an Internet survey; they could do this in the open. Another possibility is that it still was controversial and still something one did not openly talk about, but that it had (temporarily) lost ground to issues that were higher on the public agenda at that specific moment. In 2008 that was the issue of the economy and related economic disparities. It only goes to show that what people think of as influential in the future is highly related to the present and less so to the past.

The effects of ordering closed and open-ended questions in this survey are mostly in line with theory, but they are rather modest. Respondents did not give substantively different answers when asked to spontaneously mention reasons for future optimism or pessimism before or after having seen a long list of societal problems. Pessimism rose generally after respondents were presented with this list, but this rise is only weakly related to the changed question order. Almost all respondents—regardless of the motivation for their optimism or pessimism, or the order in which they answered the questions—evaluated trends in societal problems in a similar fashion. They almost all thought, for example, that phenomena such as tensions between ethnic groups would increase. Only people with a disposition to be optimistic—here labeled as generic optimists—trusted that the future would bring economic growth, yet they did so regardless of the order of the questions. The same could be said for people who indicated that they had no particular reason for their optimism or pessimism: They too trusted in economic growth regardless of the question order. Yet this group believed that all the socially problematic issues we presented, regardless of question order, would become more significant in the future.

We found two modest order effects. First a very specific effect: Respondents who spontaneously emphasized economic disparities as a reason to be optimistic or (more probably) pessimistic become more negative about prospects for economic growth after having evaluated a list of societal issues. Second, if respondents first evaluated the long list of problems, more of them indicated that they were unable to identify a reason for their optimism or pessimism about the future of Dutch society. Also, they were less outspoken in their optimism and pessimism itself. Presenting respondents with a list of societal issues that might affect society's future made respondents less affectionately outspoken and less issue-focused when assessing their own affection toward the future.

There is relevance in these findings. If questions are ordered in a way that respondents first evaluate a pre-given set of societal issues and problems, respondents who are sensitive to the issues of the times (in late October 2008, that would be people who were sensitive to economic disparities resulting from the much-debated crisis) are probably more likely to become more negative on exactly the same issues (in this case, economic growth). More generally, respondents are likely to abstain from sharply defining issues and problems in their own way if they have first seen a list of issues and problems. They do not choose different issues after having evaluated the list than they do before seeing it. There does not seem to be a priming effect. They just seem no longer able to identify specific societal issues or problems, including controversial issues. Put another way, if one aims to avoid the (modest) order effects and still tap deeper motivations and feelings with respect to sensitive issues, it is best to first pose questions in a general format and in a neutral fashion, with as little cognitive information or specific benchmark standards as possible.

An accurate correspondence between the latent and the manifest is complicated as such, and even more so when it comes to controversial issues, as we have shown. In tapping the latent regarding socially controversial (and thus often politically highly relevant) issues through the use of Internet surveys, it seems crucial to carefully balance open-ended and closed questions. In our case, with Dutch people evaluating the key social issues of the future, we found that starting with open-ended, generally phrased questions generated opportunities for Internet survey respondents to define their own future issues and at the same time to show somewhat more affection toward these future issues.

[1] Acknowledgments: Many thanks to Sybren Van der Meulen and Koen Willems for their excellent work on coding the open-ended questions. We are grateful to the MESS project and CentERdata staff for conducting this experiment.

REFERENCES

Babbie, E. R. (1973). *Survey research methods.* Belmont, CA: Wadsworth.

Blalock, H. M. (1979). Measurement and conceptualization problems: The major obstacle to integrating theory and research. Presidential address. *American Sociological Review, 44*, 881–894.

Bosnjak, M. (2001a). Teilnahmeverhalten bei Web-befragungen—Nonresponse und Selbstselektion [Participation behavior in Web surveys: Nonresponse and self-selection]. In A. Theobald, M. Dreyer, & T. Starsetzki (Eds.), *Handbuch zur online-marktforschung. beiträge aus wissenschaft und praxis* (pp. 79–95). Wiesbaden, Germany: Gabler.

Bosnjak, M. (2001b). Participation in non-restricted Web surveys: A typology and explanatory model for item nonresponse. In U.-D. Reips & M. Bosnjak (Eds.), *Dimensions of Internet science* (pp. 193–207). Lengerich, Germany: Pabst.

Brehm, S. & Brehm, J. W. (1981). *Psychological reactance: A theory of freedom and control.* New York: Academic Press.

Carmines, E. G. & Zeller, R. A. (1979). *Reliability and validity assessment.* Beverly Hills, CA: Sage Publications.

Converse, J. M. (1984). Strong arguments and weak evidence: The open/closed questioning controversy of the 1940s. *Public Opinion Quarterly, 48*, 267–282.

Couper, M. (2000). Web surveys: A review of issues and approaches. *Public Opinion Quarterly, 64,* 464–494.

Dekker, P. & Ester, P. (1989). Elite perceptions of mass preferences in the Netherlands: Biases in cognitive responsiveness. *European Journal of Political Research, 17,* 623–639.

Dillman, D. A. (2007). *Mail and Internet surveys: The tailored design method.* New York: John Wiley & Sons.

Ester, P. & Vinken, H. (2001). *Een dubbel vooruitzicht. Doembeelden en droombeelden van arbeid, zorg en vrije tijd in de 21e eeuw* [A double focus: Gloomy and dreamy perspectives on work, care, and leisure in the 21st century]. Bussum, the Netherlands: Coutinho.

Kerlinger, F. N. (1964). *Foundations of behavioral research.* New York: Holt, Rinehart, & Winston.

Knapp, F. & Heidingsfelder, M. (2001). Drop-out analysis: Effects of survey design. In U.-D. Reips & M. Bosnjak (Eds.), *Dimensions of Internet science.* Lengerich, Germany: Pabst.

Kwak, N. & Radler, B. T. (2002). A comparison between mail and Web surveys: Response pattern, respondent profile, and data quality. *Journal of Official Statistics, 18,* 257–273.

Langer, G. & Cohen, J. (2006). To editor. *Public Opinion Quarterly, 70*, 416–418.

Lee, R. M. (1993). *Doing research on sensitive topics.* London: Sage.

Lensvelt-Mulders, G. J. L. M. (2008). Surveying sensitive topics. In E. D. De Leeuw, J. J. Hox, & D. A. Dillman (Eds.), *International handbook of survey methodology* (pp. 461–478). European Association of Methodology Series. New York: Lawrence Erlbaum Associates.

Lensvelt-Mulders, G. J. L. M., Hox, J. J., Van der Heijden, P. G. M., & Maas, C. J. M. (2005). Meta-analysis of randomized response research: Thirty-five years of validation. *Sociological Methods Research, 33*, 319–348.

Lozar Manfreda, K. & Vehovar, V. (2008). Internet surveys. In E. D. De Leeuw, J. J. Hox, & D. A. Dillman (Eds.), *International handbook of survey methodology* (pp. 264–284). European Association of Methodology Series. New York: Lawrence Erlbaum Associates.

McFarland, S. G. (1981). Effects of question order on survey responses. *Public Opinion Quarterly, 45*, 208–215.

Moore, D. W. (2002). Measuring new types of question-order effects: Additive and subtractive. *Public Opinion Quarterly, 66*, 80–91.

Peeters, C. F. W. (2005). *Measuring politically sensitive behavior.* Unpublished master's thesis, Department of Political Science, Free University Amsterdam.

Rasinski, K. A., Willis, G. B., Baldwin, A. K., Yeh, W., & Lee, L. (1999). Methods of data collection, perceptions of risks and losses and motivation to give truthful answers to sensitive survey questions. *Applied Cognitive Psychology, 13*, 465–484.

Renzetti, C. M., & Lee, R. M. (1993). *Researching sensitive topics.* London: Sage Publications.

Russ-Eft, D. F. (1980). *Validity and reliability in survey research.* American Institutes for Research in the Behavioral Sciences, Palo Alto, CA; Statistical Analysis Group in Education, National Center for Education Statistics, Washington, DC.

Schaefer, D. R., & Dillman, D. A. (1998). Development of a standard e-mail methodology: Results of an experiment. *Public Opinion Quarterly, 62*, 378–397.

Schuman, H. (1992). Context effects: State of the past—state of the art. In N. Schwarz & S. Sudman (Eds.), *Context effects in social and psychological research* (pp. 5–20). New York: Springer Verlag.

Schuman, H. (2006). To editor. *Public Opinion Quarterly, 70*, 413–415.

Schuman, H., & Presser, S. (1981). *Questions and answers in attitudes surveys: Experiments on question form, wording and content.* New York: Academic Press.

Schwarz, N. (1996). *Cognition and communication: Judgmental biases, research methods, and the logic of conversation.* Mahwah, NJ: Lawrence Erlbaum Associates.

Schwarz, N. (2001). How question order affects answers. *Michigan Today*, fall issue.

Schwarz, N., Knäuper, B., Oyserman, D., & Stich, C. (2008). The psychology of asking questions. In E. D. De Leeuw, J. J. Hox, & D. A. Dillman (Eds.), *International handbook of survey methodology* (pp. 18–34). European Association of Methodology Series. New York: Lawrence Erlbaum Associates.

Sieber, J. E., & Stanley, B. (1988). Ethical and professional dimensions of socially sensitive research. *American Psychologist, 43*, 49–55.

Strack, F. (1992). "Order effects" in survey research: Activation and information functions of preceding questions. In N. Schwarz & S. Sudman (Eds.), *Context effects in social and psychological research* (pp. 23–24). New York: Springer Verlag.

Strack, F., Martin, L., & Schwarz, N. (1988). Priming and communication: Social determinants of information use in judgments on life satisfaction. *European Journal of Social Psychology, 18*, 429–442.

Sudman, S., Bradburn, N. M., & Schwarz, N. (1996). *Thinking about answers: The application of cognitive processes to survey methodology.* San Francisco: Jossey-Bass.

Tourangeau, R., Rips, L. J., & Rasinski, K. (2000). *The psychology of survey response.* Cambridge, UK: Cambridge University Press.

Tourangeau, R., & Smith, T. W. (1998). Collecting sensitive data with different modes of data collection. In M. P. Couper, R. P. Baker, J. Bethlehem et al. (Eds.), *Computer assisted survey information collection* (pp. 431–453). New York: John Wiley & Sons.

Weisband, S., & Kiesler, S. (1996). Self-disclosure on computer forms: Meta-analysis and implications. *CHI 96 Electronic Proceedings.* Retrieved from http://www.acm.org/sigchi/chi96/proceedings/papers/Weisband/sw_txt.htm

APPENDIX

Question wordings in original order (originally in Dutch):

Q1	When thinking of the Netherlands in the next 25 years, are you optimistic or pessimistic?	1 very optimistic, 2 optimistic, 3 neither optimistic nor pessimistic, 4 pessimistic, 5 very pessimistic
Q2	Can you indicate why you are optimistic, pessimistic, neither, or both regarding the Netherlands in the next 25 years?	<Open-ended>
Q3	Do you think the following situations and problems in the Netherlands will decrease, increase, or remain the same in the next 25 years?	1 unemployment, 2 poverty, 3 arrears of women, 4 old-age pension, 5 tension between religions, 6 communication possibilities, 7 work pressure, 8 economic growth, 9 war, 10 solidarity, 11 health provisions, 12 genetic manipulation, 13 environmental degradation, 14 computer literacy, 15 affordability of social provisions, 16 criminality, 17 tension between ethnic groups, 18 asylum seekers, 19 traffic jams on the highways, 20 discrimination, 21 population growth

Experimental design:

Q3 before Q1, followed by Q2

Part III

Data Quality: Problems and Solutions

11

Challenges in Reaching Hard-to-Reach Groups in Internet Panel Research

Corrie M. Vis
CentERdata
Tilburg University
Tilburg, the Netherlands

Miquelle A. G. Marchand
CentERdata
Tilburg University
Tilburg, the Netherlands

11.1 INTRODUCTION

When trying to encourage people to participate in a survey, some people are easier to reach than others. As long as the targeted population groups are sufficiently represented in the results, weighting factors can be computed. However, when hard-to-reach groups are underrepresented, the probability is high that the results will be biased. The term "hard to reach" in survey research usually refers to (1) groups within a population that are reached at less than average rates (no contact) and (2) groups that are less inclined to participate in surveys (unit nonresponse). It is not self-evident that these two groups overlap (De Leeuw & Hox, 1998).

Difficult-to-contact people generally are younger, from a higher social class, single, living in urbanized areas, or immigrants (Stoop, 2005). The most often used traditional contact methods are face-to-face or telephone contact. Over the last years, a new and steadily growing group has emerged that is difficult to contact by telephone. More and more people do not have landlines anymore, and cell phone numbers are not available in telephone directories. As a result, these people are hard to reach by telephone. People who are *less willing to participate* are most often the elderly, people with a lower education level, and, again, people living in urbanized areas. According to Stoop (2005), people become increasingly hard to reach when several of these characteristics are combined.

Some researchers argue that "hard to reach" is a stigmatizing terminology that implies homogeneity within distinct groups, which does not necessarily exist (Freimuth & Mettger, 1990). In this opinion, all groups can be reached. However, the question is at what cost this can be done in terms of money, time, and effort. When focusing on a national population, additional efforts are needed to reach small hard-to-reach groups at an additional cost. The problem of costs becomes bigger when recruiting an Internet panel that needs to be representative of a national population. Is it worthwhile to invest time, effort, and money to reach specific groups? This is not an easy question to answer, and to generate more insight in this matter we will discuss the recruitment procedure of the Dutch Longitudinal Internet Studies for the Social sciences (LISS) panel. The LISS panel is an Internet panel of about 5,000 households in the Netherlands. It is based on a household probability sample and a well-thought-out procedure of recruitment with a high panel participation response of about 50% (see Chapter 4 in this volume). To gain more insight into when and why certain groups are at risk of dropping out, we considered four stages in the recruitment process and what has been done within each stage to avoid nonresponse. Furthermore, we analyze whether the response rate and the panel attrition of the hard-to-reach groups differ from the average. Finally, strategies and challenges are discussed in the context of the participation of these groups in Internet panel research.

11.2 HARD-TO-REACH GROUPS IN INTERNET PANEL RESEARCH

The sample for the recruitment of an Internet panel is considered to be "traditionally composed" when it is based on a probability sample drawn from recorded data. The first contact with the sample members can also be traditional: by letter, by telephone, or face-to-face. When this is done, there are no substantial differences between setting up an Internet panel and a traditional survey. However, the ability and willingness of sample members to participate could be different. Focusing on data collection in an Internet panel means focusing on an interview method that leads to less participation by certain people because it combines self-administration with a visual medium and interaction with a computer (cf. Groves, 1989; Tourangeau, Rips, & Rasinski, 2000). Although Internet access has grown across the board, clear demographic gaps remain (Lenhart et al., 2003; Martin, 2003). The elderly, people with a lower household income, and people with less education often have less access to the Internet (Rookey, Hanway, & Dillman, 2008). Offering them equipment for Internet access may prevent the loss of these respondents in an Internet panel. However, it is important to realize *why* people do not have Internet access. In general, there are three reasons for not having Internet access: being unwilling to have it, being unable to have it, and just not having it (without a deliberate decision). Some people may not be willing to use the Internet at all. They make a deliberate decision not to have Internet access because they feel using the Internet has no added value, they consider it unnecessary, or they feel that alternative media are good enough for them. Others have made the decision not to have Internet access because they do not enjoy using a computer, are of the opinion that the Internet is impersonal, or are concerned about security, an involuntary confrontation with pornography, risks such as viruses, and the risk of dependence on the medium. Some people think that using a computer is too difficult for them, or they are afraid to make mistakes (Lenhart et al., 2003). Some people find it difficult to learn how to use a computer, and others think they just do not have the right skills to learn it.

There are people who may not be able to participate in Internet surveys. Dillman and Bowker (2001), for instance, mention the inability of some people to handle radio buttons, HTML boxes, and drop-down menus as the main reason for nonparticipation. In addition, lack of funds can prevent people from having Internet access.

A final group of people has made no deliberate decision not to use a computer or the Internet. They have no interest in it or simply have never been confronted with it. Some elderly use the advantages of Internet in an indirect way, because their partner is using the Internet. They will stop using the Internet after their partner has passed away. Given that women on average grow older than men, these elderly people probably form a vulnerable group (Duimel, 2007) in Internet panel research.

11.3 HARD-TO-REACH GROUPS AND THE RECRUITMENT OF THE LISS PANEL

All households in the initial LISS panel received an invitation letter and a prepaid incentive of 10 euros. Before they were asked to participate in the panel, they were asked to participate in a short interview. In the recruitment procedure, there are four different stages at which people can drop out: (1) people may not have been reached (contact stage), (2) people may refuse to participate in the interview (interview stage), (3) people may not be willing to participate in the panel (agree-to-panel stage), and (4) people may not wish to do the actual surveys in the panel (panel stage).

We will discuss which groups at which stage(s) are at risk of dropping out, and what has been done to contact them and to persuade them to participate. The results are based on analyses of the nonresponse using characteristics of households from the population register (Van der Laan, 2009), and on the reasons for not participating provided by the respondents. In two stages respondents were asked to give their own reasons for not participating: the interview stage and the agree-to-panel stage. The answers were coded by the interviewer or they were coded afterward. It should be taken into account that the responses are at a household level, whereas the reasons for nonresponse are at an individual level.

11.3.1 The Contact Stage

Examples of no contact are people who are almost never home due to work or a busy social life, or people who do not have a landline. No contact is especially apparent for young households, single-person households, and immigrants (first-generation immigrants and the second-generation children of non-Western immigrants). Members of young households are difficult to contact because they are less frequently at home, and immigrants are difficult to contact because they less often have a landline at home. Single-person households are by definition more difficult to contact, because the probability of contacting a household increases with the number of household members. Using recommendations from the literature (Groves & Couper, 1998; Snijkers & Kockelkoren, 2004; Bates, 2004), the number of contact attempts was increased to 15 times by telephone and 15 times face-to-face. In addition, the fieldwork period was extended. Attempts to contact people were fine-tuned to their situations. For example, people who work were contacted after business hours, immigrants were contacted face-to-face, and young people were contacted by telephone.

11.3.2 The Interview Stage and the Agree-to-Panel Stage

When we compare the reasons for nonresponse in the interview stage and in the agree-to-panel stage, we see that not having time is mentioned most often. Even when the recruitment interview lasts only 10 minutes and the questionnaires in the panel take a maximum of 30 minutes per month, people feel this is already taking too much of their time. Explaining the importance of the interview and the panel, offering to call back at a more convenient time or day, and offering monetary incentives all contribute to helping people understand that their time will be well spent.

Reasons for nonresponse differ significantly across different age groups: χ^2 (52, $n = 462$) = 250, $p < .001$. The elderly and single-person households show a high nonresponse rate at the agree-to-panel stage. This probably means that it is more effective to visit these people in person instead of interviewing them by phone, so that the interviewer has more time to explain the importance of panel participation. Elderly people less often say they do not have time, but mention frequently that they feel too old to participate, are physically impaired, or cannot participate due to illness. More specifically, the oldest old (ages 80 and over) give these reasons even more frequently than other elderly people (ages 65–80). Not surprisingly, most elderly people drop out in the agree-to-panel stage. Elderly people also more often state that they are not computer literate or that they do not want a computer. The agree-to-panel stage was the first time in the recruitment process that the use of the Internet and a computer were mentioned.

Providing people with a computer that has larger and more user-friendly buttons (a simPC) helped to reduce nonresponse in this group. The simPC is a simple computer with a service subscription. It was designed with limited functionality, because most elderly people will probably only use the PC for Internet access (via a browser) and e-mail. The user cannot install software on the simPC, and virus protection, security, and other maintenance issues are automatically managed remotely via update programs. If necessary, the simPC could be introduced by means of a short video at people's homes. In addition, a broadband Internet connection was provided to those who did not have access to the Internet.

Additional support was provided through a help desk and technical assistance, through a demonstration of the simPC at people's homes, and by asking a child or other family member of the potential respondent to help explain the purpose and the procedures of the LISS panel.

Other reasons for nonresponse that were mentioned were not wanting a computer and not being able to handle a simPC. When the simPC is offered to people it may therefore be more effective not to explicitly mention the use of the Internet as an advantage or reward for participating in the panel, but to emphasize that the simPC will enable them to participate in the online surveys.

Another factor in the reasons for nonresponse is type of household: χ^2 (39, n = 473) = 83.80, $p < .001$. Members of single-person households more often say they are too old, suffer from illness, are physically impaired, are not computer literate, or do not want a computer. This is consistent with the relatively high age of the members of these households.

First-generation immigrants more often drop out at the interview stage. The reason for this may be that it is difficult for them to participate in the interview due to their limited knowledge of the Dutch language. To persuade first-generation immigrants to participate in the recruitment interview, specially trained interviewers were used to support them with the interview. It appears that Western and non-Western immigrants give different reasons for nonresponse in the agree-to-panel stage. Non-Western immigrants more often give their limited knowledge of the Dutch language as a reason (as well as not having time), whereas Western immigrants more often say they are not computer literate or that they do not want a computer.

Finally, an important reason for not wanting to participate in the interview is for reasons of principle. Interestingly, this reason is also the fourth most important reason for nonresponse in the agree-to-panel stage. This suggests that these people are principled regarding the panel and not regarding the surveys, because they already had participated in the interview stage. Not surprisingly, not being willing to commit oneself to the panel is a reason for nonresponse in the agree-to-panel stage.

11.3.3 The Panel Stage

In the final stage of the recruitment process (panel stage), another issue arises. It turns out that even though households consisting of second-generation children of non-Western immigrants are relatively difficult to contact, once they have been contacted a relatively high fraction of these households agrees to participate in the panel. However, unfortunately, relatively many of these people do not register as panel members. This may be due to forgetfulness, or it may signal some other reason, such as just being evasive. Reminding people of the necessity to register helped increase the response rate in this stage. Monetary incentives sometimes appear to increase response rates (Groves & Couper, 1998; Van den Brakel & Renssen, 2000). However, the positive relationship between incentives and response rates is not evident (Cook, Heath, & Thompson, 2000; Lozar Manfreda & Vehovar, 2002; Dillman, 2000). In a study among young immigrants, an incentive of 10 euros appeared to help increase response rates of young Moroccan women but not of the average young Turkish person (Van den Brakel, Vis-Visschers, & Schmeets, 2006). In the LISS panel, an incentive of 10 euros was offered when people registered for the panel. Table 11.1 shows an overview of the hard-to-reach-groups and the chosen measures to reduce nonresponse.

11.4 HARD-TO-REACH GROUPS PARTICIPATING IN THE LISS PANEL

In March 2008, the recruitment of the LISS panel was completed. At the time, some people had been supplied with Internet access and a simPC, and the results of the first core questionnaires were becoming available. In the LISS panel, there are six core questionnaires covering different topics (see Chapter 4 in this volume). These core questionnaires were developed by researchers at CentERdata in collaboration with other experts in the field. The ethnic origin of the panel members was initially unknown. The numbers in this section about the representation of different ethnic origins in the panel are based on the response of the core questionnaire, which covers the topics of religion and ethnicity. The response rate for this questionnaire is 87%.

In the LISS panel, 3.9% of panel members (5.7% of households) were provided with a simPC. The proportion of households in the LISS panel that had no Internet access at home before becoming a member of the LISS panel is much smaller than the proportion of households without Internet

TABLE 11.1

Hard-to-Reach Groups in the Recruitment of the LISS Panel and the Chosen Solution

		Contact Stage	Interview Stage	Agree-to-Panel Stage	Join Panel Stage
Younger people	problem	sporadic at home			
	solution	many contact attempts/ tailored time of contact attempt/telephone interviewing			
Older people	problem			do not want to go online/ no Internet access	
	solution			arguments/simple device for access to the Internet/ demo at home/proxy	
Singles	problem	less chance			
	solution	many contact attempts/ telephone interviewing			
First-generation immigrants	problem	no landline	language problems		
	solution	face-to-face interview	trained interviewers/ interviewers with ethnic background		
Second-generation children of non-Western immigrants	problem	no landline			agree to panel but no registration
	solution	face-to-face interview			incentive of 10 euros

access at home in the Dutch population. In the Netherlands, 17% of private households with at least one person between the ages of 12 and 75 have no Internet access at home (Statistics Netherlands, 2008). About 5.5% of private households in the Netherlands include at least one person over the age of 75 (Statistics Netherlands, 2008). In this age group, the percentage of people that have no Internet access is probably very high. We assume that the total percentage of private households that have no Internet access at home will be not 17% but at least 20%. Under this assumption, the percentage of people who do not have Internet access in the LISS panel is about a quarter of the national percentage. The underrepresentation of households without Internet access before participating in the LISS panel correlates with an underrepresentation of people over the age of 75 (2.7% versus 8.3% in the Dutch population), but this does not explain the total underrepresentation of households without Internet access.

In 2009, with a total of 16.5 million inhabitants, the Netherlands has 3.2 million residents of foreign origin, of whom 55% are of non-Western origin. Turks, Surinamese, Moroccans, and Antilleans are by far the largest non-Western population groups. One third of the population of the big cities in the western part of the country is of non-Western origin, as opposed to one tenth for the Netherlands as a whole. The distribution of the different groups of immigrants in the panel corresponds roughly with the distribution of origin in the national population. First-generation non-Western immigrants are underrepresented most. Immigrants of Surinamese and Antillean origin are better represented than people of Turkish and Moroccan origin. The limited command of the Dutch language of these groups will play a role: Only people who can read Dutch are able to participate in the LISS panel, and the national figures of Statistics Netherlands do not include information about Dutch language skills (De Vos & Knoef, 2008). In addition, it has been shown that, of the four large groups of non-Western origin, Turks and Moroccans, in particular, rarely marry an autochthonous Dutch partner. This applies to both the first and the second generations (Jennissen & Oudhof, 2007). These groups form a more closed community (socially and cognitively) than the Surinamese and the Antillean minorities, and may therefore be less inclined to participate in a panel that serves the Dutch community. For further analyses we combine the immigrant groups into the first generation and the second generation of both non-Western and Western immigrants, because the groups of different origin are too small to be considered separately.

When we compare the distribution of education levels in the LISS panel and in the Dutch population, it appears that people with a university education are somewhat underrepresented in the LISS panel. On the other hand, people with more vocational education are overrepresented in the LISS panel. Also, people with a lower level of education (primary and lower secondary education), a category that is on average less willing to participate in survey research, is, contrary to our expectations, somewhat overrepresented in the LISS panel (De Vos & Knoef, 2008). An explanation for this could be that panel members receive a monetary incentive for every completed questionnaire. Possibly, less-educated people value the money they receive more than other people because their incomes are lower.

In addition to comparing the results of the LISS panel to the total population in the Netherlands, we can also compare it to traditional surveys and self-selection Internet surveys. Is the LISS panel closer to high-standard traditional non-Internet studies than to Internet surveys based on non-probability samples? A comparison has been made between the LISS panel and the Dutch Parliamentary Electoral Study (DPES) conducted in 2006, a major traditional national survey in the Netherlands (DPES, 2006), and between the LISS panel and a comprehensive evaluation study across 19 online panels of Dutch market research organizations, the Dutch online panel comparison study NOPVO (Vonk, Van Ossenbruggen, & Willems, 2008). Even though the elderly non-Internet group was better represented in the traditional face-to-face survey, the results show that the LISS panel was close to the traditional survey and better than the online surveys for most of the characteristics that were tested. For a more detailed description of the comparison of the LISS panel to traditional surveys and to Internet surveys, see Chapter 5 in this volume.

To assess the effect of demographic variables on the likelihood that respondents had to be provided with a simPC and a broadband connection in order to get Internet access, we performed a direct logistic regression. As shown in Table 11.2, the model as a whole, with the variables of age, origin, level of education, housing, and household composition, explains 26.8% (Nagelkerke R^2) of the variance in Internet access in the panel. The strongest predictor of using a simPC and participating in the panel is an age of 75 or over, recording an odds ratio of 12.40, followed by a primary or low secondary education, living in a rental, being single or cohabiting without

TABLE 11.2

Logistic Regression Predicting Need for a simPC (N = 7,418)

	Odds Ratio	**(S.E.)**
Age (reference: ages 16–34)		
Ages 35–54	1.435	(.213)
Ages 55–74	2.811**	(.210)
Ages 75+	12.396**	(.258)
Origin (reference: natives)		
First generation, non-Western immigrants	2.785**	(.240)
Second-generation children of non-Western immigrants	1.249	(.621)
First generation, Western immigrants	.581	(.420)
Second generation, children of Western immigrants	.405	(.296)
Education (reference: university)		
Primary	7.534**	(.404)
Lower secondary	4.391**	(.398)
Higher secondary	1.138	(.488)
Intermediate vocational training	2.320	(.416)
Higher vocational training	1.718	(.424)
Rental (reference: own house)	3.685**	(.122)
Single or cohabitants without children (reference: single or cohabitants with children)	2.884**	(.173)
Constant	.002	(.430)
Nagelkerke pseudo R^2	0.268	

Note: 0 is no simPC provided, 1 is simPC provided.
** significant ($p < .001$)

children, belonging to the age group of 55–74, or being a first-generation non-Western immigrant. The effect of the housing variable can be explained because a lower education level or being a non-Western immigrant is often correlated with living in a rental. The effect of household composition can be explained by the fact that being single or cohabiting without children correlates with old age.

Although not as well represented as in face-to-face surveys, people ages 75 and older and non-Internet-users are much better represented in the LISS panel than in other online studies (Vonk et al., 2008). We can conclude that providing people with a simPC in order to facilitate Internet access and creating the possibility of participating in the LISS panel leads to more panel participation among the very groups that are often hard to reach in survey research.

11.5 RESPONSE RATES IN THE LISS PANEL

In the period January 2008–June 2009 (17 months), a total of 8,781 panel members ages 16 and over out of a total of 5,000 households were selected for an average of 35 questionnaires covering various topics. The percentage of completed questionnaires—that is, the percentage of fully completed questionnaires among those one was selected for—was on average 64.5%; 1% of the questionnaires were started but not completed, and 34.5% of the questionnaires were not started at all. In this period of 17 months, 15.9% of panel members ended their panel participation. There is a large impact of terminated panel participation on the percentage of completed questionnaires. The mean percentage of completed questionnaires by people who are still in the panel after 17 months is 69.7%, while the percentage of completed questionnaires by people who terminated their panel participation is 33.9%. This means that people who intend to end their panel participation have not been filling out the questionnaires for quite some time.

To analyze the effect of demographic variables on the likelihood that respondents will terminate their panel participation, a direct logistic regression was performed (Table 11.3). It is remarkable that the explained variance of this model is very low (1.9%). This means there is more to be learned about nondemographic variables that influence the tendency to terminate panel participation.

Still, this model shows differences in stopping behavior between demographics. The older the members of the LISS panel, the more likely it is that they will terminate their panel participation. People ages 30–49 are 1.4 times more likely to quit than the youngest age group (ages 16–29), people ages 50–64 are 1.6 times more likely to quit, people ages 65–74 are 2.5 times more likely to quit, and people ages 75 and older are three times more likely to terminate their panel participation. Panel members with children living at home are somewhat more likely (1.3 times) to terminate their panel participation compared to panel members without children living at home. People with intermediate vocational training are less likely (0.7 times) to terminate their panel participation than people with a college education. People who were provided with Internet access by CentERdata are 0.5 times less likely to terminate their panel participation than people who already had a computer and Internet access. It is

TABLE 11.3

Logistic Regression Predicting Terminated Panel Participation (*N* = 7,418)

	Odds Ratio	(S.E.)
Age (reference: ages 16–29)		
Ages 30–49	1.369*	(.160)
Ages 50–64	1.576**	(.163)
Ages 65–74	2.499**	(.189)
Ages 75+	3.043**	(.243)
Origin (reference: natives)		
First generation, non-Western immigrants	1.185	(.193)
Second-generation children of non-Western immigrants	1.119	(.342)
First generation, Western immigrants	1.230	(.203)
Second-generation children of Western immigrants	1.108	(.166)
Education (reference: university)		
Primary	.976	(.170)
Lower secondary	.956	(.147)
Higher secondary	.805	(.177)
Intermediate vocational training	.738*	(.153)
Higher vocational training	.862	(.152)
Single or cohabitants with children (reference: single or cohabitants without children)	1.274**	(.093)
Device on loan (reference: not a device on loan)	.466**	(.193)
Women (reference: men)	.955	(.092)
Position in the household (reference: head of the household)		
Partner of the head of the household	1.033	(.540)
Child living at home	1.281	(.539)
Other housemate	1.566	(.555)
Constant	.088	(.565)
Nagelkerke pseudo R^2	0.019	

Note: 0 is participating in the panel, 1 is terminated participation.
* significant ($p < .05$)
** significant ($p < .01$)

encouraging that by providing people with Internet access, not only were we able to include more people in the panel, but also these panel members have a lower tendency to drop out.

Hierarchical multiple regression was used to see to what degree the variables age, origin, level of education, living situation, device on loan for Internet access, gender, and position in the household can predict the total percentage of completed questionnaires after controlling for the influence of terminated panel participation. The results are presented in Table 11.4.

TABLE 11.4

Regression Analysis Predicting the Percentage of Completed Questionnaires ($N = 7{,}418$)

	Model 1			Model 2		
	B	SE B	β	B	SE B	β
Terminating panel participation	−35.803	1.200	−.334**	−33.884	1.165	−.316**
Ages 30–49				7.366	1.285	.096**
Ages 50–64				18.058	1.369	.213**
Ages 65–74				24.970	1.860	.183**
Ages 75+				17.049	2.642	.078**
Origin				−.582	.402	−.015
Lower secondary				12.438	1.334	.143**
Higher secondary				18.105	1.689	.141**
Intermediate vocational training				14.707	1.388	.163**
Higher vocational training				17.698	1.415	.188**
University				13.254	1.863	.091**
Single or cohabitants with children				−8.113	.978	−.107**
Device on loan				9.749	1.700	.064**
Gender				1.583	.885	.021
Position in the household				5.036	.746	.096**
R^2	.11	.20				
F for change in R^2	890.68**	53.67**				

Note: * significant ($p < .05$)
** significant ($p < .01$)

The total variance of the model was explained by 20%, and the additional variance explained by the demographics was significant (R changed = 9%, $p < .001$). For people ages 50–64 and people ages 65–74, age contributes most to the percentage of completed questionnaires ($\beta = .213$ and $\beta = .183$, respectively). Even though extra efforts were needed to recruit the older age group into the panel, once they are in the panel they are the most reliable in responding. In other words, special efforts to recruit the elderly pay off twice. It was also found that people with the lowest level of education are difficult to recruit as panel members. Eventually their recruitment was successful and people with the lowest level of education are now sufficiently represented in the panel. However, we also found that once they are in the panel, level of education contributes significantly more to the percentage of completed questionnaires: The higher the level of education of a group, the more that group contributed to the percentage of completed questionnaires (β ranges from β = .143 to β = .188) except for the highest level of university education (β = .091). It is remarkable that both the lowest and the highest level of education have a lower response rate. This could be caused by many factors. One of the reasons may be related to the intellectual level of the content of the questionnaires and the language used in them. Researchers try to design the questions in such a way that they are understandable for the average respondent. It is possible that the questionnaires are too difficult for people with the lowest level of education and too simplistic for people with the highest level of education.

11.6 CONCLUSIONS

Internet panels that claim to be representative of a national population are criticized because of the method of recruitment of the panel members and the composition of the panel. When the sample is based on the Internet population, people without Internet access are by definition excluded. When people can register themselves as panel members, this leads to self-selection. In this study, we looked at the design and the results of the recruitment of the LISS panel in the Netherlands, an Internet panel consisting of 5,000 households. This panel was based on a probability sample from the population register. Potential panel members were contacted in a traditional manner: by letter, by telephone, or face-to-face. During the recruitment period, special efforts were made to contact low-response groups, and to point out to them that they could in fact participate in the interview and in the panel. To gain more insight into why certain groups have a higher probability of dropping out and when this is likely to happen, the recruitment process was divided in four stages: contact stage, recruitment interview stage, agree-to-panel-participation stage, and panel participation stage. It was expected that it would be difficult to achieve sufficient representation of younger people, the elderly, single people, immigrants, and less-educated people in the panel.

For younger people, the probability is higher that they cannot be reached in the contact stage, because some may almost never be home due to a busy job and social life. Because many contact attempts were made (15 by telephone and 15 face-to-face) and the contact times were spread over the day and executed with larger intervals, extra nonresponse in the contact stage of this group was ruled out. Once they were contacted, the panel participation of younger people did not differ from the average, and they are now sufficiently represented in the panel. Single people also have a lower probability of being reached in the contact stage. The reason for this is simply that the probability of reaching a household member increases with the number of household members. To recruit more panel members in this group, the same strategy was applied as for younger people, but for single people the results were less successful. Single-person households are therefore somewhat underrepresented in the panel, both for people ages 65 and older and for younger people.

It is relatively easy to contact the elderly and they are generally willing to participate in the recruitment interview. The response to a face-to-face interview is higher than to a telephone interview. The elderly have a higher probability of dropping out in the agree-to-panel stage. One of the reasons for this is their deteriorating health. Furthermore, they may feel too old to commit to the panel, they may not have Internet access at home, they think they cannot learn how to use a computer, or they may not like having a big device in their homes. Even though these people were offered the use of a user-friendly computer and broadband Internet access, it was still difficult to persuade them to participate in the panel. The response rate for this group was raised by showing them a demo video at their homes and by explaining the purpose and the procedure of the LISS panel to their relatives. It turned out that elderly people do not perceive having a computer and Internet access as an incentive, but merely consider it as facilitating their participation in the panel. It is therefore important to emphasize the latter in the recruitment interview. Also, once the elderly have the computer at home, it is of great importance to provide them with an adequate help desk (with employees with a lot of patience) and to offer computer support at their homes if necessary. Finally, people in the age group 50–65 are sufficiently represented in the panel, but we have not yet been able to avoid underrepresentation of the oldest old.

In general, immigrants are hard to contact, because they usually don't have a landline at home. Therefore, contact attempts for this group took place in face-to-face interviews. However, first-generation immigrants often do not have enough language skills in Dutch to understand the recruitment interview. Trained interviewers and interviewers with a similar ethnic background were used to help recruit this group. As a result, the response for this group rose in the recruitment stage. However, the problem with the Dutch language remains for the panel participation stage, because all questionnaires are in Dutch. The second generation—the children of non-Western immigrants—are at risk of dropping out in another stage of the recruitment process. They are willing to agree to panel participation, but they have a higher probability of dropping out when it comes to real participation. To encourage them to register as panel members, they were offered a monetary incentive of 10 euros. A fairly good representation of immigrants was accomplished. However, due to insufficient language skills and possibly due to a cultural barrier to participation in a Dutch panel, nonresponse among first-generation non-Western immigrants, particularly among Turks and Moroccans, could not be avoided.

Regarding less-educated people, after specific efforts were made to recruit this group (a large number of contact attempts, a tailor-made letter, offering them Internet access and a PC, and monetary incentives), we now have a good representation of this group in the panel.

With a total response rate of nearly 50% of the original sample combined with a good representation of the Dutch population, the recruitment of the LISS panel can be considered successful. We considered the possibility that the pressure to participate was too high, as a result of which many people might drop out with the first questionnaire or might end up participating with a low frequency. However, no evidence was found to support this hypothesis. It was shown that the older people are, the higher the probability that they will terminate their panel participation. This might be caused by deteriorating health or by a move to a retirement home. On the other hand, people ages 50 and over are much more reliable about completing the questionnaires than younger people. Less-educated people and people with the highest level of education respond less frequently in the panel than people with other levels of education. In this context, it is important to analyze the evaluation of the questionnaires in order to find possible differences between these groups in how they rate the understandability and the significance of the questions in the questionnaires.

People provided with a simPC and Internet access have a lower probability of terminating their panel participation than people who already had access to the Internet at the time of recruitment. Possibly this means that providing them with such a device may help increase the extent to which people feel committed to the panel. This may be due to a simple but powerful rule of social behavior, called the norm of reciprocity: that we treat others as they have treated us (Gouldner, 1960). In the LISS panel, people who received a simPC may feel that this gesture should be reciprocated and therefore will fill out the questionnaires more frequently and will stay in the panel longer. In addition, people may feel more committed because they have had personal contact with a member of the panel management team during the installation of the simPC at their homes, or because they frequently are in touch with the help desk by telephone.

No differences were found in panel attrition and percentage of completed questionnaires between people with first- or second-generation foreign background and natives.

We know that groups will display differences in their opinions on certain topics—for example, between people with access to the Internet and those without, between different generations, and between different ethnic groups. According to the Pew Internet and American Life Project data (2007) and other studies comparing Internet and mail respondents, it is likely that Internet users will differ substantially from those who do not use the Internet (Rookey et al., 2008), and that the differences in answers from these people cannot be explained by demographics alone. Apart from their living situations and their stages in life, different generations show differences in their opinions about society and human values. Young natives are more emancipated than young Moroccans and young Turks regarding the traditional roles within families. In addition, young Moroccans have more progressive opinions than young Turks about the position of women within families and within society (Schmeets, 2005). In light of the aging population and the growth in immigration to the Netherlands, a general Internet panel should be sufficiently represented by all age groups and groups of different ethnic origin. When Internet panel surveys are used to gain insight in opinions, attitudes, and the cultural and social development of the general population, it is of vital importance to make extra efforts to involve those people who would otherwise not participate. In this chapter we provide several ways to stimulate their participation.

REFERENCES

Bates, N. (2004). *Contact histories as a tool for understanding attrition in panel surveys.* Paper presented at the annual conference of the American Association for Public Opinion Research (AAPOR), Phoenix, Arizona.

Cook, C., Heath, F., & Thompson, R. L. (2000). A meta-analysis of response rates in Web- or Internet-based surveys. *Educational and Psychological Measurement, 60*, 821–836.

De Leeuw, E. D. & Hox, J. J. (1998). Nonresponse in surveys: Een overzicht [Nonresponse in surveys: An overview]. *Kwantitatieve Methoden, 19*, 31–53.

De Vos, K. & Knoef, M. (2008). *The representativeness of the LISS Panel.* Presentation at the MESS workshop, Zeist, the Netherlands.

Dillman, D. A. (2000). *Mail and Internet surveys.* New York: John Wiley & Sons.

Dillman, D. A. & Bowker, D. K. (2001). The Web questionnaire challenge to survey methodologists. In U.-D. Reips & M. Bosnjak (Eds.), *Dimensions of Internet science* (pp. 159–178). Lengerich, Germany: Pabst.

DPES (2006). *Dutch Parliamentary Election Study 2006* [Data file]. Retrieved from DANS EASY electronic archiving system, Data Archiving and Networked Services (DANS), http://www.dans.knaw.nl

Duimel, M. (2007). *Verbinding maken: Senioren en Internet [Connecting: Seniors and Internet*]. Netherlands Institute for Social Research, The Hague, the Netherlands.

Freimuth, V. S. & Mettger, W. (1990). Is there a hard-to-reach audience? *Public Health Reports, 105*(3), 232–238.

Gouldner, A. W. (1960). The norm of reciprocity: A preliminary statement. *American Sociological Review, 25*, 161–178.

Groves, R. M. (1989). *Survey errors and survey costs.* New York: John Wiley & Sons.

Groves, R. M. & Couper, M. P. (1998). *Nonresponse in household interview surveys.* New York: John Wiley & Sons.

Jennissen, R. P. W. & Oudhof, J. (2007). *Ontwikkelingen in de maatschappelijke participatie van allochtonen [Developments in the social participation of allochthonous people*]. The Hague, the Netherlands: BJU/CBS/WODC.

Lenhart, A., Horrigan, J. B., Rainie, L., Allen, K., Boyce, A., Madden, M. et al. (2003). *The ever-shifting Internet population: A new look at Internet access and the digital divide.* Retrieved November 2009 from http://www.pewinternet.org/~/media//Files/Reports/2003/PIP_Shifting_Net_Pop_Report.pdf

Lozar Manfreda, K. & Vehovar, V. (2002). *Survey design features influencing response rates in Web surveys.* Paper presented at the International Conference on Improving Surveys (ICIS), Copenhagen. Retrieved from http://www.icis.dk/ICIS_papers/C2_4_3.pdf

Martin, S. P. (2003). Is the digital divide really closing? A critique of inequality measurement in a nation online. *IT & Society, 1*, 1–13.

Pew Internet and American Life Project. (2007). A typology of information and communication technology users. Retrieved May 31, 2010, from http://www.pewInternet.org/Reports/2007/A_Typology_of_Information_and_Communication_Technology_Users.aspx

Rookey, B. D., Hanway, S., & Dillman, D. A. (2008). Does a probability-based household panel benefit from assignment to postal response as an alternative to Internet-only? *Public Opinion Quarterly, 72*(5), 962–984.

Schmeets, H. (2005). Culturele opvattingen van Marokkaanse en Turkse jongeren [Cultural views of young Moroccans and Turks]. In H. Schmeets & R. Van der Bie (Eds.), *Enquêteonderzoek onder allochtonen. Problemen en oplossingen* (pp. 145–152). Heerlen: Statistics Netherlands.

Snijkers, G. & Kockelkoren, S. (2004). *De gestandaardiseerde benaderingsstrategie 2003: Evaluatie en aanbevelingen [The standardized approach strategy 2003: Evaluation and recommendations]*. Report H415-04-SOO, Heerlen: Statistics Netherlands.

Statistics Netherlands. (2008). *De digitale economie 2007 [The digital economy 2007]* (p. 200). Voorburg/Heerlen: Statistics Netherlands.

Stoop, I. (2005). *The hunt for the last respondent: Nonresponse in sample surveys.* Netherlands Institute for Social Research, The Hague, the Netherlands.

Tourangeau, R., Rips, L., & Rasinski, K. (2000). *The psychology of survey response.* Cambridge: Cambridge, UK: University Press.

Van den Brakel, J. A. & Renssen, R. H. (2000). A field experiment to test effects of an incentive and a condensed questionnaire on response rates in the Netherlands Fertility and Family Survey. *Research in Official Statistics, 3*, 55–63.

Van den Brakel, J. A., Vis-Visschers, R., & Schmeets, J. J. G. (2006). An experiment with data collection modes and incentives in the Dutch Family and Fertility Survey for young Moroccans and Turks. *Field Methods, 18*, 321–334.

Van der Laan, J. (2009). *Representativity of the LISS panel.* Discussion paper 09041. The Hague/Heerlen, the Netherlands: Statistics Netherlands.

Vonk, T., Van Ossenbruggen, R., & Willems, P. (2008). A comparison study across 19 online panels (NOPVO 2006). In I. Stoop & M. Wittenberg (Eds.), *Access panels and online research: Panacea or pitfall?* (pp. 53–78). Proceedings of the DANS Symposium. Amsterdam: Aksant.

12

Mode and Context Effects in Measuring Household Assets[1]

Arthur van Soest
Netspar
Tilburg University
Tilburg, the Netherlands

and

RAND
Santa Monica, California

Arie Kapteyn
RAND
Santa Monica, California

12.1 INTRODUCTION

Differences between the distribution of answers given to the same survey question in an Internet survey and a survey using a traditional mode such as computer-assisted personal interviews (CAPI) or computer-assisted telephone interviews (CATI) can arise due to selection effects or to mode or context effects (see, e.g., Chapter 2 in this volume for a general discussion of differences between Internet surveys and surveys using other modes of administration). Selection effects arise when the Internet sample and the CAPI/CATI sample are not representative of the same population. A general concern with Internet interviewing is that even if the initial sample is a probability sample that is representative of the population of interest, households without Internet access are not covered. Since these households are in many respects not a random subpopulation, this may lead to serious selection effects (see Best, Krueger, Hubbard, & Smith, 2001; Berrens, Bohara, Jenkins-Smith, Silva, & Weimer, 2003; Denscombe, 2006; and Chapter 11 in this volume for some specific examples).

One solution to this particular selection problem is to provide Internet access (and the necessary equipment) to those who do not yet have it so that they can participate in the same way as those who already had Internet access (see, e.g., Fricker & Schonlau, 2002). This is the solution used by, for example, Knowledge Networks and the American Life Panel in the United States and the CentERpanel and the LISS panel in the Netherlands. It is an attractive solution, but it is costly—providing equipment and Internet access is not cheap. Moreover, even when a computer and Internet connection are offered for free, specific groups such as the elderly may still be reluctant to participate, leading to another selection problem due to an increase in unit nonresponse.

General socioeconomic surveys such as the Panel Study of Income Dynamics (PSID) or the Health and Retirement Study (HRS) in the United States and the European Social Survey (ESS) or the Survey of Health, Ageing and Retirement in Europe (SHARE) are traditionally administered using face-to-face (CAPI) or telephone (CATI) interviews. One suggestion to reduce the costs of these surveys has been to replace the CAPI or CATI interview by an interview over the Internet for respondents who have access to the Internet and are willing to participate in an Internet interview rather than a telephone or face-to-face interview (see, e.g., Schonlau, Asch, & Du, 2003). Since Internet interviews are generally much cheaper than CAPI or CATI interviews, this may improve cost efficiency. An important concern, however, is whether the change in interview mode may affect the survey answers. In other words, this is a feasible solution if there are no mode effects. Even if Internet answers would in some sense be better than CAPI or CATI answers (because of, for example, a reduction in social desirability bias or a reduction of random reporting errors; see Chang & Krosnick, 2009, and Yeager et al., 2009), the mixed-mode nature of the data would lead to complications for the analysis (see, e.g., Chapter 3 in this volume).

Pure mode effects arise when the same survey questions are asked in the same context to (random samples of) the same population but yield different answers. An example could be an interviewer effect such as social desirability, leading to differences in answers to the same question depending on whether or not an interviewer is present. As explained by Dillman and Christian (2005), a change of interview mode is very often accompanied by a change in question wording, question layout, or question context (e.g., a change in the preceding questions; see Schwarz, 1996; Smyth, Dillman, & Christian, 2007; and Chapter 10 in this volume). Mode effects in a broader sense also refer to the wording, layout, and context effects that are due to inevitable changes in wording, layout, or context associated with a change in mode. For example, the fact that answers in an Internet survey depend on layout (see, e.g., Christian & Dillman, 2004, and Chapter 7 in this volume) whereas layout plays no role in telephone or face-to-face interviews already implies that the effect of layout and a pure mode effect cannot be disentangled. On the other hand, the conceptual distinction between mode effects and selection effects seems much clearer, and the main goal of our analysis is to analyze mode effects in a broad sense for the population with Internet access, controlling for selection effects.

While existing studies have looked at mode effects in Internet surveys (see, e.g., Chapter 3 in this volume for an overview of some recent studies), most of these have done so under restrictive assumptions about the nature of sample selection effects. The reason is that the Internet survey and the traditional survey typically use separate independent samples, implying that mode effects and selection effects are hard to disentangle. In the ideal experiment on mode effects, the same questionnaire would be administered to the same respondents both over the Internet and using a traditional interview mode.*

In this study, we exploit the unique nature of the HRS Internet experiment carried out by RAND and the University of Michigan to analyze mode and context effects while controlling for selection effects, without making any assumptions about the nature of the selection process. In this experiment, the same respondents got CAPI or CATI interviews and Internet interviews, allowing us to control for selection effects by focusing on the same groups of respondents. The Internet survey questions and the CAPI/CATI questions overlapped, but the questionnaires were not identical, implying that context effects may play a role in addition to pure mode effects. Moreover, there were slight differences in the wordings of the questions. By looking at several waves of data we can

* In principle there may also be mode effects between CAPI and CATI. We do not pay attention to these in the current study and essentially consider CAPI and CATI as the same mode.

say something about the importance of these effects versus pure mode effects. We focus on two economic variables, in particular ownership and amounts invested in two important types of household assets (checking and savings accounts and stocks and stock mutual funds). Measuring the size and composition of household wealth is important for many economic and multidisciplinary analyses (see, for example, Guiso, Haliassos, & Jappelli, 2002). It is crucial for the economic analysis of decisions over the life cycle, such as consumption, labor supply and retirement, home ownership, financial transfers to children, and so on. At the same time, reporting asset amounts is generally known to be a demanding task for respondents in socioeconomic surveys.

The HRS is a panel study covering the U.S. population 50 years and older with regular questionnaires on health, economic status, social participation, and so on every two years. Most people are interviewed in several waves, although there is some attrition and there are refreshment samples with younger cohorts that reach the age of 50. We have two waves of regular HRS interviews, each of them followed by an Internet interview. For the first wave, we find large differences between the Internet answers and the answers to the regular interview, both in ownership and in amounts held. For the second wave, however, these differences almost completely disappear, and the Internet results for the second wave are very well in line with those of the two CAPI/CATI interviews. Our interpretation of these findings is that there is no evidence of pure mode effects, but seemingly small changes in question wordings combined with questionnaire context (the complete set of asset types considered in the survey) have a large effect on the answers, leading to a strong bias in the first Internet survey. This is not a pure mode effect but the combination of a context effect with a specific wording of the questions. When interpreting a given question, respondents use previous questions as cues, particularly if the wording of the question at hand is unclear or leaves room for different interpretations (see, e.g., Schuman & Presser, 1981). If, however, the ambiguity is removed by making the wording of the question more precise, the effect of preceding questions can be reduced. This can completely explain our main results. It is also in line with the conclusion that whether mode effects in a broad sense (not controlling for question context) play a role may strongly depend on the nature of the questionnaires and the wording of the questions (see Chapter 3 in this volume).

The remainder of this chapter is organized as follows. Section 12.2 describes the design of the HRS Internet experiment and provides detailed wordings of the main survey questions in our analysis. In Section 12.3 we describe ownership of the two types of assets we consider. In Section 12.4 we look at amounts held for those who report ownership. Section 12.5 summarizes the results of some regressions controlling for observed background characteristics, and Section 12.6 concludes.

12.2 THE HRS INTERNET EXPERIMENT

The Health and Retirement Study is a stratified random sample of the U.S. population ages 50 and older and their spouses. Once selected, the same respondents have been interviewed once every two years since 1992, with regular refreshments with new cohorts reaching the age of 50. In the years without core interviews, subsamples are often asked to participate in specific modules, usually administered by mail. Here we discuss the interviews in 2002 and 2004 (a mix of CAPI and CATI). For the purpose of the Internet experiment, these waves contained a module with questions on Internet access and willingness to participate in an Internet interview in between the biennial regular interviews. (This module was not administered in proxy interviews—interviews with relatives or others used for respondents unable to answer the questions for themselves because of physical or mental limitations.)

The first relevant question for our purposes was

> Do you regularly use the World Wide Web, or the Internet, for sending and receiving e-mail or for any other purpose, such as making purchases, searching for information, or making travel reservations?

Those who answered "yes" to this question (30%) were then asked:

> We may want to try out a procedure for asking questions of some of the participants in this study, using the Internet. Would you be willing to consider answering questions on the Internet, if it took about 15 minutes of your time?

Those who also said "yes" to this question (73%) were considered eligible for the Internet survey, and a random subset of them were sent a mailed invitation to participate. They got a URL for the survey with an ID and password. A $20 check was enclosed with the invitation letter. Up to three reminder letters were sent to those who were invited but did not log in to start the survey and to those who started but did not complete. Couper, Kapteyn, Schonlau, & Winter (2007) describe the data collection of the first wave and analyze the various steps in the selection process. Schonlau, Van Soest, Kapteyn, & Couper (2009) analyze selection effects and whether it is possible to correct for these by conditioning on a limited set of background variables. They find that propensity score weighting of the HRS Internet sample brings estimates of population means of a number of target variables closer to estimates based on the complete HRS, but differences remain. This indicates that in populations with still relatively limited Internet access, such as the population ages 50 and older, simply using Internet samples and reweighting is not a feasible procedure. One either has to provide Internet access to nonusers or employ mixed modes.

The Internet interviews were launched in 2003 and early 2006, including many questions that were also in the regular 2002 and 2004 HRS interviews, as well as specific experimental modules designed for Internet interviewing. Overall, the Internet interviews were much shorter than the regular interviews, with, for example, questions on only three types of household assets, much fewer than in the regular interviews. The two Internet questionnaires were also quite different. The first one (2003) focused on Internet and computer use, health problems, disability and work limitations, numeracy items, psychosocial items, expectations, and questions about household assets (housing, checking and savings accounts, and stocks). The second Internet interview (2006) focused on Internet and computer use, health and emotional problems, prescription drugs, social security expectations, and the same household assets.

We will consider respondents to the regular surveys in 2002 and 2004 and the Internet surveys in 2003 and 2006, which are subsamples of the 2002 and 2004 regular respondent samples, respectively. Due to the panel nature of the HRS with attrition and refreshment, there is a large subsample of 2002 HRS regular respondents who also participated in HRS 2004, and there is also some overlap between the two Internet samples. This allows for some test-retest consistency checks to compare the quality of the data collected over the Internet with the data collected in the regular CAPI or CATI interviews. We use the RAND version of HRS 2002 and HRS 2004 with 18,190 respondents.*

HRS Internet 2003 has 2,124 respondents. About 800 HRS 2002 respondents who had Internet access and were willing to participate in an Internet interview were not selected for HRS Internet 2003. These respondents served as a control group to gauge any possible adverse effects of the Internet experiment on subsequent participation in the regular HRS interviews.

HRS Internet 2006 was drawn from the subsample of HRS 2004 with Internet access. Our HRS Internet 2006 sample has 1,301 observations out of the 20,161 observations in the RAND version of HRS 2004. A second subset of HRS 2004 respondents with Internet access was interviewed over the Internet in late 2006 (HRS Internet 2006, phase 2), with a questionnaire that differed from the one used in the early 2006 Internet interviews (phase 1). The second phase data are not used for our analysis. The intersection of the four samples has 631 respondents. Many of the HRS Internet 2003 respondents are included in the phase 2 subsample of HRS Internet 2006 referred to above. They could not be interviewed in the first phase because of crowding out of the regular HRS 2006 interviews.

Compared to other general purpose socioeconomic surveys, the HRS has very extensive questions on economic aspects of the respondents and their households, with detailed questions on many components of income and wealth (see, e.g., Hurd, 2002). We present details of the question wordings, since, as we will argue below, the question wordings may have important effects on the answers.

12.2.1 HRS Regular Interviews

In the regular interviews of HRS 2002 and 2004, each financial respondent (i.e., the household member who is most knowledgeable about financial matters) answered a series of questions on household assets, starting with the following introduction:

> Savings and investments are an important part of family finances. The next questions ask about a number of different kinds of savings or investments you may have.

* The RAND version of HRS is a longitudinal user-friendly version of HRS with consistent nomenclature and imputation procedures across waves; see http://hrsonline.isr.umich.edu/index.php?p=shoavail&iyear=X7

They first got questions on real estate (other than main home), business or farm assets, and IRAs or KEOGHs (specific forms of tax-favored retirement saving in the United States) before they got the following question on stocks:

> (Aside from anything you have already told me about,) Do you (or your [husband/wife/partner]) have any shares of stock or stock mutual funds?*

Respondents who answered affirmatively immediately got a follow-up question on amounts:

> If you sold all those and paid off anything you owed on them, about how much would you have?

Respondents who did not provide an amount ("don't know" or "refuse to answer") got a series of unfolding bracket questions of the form:

> Does it amount to less than $_____, more than $_____, or what?

These unfolding bracket questions provide partial information about the amounts held by initial item nonrespondents. Juster and Smith (1997) show that many of these initial nonrespondents are willing to answer the bracket questions and that accounting for these answers changes the conclusions about the distribution of the amounts held in the population of interest, since the bracket answers suggest higher amounts held. Later studies, however, based upon an experimental module of the HRS data in which reported consumption expenditures mentioned in the bracket questions were randomized, suggest that these higher amounts may largely be due to anchoring and acquiescence bias in the answers to the bracket questions (see Hurd, 1999; Van Soest & Hurd, 2008). In this study, we will avoid these complications and consider only the respondents who answered the open-ended amount question.

After the questions on stocks, respondents were asked about bonds, and then came to a similar set of questions on checking and savings accounts:

* Shares of stock represent units of ownership in a corporation or entity; stock mutual funds are a pool of funds managed by a financial institution. They vary in the types of stocks they invest in, such as small-cap funds and growth funds, and the philosophies they use, such as aggressive or conservative.

(Aside from anything you have already told me about,) Do you (or your [husband/wife/partner]) have any checking or savings accounts or money market funds?

If "yes":

If you added up all such accounts, about how much would they amount to right now?

If "don't know" or "refuse to answer":

Does it amount to less than $_____, more than $_____, or what?

12.2.2 HRS Internet 2003

In the HRS Internet interviews, only three types of assets were considered. The series of asset questions started with the introduction:

Next we would like to ask some questions about housing, checking accounts, and stocks.

The data for housing were analyzed in an earlier version of this study; for housing we found no evidence at all of context or mode effects once selection was controlled for. To save space, these results are not presented here, but they are available upon request from the authors.

After the questions on housing, respondents then got the following questions on checking and savings accounts, with unfolding brackets for those who did not provide an amount:

Do you have any checking or savings accounts or money market funds?

If "yes":

If you added up all the checking and savings accounts and money market funds, about how much would they amount to right now?

These questions are immediately followed by similar questions on stocks and stock mutual funds:

Do you have any shares of stock or stock mutual funds?

If "yes":

If you sold all those and paid off anything you owed on them, about how much would you have?

These questions are virtually identical to those in the regular interviews, but they were not surrounded by similar questions on other types of assets. As we will argue later, this difference in context is likely to have had a major effect on the responses in the 2003 interview.

12.2.3 HRS Internet 2006

In the second Internet interview, we added a sentence asking the respondents explicitly not to include some other assets that may seem similar to the ones in the questions and that are not asked about separately in the Internet surveys. The questions on ownership and amounts of checking and savings accounts were therefore rephrased as follows:

Do you have any checking or savings accounts or money market funds? Please note: This does not include individual retirement accounts (IRAs and KEOGHs), shares of stock and stock mutual funds, corporate bonds, CDs, government savings bonds, Treasury bills, or other assets.

If "yes," then:

If you added up all the checking and savings accounts and money market funds, about how much would they amount to right now? Please note: This does not include individual retirement accounts (IRAs and KEOGHs), shares of stock and stock mutual funds, corporate bonds, CDs, government saving bonds, Treasury bills, or other assets.

Moreover, some questions on changes since the previous (regular 2004) interview were added:

Do you have more or less money in (all) your checking or savings accounts or money market funds than at the time of the HRS interview in 2004?

1. Had no checking or savings accounts or money market funds
2. More than in 2004
3. Less than in 2004
4. About the same

If "more than in 2004" or "less than in 2004":

How much [more/less] than in 2004?

The series for stocks and stock mutual funds was very similar:

Do you have any shares of stock or stock mutual funds? Please note: this does not include individual retirement accounts (IRAs and KEOGHs), checking and savings accounts or money market funds, corporate bonds, CDs, government savings bonds, Treasury bills, or other assets.

If "yes," then:

If you sold all those and paid off anything you owed on them, about how much would you have? Please note: This does not include individual retirement accounts (IRAs and KEOGHs), checking and savings accounts or money market funds, corporate bonds, CDs, government savings bonds, Treasury bills, or other assets.
Did you buy or sell stocks or stock mutual funds since the time of the HRS interview in 2004?

1. Yes, I bought and sold stocks or stock mutual funds
2. Yes, I bought stocks or stock mutual funds
3. Yes, I sold stocks or stock mutual funds
4. No, nothing bought or sold

Considering the total value of all your stocks and stock mutual funds, do you think it is more than, less than, or about the same as at the time of the HRS interview in 2004?

1. Had no stocks or stock mutual funds at that time
2. More than in 2004
3. Less than in 2004
4. About the same

If "more than in 2004" or "less than in 2004":

How much [more/less] than in 2004?

12.3 ASSET OWNERSHIP

Table 12.1 gives ownership rates for checking and savings accounts. Rows refer to time and mode of measurement, while columns refer to subsamples of respondents participating in any interview (column 1) or separately in each interview (columns 2–5). The first column shows that the raw ownership rates in the Internet interviews are substantially higher than in the regular HRS interviews. Columns 3 and 5 demonstrate that this is mainly due to selection. For example, HRS 2004 gives an ownership rate of 0.856, but if we consider the HRS 2004 ownership rate among the subsample of HRS Internet 2006 respondents, this rises to 0.967, which is actually higher than the ownership rate of 0.925 in the 2006 HRS Internet interview among the same households. Similarly, if we restrict the HRS 2002 sample to those who participated in HRS Internet 2003, the HRS 2002 ownership rate rises from 0.857 to 0.957, close to the 0.979 ownership rate in HRS Internet 2003. We can therefore conclude that once selection effects are taken out by considering the same respondents in different interviews, the differences between the four measurements are small. The selection effects are in line with the results of Schonlau et al. (2009), who find that, in general, Internet users are healthier and economically better off. It should be emphasized here that we are talking about selection in relation to participation in the Internet interview as a whole, not about selective response to the asset ownership questions of respondents who have already decided to participate in the interview. The number of "don't know" or "refuse to answer" responses on the ownership questions is very small, and the ownership rates are not sensitive to including or excluding respondents who gave such an answer in another wave.

Table 12.2 presents the ownership rates for stocks. Selection effects again play a large role, because the four samples are different and wealthier households are overrepresented in the Internet 2003 and Internet 2006 samples. In the HRS 2002 subsample of respondents who also participated in the HRS Internet 2003 interview, the ownership rate is 0.525 instead of the 0.320 ownership rate in the complete HRS 2002 sample. This difference is due to the selection effect. But this rate of 0.525 is still much lower than the ownership rate for the same respondents in HRS Internet 2003, which is 0.732. The large difference between the HRS Internet ownership

TABLE 12.1

Ownership Checking and Savings Accounts

Sample	All		HRS 02		Int 03		HRS 04		Int 06	
Variable	**Obs.**	**%Own**	**Obs.**	**%Own**	**Obs.**	**%Own**	**Obs.**	**%Own**	**Obs.**	**%Own**
HRS 2002	18,093	85.7	18,093	85.7	2,048	95.7	15,409	86.2	961	94.9
Int 2003	2,102	97.9	2,048	97.9	2,102	97.9	2,035	97.8	618	98.1
HRS 2004	19,771	85.6	15,409	86.5	2,035	96.3	19,771	85.6	1,283	96.7
Int 2006	1,288	92.5	961	92.7	618	92.6	1,283	92.5	1,288	92.5

Note: Unweighted ownership rates in % (%Own) with underlying number of observations. All: all respondents interviewed in the given wave (who answer yes or no). In HRS 02: only respondents who were interviewed in HRS 2002 and answered yes or no to the ownership question. In Int 03: same but only those with an answer in HRS Internet 2003. In HRS 04 and in Int 06: same for HRS 2004 and HRS Internet 2006.

TABLE 12.2

Ownership Shares of Stock and Stock Mutual Funds

Sample	All		HRS 02		Int 03		HRS 04		Int 06	
Variable	**Obs.**	**%Own**	**Obs.**	**%Own**	**Obs.**	**%Own**	**Obs.**	**%Own**	**Obs.**	**%Own**
HRS 2002	18,025	32.0	18,025	32.0	2,042	52.5	15,311	32.9	949	53.3
Int 2003	2,099	73.1	2,042	73.2	2,099	73.1	2,025	73.1	611	76.3
HRS 2004	19,697	30.9	15,311	31.8	2,025	53.3	19,697	30.9	1,261	49.2
Int 2006	1,272	47.9	949	49.2	611	52.0	1,261	47.7	1,272	47.9

Note: See Table 12.1.

rate and the regular HRS 2002 rate for the same households (0.732 compared to 0.525) is one of the puzzling findings of the 2002–2003 comparison. It cannot be a selection effect since the two numbers are based upon the same sample. Looking at it in isolation, it could be due to an interview mode effect, a context effect, or both.

Comparing HRS 2004 and HRS Internet 2006 does not give the same discrepancy. The selection effect is similar (a rise from 0.309 to 0.492) but once selection is controlled for, the ownership rates in HRS 2004 and HRS Internet 2006 are very similar (0.492 and 0.479). This suggests that stock ownership reported in HRS Internet 2003 is an outlier. An explanation may be the difference in context in combination with question wording. Since in HRS Internet 2003 there were no (preceding) questions on related assets (such as IRAs invested in stocks or stock mutual funds), respondents may have categorized related assets as stocks and stock mutual funds. Explicitly excluding these assets by rephrasing the question, as was done in the HRS Internet 2006 interview, solves this problem and removes the ambiguity in the wording of the question that led to the context effect. An alternative explanation might be a macroeconomic trend leading to a genuine peak in ownership of stocks and stock mutual funds in 2003, but this seems implausible given the historical trend in stock returns in the past decade.

To gain further insight into the quality of the data and possible differences between the regular interviews and the Internet interviews, we consider changes in ownership across the interviews, looking at transition rates from one wave to a later wave: Which fraction of owners in one wave do not own the same asset in the later wave, and which fraction of nonowners change to ownership? Table 12.3 presents transitions in ownership of stocks for the four waves, always using all the available observations (i.e., using the unbalanced panel). For all pairs of waves, there is a strong (and statistically significant) positive relation between owning stocks in the two waves, but there are also some substantial differences between the transition rates. For example, the transition rates from nonownership in HRS 2002 to ownership in HRS Internet 2003 are much higher than the transition rates from nonownership in HRS 2004 to ownership in HRS Internet 2006. Table 12.3, however, does not make clear which part of this is a selection effect, due to different sample compositions (the Internet 2003 sample and the Internet 2006 sample, respectively), and which part reflects mode, context, or question wording effects.

TABLE 12.3

Transitions in Stock Ownership—Unbalanced Panel

		Int 03		HRS 04		Int 06	
		No	**Yes**	**No**	**Yes**	**No**	**Yes**
HRS 02	**No**	50.83	49.17	89.55	10.45	74.04	25.96
	Yes	5.21	94.79	24.66	75.34	30.43	69.57
Int 03	**No**			89.17	10.83	88.28	11.72
	Yes			31.01	68.99	35.41	64.59
HRS 04	**No**					75.94	24.06
	Yes					27.86	72.14

Note: Transition rates in %.

Table 12.4 takes out the selection effects by considering the transition rates in the balanced sample of respondents who participated in all four surveys. It confirms that HRS Internet 2003 is different from the other surveys. While numbers of transitions in and out of ownership are roughly similar for transitions among HRS 2002, HRS 2004, and HRS Internet 2006, this is not the case for transitions involving HRS Internet 2003. For 2003, transition rates into ownership are relatively large, and transition rates out of ownership are large as well. All this could be explained by reporting errors in HRS Internet 2003 if many nonowners report ownership. However, such a reporting error does not occur in HRS Internet 2006. If the difference between HRS 2002 and HRS Internet 2003 were due to a pure effect of interview mode, we would expect a similar difference between HRS 2004 and HRS Internet 2006, but we do not find such

TABLE 12.4

Transitions in Stock Ownership—Balanced Panel

		Int 03		HRS 04		Int 06	
		No	**Yes**	**No**	**Yes**	**No**	**Yes**
HRS 02	**No**	44.53	55.47	75.09	24.91	70.94	29.06
	Yes	6.52	93.48	22.05	77.95	28.26	71.74
Int 03	**No**			89.93	10.07	87.77	12.23
	Yes			32.37	67.63	35.04	64.96
HRS 04	**No**					75.56	24.44
	Yes					23.66	76.34

Note: Transition rates in %.

TABLE 12.5

Reported Changes in HRS Internet 2006 by Ownership in 2004

Owns Stocks HRS 2004 Interview	Reported Change in Value 2004–2006				
	No Stocks in 2004	More Than in 2004	Less Than in 2004	Same as in 2004	Missing
No (154)	7.14	47.40	12.99	31.82	0.65
Yes (448)	0.89	59.38	10.27	27.90	1.56
Missing (7)	0.00	28.57	14.29	28.57	28.57
All (609)	2.46	55.99	11.00	28.90	1.64

Note: Row percentages; total number of observations for each row in parentheses. Respondents who reported owning stocks in HRS Internet 2006 interview only.

a difference there at all. This again leads us to conclude that the difference is caused by context and/or wording effects.

Table 12.5 reports the answers to the HRS Internet 2006 question: "Considering the total value of your stocks and stock mutual funds, do you think it is more than, less than, or about the same as at the time of the HRS interview in 2004?" (see Section 12.2), asked of all respondents who reported in the HRS Internet 2006 interview that they owned stocks. Although there is a significant correlation between the answer to this question and stock ownership in 2004, the correlation is far from perfect. In particular, a large majority of the 154 respondents who in 2004 reported that they had no stocks and in 2006 reported that they did have stocks did not choose the answer "had no stocks at that time," which seems the obvious answer for these people. Almost 44% of these nonowners in 2004 and owners in 2006 indicated that the value of their stocks in 2006 was about the same as or even less than the value of their stocks in 2004.

Similarly, Table 12.6 reports the answers to the question "Did you buy or sell stocks or stock mutual funds since the HRS interview in 2004?" (see Section 12.2). As expected, there is an association between the answers to this question and ownership reported in HRS 2004, though it is not very strong, and the p-value of the χ^2 test of independence is 0.032. Again, inconsistencies are revealed—half of those who reported nonownership in 2004 and ownership in 2006 said they bought no stocks or stock mutual funds in the meantime. This shows that either the retrospective questions in HRS Internet 2006 or the ownership questions in HRS 2004 (or both) suffer from substantial reporting

TABLE 12.6

Reported Buying and Selling of Stocks Since 2004, by HRS 2004 Stocks Ownership Status

Owns Stocks HRS 2004 Interview	Reported Buying and Selling 2004–2006				
	Bought and Sold	Bought, Not Sold	Sold, Not Bought	Not Bought, Not Sold	Missing
No (154)	29.22	20.13	5.19	44.81	0.65
Yes (448)	45.76	14.06	6.92	32.37	0.89
Missing (7)	57.14	14.29	0.00	28.57	0.00
All (609)	41.71	15.60	6.40	35.47	0.82

Note: Row percentages; total number of observations for each row in parentheses. Respondents who reported owning stocks in HRS Internet 2006 interview only.

errors. Although we do not find the context and wording effects that we find for HRS Internet 2003 in the later interviews, this implies that HRS Internet 2006 or HRS 2004 still suffers from reporting errors. But there are two important differences with the problems in HRS Internet 2003: First, the errors seem to be much less systematic, since they do not lead to over- or underestimation of ownership rates, and second, they may well be due to the retrospective questions only. Our data do not allow us to identify this, but in any case the results suggest that retrospective questions cannot simply replace questions asked at the time of the survey, emphasizing the need for longitudinal data collection with a genuine panel.

Table 12.7 shows that the answers to the two retrospective questions about whether respondents bought or sold assets or whether the values of assets held changed between 2004 and 2006 are associated in the expected way. For example, respondents who said they bought but did not sell often report that the value of their assets has increased. Those who reported they neither bought nor sold stocks or stock mutual funds often report that the value of the amount held has remained about the same.

Tables 12.5, 12.6, and 12.7 suggest substantial reporting errors but do not suggest that the errors are systematic. Perhaps the retrospective questions suffer from recall error, making the answers to them less accurate than those to the questions on current ownership. The tables provide no evidence that the HRS Internet 2006 answers are more or less reliable than the answers in the regular HRS 2004 interview.

TABLE 12.7

Reported Buying and Selling of Stocks and Change in Reported Value Since 2004

	Reported Change in Value 2004–2006				
Buying and Selling 2004–2006	**No Stocks in 2004**	**More Than in 2004**	**Less Than in 2004**	**Same As in 2004**	**Missing**
Bought and sold (254)	1.57	64.17	11.81	20.47	1.97
Bought, not sold (95)	5.26	74.74	8.42	10.53	1.05
Sold, not bought (39)	0.00	35.90	33.33	28.21	2.56
Not bought, not sold (216)	2.78	42.59	7.41	46.76	0.46
Missing (5)	0.00	20.00	0.00	40.00	40.00
All (609)	2.46	55.99	11.00	28.90	1.64

Note: Row percentages; total number of observations for each row in parentheses. Respondents who reported to own stocks in HRS Internet 2006 interview only.

12.4 AMOUNTS HELD

In this section we consider the amounts held for each of the two types of assets of interest, conditional on ownership. This follows the logic of the questionnaire (Section 12.2), where amount questions are asked only of respondents who have already answered the ownership question affirmatively. We only consider exactly reported amounts in the open-ended questions and do not use the information provided in follow-up unfolding brackets by respondents who do not answer the open-ended amount question.

12.4.1 Checking and Savings Accounts

Table 12.8 presents the distribution of amounts invested in checking and savings accounts, excluding zeros (i.e., only for those who own the asset) and discarding missing values. As explained in Section 12.3, we also discard the information in follow-up unfolding bracket questions and treat the bracket answers simply as missing.* The first panel considers all respondents in the unbalanced panel. There is a large difference between HRS Internet 2003 and the other three surveys, with much higher amounts in the former. To exclude the possible effect of selection, the sec-

* The existing literature suggests that item nonresponse is not random (e.g., Juster & Smith, 1997). Still, the numbers of missing values are similar in all surveys, and there is no reason why the selection effect due to nonresponse should be very different across surveys. It therefore seems very unlikely that they have an effect on our comparisons or can explain the differences in distributions across surveys.

TABLE 12.8

Amounts in Checking and Savings Accounts

All Respondents With Positive Amount

Percentile	HRS 02	Int 03	HRS 04	Int 06
10	490	2,000	300	1,000
25	2,000	8,000	2,000	3,000
50	8,000	30,000	8,000	10,000
75	26,000	100,000	25,000	40,000
90	75,000	250,000	70,000	100,000
Obs.	15,437	1,769	12,579	939

Respondents With Checking and Savings Account in HRS Internet 2003

Percentile	HRS 02	Int 03	HRS 04	Int 06
10	1,400	2,000	1,500	1,200
25	4,000	8,000	4,750	5,000
50	12,000	30,000	13,000	15,000
75	35,000	100,000	39,000	50,000
90	85,000	250,000	90,000	100,000
Obs.	1,958	1,769	1,656	468

Respondents With Checking and Savings Account in HRS Internet 2006

Percentile	HRS 02	Int 03	HRS 04	Int 06
10	1,500	3,000	1,500	1,000
25	5,000	10,000	5,000	3,000
50	12,000	35,000	13,500	10,000
75	40,000	100,000	35,000	40,000
90	90,000	250,000	80,000	100,000
Obs.	888	480	956	939

ond panel only considers the HRS Internet 2003 respondents. This leads to higher amounts for the other three surveys also, but the gap between HRS Internet 2003 and the other three surveys remains very large.

The third panel of Table 12.8 shows that this issue is specific to HRS Internet 2003 and does not play a role in HRS Internet 2006. If we consider HRS Internet 2006 participants only, the amounts reported in 2006 are distributed similarly to those in the regular HRS surveys of 2002 and 2004. For this subsample also, the amounts reported in HRS Internet 2003 have a quite different distribution, with much larger percentiles throughout.

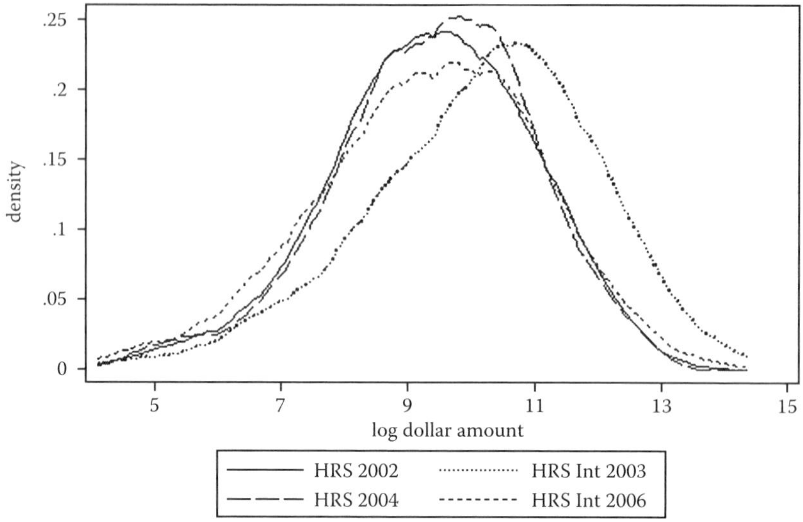

FIGURE 12.1
Checking and saving—Internet samples.

Figure 12.1 represents these findings in a slightly different way. It compares the distribution of the amounts reported in 2002 and 2003 by those who reported owning a checking or savings account in HRS Internet 2003, as well as the distribution of the amounts reported in 2004 and 2006 of those who reported ownership in HRS Internet 2006. Thus selection on Internet access is controlled for in all four distributions (the figure essentially combines the second and third panels of Table 12.8). The salient feature of the figure is the deviating pattern for HRS Internet 2003.

One way to get an impression of the stability of reported asset levels across waves is to consider rank correlations. We would of course not expect perfect correlations between waves, but broadly speaking we would expect respondents with a large amount of assets in one wave to be likely to have a large amount in the next wave. Rank correlations between amounts in checking and savings accounts reported in different waves are presented in Table 12.9. All of these are significantly positive. The rank correlation between amounts reported in the two regular interviews is highest. Correlations are lower if the time gap between waves is larger. From this table, it is not apparent that the HRS Internet 2003 data are systematically different from the other waves. It is the levels (as described in Table 12.8 and Figure 12.1) that make it different, not the relative position of each household's amount.

TABLE 12.9

Rank Correlations Between Amounts in Checking and Savings Accounts

	HRS Internet 2003	HRS 2004	HRS Internet 2006
HRS 2002	0.500	0.623	0.461
HRS Internet 2003		0.522	0.471
HRS 2004			0.559

TABLE 12.10

Changes in Amounts in Checking and Savings Accounts

Retrospective Question	Obs.	Percentiles of the Difference Between Reported Levels in HRS Internet 2006 and HRS 2004				
		10	**25**	**50**	**75**	**90**
No account in 2004	4	−8,500	−8,215	−3,465	1,675	2,350
More than in 2004	344	−35,000	−7,000	3,000	27,000	71,900
Less than in 2004	148	−57,000	−21,750	−3,000	2,600	31,000
About the same	332	−23,000	−7,000	−500	2,000	24,000
All	828	−33,500	−9,950	0	10,000	48,000

Note: Households with checking and savings accounts in HRS Internet 2006.

In HRS Internet 2006 respondents with a checking or savings account were asked, "Do you have more or less money in (all) your checking or savings accounts or money market funds than at the time of the HRS interview in 2004?" (see Section 12.2). About 43% of respondents with a checking and savings account in HRS Internet 2006 say the amount in their account(s) increased. Table 12.10 shows that, accordingly, the median difference between the amounts reported in HRS Internet 2006 and HRS 2004 is positive, but there is also a substantial number of households for which this difference is negative. This is evidence of reporting errors, due either to recall error or to errors in current amounts held. About 37% report the value is about the same at the times of the two interviews. Indeed, the median change in reported amounts is close to zero, but the variation around that median is huge. As before, we can conclude that although there is a significant association between the retrospective report of the change and the change measured as the difference in amounts held reported at the two points in time, at least one of these measures must be rather noisy.*

* After the question whether the amount held was more or less than in 2004, for those who answered "more" or "less" there was a follow-up question on the amount of change. This question is not used here.

TABLE 12.11

Amounts in Shares of Stock and Stock Mutual Funds

All Respondents With Positive Amount

Percentile	HRS 02	Int 03	HRS 04	Int 06
10	2,500	3,000	3,000	2,000
25	12,000	23,000	12,000	12,000
50	50,000	90,000	50,000	50,000
75	200,000	250,000	200,000	175,000
90	400,000	600,000	500,000	400,000
Obs.	5,798	1,262	4,063	434

Respondents Who Report That They Own Shares of Stock or Stock Mutual Funds in HRS Internet 2003

Percentile	HRS 02	Int 03	HRS 04	Int 06
10	5,000	3,000	4,600	3,000
25	20,000	23,000	20,000	15,000
50	75,000	90,000	80,000	70,000
75	200,000	250,000	249,000	200,000
90	500,000	600,000	500	400,000
Obs.	1,033	1,262	807	223

Respondents Who Report That They Own Shares of Stock or Stock Mutual Funds in HRS Internet 2006

Percentile	HRS 02	Int 03	HRS 04	Int 06
10	5,000	10,000	5,000	2,000
25	18,000	30,000	24,000	12,000
50	85,000	100,000	100,000	50,000
75	250,000	300,000	250,000	175,000
90	600,000	700,000	500,000	400,000
Obs.	366	233	349	434

12.4.2 Stocks and Stock Mutual Funds

Table 12.11 is similar to Table 12.8, but now for stocks and stock mutual funds. Comparing the first panel with the other two panels shows that the people who participated in one of the Internet interviews and had stocks at the time of the interview typically hold higher amounts in the other waves as well. Once selection on Internet access is corrected for (second and third panels), the differences between the four waves are not that large. In contrast to what was found for checking and savings accounts, the distribution in HRS Internet 2003 is not different from the other

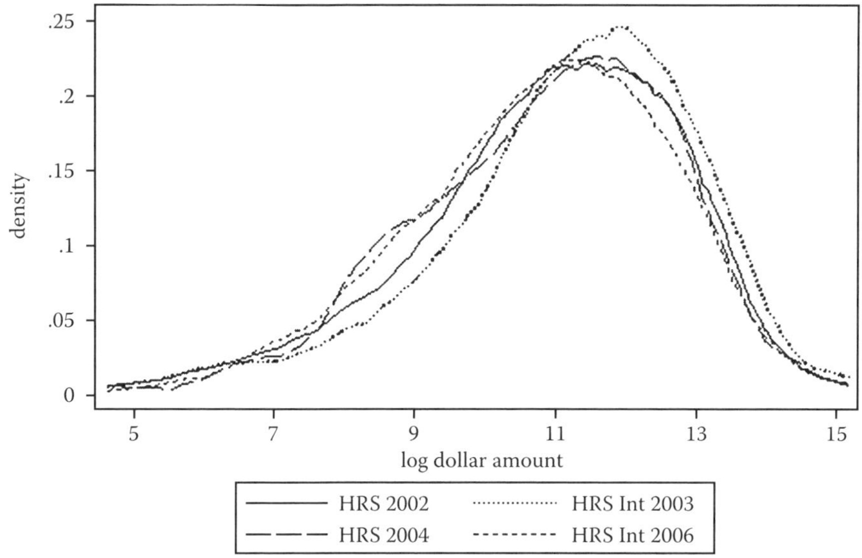

FIGURE 12.2
Stocks and stock mutual funds—Internet samples.

distributions. Still, HRS Internet 2003 shows the highest amounts. Since the other Internet interview gives the lowest amounts, this is unlikely to be due to a pure mode effect; rather, it is suggestive of a context effect.

Figure 12.2, constructed similarly to Figure 12.1, compares the distribution of the positive amounts in stocks and stock mutual funds reported in 2002 and 2003 by those who reported owning the asset in HRS Internet 2003, as well as the distribution of the positive amounts reported in 2004 and 2006 of those who reported ownership in HRS Internet 2006. Thus selection on Internet access is controlled for in all four distributions. The figure confirms that, controlling for selection, the distribution of amounts in stocks and stock mutual funds in HRS Internet 2003 is not very different from the distribution of this asset in the other three surveys.

Table 12.12 shows the rank correlation coefficients for the positive amounts for each pair of waves. There is some similarity with Table 12.9 in the sense that the highest correlation is between the two regular HRS interviews. The lowest correlation is between the two Internet interviews. Still, the rank correlations are of similar magnitude and do not suggest that there is a specific survey among the four that leads to answers that are very different from those in the other three surveys.

TABLE 12.12

Rank Correlations Between Amounts in Shares of Stock and Stock Mutual Funds

	HRS Internet 2003	HRS 2004	HRS Internet 2006
HRS 2002	0.609	0.734	0.615
HRS Internet 2003		0.649	0.557
HRS 2004			0.654

TABLE 12.13

Changes in Total Values of Shares of Stock and Stock Mutual Funds

Retrospective Question	**Obs.**	**Percentiles of Difference in Reported Levels in HRS Internet 2006 and HRS 2004**				
		10	**25**	**50**	**75**	**90**
No account in 2004	11	−2,000	1,000	7,000	50,000	60,000
More than in 2004	221	−150,000	−39,950	4,000	45,000	174,000
Less than in 2004	44	−180,000	−66,500	0	54,500	258,000
About the same	99	−300,000	−15,000	1,000	17,500	100,000
All	375	−170,000	−30,000	3,000	39,000	150,000

Note: Households with shares of stock and stock mutual funds in HRS Internet 2006.

Table 12.13 is the analog of Table 12.10 for stocks and stock mutual funds. For those who report in 2006 that the value of their stocks and stock mutual funds increased, the median difference between the reported amounts held in 2004 and 2006 is indeed positive. Still, for 37% of this group, the difference in reported amounts is negative. For those who report in 2006 that the total value has fallen, the median difference in reported amounts is zero; for those who report in 2006 that the total value of their stocks and stock mutual funds remained about the same, the median difference between amounts reported in 2006 and 2004 is $1,000. The ordering of the median differences is as expected, but the large variation at the household level is a strong indication of reporting errors in either the retrospective questions or the reports of current values (or both).

12.5 REGRESSION MODELS FOR OWNERSHIP AND AMOUNTS HELD

In this section we explain ownership and amounts held while controlling for gender, household composition, age, and education. We consider

TABLE 12.14

Ownership of Checking and Savings Accounts—Probits by Wave

	HRS 02		HRS Int 03		HRS 04		HRS Int 06	
	Coef.	***t*-val**	**Coef.**	***t*-val**	**Coef.**	***t*-val**	**Coef.**	***t*-val**
Byear	0.000	−0.06	−0.015	−1.62	−0.005	−0.77	−0.008	−0.97
Gend	−0.001	−0.01	−0.015	−0.11	−0.055	−0.56	−0.126	−1.08
Nonwh	−0.228	−1.34	−0.115	−0.47	−0.296	−1.88	−0.049	−0.26
Hispan	−0.282	−1.06	−0.318	−0.89	−0.607	−2.93	−0.345	−1.31
Edmed	−0.206	−0.85	0.396	1.66	−0.146	−0.59	0.243	0.93
Edhigh	−0.058	−0.25	0.617	2.72	−0.019	−0.08	0.536	2.09
Marr	0.032	0.28	0.318	2.24	0.146	1.34	0.193	1.51
Work	−0.143	−1.19	0.014	0.08	−0.048	−0.40	0.097	0.67
Retir	−0.101	−0.82	−0.164	−0.92	−0.141	−1.09	0.217	1.34
Intercept	1.900	5.00	1.992	3.99	2.173	5.44	1.300	2.68

Note: Respondents who participated in at least one Internet interview. Dependent variable: 1 if household reports ownership, 0 if it reports nonownership. "Don't know" and "refuse to answer" responses excluded.
Explanatory variables: Byear: year of birth; Gend: dummy for females; Nonwh: dummy nonwhite; Hispan: dummy Hispanic; Edmed, Edhig: dummies for intermediate and higher education; Marr: dummy married; Work: dummy working for pay; Retir: dummy for being retired.

models for each wave separately and random-effects models that assume slope parameters are constant across waves, with time dummies to capture differences across waves.

The goal of these regressions is to investigate whether the determinants of ownership and amounts vary across waves (which can be analyzed using separate regressions for each of the four panel waves) and whether the across-waves differences in ownership rates and amounts that were found in the previous sections remain if background characteristics are controlled for. We know that there are strong selection effects—the households with Internet access more often hold assets and hold higher amounts than those without Internet access. We do not analyze the selection effects here but control for them by including in the regressions only households who participated in at least one of the Internet interviews.

Table 12.14 presents probit results for ownership of checking and savings accounts for each wave separately. We included basic demographics such as gender, age, and ethnicity, and socioeconomic status variables including education level and employment status. Income is not included because its measure may suffer from a mode effect itself and because of a large

TABLE 12.15

Ownership of Shares of Stock and Stock Mutual Funds—Probits by Wave

	HRS 02		HRS Int 03		HRS 04		HRS Int 06	
	Coef.	***t*-val**	**Coef.**	***t*-val**	**Coef.**	***t*-val**	**Coef.**	***t*-val**
Byear	−0.008	−2.01	−0.001	−0.27	−0.015	−4.29	−0.015	−2.91
Gend	−0.004	−0.08	−0.048	−0.75	0.001	0.02	−0.031	−0.41
Nonwh	−0.247	−2.18	−0.308	−2.40	−0.259	−2.53	−0.390	−2.81
Hispan	−0.606	−3.04	−0.491	−2.38	−0.526	−3.09	−0.296	−1.30
Edmed	0.350	2.53	0.303	2.07	0.260	1.94	0.147	0.69
Edhigh	0.709	5.32	0.710	5.05	0.603	4.67	0.529	2.57
Marr	0.341	5.03	0.316	4.31	0.206	3.30	0.382	4.10
Work	−0.124	−1.77	0.079	0.99	0.036	0.54	0.081	0.81
Retir	0.061	0.84	0.140	1.66	0.103	1.48	0.116	1.08
Intercept	−0.421	−1.87	−0.151	−0.61	−0.053	−0.25	−0.101	−0.30

Note: See Table 12.14.

number of missing values. Few variables are significant, which may not be too surprising since ownership rates among households with Internet access are well over 90% in all waves (Table 12.1) and so there is not a lot of variation to explain. Still, there seem to be some substantial differences across waves. The highly educated are more likely to have checking and savings accounts in the Internet interviews (2003 and 2006) but not in the (2002 and 2004) regular HRS interviews. Hispanics are particularly unlikely to have a checking or savings account in HRS 2004.

Table 12.15 gives the results for ownership of stocks and stock mutual funds (cf. Table 12.2). The pattern is quite consistent across waves for most variables. Higher education and being married make stock ownership more likely, while nonwhites and Hispanics are less likely to own stocks than non-Hispanic whites. The effect of labor force status variables varies but is never significant. The main difference across waves seems to be the effect of birth year (or age)—it is significantly negative in all waves except the HRS Internet interview in 2003, where it is negative but small and insignificant. This suggests that the very high ownership rates reported in this interview are mainly the result of high ownership among younger age groups in comparison to the other waves.

Table 12.16 presents random effects probit models for both assets, imposing equal slope coefficients across waves. Because observations from the four panel waves are pooled now, significance levels tend to be higher than

TABLE 12.16

Asset Ownership—Random Effects Probits

	Checking & Savings		Stocks	
	Coef.	***t*-val**	**Coef.**	***t*-val**
Byear	-0.009	-1.87	-0.022	-4.06
Gend	-0.050	-0.69	-0.015	-0.18
Nonwh	-0.257	-2.07	-0.572	-3.58
Hispan	-0.496	-2.77	-0.830	-3.29
Edmed	0.059	0.36	0.600	3.00
Edhigh	0.274	1.71	1.347	6.86
Marr	0.155	1.90	0.539	5.78
Work	-0.032	-0.37	-0.018	-0.22
Retir	-0.105	-1.14	0.148	1.73
Wav2	0.419	4.59	1.122	18.66
Wav3	0.155	2.06	-0.011	-0.23
Wav4	-0.260	-3.10	-0.115	-1.81
Intercept	2.301	7.71	-0.565	-1.79
σ (ind eff)	0.721	9.81	1.670	29.14

Note: See Table 12.14. σ (ind eff) is the standard deviation of the random effect; the standard deviation of the error term is normalized to 1.

in Tables 12.14 and 12.15. The associations between ownership and socioeconomic and demographic characteristics are broadly in line with earlier studies (see, e.g., Hurd, 2002). Nonwhites and Hispanics are less likely to hold both types of assets, particularly stocks. Younger cohorts are less likely to hold stocks. Education and being married have a positive effect on holding stocks but a small and insignificant effect on holding checking or savings accounts. Labor force status plays no significant role for either type of assets. Random effects are significant in both cases, but more so for stocks than for checking and savings accounts, implying strong persistence in stock ownership. Unobserved and observed heterogeneity are the only sources of persistence incorporated in the model. More sophisticated models would also allow for state dependence: a causal effect of ownership in one wave on ownership in the next wave (see, e.g., Alessie, Hochguertel, and Van Soest, 2002).

The parameters of main interest in Table 12.16 are the coefficients on the time dummies. Keeping background variables constant, we find significant

TABLE 12.17

Log Amounts in Checking and Savings Accounts—OLS Estimates by Wave

	HRS 02		HRS Int 03		HRS 04		HRS Int 06	
	Coef.	***t*-val**	**Coef.**	***t*-val**	**Coef.**	***t*-val**	**Coef.**	***t*-val**
Byear	–0.021	–4.17	–0.027	–4.03	–0.025	–5.38	–0.033	–3.61
Gend	–0.042	–0.57	0.038	0.40	0.028	0.40	–0.209	–1.60
Nonwh	–0.345	–2.36	–0.494	–2.35	–0.203	–1.47	–0.786	–3.42
Hispan	–0.296	–1.22	–0.984	–2.91	0.063	0.28	0.057	0.15
Edmed	0.431	2.45	0.401	1.63	0.659	3.71	0.675	1.73
Edhigh	0.903	5.35	0.981	4.18	0.976	5.72	0.903	2.39
Marr	0.679	7.81	0.575	5.01	0.590	7.09	0.225	1.43
Work	–0.078	–0.86	–0.110	–0.89	0.012	0.14	–0.021	–0.12
Retir	0.264	2.78	0.246	1.90	0.283	3.03	0.013	0.07
Intercept	8.850	30.42	9.849	25.19	8.887	31.15	10.162	16.95
Root *MSE*	1.640		1.880		1.663		1.876	
R^2	0.078		0.073		0.065		0.054	

Note: Ordinary Least Squares (OLS) Estimates. Respondents who participated in at least one Internet interview, report that they own a checking or savings account, and report a positive amount. See Table 12.14 for definitions of explanatory variables.

differences in ownership rates of checking and savings accounts across waves. In particular, it seems ownership is less likely in HRS 2002 and HRS Internet 2006 than in the waves in between (HRS Internet 2003 and HRS 2004). We do not have a good explanation for this finding; it does not seem to be related to interviewing mode and may reflect a macroeconomic time effect.

As expected in view of the results in Section 12.3, the most salient feature in the ownership of stocks equation is the huge coefficient on the time dummy for 2003. This corresponds to the descriptive statistics (cf. Table 12.2)—controlling for background variables does not change the conclusion that ownership of stocks and stock mutual funds among the subpopulation with Internet access is much higher according to the reports in HRS Internet 2003 than in the other three surveys. The marginal effect (keeping everything else constant at the sample mean, and setting the individual effect to its mean of zero) is about 40 percentage points.

Table 12.17 presents the Ordinary Least Squares (OLS) estimates for a linear regression model explaining the log of the amount of money held in checking and savings accounts for each wave by the same variables as

TABLE 12.18

Log Amounts in Shares of Stock and Stock Mutual Funds—OLS Estimates by Wave

	HRS 02		HRS Int 03		HRS 04		HRS Int 06	
	Coef.	***t*-val**	**Coef.**	***t*-val**	**Coef.**	***t*-val**	**Coef.**	***t*-val**
Byear	−0.028	−3.63	−0.012	−1.46	−0.022	−3.02	−0.022	−1.46
Gend	0.143	1.30	−0.089	−0.76	0.133	1.24	−0.397	−1.94
Nonwh	−0.217	−0.86	−0.653	−2.27	−0.727	−3.10	0.211	0.47
Hispan	−0.165	−0.32	−0.395	−0.81	−0.076	−0.16	−1.700	−1.89
Edmed	0.083	0.24	0.381	1.04	0.819	2.51	−0.525	−0.82
Edhigh	0.643	1.94	1.067	3.04	1.205	3.85	0.029	0.05
Marr	0.225	1.59	0.341	2.36	0.345	2.61	−0.036	−0.13
Work	−0.172	−1.21	−0.497	−3.21	−0.333	−2.47	0.084	0.31
Retir	0.382	2.61	0.385	2.41	0.086	0.61	0.186	0.66
Intercept	10.949	22.27	10.706	20.62	10.426	22.81	12.282	12.68
Root *MSE*	1.845		1.907		1.84		1.982	
R^2	0.064		0.083		0.055		0.026	

Note: Ordinary Least Squares (OLS) Estimates. Respondents who participated in at least one Internet interview, report that they own stocks, and report a positive amount. See Table 12.14 for definitions of explanatory variables.

before. This is conditional on Internet access, ownership, and reporting a positive amount. The effects of age and education are stable over the four survey waves. Gender is never significant. Nonwhites hold lower amounts than whites, and Hispanics hold less than non-Hispanics, though this effect is often insignificant. The biggest difference between the HRS Internet 2003 wave and the other waves appears to be the coefficient on Hispanics, which is large and negative in the 2003 wave. Since the non-Hispanic whites are the reference category, this mainly suggests that the reported amounts held by non-Hispanic whites are higher in the 2003 wave.

Table 12.18 presents the same regressions for stocks and stock mutual funds. There are substantial differences across waves, particularly between the HRS Internet 2006 survey and the other three surveys. For example, the (positive) effect of education on amounts held has disappeared completely. The same applies to marital status and labor force position. The 2006 Internet wave gives the lowest R^2 and the highest estimate of the noise level (the mean squared error, *MSE*). Therefore, unlike in the previous results, it seems that when amounts in stocks and stock mutual funds are concerned, the 2006 Internet survey is more of an outlier than the 2003 Internet survey.

TABLE 12.19

Asset Amounts—Random-Effects Models

	Checking & Savings		Stocks	
	Coef.	***t*-val**	**Coef.**	***t*-val**
Byear	–0.027	–7.15	–0.023	–4.26
Gend	–0.013	–0.21	0.026	0.31
Nonwh	–0.399	–3.42	–0.482	–2.61
Hispan	–0.275	–1.46	–0.197	–0.61
Edmed	0.631	4.17	0.368	1.49
Edhigh	1.028	7.08	0.845	3.55
Marr	0.514	7.68	0.307	3.11
Work	–0.024	–0.39	–0.188	–2.18
Retir	0.151	2.42	0.233	2.69
Int 2003	0.852	21.24	0.386	7.34
HRS 2004	0.110	3.05	0.115	2.28
Int 2006	0.081	1.54	–0.116	–1.46
Intercept	9.046	39.48	10.666	31.14
σ (ind eff)	1.250		1.482	
σ (error term)	1.230		1.211	

Note: Respondents who participated in at least one Internet interview, report that they own the asset, and report a positive amount. See Table 12.14 for definitions of explanatory variables.

Table 12.19 presents the estimates of random-effects models for the log of the amounts held of both types of assets. On average over the four waves, younger households and nonwhites hold lower amounts than others. The higher educated hold higher amounts. Retired (heads of) household(s) hold higher amounts also. The estimated standard deviations of individual effects and error terms indicate high persistence of amounts held, with more than half of the unsystematic variation ascribed to the random effects.

The main parameters of interest are once again the time dummies—they clearly confirm the unusually high amounts in checking and savings accounts reported in HRS Internet 2003, keeping everything else constant. The amounts are 75% to 90% higher than in the other surveys. The amounts invested in stocks are also quite high in the 2003 Internet interview, but the difference is not as extreme as for checking and savings accounts.

12.6 CONCLUSIONS

This chapter compares the distributions of two types of assets in U.S. household portfolios, checking and savings accounts and stocks and stock mutual funds, measured in two regular HRS interviews and in two HRS Internet interviews. The design of the Internet surveys makes it possible to disentangle selection effects from mode or context effects. The main conclusions are threefold. First, we find large selection effects: Respondents with Internet access more often own stocks and stock mutual funds. They also hold higher amounts of both types of assets, conditional on ownership. Second, controlling for these selection effects, we find some salient differences between HRS Internet 2003 and the other surveys: Ownership of stocks and stock mutual funds is much larger in the 2003 survey, and the amounts held in checking and savings accounts are also much larger in that same survey. These features are specific to HRS Internet 2003 and are not shared by HRS Internet 2006. This is apparent not only from the descriptive statistics but also from regression models when background variables are controlled for. Since they are not shared by the other Internet survey, they must be interpreted as effects of context and question wording rather than as pure mode effects. Third, retrospective questions on changes since the previous interview give answers associated with the change constructed from ownership and amounts held in the two interviews, but the association is far from perfect and implies many inconsistencies in either the reported changes or the reported asset levels (or both).

The difference between the 2003 Internet interview and the two regular surveys (2002 and 2004) is primarily one of context. In the regular surveys the questions about checking and savings and about stocks and stock mutual funds are part of an exhaustive list of questions about different types of assets. It is clear from the context, therefore, that certain other assets (e.g., IRAs and KEOGHs) should not be included. In the 2003 wave that context is missing, and hence it seems likely that respondents used a broader definition of assets than in the regular HRS waves. When in 2006 these other assets were explicitly excluded by adding more explanation to the questions (see Section 12.2), the differences between the Internet responses and the responses in the regular HRS interviews disappear.

What does this imply for the future of Internet or mixed-mode surveys? First, the similarity of HRS Internet 2006 and the two regular HRS surveys suggests that pure mode effects do not play any role, implying that changing the interview mode from telephone or face-to-face to Internet by itself does not lead to comparability problems due to interviews administered with different modes. On the other hand, the large differences between HRS Internet 2003 and the regular interviews as well as HRS Internet 2006 lead to the conclusion that even for seemingly objective questions such as the household portfolio questions that we have analyzed, careful questionnaire design is crucial for the quality of the data. More specifically, when interpreting a given question, respondents use previous questions as cues, particularly if the wording of the question at hand is unclear or leaves room for different interpretations (see, e.g., Schuman & Presser, 1981). If, however, the ambiguity is removed by making the wording of the question more precise, the effect of preceding questions can be avoided. This can perfectly explain our main results. It is also in line with the conclusion that whether mode effects in a broad sense (not controlling for question context) play a role may strongly depend on the nature of the questionnaires and the wording of the questions (see Chapter 3 in this volume) and confirms a common finding in the literature on this topic (e.g., Dillman & Christian, 2005; Smyth et al., 2007): Context and question wording are crucial and deserve considerable thought, particularly since they often change as a consequence of changing interview mode. With carefully designed questionnaires, pure mode effects can be avoided, at least when measuring objective variables such as finances. The concern that measuring ownership and amounts of household assets depends too much on interviewing mode is misplaced if questions are formulated with care, accounting for preceding questions and other context.

[1] Acknowledgments: This research was funded by NIA. We are grateful to participants in the RAND/University of Michigan Internet Project meetings, and the Social Research and the Internet conferences in Mannheim for useful comments.

REFERENCES

Alessie, R., Hochguertel, S., & Van Soest, A. (2002). Household portfolios in the Netherlands. In L. Guiso, M. Haliassos, & T. Jappelli (Eds.), *Household portfolios* (pp. 341–388). Cambridge, MA: MIT Press.

Berrens, R. P., Bohara, A. K., Jenkins-Smith, H., Silva, C., & Weimer, D. L. (2003). The advent of Internet surveys for political research: A comparison of telephone and Internet samples. *Political Analysis, 11*(1), 1–22.
Best, S. J., Krueger, B., Hubbard, C., & Smith, A. (2001). An assessment of the generalizability of Internet surveys. *Social Science Computer Review, 19*(2), 131–145.
Chang, L. C. & Krosnick, J. A. (2009). National surveys via RDD telephone interviewing vs. the Internet: Comparing sample representativeness and response quality. *Public Opinion Quarterly, 73*(4), 641–678.
Christian, L. M. & Dillman, D. A. (2004). The influence of graphical and symbolic language manipulation on responses to self-administered surveys. *Public Opinion Quarterly, 68*(1), 58–81.
Couper, M. P., Kapteyn, A., Schonlau, M., & Winter, J. (2007). Noncoverage and nonresponse in an Internet survey. *Sociological Science Research, 36*(1), 131–148.
Denscombe, M. (2006). Web-based questionnaires and the mode effect: An evaluation based on completion rates and data contents of near-identical questionnaires delivered in different modes. *Social Science Computer Review, 24*(2), 246–254.
Dillman, D. A. & Christian, L. M. (2005). Survey mode as a source of instability in responses across surveys. *Field Methods, 17*(1), 30–52.
Fricker, R. D. & Schonlau, M. (2002). Advantages and disadvantages of Internet research surveys: Evidence from the literature. *Field Methods, 14*(4), 347–367.
Guiso, L., Haliassos, M., & Jappelli, T. (Eds.). (2002). *Household portfolios*. Cambridge, MA: MIT Press.
Hurd, M. D. (1999). Anchoring and acquiescence bias in measuring assets in household surveys. *Journal of Risk and Uncertainty, 19*(1–3), 111–136.
Hurd, M. D. (2002). Portfolio holdings of the elderly. In L. Guiso, M. Haliassos, & T. Jappelli (Eds.), *Household portfolios* (pp. 431–472). Cambridge, MA: MIT Press.
Juster, F. T. & Smith, J. P. (1997). Improving the quality of economic data: Lessons from the HRS and AHEAD. *Journal of the American Statistical Association, 92*, 1268–1278.
Schonlau, M., Asch, B. J., & Du, C. (2003). Web surveys as part of a mixed-mode strategy for populations that cannot be contacted by e-mail. *Social Science Computer Review, 21*(2), 218–222.
Schonlau, M., Van Soest, A., Kapteyn, A., & Couper, M. P. (2009). Selection bias in Web surveys and the use of propensity scores. *Sociological Methods and Research, 37*(3), 291–318.
Schuman, H. & Presser, S. (1981). *Questions and answers in attitude surveys: Experiments on question form, wording and content*. New York: Academic Press.
Schwarz, N. (1996). *Cognition and communication: Judgmental biases, research methods, and the logic of conversation*. Mahwah, NJ: Lawrence Erlbaum.
Smyth, J. D., Dillman, D. A., & Christian, L. M. (2007). Context effects in Internet surveys: New issues and evidence. In A. Joinson, K. McKenna, T. Postmes, & U.-D. Reips (Eds.), *The Oxford handbook of Internet psychology* (pp. 429–445). Oxford, UK: Oxford University Press.
Van Soest, A. & Hurd, M. D. (2008). A test for anchoring and yea-saying in experimental consumption data. *Journal of the American Statistical Association, 103*(481), 126–136.
Yeager, D. S. et al. (2009). *Comparing the accuracy of RDD telephone surveys and Internet surveys conducted with probability and non-probability samples*. Working paper, Stanford University.

13

Internet Survey Paradata

Dirk Heerwegh
Catholic University of Leuven
Leuven, Belgium

13.1 INTRODUCTION

A common goal of surveys is to measure theoretical concepts or constructs by means of one or several indicators. Indicators are phrased as "survey requests" (i.e., questions, such as "How often do you exercise?") or as instructions (e.g., "Report the number of people currently employed in your firm, in full-time equivalents"). The values obtained by these requests are the measurement values and constitute the primary data (sometimes also called *statistics data* because these data are relied on for the substantive statistical analysis).

Metadata describe the characteristics of the primary data. This information can, for instance, be found in code books, which report the type of variables (numeric or alphanumeric), the possible response codes and their meanings, and so on.

Paradata can be defined broadly as "data about the data gathering process itself" (Couper, 2000). Contact information, originating from call sheets (as used in face-to-face surveying) or case management software (as used in centralized computer-assisted telephone interviewing facilities), provides such data. From these data, it can be calculated how many contact attempts were needed for each sample case, why certain sample cases refused cooperation, and so forth. This information is needed to ascertain the (final) dispositions of cases, including interviews, nonresponse, cases of unknown eligibility, and cases that are not eligible. This information can subsequently be used to calculate various outcome rates for the survey as a whole. Response rates, cooperation rates, refusal rates, and contact rates can be calculated according to a set of standard definitions and formulae (AAPOR, 2008).

Paradata can also be obtained about each individual interview itself: Duration, interruptions, and other such elements can be logged either by the interviewer or by the software responsible for administering the questionnaire. This chapter focuses on paradata collected in Internet surveys. More specifically, attention is paid to paradata describing the way respondents proceed through an Internet survey and answer the questions. Moreover, the techniques covered to collect these data are themselves Internet-based and can be used on the respondents' own computer in the natural settings in which they use the Internet. In this sense, this chapter deviates from paradata resulting from eye tracking, which typically requires specialized hardware employed within a laboratory setting (see Chapter 14 in this volume).

This chapter discusses the types of Internet survey paradata, some of their uses, how they can be collected, and how they can be analyzed. This chapter also provides an example of a study to illustrate one application of Internet survey paradata.

13.2 TYPES OF INTERNET SURVEY PARADATA

13.2.1 Conceptual Distinction: Four Levels of Paradata

On a conceptual level, Kaczmirek (2008) distinguishes between four types of paradata, based on their level of aggregation. First-level paradata describe individual events within an Internet questionnaire, for individual respondents. Examples include mouse clicks, scroll movements, a key press, and the location of the event (e.g., a radio button that has been clicked). This type of paradata is characterized by its unfocused nature. All events are recorded sequentially, and the number of possible events cannot be determined in advance. Therefore, these data are typically recorded in an unstructured way, not in the convenient and familiar matrix form of most data sets.

Second-level paradata aggregate first-level paradata across a number of actions for a single respondent. Examples are the total number of times a respondent has changed an answer to a certain survey question, the total amount of time spent on a specific survey question (including time used to change answers), and the number of mouse clicks per page. This second level is characterized by a more focused type of data collection. In this case, in principle it is possible to determine before the survey starts how many variables will be needed. For instance, a research question may only require information on the total number of response changes per question. In this case, the researcher may construct a conventional matrix-formed data set with the number of variables equal to the number of questions in the Internet survey. Each of these variables will contain the number of response changes to each of the corresponding questions.

Third-level paradata aggregate data across respondents or across variables. Examples include the average time needed to answer specific survey questions (aggregated response time data across respondents, for individual survey questions) and duration of the interview (aggregated response time data across all variables for individual respondents). Fourth-level paradata aggregate data across variables and people; examples include the average amount of time needed to complete the survey. Third- and fourth-level paradata share the focused nature of second-level paradata. Consequently, these data can be recorded in a systematic way using the familiar matrix-form data sets.

Clearly, first-level paradata are the foundation of the higher levels of paradata. While one may opt not to save and analyze first-level paradata, they do have to be recorded to at least allow the Internet survey software to compute and store the higher-order paradata. However, it may be advisable to always save first-level paradata, in order to prevent being unable to answer interesting follow-up research questions that require first-level paradata or an alternative organization of first-level paradata, which cannot be arrived at from available higher-level paradata.

13.2.2 Technical Distinction: Server-Side Versus Client-Side Paradata

Traditionally, a distinction has been made between server-side paradata and client-side paradata when discussing Internet survey paradata (Heerwegh, 2003). This distinction refers to whether events on the server (which hosts the Internet survey) are logged, in which case we speak of server-side paradata, or whether events on the respondent's (or client's) computer are logged, in which case we speak of client-side paradata. The main reason for introducing this distinction was to make clear that client-side paradata are capable of logging much more detailed information than server-side paradata. Server-side paradata are restricted to logging page hits by specific respondents (identified by an IP address or a username and password if a restricted-access Internet survey is being used). This type of paradata hence provides the basis for determining in which sequence respondents visited Internet pages, whether they revisited some pages (backed up in the questionnaire), and where they left the Internet survey. Such information can provide valuable empirical information about the relative numbers of respondents falling in one of several theoretically distinguishable categories, such as lurkers—i.e., respondents going through the questionnaire without answering any of the questions (Bosnjak & Tuten, 2001). In turn, this information can be used to evaluate redesigned versions of the Internet survey, for instance by confirming that some intervention significantly reduces the number of lurkers.

In contrast with server-side paradata, client-side paradata are capable of monitoring and logging respondent's actions *within* individual Internet pages. It can, for instance, be observed which response options were clicked by an individual respondent and how much time elapsed between each of these actions. If the respondent clicked only a single response option, the data from the paradata data set will correspond to the data from the responses data set. However, if the respondent clicked two or more response options, the responses data set will contain only the final selected response option, while the paradata will contain the complete string of actions and it will be known which response options were clicked and in what order. In addition, it will be known how long it took to respond to the question. Consider as a simple example the following string of client-side paradata for a single respondent:

t=12357:q[2]=2£t=9544:q[2]=1£t=7314:q[2]=2£t=741:form submitted

This string contains the process data of one respondent's single actions. In Kaczmirek's (2008) paradata typology, these are first-level paradata because the basic data points are being collected without any form of manipulation. Collecting paradata in its raw form, without any manipulation, results in very detailed information that can be manipulated later to answer specific research questions.

In this example, question 2 (q[2]) is the survey question being monitored. The paradata string obeys certain formatting rules, which depend on the software used to create the strings. (The current string was obtained with the client-side paradata JavaScript described in Heerwegh, 2003.) In this case, each entry in the string is recorded with two components, a time component (starting with "t="), and an action identification component (starting with the variable name, e.g., "q[2]", or an expression identifying specific actions, e.g., "form submitted"). The two components are separated with a colon (":"). The times are recorded in milliseconds. Different events are separated with the pound symbol ("£"). It can thus be seen from the string of data that the respondent answered this question 12,357 ms (i.e., 12.4 seconds) after the question was displayed to the respondent. This first-time measurement includes the reading time, since the timer starts running as soon as the Internet page is downloaded and the question is presented to the respondent. Apparent from the paradata is that the respondent first clicked response option "2" (which corresponds to "rather agree"), but then changed his or her answer after 9.5 seconds to "1" ("completely agree"). About 7.3 seconds later, the respondent changed his or her mind again and changed the response back to "2" ("rather agree"). Less than one second later (0.7 seconds), the form was submitted, which means that the respondent clicked the "Next Screen" button at the bottom of the page to proceed to the subsequent question, which was located on another Internet page. From these first-level paradata, one could calculate second-level paradata. For instance, the total amount of time spent on the Internet page containing question q[2] was about 30 seconds, and the total number of changes to the response was 2. Using paradata collected from other respondents and other survey questions, one could calculate third- and fourth-level paradata (e.g., the average time needed to answer question 2, the average time needed to answer all survey questions).

A recent study confirmed that client-side paradata provide more detailed information than server-side paradata, even if they collect the same type of data (in this case, time measures; see Kaczmirek, 2008). As a consequence, tests that rely on client-side paradata are more sensitive than tests that use server-side paradata. More sensitive tests improve the power of a statistical test (Murphy, Myors, & Wolach, 2009). One implication is that fewer observations are necessary to reach statistically significant results. It is therefore recommended to use client-side paradata instead of server-side paradata whenever possible.

While client-side paradata can provide a more detailed view on respondent behavior than server-side paradata, it should be acknowledged that software used to collect client-side paradata varies in the amount of detail it can capture. One of the first released and freely online available scripts to capture client-side Internet survey paradata used JavaScript (Heerwegh, n.d.). In its earliest version, this script captured a variety of respondent actions, such as selecting response options (radio buttons, check boxes, and drop-down boxes), writing in text fields, clicking hyperlinks, and clicking submit buttons. Later on, additional events were monitored, such as scrolling. Depending on how many different event types were monitored and captured, more information would be logged and more detailed reconstructions of how respondents proceed through the Internet survey could be achieved. An extension of this script lies within the Universal Client Side Paradata (UCSP) project (Kaczmirek, 2008). This script is more general in the sense that it captures all events within an Internet page (e.g., clicking anywhere on an Internet page), whereas the earlier scripts capture only events that relate to the specific elements (e.g., radio buttons or check boxes) that have been equipped with event triggers. A more detailed technical discussion is provided by Kaczmirek (2008).

Today, very detailed reconstructions of users' actions within Internet pages can be achieved by using such tools as those provided by Clicktale (http://www.clicktale.com), Userfly (http://www.userfly.com), clickdensity (http://www.clickdensity.com), m-pathy (http://www.m-pathy.com), crazyegg (http://crazyegg.com), LEOtrace (http://leotrace.com), and others. These tools capture and record browsing data from respondents and either graphically represent these data in the form of density maps (as an overlay on the Internet pages that constitute the survey) or even let the researcher play back these data later as movies. Setup of these tools is usually straightforward, as it typically involves only adding a few lines of automatically generated code to the Internet pages one wishes to analyze. It must be noted, however, that these tools are mostly intended to evaluate Internet sites more generally. This means that some information may not be available in a useful form—for instance, a tool that provides only aggregated data may be unsuited to address research questions that require information on an individual level. Also, these tools may not provide an easy way (or any way) of downloading the captured data for further analysis.

13.3 POTENTIAL USES OF INTERNET SURVEY PARADATA

Most Internet survey paradata are collected in an unfocused way, meaning that all events are recorded. To turn these data into information, the researcher needs to ask specific research questions and extract the relevant information from the available data. This implies great flexibility, and it also means that the possible uses of paradata are virtually unlimited. This chapter will therefore discuss only a few possible uses, which should be seen as examples.

13.3.1 Testing and Evaluating Survey Questions

One obvious potential use of Internet survey paradata is to test and evaluate survey questions. As Presser et al. (2004) noted, behavior coding and response latencies can supplement conventional pretests. Recorded respondent actions that can be played back as movies can provide the raw material for behavior coding. This strategy comes very close to conventional questionnaire pretesting in laboratories. The advantage is that respondents do not need to be physically present in a research laboratory but can complete the questionnaire from anywhere in the world, in the natural environment in which they normally use their computer. In addition, a larger number of respondents can be recruited than in conventional lab pretests since there is no capacity limit imposed by the number of available computers in the laboratory. It can always be decided to select only a subset of the collected recordings for behavior coding. Potential disadvantages are the lower degree of control over the participating respondents and the lack of control over the equipment they use to access and complete the questionnaire, such as type of computer, operating system, Internet browser, screen resolution, and so on. On the other hand, this diversity makes the test more realistic and hence more valuable.

Depending on the level of detail of the collected paradata, behavior coding may be more or less of a realistic option. If response times are collected, response latencies—the time it takes for a respondent to answer a survey question—can be studied. In Internet surveys, this includes the amount of time needed to read the survey question and all possible additional instructions. This is less detailed than in interviewer-administered questionnaires where the interviewer starts the timer immediately after asking the question (Bassili & Fletcher, 1991). As a consequence, Internet survey response latencies may confound different sources of question problems. First of all, some respondents may read faster than others, contributing to shorter or longer response latencies. This problem can be overcome by accounting for baseline speed, individual differences in speed of responding that are unrelated to item content (Johnson, 2004). Second, longer response times might indicate question comprehension problems as well as retrieval problems, confounding two possible problem sources in the Tourangeau, Rips, and Rasinski (2000) cognitive model of survey question answering. This model posits that respondents must first interpret the meaning and intent of each question (step 1), after which they have to retrieve relevant information from memory (step 2). When these pieces of information are retrieved, they need to be integrated into a summary judgment (step 3), which the respondent subsequently has to map onto the provided response alternatives (step 4). Longer response times might be induced by poor question wording (e.g., use of difficult words or complex grammar) or by the fact that the information sought is cognitively less accessible.

In addition to response latencies, paradata also show whether respondents changed their responses to individual survey questions. While less research exists in this area, a number of studies have argued that changing answers could indicate lack of knowledge on a certain topic (Heerwegh, 2003) as well as problems with mapping the response on the provided response alternatives (step 4 in the cognitive model reviewed above; Stern, 2008).

A combined use of response latency analysis with answer changes might tap into most of the four steps of the cognitive question–answering model. Paradata should therefore be considered by survey researchers interested in assessing the quality of their survey questions and questionnaires. Nonetheless, while paradata do show something of the process of answering survey questions, they still hide important aspects of the process that can be accessed only via other methods, such as cognitive interviewing. Clearly, think-aloud methods or cognitive probing techniques could provide valuable additional information about the cognitive process of answering survey questions (Willis, 2005).* One of the drawbacks of cognitive probing is its labor-intensive character. Therefore, one could first screen the entire Internet questionnaire using paradata and apply cognitive interviewing techniques to only those questions with apparent problems in terms of long response times or high answer-change rates.

* Some academics argue that cognitive interviewing techniques do not provide all the answers, and that other methods (such as response time measurement) are needed to get a more complete picture (Bassili, 2000). Likewise, this chapter takes the position that both methods are limited and that their combined use is necessary to get a more complete picture.

13.3.2 Adaptive Questionnaires

While paradata could be used to test questionnaires before they are fielded, they could also be collected during the phase of data collection and used to dynamically change the behavior or content of the questionnaire. For instance, if questions are answered too quickly, they can be asked again, either immediately or at the end of the survey; this has been implemented by Conrad, Tourangeau, Couper, and Kennedy (2008). Along the same lines, it would also be possible to ask follow-up questions when short response times or a lot of answer changes to a certain question are detected. These follow-up questions could ask respondents directly about the problems they had with a question and could present the question in a different version (perhaps using a different response format).

13.3.3 Measurement of Attitude Strength

Response times have been used extensively to assess attitude strength (Bassili & Fletcher, 1991) and related issues such as activation of attitudes and related evaluations (Fazio, 2001). The concept of attitude strength is relevant in a wide range of fields, such as psychology, political science, and sociology. In political sciences, the notion of nonattitudes (Converse, 1964; Zaller, 1992) has gained some popularity, although it has also provoked a lot of controversy (Sniderman, Tetlock, & Elms, 2001; Krosnick et al., 2002). The nonattitudes problem suggests that many respondents are unlikely to hold an attitude toward many of the topics (usually related to politics) surveyors are asking questions about. This should lead to random responses, and could be picked up by longer response times and an increased rate at which answers are changed. It is important to note that while some have objected to the nonattitudes problem (Sniderman, Tetlock, & Elms, 2001; Krosnick et al., 2002), there is little if any disagreement on the position that some respondents have weaker attitudes than others (Krosnick & Abelson, 1992; Krosnick & Petty, 1995). One of the ways of measuring weaker attitudes is to use response latencies, with longer response times suggesting weaker attitudes (Bassili & Fletcher, 1991; Heerwegh, 2003).

13.3.4 Provide Context Information on Experiments and Aid in the Development of Theory

The obvious advantage of experiments is their ability to allow causal statements. Given random assignment of cases to the various conditions, one has to hold the manipulated factor(s) responsible for observed changes in behavior, opinions, or (in the case of surveys) responses to questions. One could view the manipulated factor(s) as input variables and the responses to the questions as the output variables. The intervening process is usually described in a theory, but it is not empirically observable. When the patterns in the data conform to the predictions made by the theory, it is concluded that the theory (postulating some cognitive process) cannot be refuted.

Using paradata, one could get some more insight into the intervening response process, which can strengthen the theoretical claims. An illustrative study is described in Section 13.6 of this chapter.

13.4 COLLECTING INTERNET SURVEY PARADATA

Collecting Internet survey paradata is usually easy, provided one uses software that implements this automatically. Alternatively, one could manually include the necessary paradata program code in the Internet survey files (e.g., the HTML pages containing the survey questions). Heerwegh (2003) describes in detail how client-side paradata can be collected by adding JavaScript to the HTML files of the Internet survey. To date, some software solutions have incorporated at least partial support for collecting this type of data, such as OSUCRE (http://www.osucre.be/index.php). The recorded paradata are stored either as data strings or as separate entries in a database, depending on which level of paradata are being collected (first-level versus higher-level paradata). An alternative to storing first-level paradata as strings of data (as in the example given in Section 13.2.2) is to use a relational database. In such a database, each event is stored as a separate observation (row), recording at least the respondent ID and the type and time of the event. This eliminates the need to parse data strings.

With services such as Clicktale, Userfly, and others, it is typically necessary to copy and paste just a small amount of code in the HTML files used in the Internet survey. This automatically enables the collection of the necessary data. The data are stored on the servers of the company providing the service, which could imply security risks. Because the recorded data may include clicks on response options and typed responses to open-ended questions, care should be taken that the recorded data can be seen only by the researcher's team.

Including these features to capture respondent actions and record client-side paradata typically does not affect user experience. Download speed is usually not noticeably reduced, and the responsiveness of the Internet survey in general does not typically suffer either. This means the user can be completely unaware of programs being run in the background to capture additional data. Nonetheless, respondents should be informed about the collection of process data (see also Chapter 6 in this volume).

13.5 DATA PREPARATION AND ANALYSIS

If the researcher has clear a priori assumptions about which information is important, paradata can be stored in conventional matrix form data sets. This means that second- and higher-level paradata are being collected. The variables of interest are predefined and the software is instructed to compute and record their values. These variables can then be used in analyses.

First-level paradata are collected in a relatively unstructured way. Data are collected by adding each action to a data string or as separate observations in a relational database. Since not every respondent will perform the same number of actions, or in the same sequence, the data strings will be of different lengths and their structure will vary from one observation to the next. If the data are stored in a relational database, the number of rows will differ across respondents and the sequence in which the rows appear may be different. In addition, different parts of the data strings or different data rows could be important depending on the focus of the analysis. Software capable of recognizing string patterns can be used to extract the useful information from the strings before the actual analysis is carried out, or SQL-like queries need to be performed to retrieve the relevant rows from the relational database.

After the data have been parsed or extracted, they usually need to be transformed or analyzed with specific statistical techniques. For instance, response times are typically not normally distributed and need to be transformed to more closely resemble the normal distribution. One possible transformation is to calculate the ratio 1/response time. The resulting data usually follow the normal distribution better, but the data then have to be interpreted in terms of response speed and no longer as response times (longer response times result in smaller ratios, implying slower response speeds).

The number of answer changes does not typically follow the normal distribution either, and one may need to use models suitable for count data. The Poisson model and the binomial model are frequently used to model count data, but in the case of answer changes these models may not be suitable because such data usually show a preponderance of zeros (which may not be properly modeled with the Poisson or binomial models). In this case, the overdispersed variants of the Poisson and the binomial model can be useful, since an overdispersion parameter can account for the preponderance of zeros (resulting from the majority of respondents not changing their response at all). If these models are still unable to properly model the (large) proportion of zeros in the data, a zero-inflated Poisson model can be used. (For a discussion of these models, see Gelman & Hill, 2007.) Alternatively, a simpler approach is to use logistic regression analysis and recode the dependent variable "answer changes" to 0 (no changes) and 1 (one or more changes). This is appropriate if most respondents who changed their response did so only once (so that the data show a natural tendency of having only zeros and ones).

13.6 EXAMPLE STUDY: USE OF PARADATA TO ASSIST IN THE DEVELOPMENT OF THEORY

This section describes an application of Internet paradata to assist in the development of theory. First, some background is given on a survey design issue regarding response formats and labeling of response scales. Next, a tentative theoretical explanation is given for the observed phenomena, which leads to a specific hypothesis to be tested. Subsequently, an experiment supplemented with Internet paradata is conducted to test the hypothesis. It is shown how the paradata make a crucial contribution to the test of the theoretical explanation.

13.6.1 Background

It has repeatedly been reported in the literature that using a number box instead of a polar point scale significantly increases the mean score obtained on the variables (Christian & Dillman, 2004; Stern, Dillman,

A. How important is music to you, on a scale from 1 to 5, with 1 being "very important" and 5 being "not important at all"?

- ○ 1 very important
- ○ 2
- ○ 3
- ○ 4
- ○ 5 not important at all

B. How important is music to you, on a scale from 1 to 5, with 1 being "very important" and 5 being "not important at all"?

[ ]

FIGURE 13.1
Illustration of the experimental manipulation. Version A is the polar point response scale (using radio buttons), and version B is the number box version.

& Smyth, 2007; Stern, 2008). An illustration of the manipulation is shown in Figure 13.1.

Christian and Dillman (2004), Stern et al. (2007), and Stern (2008) entertained the hypothesis that removal of the graphical and symbolic language elements by moving from the polar point scale to the number box format might have caused respondents to become confused about the direction of the scale, leading to the differences in response distributions across the experimental groups.

This hypothesis makes theoretical sense. As illustrated in Figure 13.1, the cited studies used response scales with 1 being the most positive pole ("very satisfied," "outstanding," "a lot") and 5 being the most negative pole ("very dissatisfied," "terrible," "not at all"). Higher numbers were hence associated with more negative ratings, which might be counterintuitive, and consequently confusing, for many respondents. While the polar point format provides additional supporting (graphical and symbolic) cues during the step in which the respondent actually selects an answer (which potentially reduces or eliminates respondent confusion), this is absent in the number box format. It is this difference between the response formats that may have led to the observed differences.

An experiment can be set up to test whether this hypothesis holds when confronted with empirical data. In essence, testing the hypothesis requires extending the experiments used in previous research with a single factor with two levels: whether higher numbers in the response scale are associated with higher ratings (the intuitive scale), or whether higher numbers are associated with lower ratings (the counterintuitive scale, as used in the cited previous studies). This manipulation allows testing of whether respondent confusion is likely to have led to the observed differences, for the assumed cause of respondent confusion (association of higher numbers with lower ratings) has been eliminated in specific conditions. The following sections describe the method and data, the results of the experiment, and the added benefit of using paradata.

13.6.2 Method and Data

An experiment was set up in March 2008 at the Catholic University Leuven (Belgium) to test the confusion hypothesis. A random sample of 2,500 first- and third-year university students at the Catholic University Leuven was drawn.* Prior to fielding the Internet survey, each of the 2,500 sample cases was randomly assigned to one of four conditions: the polar point format with intuitive scale, the polar point format with counterintuitive scale, the number box with intuitive scale, and the number box with counterintuitive scale. Five survey questions were included in the experiment (see appendix).

13.6.3 Results

In total, 1,421 respondents logged on to the Internet survey, representing 57% of the 2,500 invited respondents. Of those logging on, 1,341 (94.4%) completely filled in the survey (i.e., reached and answered the last survey question). This represents a response rate of 54% when calculated according to the response rate calculation 1 formula described by AAPOR (2008). On average, the Internet survey took approximately 23 minutes to complete. The Internet survey respondents were on average 19.6 years old, and 60% of them were female.

The response did not depend on the experimental condition to which the respondents were assigned. Each of the experimental conditions had a very similar login rate, ranging from 55 to 58% ($\chi^2(3) = 2.02$; $p = .56$; $n = 2{,}500$). More importantly, the percentage of respondents completing the Internet survey once they logged in did not depend on the experimental conditions either. Each of the conditions had a completion rate ranging from

* The total number of first- and third-year students equaled 14,413 (i.e., the sample frame).

92% to 96% ($\chi^2(3) = 4.53$; $p = .21$; $n = 1{,}421$). These results indicate that the randomization procedure was not disturbed by differential nonresponse.

To analyze the effects of the experimental treatments on the response distributions, *t*-tests were conducted. The left part of Table 13.1 (column A) shows the effect of the response format on the response distributions for the counterintuitive scales, which associate higher numbers with lower (more negative) ratings. This analysis serves as a check of whether the current experiment replicates the findings of Christian and Dillman (2004) and those of Stern et al. (2007). Three of the five questions in the experiment (Q17b, Q18, and Q29) showed the expected significant response distribution differences. For these three questions, using the number box produces significantly more negative evaluations.* (The same is true for the other two questions, but the differences do not achieve statistical significance.) As such, this experiment exactly replicates the results of the earlier studies.

The right part of Table 13.1 (column B) shows that the response distributions of the intuitive response scales (which associate higher numbers with higher ratings) are not influenced by changing from one response format to another. None of the five tested variables shows a significant difference across the two response formats.† These results indicate that a change of response format does not imply different response distributions if the assumed cause of respondent confusion (a counterintuitive scale) is removed.

Even though these findings are consistent with the theoretical assumption that respondent confusion is an important cause for the differences in responses between the response formats, respondent confusion has not actually been observed. In other words, the input variables have been manipulated and it has been observed that the output variables behave in accordance with the theory, but the intervening process itself has remained hidden from view. This is where the Internet survey paradata have a role to play, since they could provide more direct measures of respondent confusion.

Confusion about the direction of the response scale could be measured by what Stern (2008) has termed "reciprocal changes." These are response

* Prior to the analysis, data were reverse-coded for the conditions where lower numbers reflected more positive evaluations. This data preparation step ensured that higher values reflected more positive ratings in all conditions, enabling meaningful experimental comparisons.

† Five ANOVA analyses (one per survey variable) were conducted with two independent variables: response format and response scale. These analyses confirmed the results presented in Table 13.1.

TABLE 13.1

Average Scores for Five Survey Questions by Response Format

	A. Counterintuitive Response Scale (e.g., 1 = a lot and 5 = not at all)			B. Intuitive Response Scale (e.g., 1 = not at all and 5 = a lot)		
Survey Question	**Polar Point Scale**	**Number Box**	***t*-Test**	**Polar Point Scale**	**Number Box**	***t*-Test**
Q17a	3.73	3.60	$t(687) = 0.83, p = 0.4088$	3.85	3.96	$t(683) = -0.67, p = 0.5007$
Q17b	6.24	5.64	$t(472) = 4.14, p < .0001$	5.81	5.81	$t(635) = -0.01, p = 0.9921$
Q18	5.14	4.85	$t(684) = 2.48, p = .0130$	5.14	5.12	$t(681) = 0.12, p = 0.9070$
Q29	4.03	3.95	$t(680) = 2.56, p = .0107$	4.16	4.08	$t(681) = 1.14, p = 0.2532$
Q31	4.40	4.33	$t(684) = 0.80, p = .4229$	4.56	4.47	$t(685) = 1.16, p = 0.2470$

Note: Exact wording of survey questions can be found in the appendix.

TABLE 13.2

Proportion of Reciprocal Changes to Each of the Survey Questions

	Polar Point Scale		Number Box	
Question	Intuitive Response Scale	Counterintuitive Response Scale	Intuitive Response Scale	Counterintuitive Response Scale
Q17a	.01 (n = 5 out of 355)	.04 (n = 15 out of 349)	.00 (n = 0 out of 329)	.02 (n = 8 out of 336)
Q17b	.00 (n = 0 out of 331)	.02 (n = 5 out of 241)	.00 (n = 0 out of 290)	.04 (n = 9 out of 230)
Q18	.00 (n = 1 out of 351)	.00 (n = 0 out of 348)	.00 (n = 0 out of 326)	.00 (n = 0 out of 327)
Q29	.00 (n = 0 out of 357)	.08 (n = 28 out of 349)	.00 (n = 0 out of 322)	.04 (n = 12 out of 330)
Q31	.01 (n = 3 out of 356)	.03 (n = 10 out of 348)	.00 (n = 0 out of 325)	.05 (n = 16 out of 334)

changes whereby the respondent switches from one side of the response scale to the other (e.g., changing from 5 to 1 or vice versa on a 5-point response scale). The current Internet survey used JavaScript to collect client-side paradata available from Heerwegh (2003).* As the number of reciprocal changes per survey question never exceeded 1, the dependent variable was recoded to 0 if no reciprocal changes had occurred and 1 if one such change had occurred. Table 13.2 reports the proportion of reciprocal changes per survey question. For Q17a, which used the polar point scale, where higher numbers refer to more positive ratings, the proportion is .01, meaning that just 1 percent of all respondents made a reciprocal change at this question in this condition. Even though no statistical test is provided yet, a clear pattern emerges in these results. In keeping with the hypothesis, reciprocal changes are less likely when using intuitive response scales than when counterintuitive response scales are used.

Because of the small number of reciprocal changes, all five questions were grouped together for further analysis using logistic regression analysis. The dependent binary variable was coded 0 if the respondent had not made any reciprocal change to any of the five survey questions, whereas it was coded 1 if the respondent had made at least one such change to at

* The original script was modified to check every half second whether the response in the answer box had been changed, because tests showed that response changes to number boxes were not registered if the respondent did not first click outside of the box before changing the response. This ensured that all response changes would be detected.

least one of the five variables. Two dummy-coded variables were used as the independent variables: whether a number box was used (as opposed to a polar point scale) and whether the numeric labeling of the response scale was intuitive (as opposed to not).* The results of the logistic regression analysis indicated that the number box elicited fewer reciprocal changes, although the effect was not statistically significant (standardized $\beta = -.11$, $p = .11$). In keeping with the pattern observed in Table 13.2, counter-intuitive response scales led to a dramatically increased probability of making reciprocal changes (standardized $\beta = .71, p < .0001$). The odds ratio indicates that using a counterintuitive scale makes it 13 times more likely that a respondent will make reciprocal changes. This finding clearly shows that counterintuitive scales lead to respondent confusion, as witnessed by an increased probability of answer changes. As such, the Internet survey paradata provided more context for interpreting the results of the experiment. The intervening process, speculated to be respondent confusion, has actually been operationalized and directly tested. This strengthens the theoretical claim.

13.7 CONCLUSIONS

This chapter defined Internet survey paradata and discussed some of the possible uses. While paradata could be used for a very wide array of objectives, a few obvious application areas exist, such as pretesting and attitude strength measurement. Paradata present some useful opportunities in the field of pretesting since they are less labor intensive to collect. It is therefore of importance to study the extent to which paradata lead to the same conclusions as traditional pretesting (e.g., cognitive interviewing). If signals obtained from paradata echo those obtained from more traditional methods, then a considerable amount of time and energy can be saved by relying on paradata. Consequently, the research agenda in this field could prioritize questions such as these: Do paradata lead to the same substantive conclusions as conventional pretesting methods? Which paradata should be used (response times, answer changes, a combination

* An analysis not reported here also included the interaction term. This term was not statistically significant, while the other effects remained the same as those reported here.

of both)? Do paradata highlight problems that are not detected with conventional pretests? Do paradata miss certain problems that conventional pretests do identify? Can paradata assist in making the pretesting procedure more standardized?

In the field of attitude strength measurement, a strong tradition already exists of using response times. As a consequence, this field could focus on whether findings from interviewer-based surveys carry over to Internet surveys. Two specific problems involve adjusting for the fact that reading times are included in response times and determining whether answer changes can also be understood as expressions of lower attitude strength.

Other ways of using paradata are less well explored, such as using it to dynamically adapt Internet questionnaires. This field is very much uncharted, and there are many potential research questions. First of all, while there are few technical limits, methodological research is very much needed to ascertain whether and which strategies of dynamically adapting survey questionnaires increase data quality. For instance, should questions that are answered too quickly be asked again immediately, or should they be postponed until the end of the survey? Should survey designers repeat the questions in the same form, or should they be adapted slightly? In general, it is necessary to investigate whether dynamic surveys obtain more accurate responses (less measurement error) while keeping other sources of error (e.g., due to partial nonresponse) in check. Also, making survey questionnaires more dynamic may imply a certain loss of the standardized nature of the survey interview, which may in itself lead to higher or lower data quality.

A final area in which paradata could be useful is that of experimental research. In this area, paradata can provide more direct tests of hypotheses that involve processes that usually remain hidden from the researcher. This chapter provided an example in which it was shown that the paradata allowed a more direct test of the confusion hypothesis than the experimental data alone. While the experiment showed a causal link between counterintuitive response scales and response differences, it was the paradata that provided the data needed to link counterintuitive scales with respondent confusion. This considerably strengthened the claim made by the confusion hypothesis.

Many other uses of Internet paradata could be thought of besides those mentioned in this chapter. These could include applications such as using response times to calibrate progress indicators (Heerwegh, 2004), observing navigational errors or potential tendencies of respondents to back up in a questionnaire and changing an answer to avoid follow-up questions (Peytchev, Couper, McCabe, & Crawford, 2006), and detecting whether error messages are triggered by improper input in answer boxes and how users deal with them (Haraldsen, 2004; Peytchev & Crawford, 2005). Their flexibility make paradata useful in many areas, and novel applications of Internet survey paradata will undoubtedly appear and command research attention.

DISCLAIMER

All references to software and Internet sites are intended for informational purposes only. With the exception of the client-side paradata JavaScript, which is provided for free and without any warranty (Heerwegh, 2003), the author is not involved in any of the mentioned software or Internet sites. Use of the software and Internet sites is at one's own risk.

REFERENCES

AAPOR. (2008). *Standard definitions: Final dispositions of case codes and outcome rates for surveys* (5th ed.). Lenexa, KS: AAPOR. Retrieved from http://www.aapor.org/uploads/Standard_Definitions_07_08_Final.pdf

Bassili, J. N. (2000). Editor's introduction: Reflection on response latency measurement in telephone surveys. *Political Psychology, 21*(1), 1–6.

Bassili, J. N. & Fletcher, J. F. (1991). Response-time measurement in survey research: A method for CATI and a new look at nonattitudes. *Public Opinion Quarterly, 55*(3), 331–346.

Bosnjak, M. & Tuten, T. L. (2001). Classifying response behaviors in Web-based surveys. *Journal of Computer Mediated Communication, 6*(3). Retrieved from http://www.ascusc.org/jcmc/vol6/issue3/boznjak.html

Christian, L. M. & Dillman, D. A. (2004). The influence of graphical and symbolic language manipulations on responses to self-administered questions. *Public Opinion Quarterly, 68*(1), 57–80.

Conrad, F. G., Tourangeau, R., Couper, M. P., & Kennedy, C. (2008). *Interactive interventions in Web surveys can improve data quality.* Paper presented at the 7th International Conference on Social Science Methodology, Naples, Italy.

Converse, P. (1964). The nature of belief systems in mass publics. In D. Apter (Ed.), *Ideology and discontent* (pp. 206–261). New York: Free Press.

Couper, M. P. (2000). Usability evaluation of computer-assisted survey instruments. *Social Science Computer Review, 18*(4), 384–396.

Fazio, R. H. (2001). On the automatic activation of associated evaluations: An overview. *Cognition and Emotion, 15*(2), 115–141.

Gelman, A. & Hill, J. (2007). *Data analysis using regression and multilevel/hierarchical models.* Cambridge, UK: Cambridge University Press.

Haraldsen, G. (2004). Identifying and reducing response burdens in Internet business surveys. *Journal of Official Statistics, 20*(2), 393–410.

Heerwegh, D. (2003). Explaining response latencies and changing answers using client-side paradata from a Web survey. *Social Science Computer Review, 21*(3), 360–373.

Heerwegh, D. (2004). *Uses of client side paradata in Web surveys.* Paper presented at the international symposium in honor of Paul Lazarsfeld, Brussels, Belgium. Retrieved from https://perswww.kuleuven.be/~u0034437/public/papers.htm

Heerwegh, D. (n.d.). *The CSP Project.* Retrieved from https://perswww.kuleuven.be/~u0034437/public/csp.htm

Johnson, M. (2004). Timepieces, components of survey question response latencies. *Political Psychology, 25*(5), 679–702.

Kaczmirek, L. (2008). *Human-survey interaction: Usability and nonresponse in online surveys.* Unpublished doctoral dissertation, University of Mannheim. Retrieved from http://madoc.bib.uni-mannheim.de/madoc/volltexte/2008/2150

Krosnick, J. A. & Abelson, R. P. (1992). The case for measuring attitude strength in surveys. In J. M. Tanur (Ed.), *Questions about questions: Inquiries into the cognitive bases of surveys* (pp. 177–203). New York: Russell Sage Foundation.

Krosnick, J. A., Holbrook, A. L., Berent, M. K., Carson, R. T., Hanemann, W. M., Kopp, R. J. et al. (2002). The impact of "no opinion" response options on data quality: Non-attitude reduction or an invitation to satisfice? *Public Opinion Quarterly, 66*(3), 371–403.

Krosnick, J. A. & Petty, R. E. (1995). Attitude strength: An overview. In R. E. Petty & J. A. Krosnick (Eds.), *Attitude strength: Antecedents and consequences* (pp. 1–24). Hillsdale, NJ: Lawrence Erlbaum Associates.

Murphy, K. R., Myors, B., & Wolach, A. (2009). *Statistical power analysis: A simple and general model for traditional and modern hypothesis tests.* New York: Routledge.

Peytchev, A., Couper, M. P., McCabe, S. E., & Crawford, S. D. (2006). Web survey design: Paging versus scrolling. *Public Opinion Quarterly, 70*(4), 596–607.

Peytchev, A., & Crawford, S. D. (2005). A typology of real-time validations in Web-based surveys. *Social Science Computer Review, 23*(2), 235–249.

Presser, S., Couper, M. P., Lessler, J. T., Martin, E., Martin, J., Rothgeb, J. et al. (2004). Methods for testing and evaluating survey questions. *Public Opinion Quarterly, 68*(1), 109–130.

Sniderman, P. M., Tetlock, P. E., & Elms, L. (2001). Public opinion and democratic politics: The problem of nonattitudes and the social construction of political judgment. In J. H. Kuklinski (Ed.), *Citizens and politics: Perspectives from political psychology* (pp. 254–288). Cambridge, UK: Cambridge University Press.

Stern, M. J. (2008). The use of client-side paradata in analyzing the effects of visual layout on changing responses in Web surveys. *Field Methods, 20*(4), 377–398.

Stern, M. J., Dillman, D. A., & Smyth, J. D. (2007). Visual design, order effects, and respondent characteristics in a self-administered survey. *Survey Research Methods, 1*(3), 121–138.

Tourangeau, R., Rips, L. J., & Rasinski, K. A. (2000). *The psychology of survey response.* Cambridge, UK: Cambridge University Press.

Willis, G. B. (2005). *Cognitive interviewing: A tool for improving questionnaire design.* London: Sage.

Zaller, J. R. (1992). *The nature and origins of mass opinion.* Cambridge, UK: Cambridge University Press.

APPENDIX: SURVEY QUESTIONS INVOLVED IN THE EXPERIMENT

Questions were translated from Dutch. Conditions A and B used radio buttons to register the responses. The radio buttons were located to the left of the numerical labels. Question Q17b was not asked if respondents answered "very high" on question Q17a.

Condition A: Polar point format with intuitive response scale
Condition B: Polar point format with counterintuitive response scale
Condition C: Number box format with intuitive response scale
Condition D: Number box format with counterintuitive response scale

Q17a. How high do you think the likelihood is that you will pass the exams in the first exam period, on a scale from 1 to 7 [conditions A and C] with 1 being "very low" and 7 being "very high" / [conditions B and D] with 1 being "very high" and 7 being "very low"?

TABLE 13.3

Condition A	Condition B	Condition C	Condition D
1 very low	1 very high		
2	2		
3	3		
4	4		
5	5		
6	6		
7 very high	7 very low		

Q17b. How high do you think the likelihood is that you will pass the exams in the first or in the second exam period, on a scale from 1 to 7 [conditions A and C] with 1 being "very low" and 7 being "very high" / [conditions B and D] with 1 being "very high" and 7 being "very low"?

TABLE 13.4

Condition A	Condition B	Condition C	Condition D
1 very low	1 very high		
2	2		
3	3		
4	4		
5	5		
6	6		
7 very high	7 very low		

Q18. How high do you think the likelihood is that you will quickly find a job after graduating, on a scale from 1 to 7 [conditions A and C] with 1 being "very low" and 7 being "very high" / [conditions B and D] with 1 being "very high" and 7 being "very low"?

TABLE 13.5

Condition A	Condition B	Condition C	Condition D
1 very low	1 very high		
2	2		
3	3		
4	4		
5	5		
6	6		
7 very high	7 very low		

Q29. How important is music to you, on a scale from 1 to 5 [conditions A and C] with 1 being "not important at all" and 5 being "very important" / [conditions B and D] with 1 being "very important" and 5 being "not important at all"?

TABLE 13.6

Condition A	Condition B	Condition C	Condition D
1 not important at all	1 very important		
2	2		
3	3		
4	4		
5	5		
6	6		
7 very important	7 not important at all		

Q31. Generally speaking, how trustworthy do you think other people are, on a scale from 1 to 7 [conditions A and C] with 1 being "not trustworthy at all" and 7 being "completely trustworthy" / [conditions B and D] with 1 being "completely trustworthy" and 7 being "not trustworthy at all"?

TABLE 13.7

Condition A	Condition B	Condition C	Condition D
1 not trustworthy at all	1 completely trustworthy		
2	2		
3	3		
4	4		
5	5		
6	6		
7 completely trustworthy	7 not trustworthy at all		

14

Use of Eye Tracking for Studying Survey Response Processes[1]

Mirta Galesic
Max Planck Institute for Human Development
Berlin, Germany

Ting Yan
NORC at the University of Chicago
Chicago, Illinois

14.1 INTRODUCTION

Survey data are often collected via electronic devices that enable visual presentation of questions, such as personal computers, PDAs, and cell phones. These surveys are often self-administered, highlighting the importance of a clear and neutral question design. This is difficult to achieve, however. Numerous elements of a questionnaire need to be attended to: graphic design (logos, pictures, banners, background), question layout (grids or single questions, one or multiple questions per screen), design of answer options (number and order, radio buttons versus drop-down lists versus slider bars, check boxes, drag-and-drop tasks), instructions and definitions (always on or on demand, the position of instructions and definitions), progress indicators, error messages, and plausibility checks. Each of these elements could affect answers in unwanted ways, and their interactions can have further unforeseeable consequences.

Empirical studies have demonstrated that visual features of Web surveys such as spacing, position, order, and even color of response options can affect survey responses (e.g., Tourangeau, Couper, & Conrad, 2004, 2007). The presence of pictures affects how survey respondents interpret and answer survey questions (Couper, Tourangeau, & Kenyon, 2004; Couper, Conrad, & Tourangeau, 2007). New ways to help people understand questions and navigate through the survey in the absence of survey interviewers—such as the interactive provision of survey definitions, progress indicators, and running tallies—can lead to different response behaviors, and eventually different survey responses. For instance, the accessibility of definitions affects the frequency with which survey respondents retrieve and read the definitions (Conrad, Couper, Tourangeau, & Peytchev, 2006). The format of progress indicators, the frequency with which they are displayed, and the speed of progress they suggest affect people's decision to stay in or to quit and drop out of the survey (Conrad, Couper, Tourangeau, & Peytchev, 2005; Heerwegh & Loosveldt, 2006; Kaczmirek & Faass, 2008; Yan, Conrad, Tourangeau, & Couper, 2007). Effects sizes reported in these studies range from small to large.

One problem with most of the empirical studies so far is that the findings are based on indirect data about respondent behavior and the underlying survey response processes. In other words, respondents' behaviors were typically not directly observed and studied while they were completing the questionnaire. Instead, their behaviors and the underlying response processes were reconstructed based on the traces they left. For instance, to infer how much cognitive effort respondents have put into answering the questions, their responses are typically examined for the number of "don't know" answers provided, the number of nondifferentiated responses given, and the length of answers to open-ended questions. If a particular respondent provides many "don't know" answers, gives the same rating scores to all rating tasks, or skips the open-ended questions, we assume that this person is not investing much cognitive effort in answering survey questions. Some authors label such respondents as "satisficers" who take an easy but suboptimal route (Cannell, Miller, & Oksenberg, 1981; Krosnick, 1991, 1999).

Paradata—data generated directly by the survey data collection process and used to evaluate that process—are sometimes analyzed to infer about the survey response processes. Mouse movements, clicks, and response times are examples of paradata that have been used to measure and describe response behavior and survey response process (see Chapter 13 in this volume; Kaczmirek & Faass, 2008; Yan & Tourangeau, 2008). For instance, when response time data show that a respondent spent two seconds to answer a question of 20 words, we infer that this person probably did not read or did not finish reading the survey question before choosing an answer.

All these traditional methods used to study respondent behavior are indirect methods through which we try to infer what is going on with respondents when they answer the questions. The true response behavior and processes—whether respondents ever bother to finish reading a question, whether respondents take the trouble to search their memories for cues, whether respondents use the cues to form an answer, and how they edit and map their answers to the required response format—are largely unknown.

Eye tracking, by contrast, provides a direct window into the way the respondents see and process survey questions. As the name implies, eye tracking tracks respondents' eye movements while respondents are reading and answering survey questions. Recorded in the eye-tracking data are the exact location of eye gaze, the length of the fixation, and the sequence of eye gazes. In other words, through eye-tracking data, one knows exactly where respondents look and for how long they look while they are completing the survey questionnaire. Therefore, this technique helps resolve ambiguities in data collected by the traditional indirect methods. In addition, the richer and more direct data on where people look and for how long provide additional insight to the survey response processes. They allow survey researchers to generate and test new hypotheses.

In Section 14.2, we describe what eye tracking is and how it is done. Section 14.3 talks about various ways eye tracking can be used in survey methodology, while Section 14.4 discusses how eye tracking differs from other traditional methods used to study respondent behaviors. Two experiments in which eye tracking was actually employed to study effects of order and format of response options are described in Section 14.5. Section 14.6 concludes with a discussion of the usefulness of eye tracking in survey research and offers directions for future research.

14.2 WHAT IS EYE TRACKING?

The basic mechanism underlying human vision is well studied. Light enters the eye through the cornea, passes through the pupil and the lens behind it, and ends on the retina, where photosensitive rod and cone cells transform it into neural signals. The central part of the retina, called the fovea, is densely packed with cone cells, enabling the high-acuity vision needed for reading. Peripheral parts of the retina have a higher proportion of rod cells that are highly sensitive to light but have lower visual acuity. To determine which objects are present in the particular parts of the visual field, people use eye, head, and body movements. These movements act in a complex coordination that is still not completely understood.

There are several different classes of eye movements, ranging from very fast and small to slow and large (Rayner, 1998). For the purposes of eye-tracking studies of survey response processes, we are most interested in saccades—rapid movements of the eyes occurring in reading, looking at a scene, and searching for an object. Unlike some other eye movements, saccades are usually under voluntary control and are used to place the retinal image within the fovea, the part of the retina where visual acuity is highest. Between the saccades, the eyes remain relatively still during fixations. Length of saccades and duration of fixations depend on the properties of visual stimuli.

For more than a century, tracking of eye movements has been used in studies of cognitive processes in reading, visual search, scene perception, and face recognition (cf. Rayner, 1998). Eye tracking is also often used in studying cognition in real-world situations such as watching TV commercials (Woltman-Elpers, Wedel, & Pieters, 2003), reading print advertisements (Liechty, Pieters, & Wedel, 2003; Pieters, Rosbergen, & Wedel, 1999; Rayner, Rotello, Stewart, Keir, & Duffy, 2001; Wedel & Pieters, 2000), making a sandwich (Land & Hayhoe, 2001; Land, Mennie, & Rusted, 1999), flying a plane (Thomas & Wickens, 2004) and driving a car (Ho, Scialfa, Caird, & Graw, 2001). Eye tracking is seldom used in survey methodological research, even though the processing of self-administered survey questions involves reading and visual search (for two exceptions, see Redline & Lankford, 2001, and Graesser, Cai, Louwerse, & Daniel, 2006).

The first eye-tracking measurements were done more than a hundred years ago through a very light stylus attached to a cup placed over the cornea. As the eye moved, the stylus left traces on a smoked drum (Delabarre, 1898; Huey, 1898). Orchansky (1898) made the first photographs of eye movements. He attached a small mirror to a cup placed on the cornea and directed a small source of light to the mirror. The mirror reflected light under different angles to a moving film as the eye moved. Dodge and Cline (1901) were the first to record eye movements without any attachments to the eye. They photographed a bright vertical line reflected directly from the cornea, establishing the corneal reflex method, which is still used today.

Important to eye tracking is the ability to differentiate between movements of eyes and movements of the head, both of which cause shifts in the direction of light reflected from the eye. As the head movements are not of interest to researchers, different methods have been tried to either constrain the head or to measure its movements so that they can be accounted for in the analysis. For example, Marx and Trendelenburg (1911) used a biting board to keep the head still and a small mirror on the nose to record head movements. For more details on the history of eye-tracking methods, see Lord and Wright (1950).

Today, eye tracking employs a variety of techniques that differ in technical solutions, ease of use, and level of precision. Some techniques are very precise but are complex to implement and somewhat uncomfortable for participants. For instance, electro-oculographic methods use tiny electrodes attached to the skin at the inner and outer corners of the eye. As the eye moves, the electric potential between these electrodes changes and provides information about eye position. Other techniques use contact lenses to hold a mirror next to the pupil. The mirror reflects the light directed from an independent source to the eye, and the reflections are recorded. The most precise measurements are obtained by attaching magnetic field sensor coils to the eye and to the head. The participants themselves are placed within a revolving magnetic field, which causes an induced current within the coils, depending on their spatial orientation. Such systems can enable measurements in 2 millisecond (ms) intervals with a margin of error of +/– 1/60 of a degree (cf. Epelboim et al., 1995). These techniques enable very detailed insight into the dynamics and physiology of eye movements, but they require sophisticated technical equipment and knowledge on how to use them. They also tend to induce a considerable level of discomfort for the participants.

A method widely used in today's applied research settings is the corneal reflex method, which does not require any attachments to the eye. Beams of infrared light are directed at the boundary between the iris and the white part of the eye. The reflected light is picked up by infrared detectors, and the signal is analyzed to provide the position of the eyes. In many systems, the head does not need to be restrained. Instead, head movements are recorded, either by attaching a magnetic detector to the head (e.g., on a cap) or by a camera, and accounted for in the analysis.

The unobtrusive eye tracking enabled by modern corneal reflex methods comes at the price of a lower precision of recordings; the measurement intervals range from every 20 ms to less than every 10 ms, and the margin of error ranges from +/– 0.5 to +/– 1 degree. Such a level of spatial precision may not be enough to distinguish which exact words respondents read when the words are in normal font size. In addition, without a head constraint, calibration (the position of respondents' eyes) tends to decrease in accuracy with time. That implies that calibration needs to be done several times during the same session (e.g., every 10–15 minutes). However, these measurement properties are satisfactory for most practical applications and are more than compensated for by the higher level of freedom and comfort for the participants.

14.3 WHAT CAN EYE TRACKING DO?

Eye tracking can be used in both practical and theoretical research. It is a useful pretesting tool for visual instruments such as Web or self-administered questionnaires. It can also address theoretical questions about response behaviors and the underlying survey response processes.

Nowadays more and more surveys rely on self-administered questionnaires. The LISS panel is a prime example of a highly sophisticated data collection system involving computerized self-administered questionnaires presented to a large national probability sample. Reliance on self-administration puts especially high demands on the need for clear and neutral questionnaire design. The design elements should be easy to understand and should not affect the answers in systematic ways.

In pretesting self-administered questionnaires, eye tracking can help in improving both their visual design and their substantive content. It helps detect elements on the screen—pictures or definitions—that are given too much or too little attention. It can also be used to determine whether respondents read the questions and response options in the intended order, and whether they read all options and necessary instructions before marking their answer. Finally, as novel and complex words are typically fixated upon for a longer time than simple and common words (cf. Rayner, 1998), researchers can use eye tracking to detect difficult and flawed questions.

In addition to answering practical usability questions, eye tracking is a useful tool in answering general theoretical questions about underlying survey response processes. One example is the investigation of the mechanisms underlying response order effects. Response order effects occur when the order of the response categories affects the distribution of the answers, producing either primacy effects in visual modes or recency effects in aural modes (Krosnick & Alwin, 1987; Miller & Krosnick, 1998). There are at least two mechanisms that can account for the primacy effects in visual modes. Krosnick and his colleagues argue that working memory is limited and that respondents are unable to give later options as much attention as earlier ones. Because respondents are prone to confirmation bias, this deeper scrutiny makes respondents more likely to select the first options they consider. A different though related possibility is that some respondents process only part of the answers, discarding further options completely once they come to an answer that is good enough (Tourangeau, 1984); such respondents never even read and process later options after they have chosen one. Eye tracking helps disentangle these two mechanisms, as shown in a later section.

Another theoretical question that could be addressed with eye tracking is under which conditions pictures and other nontextual elements on the screen affect answers. Couper et al. (2007) conducted a series of Web experiments in which they have manipulated the content and position of a picture accompanying self-ratings of health. One group of respondents got the image of an obviously healthy person (a woman jogging) and the other group saw the image of an obviously ill person (a woman lying in a hospital bed). In all three experiments, they observed contrast effects of the pictures on the health ratings—those respondents who got the picture of the sick woman rated their health as significantly better than those who got the picture of the healthy woman. In addition, they found that the placement of the picture moderated its impact on survey responses: In two of the three experiments, the contrast effect was not observed when the picture was placed in the header area of the computer screen rather than next to the question text. The authors attributed this finding to "banner blindness"—that is, the tendency for all people to ignore ads or other material presented at the top of Web pages. Another hypothesis that could explain the results is that people do look at the material in the banners but then disregard it when interpreting the meaning of the question. The existing data from the Internet surveys conducted by Couper and colleagues are unable to disentangle the effect of these two related accounts and to determine which one offers the best explanation for the contrast effects. Eye tracking, by contrast, is able to determine the correct mechanism underlying the contrast effects.

14.4 WHAT CAN EYE TRACKING DO THAT THE OTHER METHODS CANNOT?

Compared to traditional mechanical methods for tracking respondent behavior, such as response latencies and mouse traces, the key methodological advantage of eye tracking lies in its ability to provide a direct window into where people look and for how long. By contrast, the traditional methods only produce indirect data about response processes, introducing ambiguities into the interpretation of findings. For instance, response times measure the amount of information processing needed to answer a survey question. Short response times could imply a faster reader or a satisficing respondent skipping some or all parts of the question. Similarly, with mouse movement data, which can be used to track where on the screen people look and read, an idle mouse could signal lack of attention to questions or active reading without mouse movements. Paradata may show that a respondent has changed an answer from 2 to 3, but it cannot tell when that change happened; did it occur after the respondent finished reading the question or during the question reading? Eye-tracking data fill the holes and clear up the ambiguities inherent in these indirect methods. It paints a complete and direct map of people's eye movements and can be used to describe and measure cognitive processes related to survey response.

Cognitive interviewing is another method that is frequently used to understand how respondents process survey questions. During these in-depth individual interviews, respondents are often asked to "think aloud" or to answer probing questions. The verbal reports generated by thinking aloud or in response to specifically designed probes are thought to provide important clues about how respondents come up with their answers and about potential problems with those processes. However, verbally reporting on such response processes is especially taxing for people with low education, low cognitive skills, and less experience with surveys. And the quality of the verbal reports depends on respondents and cognitive interviewers. By contrast, the quality of eye-tracking data does not depend on participants' training, abilities, and skills. Eye-tracking data are not contaminated by participants' subjective interpretation; they provide an objective trace of cognitive processes occurred during survey response.

Eye tracking also has analytical advantages since the data include the location of each gaze, the sequence of gazes, and the amount of fixation at each gaze. Depending on specific research questions to be tested, the data can be analyzed using simple statistical techniques or by means of more advanced methods such as cluster, sequence, or homogeneity analyses. Furthermore, analysts can use them in conjunction with survey responses to test hypotheses regarding response processes.

There are analytical challenges to the eye-tracking data as well. For instance, it is important to make an informed decision on how to define a fixation—that is when it starts and when it ends. A number of algorithms for determining fixations, based on different spatial and temporal properties of eye movements, have been proposed in the literature (cf. Salvucci & Goldberg, 2000). Applying different algorithms can produce different numbers of fixations: Some can result in too many fixations (e.g., when saccades are mistaken for fixations) and some in too few fixations (when some are missed). Researchers need to choose the appropriate algorithm depending on the level of spatial and temporal resolution they require to answer a particular research question. It is also important that they report which algorithm was used to enable proper replication of their results.

14.5 WHAT HAS BEEN DONE WITH EYE TRACKING?

In this section, we present a condensed description of a couple of recent experiments employing eye tracking. These experiments were designed to answer previously unresolved questions such as whether primacy effects are mostly due to shallower processing of response options positioned lower on the list or to skipping later response options altogether, and whether or not initially hidden response options receive the same amount of attention as options that are immediately visible. We also analyzed response styles of individual respondents and examined whether respondents differ in the overall level of effort they invest in reading the questions and the accompanying instructions.

These experiments manipulated response order, the format of response options, and the accessibility of definitions of key concepts. Previous studies have shown that these manipulations produce changes in the answers (Couper et al., 2004; Conrad et al., 2006; Krosnick & Alwin, 1987; Schuman & Presser, 1981). There were five experiments, two of which are described here. Each contains about 20 questions and takes about 10 minutes to complete.

14.5.1 Methods

The Tobii 1750 eye-tracking system was used in this study (www.tobii.com). The Tobii 1750 includes hardware for unobtrusive tracking of eye movements, and software for data analysis. The hardware resembles an ordinary computer monitor and uses near-infrared beams and video images to capture the respondent's eye movements; no special helmets, lenses, or other equipment is needed. The accuracy of recordings is satisfactory for our purposes and for most practical applications: the margin of error for timing of eye movements is +/– 3 ms and for position of eye fixations +/– 0.5–1 degree. The frame rate is 50 Hz, meaning that a data point is produced every 20 ms. In all analyses, we took into account all fixations that lasted at least 100 ms and encompassed 20 pixels (about one word of text) in our questionnaire.

The study was conducted on 120 respondents recruited from the local community of the University of Maryland, College Park. Technical difficulties prevented recording of eye movements for four of the respondents. In addition, eight respondents had recordings that were not of satisfactory quality due to systematic shifts in the tracking of the eye movements relative to the probable locations of the fixations and/or due to unreliable tracking measures (with high unsystematic error). The systematic shifts were easy to spot visually—the apparent positions of the fixations were consistently a fixed distance above (or below) the lines of text on the screen. These recordings were excluded from the subsequent analyses, leaving 108 respondents with good-quality recordings. Of those 108, 50% were between 18 and 24 years old, 35% between 25 and 34, and 15% between 35 and 64; 51% were male; 13% had only a high school education, 52% some college, and 35% a college degree. Most (83%) used the Internet every day, 60% considered themselves advanced or expert users of the Internet, and 77% had already participated in at least one prior Internet survey.

14.5.2 Effects of Order of Response Options

As mentioned before, with response options presented visually (rather than aurally), it is often observed that the options near the top of the list are more likely to be selected than those closer to the bottom (Krosnick, 1991, 1999). As we noted earlier, there are at least two possible mechanisms underlying such primacy effects. First, respondents may simply select the first acceptable answer they read, not bothering to read the later options at all. On the other hand, respondents may read all the options but spend fewer cognitive resources processing the later options compared to those presented earlier (cf. Krosnick & Alwin, 1987; Krosnick, 1991). Either way, if eye fixations reflect the amount of attention given to a response option, both accounts suggest that respondents spend more time looking at the top options. However, the first mechanism would predict very little or no time at all spent on looking at the options that come after the chosen one.

To study these mechanisms, we used four questions on different topics and with a varying number of options (see Figure 14.1 for screenshots). We reversed the order of the response options for a random half of the respondents and measured the time they spent looking at the options in the first and the second half of the response option list. One question asked about desirable qualities of a child and had twelve response options; the other three questions asked about trust in police officers with five options, and attitudes toward crime and morality with two options each. All of these questions were positioned in the second half of the questionnaire and each question was shown on a separate screen.

As observed in the previous studies, respondents were more likely to choose the options in the first half of the list than the second half for all four items, independently of the content of options and the length of the list. What is important, however, is that eye-tracking data showed that respondents spent more time looking at the response options in the first half of the list than those in the second. As shown in Figure 14.2, the larger the proportion of time respondents spent looking at the top half of the options, the more likely they were to choose an option from that part. If we assume that the time spent fixating on an option reflects, at least in part, the time spent on processing that option (Just & Carpenter, 1980),

Which one quality listed below would you say is the most desirable for a child to have?

- That he is interested in how and why things happen
- That he is considerate of others
- That he is responsible
- That he obeys his parents well
- That he gets along well with other children
- That he acts like a boy or she acts like a girl
- That he has self-control
- That he has good sense and sound judgement
- That he is neat and clean
- That he is honest
- That he tried hard to succeed
- That he has good manners

Next, we would like you to think about the amount of trust you have that the police officers in your area will always do what is right. Would you say you have–

- A great deal of trust
- A moderate amount of trust
- Equal amounts of trust and distrust
- A moderate amount of distrust
- A great deal of distrust

Some say individuals are more to blame than social conditions for crime and lawlessness in this country. Others say the contrary—social conditions are more to blame than individuals for crime and lawlessness in this country. Which one of these two statements comes closest to your opinion on this issue?

- Individuals are more to blame
- Social conditions are more to blame

In your opinion, should government (federal, state, or local) have some responsibility for preventing the breakdown of morality, or should private organizations and individuals be entirely responsible for preventing the breakdown of morality?

- Government is responsible
- Private organizations and individuals are responsible

FIGURE 14.1
Screenshots of the questions used in the response order experiment.

this lends support to the idea that primacy effects are partially caused by processing the later options less deeply than the earlier ones.

In addition, some respondents did not look at the later options at all. For example, with the question item listing 12 characteristics of children, 10% of the respondents did not fixate on either of the last two options. For the question about trust in police officers, which used an ordered 5-point response

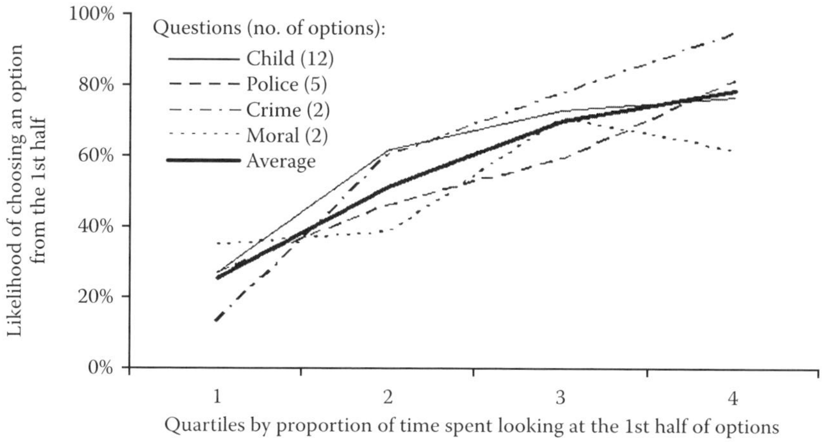

FIGURE 14.2
Relationship between the proportion of time spent looking at the top half of response options and likelihood of choosing an option from the top half, for each question.

scale (from "great deal of trust" to "great deal of distrust"), the results were more dramatic. Only 54% fixated on the last option of the scale. These results support the idea that the observed primacy effects are a product of two behavioral patterns: reading all options but paying more attention to the first ones on the list, and skipping the latter options altogether. Figure 14.3 gives examples of two respondents with different behavioral patterns.

14.5.3 Effects of Response Format

As noted by Couper, Tourangeau, Conrad, and Crawford (2004), some response formats are more prone to primacy effects than others. For drop-down lists in which some of the options are immediately visible but others need to be uncovered by a mouse click or by scrolling, primacy effects are much stronger than for drop-down lists with no options visible immediately or with radio button lists in which all response options are visible at the outset.

There are two possible explanations for this difference across response formats. First, the respondents might never activate the drop-down list to reveal the options that were not visible initially—either because they are unwilling to expend the additional effort or because they do not know how to activate the list. Second, even if they do uncover the bottom options, it is possible that they still pay more attention to the options that

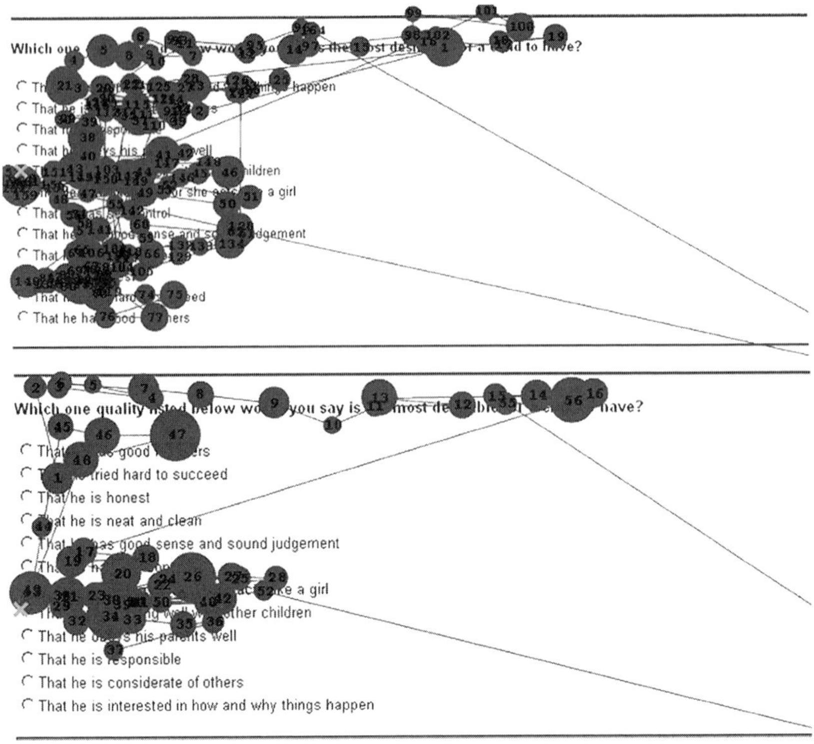

FIGURE 14.3
Gaze plots of two different respondents to the question about child qualities. Each circle denotes a fixation, and lines are saccades. Numbers within the circles show the order of the fixations, and the size of each circle is proportional to the fixation duration. The respondent in the top panel fixated on all the response options; the respondent in the bottom did not fixate on the last two options. The order of options in the two examples is reversed, reflecting the order manipulation in this experiment.

were visible from the outset. Eye tracking can help us to resolve this issue by revealing not only how many people activated the list but also how long they looked at different parts of the list.

We replicated the Couper, Tourangeau, Conrad et al. (2004) experiment mentioned above, this time recording the respondents' eye movements. We used two questions with 10 substantive response options each. One question asked about the nutrients that were important in choosing a breakfast cereal and the other asked about features that were important when deciding on which automobile to purchase. We reversed the order of the substantive options for half of the respondents; the option "none of the above" was always at the end of the list. The questions were presented in three formats

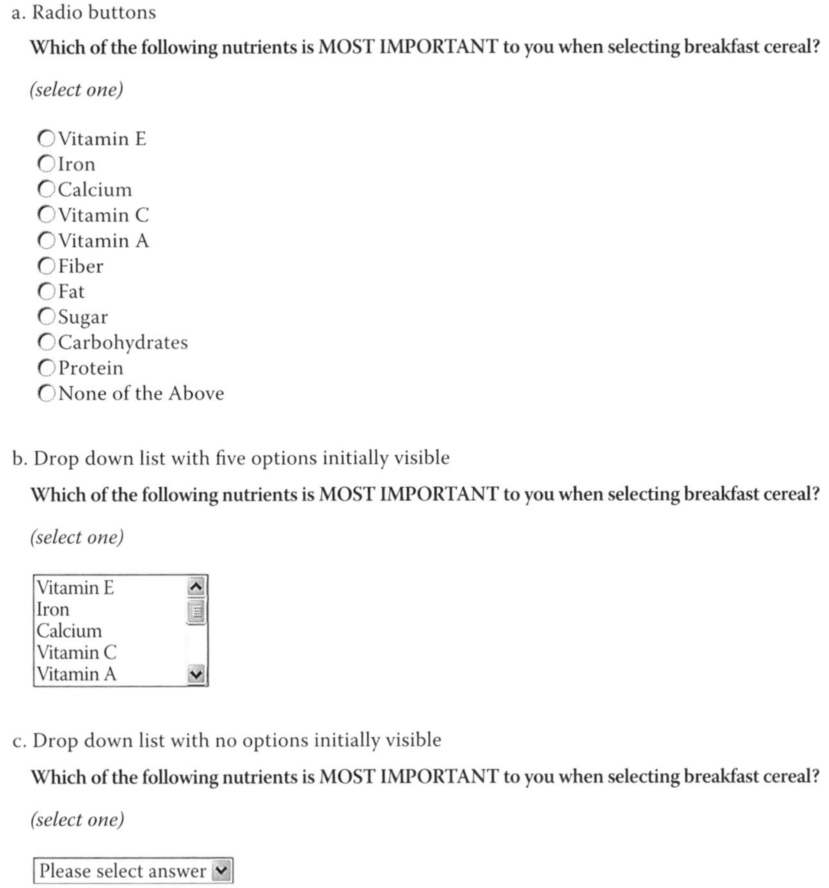

a. Radio buttons
Which of the following nutrients is MOST IMPORTANT to you when selecting breakfast cereal?
(select one)
Vitamin E
Iron
Calcium
Vitamin C
Vitamin A
Fiber
Fat
Sugar
Carbohydrates
Protein
None of the Above
b. Drop down list with five options initially visible
Which of the following nutrients is MOST IMPORTANT to you when selecting breakfast cereal?
(select one)
Vitamin E
Iron
Calcium
Vitamin C
Vitamin A
c. Drop down list with no options initially visible
Which of the following nutrients is MOST IMPORTANT to you when selecting breakfast cereal?
(select one)
Please select answer

FIGURE 14.4
Response formats used in the second experiment.

(Figure 14.4). A third of the respondents got the response options for both questions in radio button format with all options immediately visible; a third received both questions as drop-down lists with five options visible initially; and the final third got drop-down lists with no immediately visible options. The respondents answered both questions in the same format.

For both questions, the options in the top part of the list were chosen more often than those in the bottom half. Of the respondents who selected one of the substantive answers, 55% across the three versions chose one of the top five options in the question about breakfast cereal and 66% did so in the question about automobiles. This effect was more pronounced, however, when only five options were visible initially than when all of the

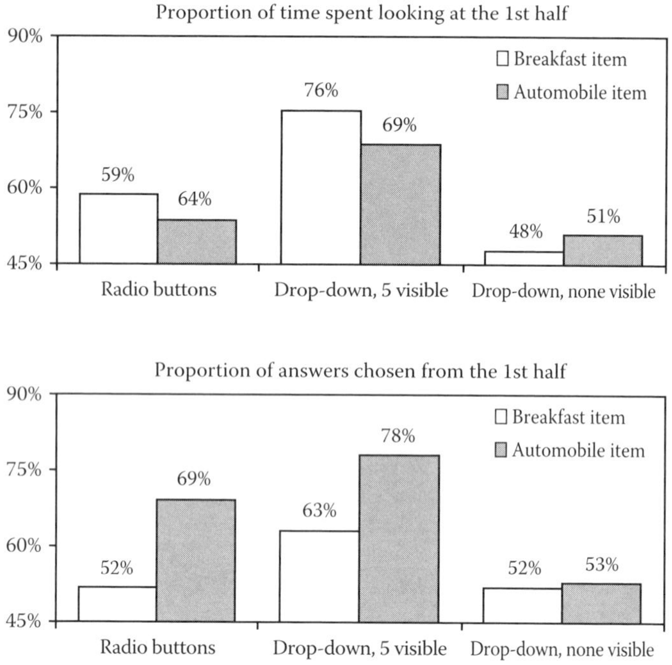

FIGURE 14.5
Proportion of time spent looking at the top half of the options (top panel), and proportion of answers chosen from the top half (bottom panel).

options or none of them were visible at the outset (see the bottom panel of Figure 14.5). How are these findings related to fixation times?

The top panel of Figure 14.5 shows that respondents looked longer at the first half of the list of response options in most conditions. On average, the respondents spent 61% (for the question about cereal) and 57% (for the question about automobiles) of their time looking at options in the top half of the list. This difference was most pronounced, however, when five options were visible initially (for cereal: 76%, $t(29) = 5.40$, $p = .001$; for automobiles: 69%, $t(32) = 4.61$, $p = .001$). Some respondents never activated the drop-down list and thus never saw the bottom options (43% for breakfast cereal and 41% for automobiles, respectively). Even those who did activate the list spent more time looking at the first five than at the second five options (64%, $t(16) = 2.42$, $p = .03$; and 60%, $t(20) = 3.10$, $p = .006$, respectively).

As in the first experiment, the longer respondents looked at the response options in the top part, the more likely they were to choose one from them. Regression analyses controlling for question format showed that the respondents who fixated more than half of the time on the first half of the options were much more likely to choose one of those options for both questions (odds ratios obtained in logistic regressions were 15.00 and 5.43 for the cereal and automobiles questions, respectively; $p = .01$ for both).

14.5.4 General Observations About Respondents' Answering Styles

In addition to answering these and other specific research questions, we were also able to observe some more general characteristics of respondents' survey response behavior. Respondents tended to read response options from top to bottom, and only about half of them revisited options they had read before (from 43% for the question about trust in police officers to 57% for the question about child qualities). Some respondents, however, merely skimmed through the response options, especially when the lists were longer. For example, only 75% of all respondents fixated for at least 100 ms on each of the 12 options for the question on desirable qualities for children. Even in the two questions with only two response options (about attitudes related to crime and morality), only 80% and 77% fixated on both options. Finally, when the response options were ordered, forming a graded scale, such as in the question that asked about level of trust in police officers, only 26% of the respondents fixated on each one of them; the remaining respondents appeared to have inferred what the rest of the options were from reading just a few. This is reminiscent of the eye-tracking results reported by Graesser et al. (2006). They found that respondents frequently answered the question before finishing reading the entire question stem, especially when the question syntax was complex, and especially among respondents who had scored poorly on an intelligence test.

Some respondents seemed to adopt a particular style for working through questions. The average correlation between the number of options that were fixated on in the four questions mentioned above was $r(105) = .57, p = .001$. This means that some respondents were more likely than others to skim through the options. In fact, only 23% of the respondents fixated on every one of the options in all four of those questions; the remaining 77% skipped at least one option. Those who fixated on all options were also more conscientious when answering other questions. For example, they retrieved more definitions in the rollover condition (1.9 vs. 0.4 definitions, $t(52) = -2.88$,

$p = .01$), and when they retrieved them, they spent more time reading the definitions (20.8 vs. 4.9 seconds on average, $t(13) = -1.84$, $p = .09$). They also spent more time reading the general instructions on the very first page of the questionnaire (11.7 vs. 7.7 seconds, $t(105) = -2.69$, $p = .01$).

These results suggest that some respondents were more prone than others to satisficing behavior (cf. Krosnick & Alwin, 1987), which was reflected in different ways throughout the survey. These patterns of behavior are usually undesirable in survey research. We did not find any significant demographic differences between the conscientious respondents and the other respondents, nor did we observe any difference in their previous experience with Internet surveys. However, survey literature indicates that motivational and personality variables are correlated with the amount of cognitive capacity and the depth of cognitive processing. For instance, older people are shown to be more susceptible to response effects than younger people due to lack of cognitive capacity (Knäuper, 1999). Furthermore, people with a high need for cognition are more likely to engage in deeper cognitive processing than those with a low need for cognition (Cacioppo & Petty, 1982). However, the exact relationships of these personality and motivation variables to different eye movement patterns are yet to be explored.

14.6 CONCLUSIONS

This chapter describes eye tracking as a promising new method for studying survey responses. We began the chapter with examples of the type of research questions eye tracking can help address, proceeded with a short history of techniques for tracking eye movements and a comparison of eye tracking to traditional methods, and ended with examples of experiments employing eye tracking to study survey response. Current eye-tracking equipment no longer requires awkward and invasive apparatus such as special lenses or helmets. Instead, the combination of near-infrared beams that reflect off the retina and digital cameras that track head position makes it possible to record eye movements more or less unobtrusively with adequate precision for most applications in survey methodology.

Information on eye movements provides direct insights into how respondents read and process survey questions. The two experiments described in this chapter are examples of the ongoing research effort in employing eye tracking to deepen our understanding of survey response processes. Eye-tracking data can also be used for question pretest and evaluation and assessments of questionnaire usability. For instance, as people tend to fixate longer on difficult words and complex sentences, fixation durations can be used to identify bad question wordings. In addition, eye tracking records whether people look at numerical scale points and/or scale labels when answering survey questions. Question writers can take advantage of this feature of eye tracking to determine whether a particular scale should be fully labeled or not. Similarly, eye tracking can show how many response options most respondents read before providing an answer and help question writers determine how many points a particular scale should have.

Despite the apparent analytic advantages of eye-tracking data, we do not believe that eye tracking will ever completely replace other methods for studying response behavior. First, the initial cost of eye tracking is probably much higher than the initial cost of some of the traditional methods, such as the collection of paradata. Second, eye tracking is not able to answer all interesting research questions. For instance, eye tracking probably will not be able to tell whether an answer provided by a respondent is true, or whether a respondent acquiesces by choosing the "yes" option. Traditional indirect analyses of response patterns and external data sets should be used in combination with eye tracking to thoroughly study these phenomena.

Future research using eye tracking should explore the relationship of eye movements (e.g., the order and duration of fixations), response processes (e.g., attending to different parts of the questionnaire, speed and thoroughness of reading, editing the response), and respondent characteristics (e.g., education, cognitive abilities, motivation, and expertise with surveys). As these relationships are better understood, eye tracking will bring added value to the research uncovering survey response processes.

[1] Acknowledgments: The eye-tracking experiments presented in this chapter were supported by a grant from the National Institute for Child Health and Human Development (R01 HD041386-01A1) to Roger Tourangeau, Mick Couper, Fred Conrad, and Reg Baker. We would like to thank them for their support. A more complete report on these studies can be found in Galesic, Tourangeau, Couper, and Conrad (2008).

REFERENCES

Cacioppo, J. T. & Petty, R. E. (1982). The need for cognition. *Journal of Personality and Social Psychology, 42*, 116–131.

Cannell, C. F., Miller, P. V., & Oksenberg, L. (1981). Research on interviewing techniques. In S. Leinhardt (Ed.), *Sociological methodology* (pp. 389–437). San Francisco: Jossey-Bass.

Conrad, F. G., Couper, M. P., Tourangeau, R., & Peytchev, A. (2005). Impact of progress feedback on task completion: First impressions matter. In *Proceedings of the CHI* (pp. 1921–1924), Portland, OR.

Conrad, F. G., Couper, M. P., Tourangeau, R., & Peytchev, A. (2006). Use and non-use of clarification features in Web surveys. *Journal of Official Statistics, 22*, 245–269.

Couper, M. P., Conrad, F. G., & Tourangeau, R. (2007). Visual context effects in Web surveys. *Public Opinion Quarterly, 71*, 623–634.

Couper, M. P., Tourangeau, R., Conrad, F. G., & Crawford, S. (2004). What they see is what we get: Response options for Web surveys. *Social Science Computer Review, 22*, 111–127.

Couper, M. P., Tourangeau, R., & Kenyon, K. (2004). Picture this! Exploring visual effects in Web surveys. *Public Opinion Quarterly, 68*, 255–266.

Delabarre, E. B. (1898). A method of recording eye-movements. *American Journal of Psychology, 9*, 572–574.

Dodge, R. & Cline, T. S. (1901). The angle velocity of eye movements. *Psychological Review, 8*, 145–157.

Epelboim, J., Steinman, R. M., Kowler, E., Edwards, M. E., Pizlo, Z., Erkelens, C. J. et al. (1995). The function of visual search and memory in sequential looking tasks. *Vision Research, 35*, 3401–3422.

Galesic, M., Tourangeau, R., Couper, M. P., & Conrad, F. G. (2008). Eye-tracking data: New insights on response order effects and other cognitive shortcuts in survey responding. *Public Opinion Quarterly, 72*, 892–913.

Graesser, A. C., Cai, Z., Louwerse, M. M., & Daniel, F. (2006). Question understanding aid (QUAID): A Web facility that tests question comprehensibility. *Public Opinion Quarterly, 70*, 3–22.

Heerwegh, D. (2003). Explaining response latencies and changing answers using client-side paradata from a Web survey. *Social Science Computer Review, 21*(3), 360–373.

Heerwegh, D. & Loosveldt, G. (2006). An experimental study on the effects of personalization, survey length statements, progress indicators, and survey sponsor logos in Web surveys. *Journal of Official Statistics, 22*(2), 191–210.

Ho, G., Scialfa, C. T., Caird, J. K., & Graw. T. (2001). Visual search for traffic signs: The effects of clutter, luminance, and aging. *Human Factors, 43*, 194–207.

Huey, E. B. (1898). Preliminary experiments in the physiology and psychology of reading. *American Journal of Psychology, 9*(4), 575–586.

Just, M. A. & Carpenter, P. A. (1980). A theory of reading: From eye fixations to comprehension. *Psychological Review, 87*, 329–354.

Kaczmirek, L. & Faass, T. (2008). *Data quality of paradata: A comparison of three response time measures in a randomized online experiment.* Paper presented at the General Online Research conference (GOR '08), Hamburg, Germany.

Knäuper, B. (1999). The impact of age and education on response order effects in attitude measurement. *Public Opinion Quarterly, 63*, 347–370.

Krosnick, J. A. (1991). Response strategies for coping with the cognitive demands of attitude measures in surveys. *Applied Cognitive Psychology, 5*, 213–236.

Krosnick, J. A. (1999). Survey research. *Annual Review of Psychology, 50*, 537–567.

Krosnick, J. A. & Alwin, D. (1987). An evaluation of a cognitive theory of response-order effects in survey measurement. *Public Opinion Quarterly, 51*, 201–220.

Land, M. F. & Hayhoe, M. (2001). In what ways do eye movements contribute to everyday activities. *Vision Research, 41*, 3559–3565.

Land, M. F., Mennie, N., & Rusted, J. (1999). The roles of vision and eye movements in the control of activities of daily living. *Perception, 28*, 1311–1328.

Liechty, J., Pieters, R., & Wedel, M. (2003). Global and local covert visual attention: Evidence from a Bayesian hidden Markov model. *Psychometrika, 68*, 519–541.

Lord, M. P. & Wright, W. D. (1950). The investigation of eye movements. *Reports on Progress in Physics, 13*, 1–23.

Marx, E. & Trendelenburg, W. (1911). Ueber die Genauigkeit der Einstellung des Auges beim Fixieren. *Zeitschrift fuer Sinnesphysiologie, 45*, 87–102.

Miller, J. M. & Krosnick, J. A. (1998). The impact of candidate name order on election outcomes. *Public Opinion Quarterly, 62*, 291–330.

Orchansky, J. (1898). Eine Methode die Augenbewegungen direkt zu untersuchen (Ophthalmographie). *Zentralblatt Physiologie, 12*, 785.

Pieters, R., Rosbergen, E., & Wedel, M. (1999). Visual attention to repeated print advertising: A test of scanpath theory. *Journal of Marketing Research, 36*, 424–438.

Rayner, K., (1998). Eye movements in reading and information processing: 20 years of research. *Psychological Bulletin, 124*, 372–422.

Rayner, K., Rotello, C. M., Stewart, A. J., Keir, J., & Duffy, S. A. (2001). Integrating text and pictorial information: Eye movements when looking at print advertisements. *Journal of Experimental Psychology Applied, 7*, 219–226.

Redline, C. D. & Lankford, C. P. (2001). Eye-movement analysis: A new tool for evaluating the design of visually administered instruments (paper and Web). In *Proceedings of the Section on Survey Research Methods of the American Statistical Association*. Retrieved from www.amstat.org/Sections/Srms/Proceedings/y2001/Proceed/00248.pdf

Salvucci, D. D. & Goldberg, J. H. (2000). Identifying fixations and saccades in eye-tracking protocols. In *Proceedings of the Eye Tracking Research and Applications Symposium* (pp. 71–78). New York: ACM Press.

Schuman, H. & Presser, S. (1981). *Questions and answers in attitude surveys*. New York: Academic Press.

Thomas, L. C. & Wickens, C. D. (2004). *Eye-tracking and individual differences in off-normal event detection when flying with a synthetic vision system display*. Paper presented at the 48th annual meeting of the Human Factors and Ergonomics Society, Santa Monica, California.

Tourangeau, R. (1984). Cognitive science and survey methods. In T. B. Jabine, M. L. Straf, J. M. Tanur, & R. Tourangeau (Eds.), *Cognitive aspects of survey methodology: Building a bridge between disciplines* (pp. 73–100). Washington, DC: National Academy Press.

Tourangeau, R., Couper, M. P., & Conrad, F. G. (2004). Spacing, position, and order: Interpretive heuristics for visual features of survey questions. *Public Opinion Quarterly, 68*, 368–393.

Tourangeau, R., Couper, M. P., & Conrad, F. G. (2007). Color, labels, and interpretive heuristics for response scales. *Public Opinion Quarterly, 71*, 91–112.

Wedel, M. & Pieters, R. (2000). Eye fixations on advertisements and memory for brands: A model and findings. *Marketing Science, 19*, 297–312.

Woltman-Elpers, J. L. C. M., Wedel, M., & Pieters, F. G. M. (2003). Why do consumers stop viewing television commercials? Two experiments on the influence of moment-to-moment entertainment and information value. *Journal of Marketing Research, 40*, 437–453.

Yan, T., Conrad, F. G., Tourangeau, R., & Couper, M. P. (2007). *Should I stay or should I go: The effects of progress indicators, promised duration, and questionnaire length on completing Web surveys.* Paper presented at the annual conference of the American Association for Public Opinion Research (AAPOR), Anaheim, California.

Yan, T. & Tourangeau, R. (2008). Fast times and easy questions: The effects of age, experience and question complexity on Web survey response times. *Applied Cognitive Psychology, 22*, 51–68.

15

Can Biomarkers Be Collected in an Internet Survey? A Pilot Study in the LISS Panel[1]

Mauricio Avendano
Department of Public Health
Erasmus MC Rotterdam
Rotterdam, the Netherlands

and

Center for Population and Development Studies
Harvard School of Public Health
Boston, Massachusetts

Annette C. Scherpenzeel
CentERdata
Tilburg University
Tilburg, the Netherlands

Johan P. Mackenbach
Department of Public Health
Erasmus MC Rotterdam
Rotterdam, the Netherlands

15.1 INTRODUCTION

Research during the last decades has shown that social and economic factors such as educational level, income, and psychosocial well-being have a major impact on disease risk (Avendano, Kawachi et al., 2006; Avendano,

Kunst et al., 2006; Cohen et al., 2006). Simultaneously, health and disease influence individuals' income, wealth, and psychological well-being (Smith, 2005). Research in this area has primarily focused on examining associations of social and economic factors with disease incidence, mortality, and self-rated health (Avendano, Kawachi et al., 2006; Avendano et al., 2005; Smits, Westert, & Van den Bos, 2002; Steenland, Henley, & Thun, 2002; Steptoe & Marmot, 2002). These measures, however, reflect the final stage of disease progression but tell us little about the biological mechanisms that precede disease. Biomarkers are more detailed and objective measures of the biological processes that underlie an individual's health.

Available population studies typically rely on self-reports or national mortality registries to measure health outcomes (Avendano et al., 2004; Avendano et al., 2005; Börsch-Supan et al., 2005; Juster & Suzman, 1995; Marmot, Banks, Blundell, Lessof, & Nazroo, 2002; Wilson & Howell, 2005), but few social surveys comprise detailed data on the biological mechanisms of disease. Recent population surveys have started to collect data on biomarkers, but most have focused on localized populations, primarily in the United States and the United Kingdom (Alley et al., 2006; Banks, Marmot, Oldfield, & Smith, 2006). The lesson from these studies is that to understand how health is shaped by social and economic experiences, better data on the biology underlying disease are essential (Cohen et al., 2006; Dowd & Goldman, 2006; Kristenson, Eriksen, Sluiter, Starke, & Ursin, 2004).

In this chapter, we explore the methodological challenges involved in the collection of biomarkers in population surveys, with particular emphasis on Internet surveys. The chapter is divided into three sections. Section 15.2 presents an overview of biomarker measurement and discusses the potential advantages and challenges of measuring biomarkers in population surveys. Section 15.3 discusses the types of biospecimens and biomarkers of potential interest and existing measurement techniques. In this section, the feasibility of collecting different biospecimens in an Internet survey is discussed. Section 15.4 presents the results of a pilot study conducted in the Netherlands to examine the feasibility of collecting three specific biomarkers in an Internet survey. In this pilot, we examine the overall quality of biomarker data obtained using self-collection methods. We also examine distributions of biomarkers and their association with demographic factors, and compare these to results reported in previous studies that are based on traditional methods.

15.2 RATIONALE FOR THE COLLECTION OF BIOMARKER DATA

15.2.1 Biomarkers

A biological marker (biomarker) is a characteristic that is objectively measured and evaluated as an indicator of normal biological processes, pathogenic processes, or pharmacological responses (Biomarkers Definitions Working Group, 2001). Biomarkers have many valuable applications in disease detection and monitoring of health status: They serve as diagnostic tool for the identification of patients with a disease or abnormal condition (e.g., elevated blood glucose concentration for the diagnosis of diabetes mellitus), provide information about the staging of a disease (e.g., in cancer), act as indicators of disease prognosis, and are a useful tool in the prediction and monitoring of clinical response to an intervention (e.g., reducing cholesterol levels) (Biomarkers Definitions Working Group, 2001). Table 15.1 presents an overview of some of the biospecimens most commonly collected in population surveys.

Table 15.1 shows that there are many different biospecimens, each of which yields data on different biomarkers. Table 15.2 presents the most important categories of biomarkers. Depending on the purpose for which they are collected in population surveys, they can be grouped into two broad categories. *Standard biomarkers* are those that are incorporated into most epidemiological surveys that collect data on biomarkers. Practically all population epidemiological surveys collect information on anthropometrics and body fat. This includes height and weight, with several of them also incorporating measurements of waist/hip ratio or waist circumference in their recent measurements. Furthermore, the majority of existing population epidemiological surveys have focused their attention primarily on cardiovascular-, metabolism-, and inflammation-related biomarkers, including measurements such as blood pressure, cholesterol, glucose, and C-reactive protein. The category *biomarkers for specific purposes* comprises biomarkers that are collected mostly in specific surveys and which address relatively more specific research questions (e.g., psychobiological pathways, genetic interactions). In this group are biomarkers of the hypothalamic-pituitary-adrenal (HPA) axis and the sympathetic nervous system, genetic biomarkers, and biomarkers of performance.

TABLE 15.1

Biospecimens for the Collection of Biomarkers

Measurement	Advantages	Disadvantages
Blood samples/ dried blood spots	Ample source for various materials that can be used for multiple purposes, including recent or remote exposures, pathological markers, physiological markers and genetic markers (Survey and Measurement Core, 2005).	It is the most invasive biomarker taken during surveys, achieving the lowest response rates (Kumari, Wadsworth, Blake, Bynner, & Wagner, 2006).
Anthropometrics, e.g., height, weight, waist circumference	They are relatively easy to measure by respondents and involve no risks.	As opposed to blood or saliva samples, which provide information on a wider array of biomarkers, anthropometrics are a specific measurement referring to a single specific aspect of human health.
Saliva samples	Efficient way to obtain higher response rates as compared to blood samples. It provides information on recent or remote exposures, pathological markers, physiological markers including hormones, and genetic markers (Survey and Measurement Core, 2005).	Relatively smaller numbers of parameters measurable, compared to blood (Kumari et al., 2006).
Urine samples	Urine samples can be used to collect a wider array of biomarkers including recent or remote exposures, pathological and physiological markers including hormones, rhythms, and genetic markers.	Adequate collection may be inconvenient for participants (e.g., timed 24-hour collections).
Hair	It provides information on disease conditions, levels of trace elements that reflect internal metabolism or external exposures, and genetic markers from cells at the hair roots. It is painless to collect, inexpensive, and particularly apt for occupational and environmental exposures.	It is susceptible to external contamination from air, shampoos, and chemicals used in processing. In drug testing studies, the response rate is about 69%, with 13% refusing and 19% judged as having insufficient hair (Fendrich, Johnson, Wislar, Hubbell, & Spiehler, 2004).

continued

TABLE 15.1 (continued)

Biospecimens for the Collection of Biomarkers

Measurement	Advantages	Disadvantages
Nail clippings	It provides information on levels of trace elements that reflect internal metabolism or external exposures. It is painless and accessible, inexpensive to collect, handle, store and ship, and less likely to be contaminated by external exposures compared to hair.	They require multiple steps for analysis in the lab, and provide data on relatively specific biomarkers of exposure only.
Adipose tissue	Provides information on long-term exposure, especially of fat-soluble chemicals (e.g., fatty acids) in highly concentrated forms compared to blood. It reflects stable, long-term exposures.	Invasive and not routinely collected. It must be collected by a technician and it requires immediate processing.
Performance measures, e.g., grip strength, walking speed, lung function	They provide objective information on functioning outcomes and do not involve major risks.	Outcomes are highly sensitive due to variations in protocol.

Despite their advantages for health research, it is also important to understand that biomarkers have some limitations. One of their key limitations is that they are markers of specific biological processes that generally precede clinical diagnosis. For instance, markers of inflammation can be related to several medical conditions rather than being markers of a single disease process. Furthermore, biomarker data are relatively specific in the sense that they provide information about particular biological processes, as opposed to reflecting the general state of health of an individual. For instance, grip strength is a generic health indicator strongly predictive of mortality and disability. However, this biomarker is likely to reflect specific processes influencing the motor function without fully encompassing other morbidities for which grip strength is not a marker.

15.2.2 Can Biomarkers Be Collected in an Internet Panel?

The collection of biomarkers by a nurse or trained interviewer has become relatively standard practice in several epidemiological and social surveys. Some studies have also collected data on biomarkers using

TABLE 15.2

Most Common Biomarkers Collected in Population Surveys

Classification	Biomarker	Description and Scientific Relevance
Cardiovascular disease	Blood pressure	Index of cardiovascular activity, composed of systolic and diastolic blood pressure.
	Pulse	Pulse measurement is performed to determine the heart rate and rhythm.
	Heart rate variability (HRV)	Beat-to-beat alterations in heart rate.
Metabolism-related biomarkers	High-density lipoproteins (HDL), low-density lipoproteins (LDL), and total cholesterol	A cholesterol test, also called lipid test and lipoprotein test, measures the amount of cholesterol and triglycerides in the blood serum. It is a strong predictor of cardiovascular (especially heart) disease.
	Glycosylated hemoglobin	Measure of the amount of sugar that is attached to the hemoglobin in red blood cells. Higher test values are associated with higher risk of complications from diabetes (eye disease, kidney disease, nerve damage, heart disease, and stroke).
	Glucose	Measured to determine if the blood glucose level is within healthy ranges, and to screen for, diagnose, and monitor hyperglycemia (high blood glucose), hypoglycemia (low blood glucose), diabetes, and prediabetes.
	Insulin	Hormone produced and stored in the beta cells of the pancreas. Insulin is vital for the transportation and storage of glucose at the cellular level.
Inflammatory/immune system biomarkers	C-reactive protein (CRP)	Acute phase response protein that indicates blood levels of inflammation.
	Interleukin-6 (IL-6)	Protein produced throughout the body as part of the immune response. IL-6 is one of a class of immune system regulators called cytokines that serve a variety of immune functions in response to acute illness or injury.

	Fibrinogen	Protein produced by the liver that helps stop bleeding by helping the formation of blood clots. It is a strong predictor of mortality and cardiovascular disease.
Hypothalamic-pituitary-adrenal (HPA) axis	Cortisol	Steroid hormone produced by the adrenal cortex. Levels of cortisol and its antagonist dehydroepiandrosterone sulfate (DHEA-S) are indicators of HPA activity. The HPA axis is one of two major stress-responsive physiological systems of the body, and cortisol is the end product of the HPA system. It influences human health and behavior, reaching almost every body cell, and influencing major physiological systems including growth, metabolic function, inflammation, sleep timing and quality, cognition and mood, and cellular function and damage. There is extensive evidence relating cortisol to chronic stress from work or emotional strain.
	Dehydroepiandrosterone sulfate (DHEA-S)	Hormone produced by the adrenal gland. Indicator of hypothalamic-pituitary axis activity.
	Adrenocorticotropic hormone (ACTH)	Stimulates the adrenal cortex. More specifically, it stimulates secretion of glucocorticoids such as cortisol.
	Epinephrine	Stress hormone important to the body's metabolism, also known as adrenaline. Heightened secretion caused by fear or anger, will result in increased heart rate and the hydrolysis of glycogen to glucose.
	Norepinephrine	Neurotransmitter in the catecholamine family. It mediates chemical communication in the sympathetic nervous system.
Anthropometrics and body fat	Height	Related to the risk of chronic conditions, diseases, and death among older people.
	Weight, body mass index (BMI)	These adiposity measures indicate the balance between energy intake and energy expenditure.
	Waist circumference/hip size	Measures the distribution of fat and predicts adiposity-related diseases and mortality.

continued

TABLE 15.2 (continued)

Most Common Biomarkers Collected in Population Surveys

Classification	Biomarker	Description and Scientific Relevance
	Body fat (bioelectrical impedance analysis)	Calculates fat levels using hand-held scales.
	Leg length	Also called leg height and lower limb development; thought to be affected by adverse childhood circumstances. Adult leg length is particularly sensitive to diet (breastfeeding and energy intake) in early childhood.
	Demispan	Sternal notch to finger roots with arm outstretched laterally.
Genetics-related biomarkers	Apolipoprotein E (APOE)	Gene that produces a protein called apo-epsilon. Working with another protein (apo-beta), apo-epsilon modulates the uptake of triglyceride-rich lipoproteins. APOE has been shown to be associated with a higher risk of late-onset Alzheimer's disease, heart disease, stroke and coronary artery disease. It is also related to family hyperlipidemia.
	Angiotensin I converting enzyme (ACE)	This gene encodes an enzyme involved in catalyzing the conversion of angiotensin I into a physiologically active peptide angiotensin II, which is a potent vasopressor and aldosterone-stimulating peptide that controls blood pressure and fluid–electrolyte balance.
Performance measures	Lung function/peak flow	Measure of lung function.
	Walking speed	Measure of functioning and walking ability, particularly among the very old. It is based on a measurement of walking speed in a short distance.
	Grip strength	Measure of motor function of the upper part of the body used as an indicator of physical disability.

Other biomarkers	Homocysteine	Amino acid measured in plasma that is related to a higher risk of coronary heart disease, stroke, and peripheral vascular disease.
	Albumin	Protein that transports many small molecules in the blood, e.g., bilirubin, calcium, progesterone, and drugs.
	Potassium	Used to detect concentrations that are too high (hyperkalemia) or too low (hypokalemia). The most common cause of hyperkalemia is kidney disease.
	Sodium	Used to detect hyponatremia (low sodium) or hypernatremia (high sodium) associated with dehydration, edema, and a variety of diseases.
	Oxidative stress	General term used to describe the steady-state level of oxidative damage in a cell, tissue, or organ, caused by the reactive oxygen species (ROS).
	Complete blood count	Provides information on general health status and is a tool for checking disorders such as anemia, infection, and thrombocytopenia.

self-administration methods. For example, a study showed that collecting saliva by mail for cotinine and DNA analysis in participants recruited through the Internet was feasible and cost-effective (Etter, Neidhart, Bertrand, Malafosse, & Bertrand, 2005). The Health and Retirement Survey (HRS) used self-administered blood test kits to collect glycosylated hemoglobin (HbA1c) in a subsample of diabetic patients and obtained a net participation rate of 52% (Weir, 2008). The Rotterdam study (Dekker et al., 2008) asked participants to collect four saliva samples in one day using salivettes and obtained a response rate of 78%. To our knowledge, however, there are no nationally representative Internet surveys collecting a wide array of biomarkers using self-administered methods.

In this chapter, we conceive two ways in which the Internet can be used to collect biomarker data. First, some biomarkers may be collected using computer technology and be sent directly via the Internet from the respondent to the investigators. For example, devices have been developed to measure body weight using an electronic scale that directly reports the results via the Web system. Second, the Internet can be used to record the results of biomarker measurements that are performed by the respondent using noncomputerized devices. For example, respondents may be asked to measure their waist circumference with a standard measuring tape and asked to report the results via the Internet. In the present chapter, we focus particularly on the latter category, as computer technologies for the first type of measurement that are endorsed by the medical community are at this point limited for most biomarkers. Future studies should examine the feasibility of collecting biomarkers using computer technologies as they start to become available and approved for research purposes.

The possibility of introducing biomarkers into an Internet survey is partly determined by the methods of data collection that can be applied in this particular context. There are at least three major aspects to consider regarding the feasibility of collecting biospecimens in an Internet survey:

- *Respondent burden and invasiveness.* There are large differences in the level of invasiveness of different biomarkers. Blood samples are highly invasive and tend to have the lowest response rates (Kumari, Wadsworth, Blake, Bynner, & Wagner, 2006). As an alternative, dried blood spots (DBS), whereby a finger is pricked with a disposable lancet and blood drops are applied to filter paper and allowed to dry, are often used. Although less invasive than blood samples, they are in general more invasive than several other biospecimens. Although urine samples are often classified as noninvasive, cooperation rates in drug studies tend to be lower than for other biospecimens such as saliva, suggesting that it may still be perceived as invasive by participants. Saliva samples appear to be the least invasive and in drug testing studies have the highest cooperation rates, around 90% (Fendrich, Johnson, Wislar, Hubbell, & Spiehler, 2004). In addition, nail clippings and some external physical measurements such as waist circumference are also noninvasive and collection by the respondent is feasible.

- *Health risks.* The collection of blood carries the highest risk due to the possibility of infection or bleeding. However, even though the risks might be higher as opposed to other fluids, dried blood spots reduce this risk considerably.
- *Ease of sample collection.* Some biomarkers require relatively simple protocols and can easily be performed by the respondent. Most biomarkers, however, are collected following relatively strict protocols. For example, intravenous blood can only be collected by a trained nurse and requires a detailed protocol for safety. Blood pressure measurements are generally considered valid only if performed according to a strict protocol.

Up till now, no studies have examined whether biomarkers can be collected in the context of an Internet survey. In the next section, we present the results of a pilot to examine the feasibility of collecting biomarkers in an Internet survey in the Netherlands.

15.3 THE LISS PANEL BIOMARKER PILOT

15.3.1 Introduction and Rationale

Recent years have seen an increased interest in the implementation of new techniques to conduct research in epidemiology and the social sciences using the Internet. This new medium of data collection has become of interest due to an increase in access to both personal computers and the Internet. In 2008, 91% of the total Dutch population had Internet access

(Statistics Netherlands, 2008), which makes the Internet a potentially major tool to conduct population surveys aimed to study population health. This method of data collection provides several advantages over traditional survey methods, including convenience for the participant, relatively low costs for the researcher, efficiency in data collection, higher data quality, and the ability to increase response rates (Ekman, Dickman, Klint, Weiderpass, & Litton, 2006; Smith, Smith, Gray, Ryan, & Millennium Cohort Study Team, 2007; Truell, Bartlett, & Alexander, 2002). On the other hand, Internet surveys face substantial challenges that are not faced by regular surveys. In particular, what distinguishes Internet surveys from other biomarker surveys is that in Internet surveys respondents are asked to carry out the tests on their own, without the help of an interviewer or nurse. This implies that Internet surveys need to make use of all available Internet resources, such as Internet videos to supplement instructions for measurement.

The objective of this pilot is to establish whether collection of blood cholesterol, salivary cortisol, and waist circumference using self-collection methods is feasible in an Internet survey in the Netherlands. This study focuses on examining response and participation rates for the collection of these biomarkers in the Dutch LISS (Longitudinal Internet Study for the Social sciences) panel. The specific objectives of this pilot are threefold:

- To examine the feasibility of collecting blood cholesterol, saliva samples, and waist circumference using self-collection methods in an Internet survey
- To examine the overall quality of data on blood cholesterol, saliva samples, and waist circumference obtained using self-collection methods in an Internet survey
- To examine the general distributions of biomarkers and their association with demographic factors, and to establish whether they show the expected pattern as observed in previous studies

Blood cholesterol and waist circumference are strong predictors of cardiovascular disease and are routinely included in major epidemiological population surveys such as the Whitehall study, the Rotterdam study, the McArthur Study of Successful Aging, and the National Health and Nutrition Examination Survey (NHANES). Cortisol is the end product of one of two major stress-responsive physiological systems of the body.

It influences human health and behavior, reaching almost every body cell, and affecting the major physiological system (Table 15.2). Cortisol is the most common HPA axis biomarker collected in epidemiological surveys, including the Whitehall II study, the English Longitudinal Study of Ageing (ELSA), the McArthur Study of Successful Aging, and the Social Environment and Biomarkers of Aging Study (SEBAS).

15.3.2 Design and Population

The pilot was conducted among a group of participants of the LISS panel, an ongoing study in a representative sample of the Dutch population. This LISS panel consists of almost 8,000 individuals who complete online questionnaires every month. To recruit panel members, a traditional random sample was drawn from the population registers, in collaboration with Statistics Netherlands. If a respondent did not have Internet access at the time of recruitment, he or she was provided with a simPC (a basic PC with the ability to surf the Internet and some other functionalities). All households in the sample were approached in traditional ways (by letter, followed up by telephone call or house visit) with an invitation to participate in the panel. The sample unit was the household because it was the intention to build a panel including all members of a household living at a given address. More details on the LISS panel can be found in Chapter 4 of this volume.

The present pilot was based on three random subsamples of 200 participants ages 18 and older who had agreed to take part in the LISS panel. Selected participants were asked to perform a measurement of one of the three biomarkers and to complete a short survey to report the results of the measurement at one point in time.

This study was reviewed and approved by the Medical Ethical Commission (METC) of Erasmus MC Rotterdam, the Netherlands (file number NL21289.078.08).

15.3.3 Study Protocol

In the LISS panel, participants are asked every month to complete questionnaires through the Internet. The study protocol for the present pilot comprised the following steps:

1. *Web message informing about invitation to participate.* Selected participants received an online message and information about the study through the LISS Internet account. Participants were asked whether they would agree to receive further information about the study. If participants agreed, they were informed that an invitation to participate in the pilot would be sent by regular mail. Following the standard level of incentives of the LISS panel, participants were offered an incentive of 5 euros for participation in the study.
2. *Eligibility (for blood cholesterol only).* Participants in the blood cholesterol pilot were also asked via the LISS Internet account whether they had hemophilia (a disorder that impairs the body's ability to control blood clotting and coagulation) or were using antiplatelets (a drug that inhibits platelets from aggregating to form a plug and used to prevent clotting). Those with any of these two conditions were not eligible to use the cholesterol self-test and were therefore excluded from this study.
3. *Information brochure and consent form.* Participants received a letter of invitation to take part in the study, a brochure with information about the pilot study, and an informed-consent form by regular mail. They also received a prepaid envelope and were asked to return the signed consent form to the researchers. Only participants who signed and returned the informed-consent form indicating their agreement with all points were included. Participants who did not agree to participate were asked why they were not interested in participating. In the information brochure, participants were provided with a telephone number for the LISS panel help desk if they had questions about the study. In addition, participants were given the contact details of an independent medical doctor who would be available to answer questions or address problems related to participation in the study. The latter was required as part of the protocol by the Medical Ethical Commission. However, the independent doctor received no requests for information, while the LISS panel help desk received only a limited number of calls with questions on the pilot.
4. *Home kit for self-collection.* Eligible participants who formally agreed to participate were sent another letter reminding them about the study, explaining the device for measurement, and providing written instructions. Participants were asked to log in to their LISS Internet

account and view the supporting instructional video before taking the measurement. Videos presented precise instructions and steps on how measurements should be performed. Videos were targeted to minimize errors in measurement, such as taking an inadequate amount of blood for the cholesterol test, inadequate reading of the blood cholesterol test result, inadequate timing of collection of the saliva sample, or misidentification of the waist for the waist circumference measurement. Participants could watch the video as many times as they wanted. Videos are available on the online supplement to this book. Both the written and the video instructions contained detailed information on how to avoid errors and perform precise measurements. An online supplement is available on CentERdata's Web site (http://www.centerdata.nl/link/sbri).

5. *Measurement of outcomes.* Participants were asked to take the corresponding measurements after seeing the video and reading the instructions. For all three substudies, participants were asked to perform the corresponding measurement within two weeks after receiving the device and instructions. Participants in the blood cholesterol and waist circumference tests were asked to register online the day and time of completion of the measurements, after which they were asked to report the results. Participants in the waist circumference study were asked to perform two measurements. If the first two measurements differed by more than one centimeter, they were asked to perform and report on a third measurement. Participants in the salivary cortisol study were asked to collect five saliva samples on a single day and to register online the day and time when the samples were collected. They were then requested to return the saliva samples in a prepaid envelope.
6. *Returning and analyzing samples (for salivary cortisol only).* The returned saliva samples were sent to the laboratory of the Technical University of Dresden in Germany for analysis.
7. *Questionnaire about the test.* A few questions about their participation in the study were asked to the participants through their LISS Internet account. These questions were to determine their satisfaction with the test and to identify possible problems in the measurements.
8. *Feedback on test results (for cholesterol and waist circumference only).* A letter was sent to participants whose test indicated an abnormal cholesterol level or waist circumference, informing them of this

> and advising them to contact their general practitioner. The letter also included information about the study and the result of the test, which they could present to their general practitioner.

Because the pilot was carried out in the Netherlands, all documents including the questionnaires and the information brochure were in the Dutch language, and are available upon request.

15.3.4 Measurement Instruments: Self-Tests

Self-tests are devices that collect and analyze a sample or biospecimen at home without the need for trained personnel (Everdigen, Georgie, Beukema, & Pekelharing, 2003). Results are available within minutes, or a sample can be sent to a laboratory for analysis. The present pilot was based on existing technology tailored for home self-measurement. There are three main advantages of this approach. First, because the tests are tailored for home use, instructions for measurement are available, and devices are designed for self-collection by the respondent without the presence of trained personnel. Second, results are available within minutes, and participants report them directly through the Internet. Finally, these tests are legally approved for use in the Netherlands (Everdigen et al., 2003).

Blood cholesterol was measured using a device specifically designed for self-administration at home. The test is distributed in the Netherlands by the company Easy Home Test and is denominated Easy Home Test Cholesterol HVZR (see http://www.easyhometest.eu). This is a self-test to establish the level of cholesterol in the blood and comprises two tests to examine HDL as well as total cholesterol. Participants received the kit for the assessment of cholesterol at home, including detailed instructions for utilization. In short, participants are asked to puncture their finger with a small lancet contained in the testing device and to place a drop of blood on the test device spot. Participants must then activate the test within three to four minutes. The analysis of blood cholesterol is performed directly on the device. In a first step, the plasma is separated from the blood cells. Following the activation of the test, the present cholesterol is transformed into hydrogen peroxide, which in turn generates a color reaction. The height of the colored section is proportional to the concentration of cholesterol present in the blood. Participants were asked to report the results of the self-testing via the LISS Internet account. The procedure described above is performed twice, once for HDL and once for total cholesterol. Participants were provided with detailed written and video instructions on how to perform the test.

For *salivary cortisol*, saliva samples were collected using plastic tubes with a cotton roll (salivettes) on which participants had to chew for 45 seconds. They were asked not to eat or brush their teeth in the 15 minutes before chewing on the salivette. Samples were collected at five different times during a single day: right after waking up, 30 minutes after waking up, at 9:00 a.m. (if the participant woke up after 9:00 a.m., he or she was asked to chew this salivette together with salivette 1), at 5:00 p.m., and before going to sleep. The multiple measurements aimed at obtaining a representation of the cortisol rhythm over the day (cortisol day curve). In order to control for possible deviations in the time of measurement, participants were asked to note on a form the times at which all measurements were taken. Participants were provided with detailed written and video instructions on how to take measurements. They were asked to return the saliva samples in a prepaid envelope.

For *waist circumference*, we used a device designed at the Centre for Obesity Research and Education of Queen's University in Canada and specifically tailored for self-measurement. The kit was designed in the context of lifestyle-based strategies to prevent and reduce obesity. The device consists of a measuring tape in a special holder allowing people to measure their own waist circumference without assistance. The participants were provided with detailed written and video instructions on how to take measurements.

15.3.5 Methods of Analysis

We started by examining response and participation rates among all participants for each group, as well as by basic demographics. We then examined the range and distributions of outcome values in order to determine whether individual outcomes fell within expected ranges. At a second stage, we examined associations of biomarkers with basic demographics including age, sex, and educational level. Logistic and linear regression techniques were used to examine all associations, controlling for demographics and relevant confounders.

15.4 RESULTS

For each of the three biomarkers this section presents the results on response and participation rates, associations of biomarker values with demographic characteristics, and range and mean of biomarker values in comparison to those reported in previous studies. It is important to bear in mind that results on associations with demographic variables should be interpreted with caution, because sample sizes were very small.

15.4.1 Cholesterol Test

15.4.1.1 Overall Response and Participation

Figure 15.1 shows a diagrammatic representation of response and participation in the biomarker pilot for cholesterol testing. Out of the total sample of selected LISS panel members, eight were excluded because they were taking medications or had conditions that rendered them ineligible to participate in the study. Of all selected panel members, 69.5% responded to the invitation, and out of these 82 (41%) agreed to participate in the study. Thirty-eight participants (19%) actually carried out the test, completed the form, and sent back the results of the measurement through the LISS Internet account. About a fifth of these participants (7 participants) reported results that indicated the test might not have been carried out properly. The final sample of valid responses comprised 31 participants, that is, 15.5% of the original sample.

It is important to consider that although participation rates are relatively low, the denominator used includes all participants who were invited to participate (including those who were not eligible because of health reasons). In addition, the LISS panel always comprises a group of nonrespondents to the monthly questionnaire (ranging from 20% to 30%), which is also reflected in the low response and participation rates. Among those who were eligible and responded to the first invitation (n = 139), the participation rate was 22% (n = 31). All participants who took part in the pilot had to pass through a Web page showing the instructional video before they could complete the electronic form with the results of the test.

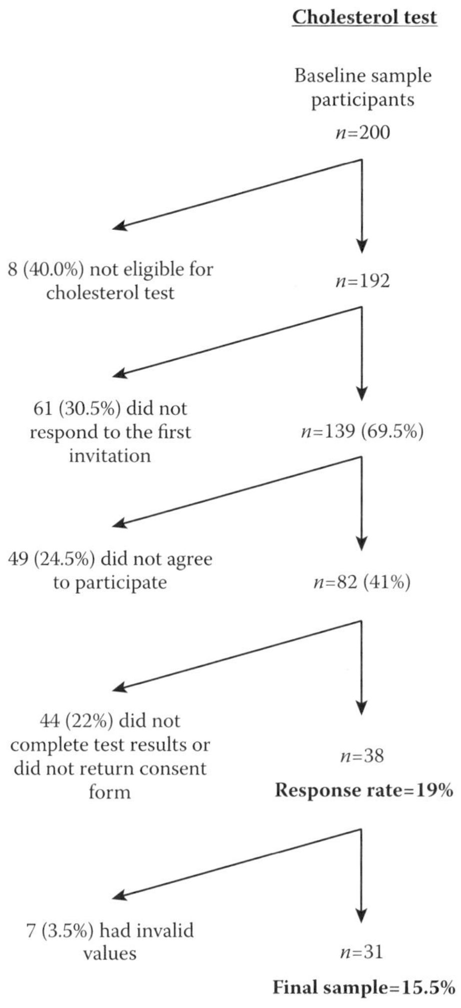

FIGURE 15.1
Response, participation, and final sample in the LISS biomarker pilot for total and HDL cholesterol.

In total, 49 participants explicitly refused to take part in the study. These participants were asked to provide the reasons why they decided not to join the pilot. Over a third (38%) of these participants indicated that they did not participate because they already knew their cholesterol level and they did not find it necessary to use a self-test. Another 22% of participants refused because they thought that the test would take too much of their time. Only five participants (10%) reported that they refused because they disliked the idea of pricking their finger.

Participants who took part in the pilot (n = 38) were asked to rate their experience with the measurement of cholesterol on a 5-point scale (see appendix). Of this group, 45% of respondents reported that the experience was "positive" or "very positive"; 29% reported a neutral position; and 21% were "negative," whereas 5% were "very negative." About a quarter (24%) of the participants reported that the test was "difficult" to conduct, while 37% reported that it was "easy" or "very easy."

15.4.1.2 Demographic Factors Related to Study Participation

Table 15.3 shows participation rates categorized according to demographic characteristics. Results are presented separately for the measurement of HDL and total cholesterol, although practically all participants who participated in one measurement took part in the other measurement

TABLE 15.3

Participation Rates for Cholesterol Test According to Basic Demographics

	Total Cholesterol		HDL Cholesterol	
Demographic Characteristics	**Number**	**% (95% CI)**	**Number**	**% (95% CI)**
Sex				
Male	17	20 (11, 28)	18	21 (13, 29)
Female	21	18 (11, 26)	20	17 (10, 25)
Age				
19–34	6	14 (2, 26)	7	16 (4, 28)
35–59	23	20 (12, 27)	22	19 (12, 26)
60+	9	23 (10, 35)	9	23 (10, 35)
Living with partner				
Yes	11	19 (13, 26)	12	19 (12, 26)
No	27	19 (9, 30)	26	21 (11, 32)
Education				
Elementary or lower secondary	8	14 (3, 25)	9	17 (6, 28)
Higher secondary	13	19 (10, 29)	12	18 (8, 27)
Postsecondary	17	23 (14, 32)	17	23 (14, 32)
Income				
Lowest 33%	8	15 (5, 26)	9	18 (7, 28)
33 < 66%	12	16 (7, 26)	11	15 (6, 24)
Top 33%	18	26 (16, 35)	18	26 (17, 35)

Note: All percentages are standardized by age and sex.

as well. Overall, it is remarkable to see that there is no clear evidence of systematic nonresponse according to sex, age, or living with a partner. Although not significant, due to the small sample size, there is some indication that participants with postsecondary education were about 60% more likely to participate in the survey (response ratio = 1.6, 95% CI [0.7, 3.5]) as compared to participants with only elementary or lower secondary education. Similarly, although not statistically significant, participants in the highest income tertile were about 68% more likely to respond (response ratio = 1.68, 95% CI [0.8, 3.6]) than participants in the lower income tertile.

15.4.1.3 Mean Cholesterol and Prevalence of High-Risk Levels

Table 15.4 shows that in the sample of participants with valid responses ($n = 31$, mean age = 47.6 years), the mean HDL cholesterol was 1.0 mmol/l ($SD = 0.4$), while the mean total cholesterol was 4.4 mmol/l ($SD = 1.1$). We compared the means observed in our pilot with means reported for the Netherlands in a previous study among the Dutch population based on a random sample of 21,451 individuals ages 20–59 (Houterman, Verschuren, Oomen, Boersma-Cobbaert, & Kromhout, 2001). At these ages, the Dutch study reported a mean total cholesterol value of 5.08 ($SD = 1.05$) for the year 1997. In our data, the corresponding figure was 4.4 ($SD = 1.0$). This may reflect some measurement error in our study. However, this difference is also consistent with a decline in mean cholesterol levels in the Dutch population during the last two decades. The proportion of the population in Houterman et al. with a high cholesterol level (> 6.5 mmol/l) was 9.8%, very close to the value observed in our study (9.1%).

TABLE 15.4

Mean Values of Total and HDL Cholesterol Among Respondents of the Biomarker Pilot

Age		Mean (mmol/l)	*SD*	Minimum	Maximum	% High-Risk Cholesterol (95% CI)
19–80	Total cholesterol	4.4	1.1	3.1	7.1	9.6 (0.0, 20.7)
	HDL cholesterol	1.0	0.4	0.5	2.0	38.7 (20.5, 57.0)
20–59	Total cholesterol	4.4	1.0	3.1	6.5	9.1 (0.0, 22.1)
	HDL cholesterol	1.1	0.4	0.5	2.0	36.3 (14.5, 58.2)

Note: All values are standardized by age and sex.

Similar results are available from this survey for the HDL cholesterol level. Between ages 20 and 59, mean HDL cholesterol was 1.19 ($SD = 0.30$) in the year 1997. This is slightly higher but close to the value observed in the LISS biomarker pilot (mean = 1.08, $SD = 0.42$). In 1997, 12.6% of the population ages 20–59 had HDL cholesterol lower than 0.9 mmol/l, while the corresponding percentage in the LISS biomarker pilot was 36.3%, which is considerably higher. This suggests that there may be an overestimation of lower HDL cholesterol levels in our study.

15.4.1.4 Associations Between Demographics and Cholesterol Level

Based on previous studies, we expected total cholesterol levels to be similar among men and women, but HDL cholesterol to be higher among women. We expected cholesterol levels to vary by age, education, and income (Verschuren, Boerma, & Kromhout, 1994), although not all studies have found such associations. Table 15.5 shows mean cholesterol values according to these and other basic demographics.

TABLE 15.5

Mean Total and HDL Cholesterol Levels According to Basic Demographics

	Total Cholesterol		**HDL Cholesterol**	
Demographic Characteristics	**Number**	**% (95% CI)**	**Number**	**% (95% CI)**
Sex				
Male	4.5	(3.9, 5.1)	0.9	(0.7, 1.1)
Female	4.4	(3.8, 4.9)	1.2	(0.9, 1.4)
Age				
18–34	4.5	(3.3, 5.7)	1.2	(0.8, 1.6)
35–59	4.3	(3.8, 4.9)	1.0	(0.8, 1.2)
60+	4.7	(3.9, 5.6)	1.0	(0.7, 1.3)
Living with partner				
Yes	4.3	(3.8, 4.8)	1.0	(0.8, 1.2)
No	4.9	(4.1, 5.7)	1.2	(0.9, 1.5)
Education				
Elementary or lower secondary	4.0	(3.1, 5.0)	1.2	(0.8, 1.5)
Higher secondary	4.8	(4.1, 5.4)	1.0	(0.8, 1.3)
Postsecondary	4.3	(3.7, 5.0)	1.0	(0.7, 1.2)
Income				
Lowest 33%	4.4	(3.5, 5.2)	1.1	(0.7, 1.4)
33 < 66%	4.6	(3.7, 5.4)	1.0	(0.7, 1.3)
Top 33%	4.4	(3.7, 5.1)	1.0	(0.8, 1.3)

Note: All values are standardized for age and sex.

As expected, we found no evidence of gender-related differences in total cholesterol. Although not significant, HDL cholesterol levels were higher among women (mean = 1.2, *SD* = 0.4) than men (mean = 0.9, *SD* = 0.4), which is consistent with previous studies (Houterman et al., 2001; Verschuren et al., 1994). There were no clear differences in mean cholesterol by age, although there was a tendency toward higher levels of total cholesterol and lower levels of HDL cholesterol at older ages. There were no clear variations in mean cholesterol levels by education or income. These results tend to indicate that some of the expected associations were not replicated. This may also be attributable to the small number of observations in the sample, so that power is not sufficient to detect associations. On the other hand, these discrepancies may also be explained by sample selection or systematic differences in the quality of measurement according to basic demographics (e.g., less-educated individuals may be more likely to perform the test incorrectly, which might bias differences in cholesterol level according to educational level).

15.4.2 Waist Circumference Test

15.4.2.1 Overall Response and Participation

Figure 15.2 shows the diagrammatic representation of response and participation in the LISS biomarker pilot for waist circumference. About one-quarter of the selected LISS panel members did not respond to the first invitation and were therefore dropped from the study. Among the selected LISS panel members, a positive response to participation after the first invitation was 43.5% (*n* = 87). However, about 34 of these participants (17%) did not return the consent form to participate in the study or did not register the measurement in the LISS Internet account. In total, 53 panel members (26.5%) participated in the pilot.

Six participants who provided a waist circumference measurement had observations that were unlikely to be expressed in centimeters. An assumption was made that these participants mistakenly reported the measurement indicated by the inches portion of the device provided (it contained both units). Transforming these values into centimeters yielded potentially valid values. Therefore, we concluded that all or most values provided by the participants were valid. Nevertheless, this illustrates the importance of using a process that contains only centimeters to avoid confusion.

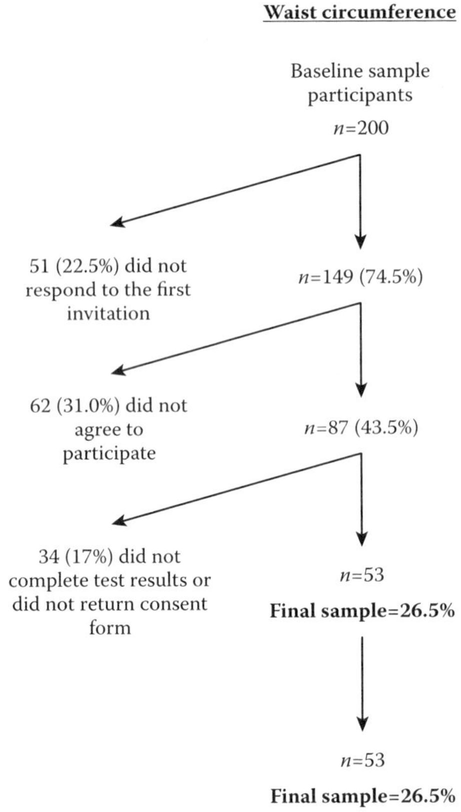

FIGURE 15.2
Response, participation, and final sample in the LISS biomarker pilot for waist circumference.

All participants were initially asked to take two measurements, and only if the difference between these measurements was larger than 1 centimeter were they asked to take a third measurement. Four participants had two measurements that differed by more than 1 centimeter, and all of these carried out a third measurement. The mean value of all measurements was used for analysis.

In total, 62 participants did not agree to take part in the waist circumference measurement. These participants were asked to report why they refused to participate, either by choosing one of four options or by specifying any reason not listed. The reason given by 26% of these participants was that it would take too long to perform the test. Another 26% reported that they did not like to perform this type of measurement. Two participants reported that they refused because they already knew their waist circumference, and 22% of the participants reported other reasons, mostly indicating that they were not interested in performing the test.

Participants who took part in the pilot (*n* = 53) were asked to assess their experience with the test on a 5-point scale (appendix). Of these, 43% reported that their experience was "positive," while 50% reported that it was neutral. In addition, 77% of respondents reported that measuring their waist circumference was "easy," while only 2% reported that it was "difficult" to measure it.

15.4.2.2 Demographic Factors Related to Study Participation in the Waist Circumference Pilot

There was no evidence of study participation selection according to sex, living with partner, education, or income (see Table 15.6). However, there was a clear tendency for an increasing age-related trend in participation: Participants over 60 years were almost three times more likely to

TABLE 15.6

Participation Rates for Waist Circumference Measurement According to Basic Demographics

Demographic Characteristics	Number	% (95% CI)
Sex		
Male	23	24 (15, 32)
Female	30	29 (21, 37)
Age		
18–34	7	15 (2.4, 28)
35–59	26	24 (16, 32)
60+	20	42 (29, 54)
Living with partner		
Yes	16	27 (20, 34)
No	37	28 (16, 40)
Education		
Elementary or lower secondary	24	24 (17, 37)
Higher secondary	14	28 (16, 39)
Postsecondary	15	27 (15, 39)
Income		
Lowest 33%	21	25 (15, 35)
33 < 66%	14	28 (16, 40)
Top 33%	18	29 (19, 40)

Note: All percentages are standardized by age and sex.

take part in the measurement than participants who were in the 18–34 age group (response ratio = 2.7, 95% CI [1.28, 5.8]). On a linear scale, the increase-response trend with increasing age was significant ($p = .0003$).

15.4.2.3 Mean Waist Circumference and Prevalence of High-Risk Levels

Table 15.7 shows that in the sample of respondents with valid values ($n = 53$, mean age = 53.1), mean waist circumference was 94.7 cm (95% CI [90.8, 98.7]) among men and 89.8 cm (95% CI [86.4, 93.3]) among women. We compared data from our sample to data from a study (Visscher & Seidell, 2004) based on a sample of 17,824 men and women ages 20–59 living in three Dutch cities (Amsterdam, Doetinchem, and Maastricht) in the period 1993–1997. At these ages, age-standardized mean values for waist circumference were 90.4 cm among men and 79.9 cm among women. This is relatively consistent with findings from our study for the same age group (95.9 cm for men and 88.0 cm for women). Our slightly higher values may be explained by sample selection or may also reflect, at least partly, the increasing trend in waist circumference that has taken place during the last decades (Visscher & Seidell, 2004). The fact that values for women are relatively high in our study, as compared to the study by Visscher and Seidell, suggests that this discrepancy might partly be the consequence of higher participation among older than younger women (see Table 15.6), leading to higher average mean values of waist circumference. It may also reflect the fact that Visscher and Seidell's study was not based on a representative sample of the Dutch population but comprised only three cities. On the other hand, our results are consistent with the findings from Visscher and Seidell and other studies (Bos et al., 2007), showing that waist circumference is higher for women.

TABLE 15.7

Mean Waist Circumference and Prevalence of Abdominal Obesity

Age	Sex	Mean	95%CI	Minimum	Maximum	Abdominal Obesity*
19–80	Males	94.7	(90.8, 98.7)	80	110	19.5 (8.0, 40.3)
	Females	89.8	(86.4, 93.3)	77	117	51.1 (32.8, 69.2)
20–59	Males	95.9	(91.4, 100.1)	85	110	12.6 (2.9, 40.9)
	Females	88.0	(84.2, 91.8)	77	103	53.7 (28.4, 77.2)

Note: * Waist > 102 cm (men), > 88 cm (women)
All values are standardized by age and sex.

The prevalence of abdominal obesity was 12.6% for men ages 20–59, which is close to the value (14.8%) reported by Visscher and Seidell for the Netherlands. Among women, the prevalence of abdominal obesity was substantially larger in our study (53.7%) than in the study by Visscher and Seidell (21%). This may partly reflect random variation and the trend toward increasing abdominal obesity during the last decades. However, it may also point at a possible selection effect. For example, below age 60, response rates for the study were lower. It is plausible that only individuals concerned about their own waist measurement took part in the study, boosting the mean values for waist circumference in the sample. Another possibility is that there was more error in the measurement of waist circumference for women than for men.

15.4.2.4 Associations Between Demographics and Waist Circumference

Based on previous studies, we expected waist circumference to increase with age and to be inversely related to educational level and income. Table 15.8 summarizes mean waist circumference according to these and other basic demographic variables.

TABLE 15.8

Mean Waist Circumference and Prevalence of Abdominal Obesity According to Basic Demographics

Demographic Characteristics	Mean	(95%CI)	Abdominal Obesity, % (95%CI)
Age			
18–34	83.2	(76.3, 90.0)	9.7 (1.2, 49.2)
35–59	93.4	(89.9, 97.0)	37.0 (20.1, 57.8)
60+	98.8	(89.8, 97.9)	40.6 (20.8, 63.9)
Living with partner			
Yes	90.4	(87.1, 93.7)	39.1 (17.1, 66.7)
No	89.5	(84.4, 95.6)	31.4 (17.8, 49.1)
Education			
Elementary or lower secondary	90.0	(85.7, 94.4)	29.1 (13.4, 51.9)
Higher secondary	88.2	(83.4, 93.1)	32.1 (11.6, 63.0)
Postsecondary	92.6	(87.6, 97.5)	41.2 (18.8, 67.9)
Income			
Lowest 33%	89.1	(84.7, 93.5)	29.4 (13.0, 57.8)
33 < 66%	87.6	(82.6, 92.5)	22.7 (6.8, 53.9)
Top 33%	93.2	(88.9, 97.6)	47.4 (24.5, 71.4)

Note: All values are standardized by age and sex.

As expected, waist circumference increased linearly with age ($p = .0075$). Although not significant, the point estimates of the prevalence of abdominal obesity was considerably higher at ages 60+ than at ages 18–34. There was no evidence of waist circumference variations among those living with or without a partner. Although differences did not reach statistical significance, there was a tendency for higher waist circumference and abdominal obesity among those with higher education or income compared to participants with low education or income. This is contrary to findings from previous studies showing a negative association of education or income with waist circumference. This finding may be attributable to sample selection or systematic differences in the quality of measurement according to educational level or income.

15.4.3 Cortisol Level Measurement

15.4.3.1 Overall Response and Participation

Figure 15.3 shows the diagrammatic representation of response and participation in the LISS biomarker pilot for cortisol levels. About a third of the selected LISS panel members did not respond to the first online invitation to participate in the project, and more than a third did not agree to participate in the study. In total, only 63 participants (31.5%) agreed to take part in the pilot after the first online invitation, but about half of these participants did not return the consent form or did not send back saliva samples. In total, 30 participants (15.0%) completed the saliva measurements and sent back the results for analysis in the lab. All of these participants watched the instructional video before completing the test, as this was a required step before completing the questionnaire with the test results. One of these respondents, however, did not complete the questionnaire on measurement time. Therefore, the final sample for analysis was 29.

Participants who took part in the pilot ($n = 29$) were asked to rate their experience with the collection of saliva samples on a 5-point scale (see appendix). Over a third of the participants (34%) reported that their experience was "negative," while 27% reported that it was "positive" or "very positive"; 90% of the participants reported that collecting the saliva samples was "easy" or "very easy," while only 3% reported that it was "difficult."

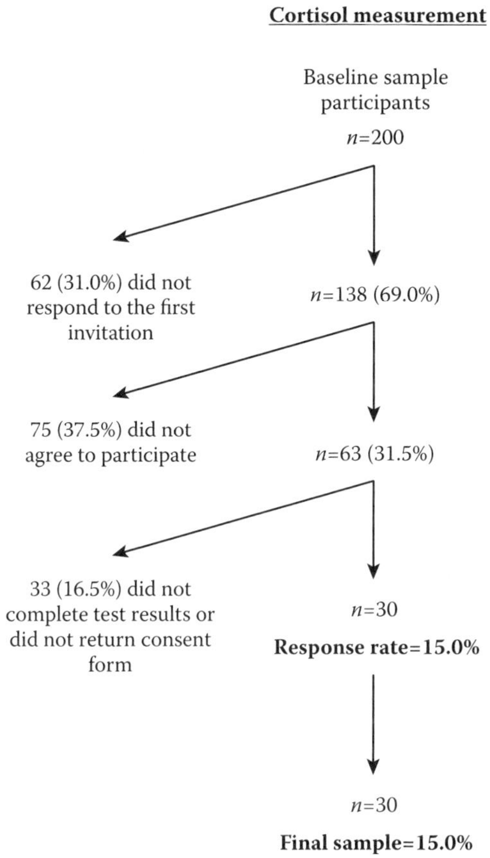

FIGURE 15.3
Response, participation, and final sample in the LISS biomarker pilot for cortisol levels.

15.4.3.2 Study Participation in the Cortisol Pilot According to Demographic Factors

Table 15.9 summarizes participation rates according to basic demographics. Response rates were not significantly different according to sex or between those living with or without a partner. There was a significant increasing age trend in participation rates (p = 0.005). Participants ages 60+ were four times more likely to take part in the study (participation ratio = 4.0, 95% CI [1.41, 11.5]) as compared to participants between 18 and 34. Participation rates were higher among those with only higher secondary education and those in the second tertile of income, but these differences did not reach statistical significance.

TABLE 15.9

Participation Rates for Cortisol Level Measurement According to Basic Demographics

Demographic Characteristics	Number	% (95%CI)
Sex		
Male	14	12 (7, 20)
Female	15	17 (14, 27)
Age		
18–34	4	7 (3, 17)
35–59	12	13 (7, 21)
60+	13	27 (17, 42)
Living with partner		
Yes	19	13 (9, 21)
No	10	17 (9, 30)
Education		
Elementary or lower secondary	9	16 (8, 28)
Higher secondary	11	25 (14, 40)
Postsecondary	9	8 (4, 17)
Income		
Lowest 33%	6	9 (4, 19)
33 < 66%	14	18 (11, 29)
Top 33%	9	16 (9, 28)

Note: Table includes participants who returned saliva samples and completed online questionnaire on time of measurements ($n = 29$). All percentages are standardized by age and sex.

15.4.3.3 Reasons for Not Taking Part in the Cortisol Pilot

In total, 75 participants explicitly refused to take part in the cortisol pilot. These participants were asked to provide the reason why they decided not to join the study. The most common reasons were difficulty in planning the collection of saliva samples during the day (15%) and the collection and reporting taking too much time (5%). Some participants reported disliking collecting saliva samples using the salivettes (9%). The majority of other participants (59%) did not provide a reason.

15.4.3.4 Time of Collection of Saliva Samples

Participants were asked to complete a questionnaire online where they indicated the precise time at which measurements were taken. This

TABLE 15.10

Windows of Measurement Times for Each Cortisol Sample

Targeted Time	Window of Accepted Times	Mean	Minimum	Maximum	# Outside Acceptable Window
1. Wake up	—	7:31 a.m.	6:15 a.m.	9:30 a.m.	—
2. + 30 min.	15 to 90 min. after wake up	8:03 a.m.	6:45 a.m.	10:00 a.m.	0
3. 9:00 a.m.	8:30 a.m. to 10:00 a.m.	9:03 a.m.	8:55 a.m.	9:30 a.m.	0
4. 5:00 p.m.	4:00 p.m. to 6:00 p.m.	5:09 p.m.	4:55 p.m.	8:15 p.m.	1
5. Bedtime	—	11:14 p.m.	8:40 p.m.	1:45 a.m.	—

information was required in order to examine deviations between the required and actual time of measurement. Table 15.10 summarizes the mean and ranges of measurement times as well as the number of measurements outside the acceptable window according to prespecified criteria (Cohen et al., 2006). Compliance with requested measurement times was very high. There was only one measurement that fell outside the defined acceptable window. In addition, the mean measurement time was almost similar to the required time specified for each sample collection.

15.4.3.5 Slope of Diurnal Cortisol

Cortisol levels have been shown to vary systematically over the day, starting at high levels just before waking, reaching a peak shortly after waking, declining thereafter linearly, and reaching the lowest levels before bedtime (Cohen et al., 2006). Thus, the main focus of interest is in variations in the slope of diurnal cortisol rhythm, rather than on overall mean cortisol.

Figure 15.4 shows mean cortisol levels by gender for each of the five measurements among participants that responded to the survey. The pattern is consistent with the expected diurnal rhythm of cortisol levels, starting at high levels before waking, reaching a peak shortly after waking up, and decreasing monotonically thereafter. Results indicate that this pattern is consistent for both men and women. Over most of the day, mean cortisol levels were higher among men than women, but at bedtime cortisol

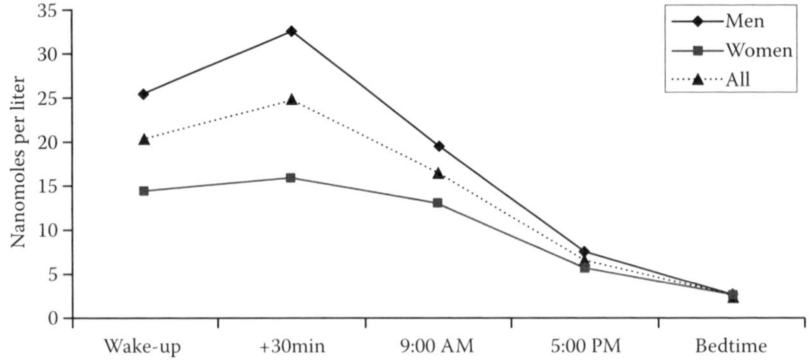

FIGURE 15.4
Mean diurnal salivary cortisol levels for men and women.

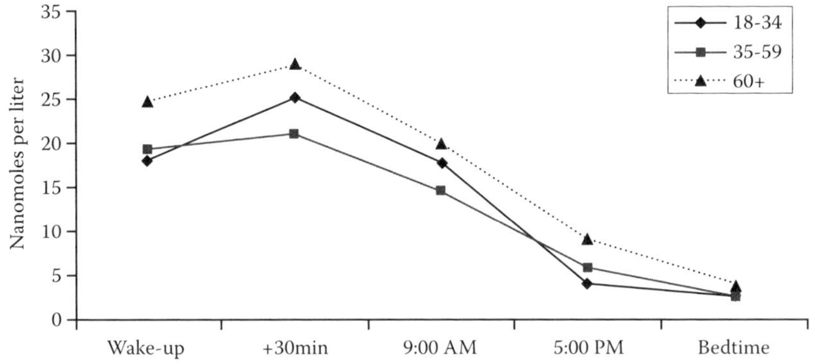

FIGURE 15.5
Mean diurnal salivary cortisol levels by age.

levels were similar, due to a steeper slope for men than women. Previous studies on sex differences in diurnal cortisol levels have been controversial (Cohen et al., 2006; Goldman et al., 2004), as sex differences may differ across populations depending on the level of activity and stress at different times of the day for both groups. Yet it is reassuring to find a similar diurnal pattern over the day for both men and women.

Figure 15.5 shows diurnal salivary cortisol levels for three age groups. Although differences did not reach statistical significance, cortisol levels were consistently higher among older participants over most of the day, but reached similar levels toward the end of the day. This may suggest higher hypothalamic-pituitary-adrenal axis activity at old ages, which has been observed in some studies (Van Cauter, Leproult, & Kupfer, 1996).

15.5 CONCLUSIONS

The recent increase in the number of studies incorporating biomarkers into large population surveys has contributed substantially to understanding links between specific biological processes and various social, economic, psychological, and behavioral characteristics. Understanding these links is an essential step in disentangling the mechanisms through which these social processes relate to health and aging. Internet surveys have proved to be capable of providing high-quality data on a variety of areas including economic factors, behavior, psychosocial well-being, and self-reported health. However, it remains unknown whether the collection of biomarkers is feasible in the context of an Internet survey.

In this pilot we made a first attempt to examine whether biomarkers can be collected in an Internet survey, focusing on three biomarkers commonly collected in face-to-face interview surveys. The conclusions on the feasibility of incorporating these biomarkers in an Internet survey are mixed. On one hand, we found that participation rates are much lower than those reported in face-to-face interviews or regular mail surveys. Participation rates ranged from 15% for the cholesterol and cortisol measurements to 26.5% for the waist circumference measurement. This is much lower than participation rates in the HRS diabetes study (52%; Weir, 2008), the subsample of the Rotterdam study on salivary cortisol (78%; Dekker et al., 2008), or the biomarker component of the HRS study which included blood and saliva sample collection (around 80% for those who agreed to face-to-face interviews; Weir, 2008). Although there was no major evidence of selective response for some of the major demographic characteristics, participation rates in our pilot are insufficient and may compromise the validity of findings. In addition, although most associations of biomarkers with demographic variables showed the expected pattern, there were some unexpected variations in waist circumference by gender, education and income, which may be attributable to sample selection or systematic differences in the quality of measurement. On the other hand, we found that it is feasible for people to collect biomarkers on their own, using self-tests with the support of video instructions provided via the Internet. This is supported by the fact that most measurements fell within the expected ranges and, in many cases, showed the expected associations with basic demographic factors. Measurement of blood cholesterol levels proved more difficult for respondents than measurement of cortisol and waist circumference. In addition, we received informal reports from a few participants indicating that the test did not yield valid values despite them having followed the instructions correctly. This suggests that more trials may be needed in order to ensure that all tests yield valid results. Yet, it is reassuring that a majority of respondents were able to perform the test and report valid cholesterol values.

It is important to distinguish three major mechanisms that contribute to the low participation rates. First, about 30% of respondents in the LISS panel did not respond to the first invitation and therefore were not informed about the topic or requirements for participation in the study. This suggests that their lack of motivation to participate lies outside the particular difficulties perceived in the collection of biomarkers. The LISS panel is a panel in which members respond to survey questions on a monthly basis. Among this group, there is always a fraction that does not complete the monthly questionnaire.

The second mechanism that drives low response rates is directly related to the collection of data on biomarkers. Approximately a third of the respondents in each pilot explicitly refused to take part in the study, which is a relatively high number considering that these participants have already agreed to participate as regular respondents in the LISS panel. The main reasons for not taking part in the study are related to the large amount of time needed to take the measurements and to a general lack of personal interest in taking these measurements. Participants seem to weight their decision to participate on the basis of the potential benefit of taking a particular measurement. For example, already knowing their cholesterol was a major motivation for participants' refusal to participate. This is likely to induce selection in the sample, because participants who are not aware of their cholesterol (and who are more likely to be healthier) will be more likely to participate in the study. Similarly, many participants did not perceive any benefit from measuring their cortisol levels, which led to low participation rates in this particular measurement.

The third driving force of participation rates refers to the requirement to complete and return a signed consent form in a separate step of the pilot. About half of the participants who initially agreed to participate in the study eventually did not return the signed form and therefore did not receive a home kit for taking the measurements. A crucial challenge is therefore to find a mechanism through which participants do not have to return signed forms before receiving the test—for example, by expressing their willingness to participate via the LISS Internet account. However, this will be possible only if the online system is upgraded to ensure that individuals can identify themselves (e.g., through a personal ID document) and are the only ones able to give their consent.

Surprisingly, we found that older age is associated with higher participation rates in the waist circumference and cortisol pilot. A possible explanation for this finding is that older participants (60+ years) are retired and may have more time to perform these measurements. Many participants of working age may find it difficult to collect saliva samples during their workday. It is important to mention that this is a general pattern observed in the LISS panel and is not unique to this pilot. Once in the panel, older participants have higher participation rates in the monthly questionnaire.

One of the positive outcomes of our pilot was that the majority of respondents who agreed to participate reported the results of the measurements via the LISS Internet account and returned the saliva samples for analysis in the laboratory. Practically all the saliva samples were of sufficient quantity and quality. In particular, only two of the 150 saliva samples were ineligible for analysis, and the diurnal cortisol rhythm was consistent with the expected pattern. Many of the expected associations between biomarkers and demographic factors were also reproduced in our data, and overall levels correspond well with those observed in previous surveys. Although there were some deviations in mean values and demographic variations, these may be due to selective response on some characteristics such as age, rather than on incorrect measurements.

Several recommendations for future full-scale studies collecting biomarkers in an Internet panel can be derived from our study. First, our findings suggest that the main challenge for collecting biomarkers lies in increasing response and participation rates. In order to achieve this, the following potential strategies might help to improve the quality of biomarker data. It may be necessary to provide respondents with larger incentives to increase participation and cooperation rates. The most obvious type of incentive is financial: The regular incentives for participation in the monthly LISS panel (7.50 euros for 30 minutes) might be insufficient to yield acceptable response and cooperation rates for the collection of biomarkers. For the biomarker pilot, an incentive of 5 euros was provided, based on an estimation of the total time required to complete the measurements. Although this may be correct for the cholesterol and waist circumference measurement, the time required for the cortisol measurements is likely to be higher. There is no convention about what financial incentive should be provided to participants in studies that collect data on biomarkers, and our study did not experiment with incentives and therefore cannot offer certainty on the impact of higher incentives. However, it is worth comparing our study with more traditional surveys. In pharmaceutical studies, incentives can be as high as several hundreds or thousands of euros, but this is mostly for studies that experiment with new drugs. Population studies collecting biomarker data in the United States have typically higher incentives than in the LISS panel. For example, the HRS provided $40 incentives for their mail diabetes study involving use of blood test kits. This was twice the regular incentive of $20 for an HRS mail survey. Although we did not experiment with higher incentives in this pilot, and there may be different incentive thresholds in the Netherlands than in the United States, it seems plausible that increasing financial incentives (regardless of the time required to complete the measurements) will reduce the number of participants who refuse to participate after the first online invitation. Nevertheless, more experimentation is needed to ascertain the role of incentives.

Second, a large number of nonparticipants stated that they did not take part in the pilot because there was no clear benefit for them. This suggests that participation may be enhanced by providing respondents with more concrete information on the potential benefits of taking measurements. For example, providing more didactic information through a video in the initial invitation about the benefits of regularly monitoring cholesterol may motivate participation among potential respondents who feel that they have little to gain from taking part in this study. In addition, participation rates may be improved by further clarifying the goal of and motivation for measuring biomarkers.

Third, the three pilots followed a structure that takes participants through different steps and asks them to actively state whether they are willing to participate. These steps were either required because of ethical reasons or necessary in order to establish contact with participants through the LISS Internet account. However, at each step, we lost a large number of participants. This suggests that response rates are likely to improve by aggregating these steps and diminishing the number of stages at which participants are expected to provide a response. This is particularly important at two different stages:

1. In this pilot, participants were first presented with an online invitation to take part in the study. Surprisingly, a large proportion of participants did not respond to this initial invitation or refused to participate in the study at this relatively early stage. An alternative to reduce nonresponse would be to replace this initial invitation with an online message to inform subjects that they will be invited to participate in the study and that they will receive further information and an informed-consent form where they will be asked whether they would agree to participate. Participants can then be expected to formally express their willingness to participate at the second stage, using the consent form. By replacing the initial invitation with an online message to inform participants that they will be formally invited, we expect to diminish nonresponse rates somewhat and potentially increase the proportion of participants willing to participate in the study.
2. Our study shows that it is unlikely that high participation rates will be obtained if the completion of the informed-consent form takes place as a separate step in the protocol. Had all participants who agreed to participate in the first invitation returned the consent form and performed the tests, participation rates would have been as much as 40% for the cholesterol and waist circumference measurements and 30% for the cortisol study. Unfortunately, the Medical Ethical Commission did not approve the completion of this form electronically. The commission required participants to complete the informed-consent form in a separate step and return it by mail before they could move on to the next step in the pilot. The Medical Ethical Commission rejected our proposal to ask respondents to agree electronically to participate in the pilot, because it was felt that the online system would not allow for adequately controlling the identity of each participant, such as by personally signing the form or showing a copy of their passport. In addition, the Medical Ethical Commission considered that participants should personally be informed about the study, thus giving them the opportunity to pose questions before deciding to participate. A possible strategy would

> be to implement an electronic system that allows controlling the identity of each participant (as opposed to each household) and that is agreeable to the Medical Ethical Commission, such as through the use of the Dutch DIGID unique identification system. To comply with the requirements of the Medical Ethical Commission, individuals could be offered the possibility to ask questions electronically about the study or chat through the LISS Internet account before deciding to participate. We expect response and participation rates to increase substantially if participants are offered the possibility to complete the informed-consent form through the online system.

Among participants who agreed to participate, we did not detect major problems in the performance of the measurements using the self-test devices. Values from waist circumference and cortisol levels fell within the expected ranges and followed expected patterns. However, a relatively large number of cholesterol values (20%) indicated that the test was not performed adequately. Despite being based on a self-test device that had been tested for use by the general population, some participants may ultimately have been unable to follow the relatively complex instructions of this test. Furthermore, there are some indications that the test itself did not work properly despite being carried out according to the instructions. Use of this device will require further testing and liaison with the manufacturer. Yet the fact that a majority (80%) of all those who took the test reported valid values shows that it may be feasible to implement this at a larger scale. A possible alternative would be to include a step in the Internet protocol in which the reporting of invalid values automatically informs the participant that a second device will be sent for them to do the test again.

The Medical Ethical Commission explicitly requested that we provide feedback to respondents on the results of the cholesterol and waist circumference test. The advantage of this approach is that by informing participants that they have a elevated risk of getting a disease we may induce preventive action on their part and thus contribute to the respondent's health. The disadvantage, however, is that our measurements may introduce behavioral changes in the sample, which may bias observational studies. In addition, although we had no such negative experiences, some participants may feel uncomfortable when given feedback about their health. Participants may also take measurements incorrectly and receive feedback on their health that is not confirmed by a medical professional. Thus, the benefits of providing feedback to respondents should be balanced against unwanted consequences, and this issue should be carefully discussed with the Medical Ethical Commission.

Overall, the present study shows that response and participation rates for collecting biomarkers in an Internet survey are relatively low. This appears to be driven primarily by the lack of incentives and the number of steps between the first invitation, the completion of the consent form, and the performance of the biomarker measurement. Although some of these steps are required for ethical reasons, we believe strategies can be implemented to simplify the process. It is reassuring that participants are able to adequately collect data on cholesterol level, waist circumference, and cortisol level using self-test devices tailored for this purpose. The key challenge remains implementing mechanisms that will enhance response and participation rates, and that will allow us to gain consent for participation in a simpler set of steps. We believe that these strategies may contribute to increasing response rates to the levels required for an appropriate measurement of the biological markers of disease. However, it will be necessary to further experiment with both higher incentives and simplified versions of the protocol acceptable to the Medical Ethical Commission before fully implementing biomarker data collection in an Internet survey.

[1] Acknowledgments: This study was supported by CentERdata at Tilburg University, the Netherlands. We would like to acknowledge the support of Eveline Bunge in the organization and design of the study. We acknowledge the support of Henning Tiemeier in the design of the salivary cortisol pilot, and Rianne Vaneijsden for her support in the implementation of the salivary cortisol pilot. We are grateful for the support of CentERdata and the MESS project team in the implementation and data collection for the biomarker pilot. Mauricio Avendano is supported by a VENI grant from the Netherlands Organisation for Scientific Research (NWO, grant no. 451-07-001) and a Bell Fellowship from the Harvard Center for Population and Development Studies.

REFERENCES

Alley, D. E., Seeman, T. E., Ki Kim, J., Karlamangla, A., Hu, P., & Crimmins, E. M. (2006). Socioeconomic status and C-reactive protein levels in the US population: NHANES IV. *Brain, Behavior, and Immunity, 20*(5), 498–504.

Avendano, M., Kawachi, I., Van Lenthe, F., Boshuizen, H. C., Mackenbach, J. P., Van den Bos, G. A. M. et al. (2006). Socioeconomic status and stroke incidence in the US elderly: The role of risk factors in the EPESE study. *Stroke, 37*, 1368–1373.

Avendano, M., Kunst, A. E., Huisman, M., Van Lenthe, F., Bopp, M., Borrell, C. et al. (2004). Educational level and stroke mortality: A comparison of 10 European populations during the 1990s. *Stroke, 35*(2), 432–437.

Avendano, M., Kunst, A. E., Huisman, M., Van Lenthe, F., Bopp, M., Regidor, E. et al. (2006). Socioeconomic status and ischaemic heart disease mortality in 10 Western European populations during the 1990s. *Heart, 92*(4), 461–467.

Avendano, M., Kunst, A. E., Van Lenthe, F., Boss, V., Costa, G., Valkonen, T. et al. (2005). Trends in socioeconomic disparities in stroke mortality in six European countries between 1981–1985 and 1991–1995. *American Journal of Epidemiology, 161*(1), 52–61.

Banks, J., Marmot, M., Oldfield, Z., & Smith, J. P. (2006). Disease and disadvantage in the United States and in England. *Journal of the American Medical Association, 295*(17), 2037–2045.

Biomarkers Definitions Working Group. (2001). Biomarkers and surrogate endpoints: Preferred definitions and conceptual framework. *Clinical Pharmacology & Therapeutics, 69*(3), 89–95.

Börsch-Supan, A., Brugiavini, A., Jürges, H., Mackenbach, J., Siegrist, J., & Weber, G. (2005). *Health, ageing and retirement in Europe*. Morlenbach, Germany: Strauss.

Bos, M. B., De Vries, J. H., Wolffenbuttel, B. H., Verhagen, H., Hillege, J. L., & Feskens, E. J. (2007). The prevalence of the metabolic syndrome in the Netherlands: Increased risk of cardiovascular diseases and diabetes mellitus type 2 in one quarter of persons under 60. *Nederlands Tijdschrift voor Geneeskunde, 151*(43), 2382–2388.

Cohen, S., Schwartz, J. E., Epel, E., Kirschbaum, C., Sidney, S., & Seeman, T. (2006). Socioeconomic status, race, and diurnal cortisol decline in the Coronary Artery Risk Development in Young Adults (CARDIA) study. *Psychosomatic Medicine, 68*(1), 41–50.

Dekker, M. J., Koper, J. W., Van Aken, M. O., Pols, H. A., Hofman, A., De Jong, F. H. et al. (2008). Salivary cortisol is related to atherosclerosis of carotid arteries. *Journal of Clinical Endocrinology & Metabolism, 93*(10), 3741–3747.

Dowd, J. B. & Goldman, N. (2006). Do biomarkers of stress mediate the relation between socioeconomic status and health? *Journal of Epidemiololgy and Community Health, 60*(7), 633–639.

Ekman, A., Dickman, P. W., Klint, A., Weiderpass, E., & Litton, J. E. (2006). Feasibility of using Web-based questionnaires in large population-based epidemiological studies. *European Journal of Epidemiology, 21*(2), 103–111.

Etter, J. F., Neidhart, E., Bertrand, S., Malafosse, A., & Bertrand, D. (2005). Collecting saliva by mail for genetic and cotinine analyses in participants recruited through the Internet. *European Journal Epidemiology, 20*(10), 833–838.

Everdigen, J., Georgie, D., Beukema, A., & Pekelharing, M. (2003). *Test uw gezondheid* [*Test your health*]. The Hague, the Netherlands: Consumentenbond.

Fendrich, M., Johnson, T. P., Wislar, J. S., Hubbell, A., & Spiehler, V. (2004). The utility of drug testing in epidemiological research: Results from a general population survey. *Addiction, 99*(2), 197–208.

Goldman, N., Weinstein, M., Cornman, J., Singer, B., Seeman, T., & Chang, M.-C. (2004). Sex differentials in biological risk factors for chronic disease: Estimates from population-based surveys. *Journal of Women's Health, 13*(4), 393–403.

Houterman, S., Verschuren, W. M., Oomen, C. M., Boersma-Cobbaert, C. M., & Kromhout, D. (2001). Trends in total and high density lipoprotein cholesterol and their determinants in the Netherlands between 1993 and 1997. *International Journal of Epidemiology, 30*(5), 1063–1070.

Juster, F., & Suzman, R. (1995). An overview of the Health and Retirement Study. *Journal of Human Resources, 30*, S7–S56.

Kristenson, M., Eriksen, H. R., Sluiter, J. K., Starke, D., & Ursin, H. (2004). Psychobiological mechanisms of socioeconomic differences in health. *Social Science and Medicine, 58*(8), 1511–1522.

Kumari, M., Wadsworth, M., Blake, M., Bynner, J., & Wagner, G. G. (2006). *Biomarkers in the proposed UK longitudinal household study*. London: Longview.

Marmot, M., Banks, J., Blundell, R., Lessof, C., & Nazroo, J. (2002). *Health, wealth and lifestyles of the older population in England: The 2002 English Longitudinal Study of Ageing*. London: University College London.

Smith, B., Smith, T. C., Gray, G. C., Ryan, M. A., & Millennium Cohort Study Team (2007). When epidemiology meets the Internet: Web-based surveys in the Millennium Cohort Study. *American Journal of Epidemiology, 166*(11), 1345–1354.

Smith, J. (2005). Unraveling the SES-health connection. In L. Waite (Ed.), *Aging, health, and public policy: Demographic and economic perspectives* (pp. 108–132). New York: Population Council.

Smits, J., Westert, G. P., & Van den Bos, G. A. (2002). Socioeconomic status of very small areas and stroke incidence in the Netherlands. *Journal of Epidemiology and Community Health, 56*(8), 637–640.

Statistics Netherlands. (2008). *Mediaproducten steeds meer via Internet* [*Media products more and more through Internet*]. CBS press release PB08-071. The Hague: Statistics Netherlands.

Steenland, K., Henley, J., & Thun, M. (2002). All-cause and cause-specific death rates by educational status for two million people in two American Cancer Society cohorts, 1959–1996. *American Journal of Epidemiology, 156*(1), 11–21.

Steptoe, A. & Marmot, M. (2002). The role of psychobiological pathways in socio-economic inequalities in cardiovascular disease risk. *European Heart Journal, 23*(1), 13–25.

Survey and Measurement Core. (2005). Introduction to biomarker measurement. Retrieved February 27, 2007, from http://www.dfhcc.harvard.edu/fileadmin/DFHCC_Admin/Cores/SurveyMeas/Survey_Biomarkers.doc

Truell, A. D., Bartlett, J. E., II, & Alexander, M. W. (2002). Response rate, speed, and completeness: A comparison of Internet-based and mail surveys. *Behavior Research Methods, Instruments, & Computers, 34*(1), 46–49.

Van Cauter, E., Leproult, R., & Kupfer, D. J. (1996). Effects of gender and age on the levels and circadian rhythmicity of plasma cortisol. *Journal of Clinical Endocrinology & Metabolism, 81*(7), 2468–2473.

Verschuren, W. M., Boerma, G. J., & Kromhout, D. (1994). Total and HDL-cholesterol in the Netherlands: 1987–1992. Levels and changes over time in relation to age, gender and educational level. *International Journal of Epidemiology, 23*(5), 948–956.

Visscher, T. L. & Seidell, J. C. (2004). Time trends (1993–1997) and seasonal variation in body mass index and waist circumference in the Netherlands. *International Journal of Obesity and Related Metabolic Disorders, 28*(10), 1309–1316.

Weir, D. (2008). Elastic powers: The integration of biomarkers into the Health and Retirement Study. In M. Weinstein, J. W. Vaupel, & K. W. Wachter (Eds.), *Biosocial surveys* (pp. 78–95). Washington, DC: National Academies Press.

Wilson, S. E. & Howell, B. L. (2005). Do panel surveys make people sick? US arthritis trends in the Health and Retirement Study. *Social Science & Medicine, 60*(11), 2623–2627.

APPENDIX

Self-reports of participants' overall experience (A) and level of difficulty (B) taking measurements in the biomarker pilot.

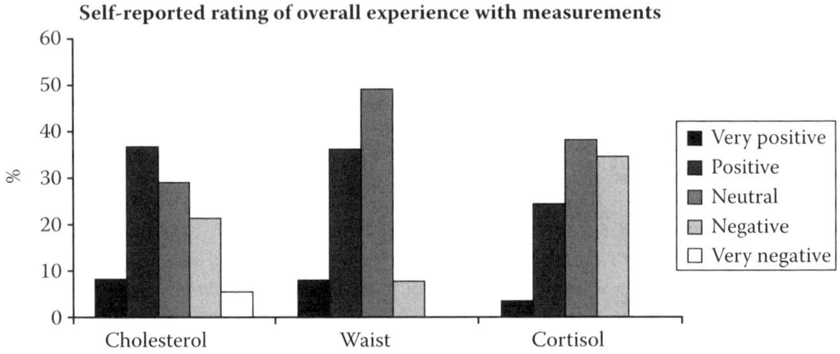

(a)

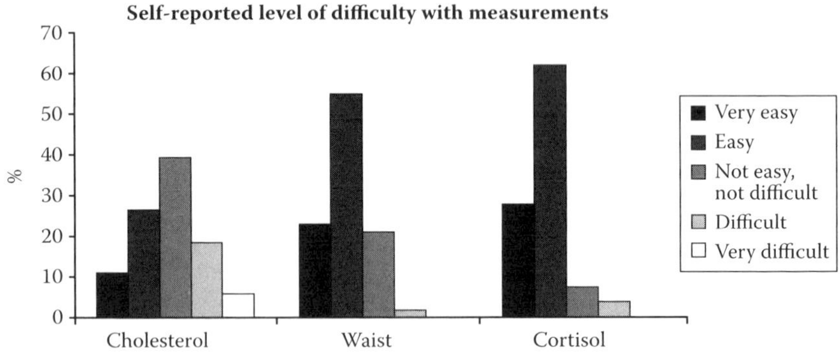

(b)

16

Discussion and Conclusions

Marcel Das
CentERdata and Tilburg School of Economics and Management
Tilburg University
Tilburg, the Netherlands

Peter Ester
Rotterdam University
Rotterdam, the Netherlands

Lars Kaczmirek
GESIS—Leibniz Institute for the Social Sciences
Mannheim, Germany

The contributions in this book cover a wide range of topics in Internet survey research. The overall goal is to show how researchers can benefit from the advantages of the Internet mode and how to tackle problems that sometimes are misinterpreted as inherent disadvantages to Internet survey methodology. Furthermore, the project fosters the discussion of new Internet survey developments and unique research opportunities. This final chapter draws the main conclusions of the book and discusses the consequences for the research agenda on the use of Internet surveys in social and behavioral research.

Part I of the book reviewed the weaknesses, strengths, and feasibility of Internet surveys. This is done in an overall assessment of survey errors, as part of a mixed-mode design, in a panel context, and with respect to ethical issues. Compared to other modes, two of the most obvious benefits of Internet surveys are the low costs and the (much) shorter time needed to collect data. Chapter 2 showed that Internet surveys offer a feasible alternative to traditional modes of data collection, although the weaknesses and strengths of this mode vary to a great extent with different situations. For some target populations the mode is less suitable and there is still a need to study and grasp the effects of Internet survey design and implementation decisions for this mode. But vast progress has been made, and the Internet mode is nowadays a serious competitor to other modes of data collection in scientific (both fundamental and applied) research projects.

To benefit from the convincing advantages of Internet surveys while trying to limit the effects of weaknesses such as coverage and nonresponse error, a researcher may decide to use a mixed-mode design. Chapter 3 focused on the optimal design strategy and provides a framework for how to solve open issues in a specific project. Where a mix of modes may lead to problems of data integrity, combining visual self-administered modes, such as Internet and paper mail surveys, may be the best feasible way of minimizing measurement error. For more demanding administrative tasks in particular, this combination is an interesting option. In a panel context with frequent data collection, however, this combination may be problematic, mostly in terms of logistics and management. Providing hardware and Internet access in such a situation, as is done in the LISS panel, is an interesting alternative (Chapter 4).

Working with a panel obviates the need to collect standard background variables in each interview. Furthermore, background variables can be used to stratify the sample and to tailor interviews to the characteristics of a respondent. When the panel is combined with the Internet as a mode of data collection, the possibilities for real-time quality control and automatic preloading of existing information are enormous. In practice this has led to online volunteer and access panels popping up like daisies, making them easily available for every researcher. But one needs to be very careful. Decision makers must be cautious about results from such surveys and should carefully consider the impact of coverage and self-selection risks on data quality (Chapter 5).

In contrast to other modes of data collection, one of the additional features of Internet surveys is the possibility to collect process data unnoticed by respondents. Researchers may become very enthusiastic and use data about the data-gathering process itself (i.e., paradata) for purposes beyond the aim of monitoring data collection to ensure that it is methodologically sound. Although informed consent about which data are collected is a prerequisite for survey researchers, issues of consent become even more salient if paradata are used in substantive domains. The results presented in Chapter 6 suggest that there may be a potential conflict between research considerations and obligations to respondents, because informing them appears to reduce both their willingness to participate in the research and, more substantially, permission to use the paradata collected. This point should be taken seriously, and more research and insights into ethical issues are warranted.

Part II of the book focuses on advanced methods and applications. Two characteristics of Internet surveys are central in this part of the book: the visual presentation of questions, and self-administration. The Internet seemingly offers many possibilities to present questions and enrich them with graphical details, but research has shown that different visual layouts produce different answers for all types of survey questions. Therefore, it is very important to understand how visualization affects the answering process. However, the number of arguments in favor of or against specific implementations may seem endless. Here, Chapter 7 structured the body of knowledge around the design of questions by providing an in-depth literature review and design guidelines. Research should continue, particularly on assessing the relative importance of visual factors influencing answers in surveys.

With respect to survey questions, a specific advantage of Internet surveys is the possibility to dynamically interact with respondents. Good design can be very helpful in improving data quality. Survey researchers have learned to benefit from areas such as cognitive psychology and usability theory. All sorts of visual feedback and interactive probing may help to motivate respondents and reduce measurement error and nonresponse (Chapters 8 and 9). Future research is needed in these areas to fine-tune the specific implementations of interactive feedback.

The self-administered character of this mode is the focus of Chapter 10. Because no interviewer is present, answers are less affected by social desirability bias, which is particularly important for attitude research on controversial issues. It has been shown that respondents are not reluctant to give an extended response to open-ended questions on the Internet. However, we should not forget that the role of the interviewer is also to motivate the respondent to answer all items and complete the survey. This would be missing in a self-administered mode. Nevertheless, the chapters in Part II show that there are clear possibilities for successfully incorporating interactive elements and feedback in an Internet survey, mimicking some aspects of an interviewer. This is a very challenging direction, and the increasing number of innovative technical features suggests that much can be gained.

Part III of the book discusses problems and solutions with respect to data quality in Internet surveys and provides research insights into new, promising applications and methods. As mentioned above, for some target populations the Internet as interview mode may be less suitable, and some groups are not able or willing to answer questions over the Internet. Research has produced evidence that ignoring such groups may lead to biases in the results (Chapter 11). A mixed-mode design may be helpful here, at least for including groups that are not able to participate using the Internet. But that raises the issue of possible mode effects. Differences in answers in Internet and traditional surveys are easily interpreted as mode effects, but these differences can also be due to selection, question-wording effects, or context effects (Chapter 12).

In terms of research insights into new and promising applications, the use of paradata opens up a wide range of possibilities for learning more about the quality of the data, the optimal construction of the questionnaire, and the actual behavior of respondents (Chapter 13). Paradata can be collected indirectly by registering mouse clicks, keystrokes, times, and so on, but also directly with eye-tracking methodology (Chapter 14). Currently, eye tracking requires specialized hardware employed within a laboratory setting, but in the future new technological developments may simplify the collection of this kind of paradata. And much is to be learned from such data. The improvements in technology make it possible to employ it as a standard methodology in the toolbox of survey researchers. Several statistics bureaus around the world use eye-tracking paradata to optimize their questionnaires. Apart from helping to understand how a questionnaire is processed, eye tracking reveals the difference between good and bad questions, pinpoints bad design and poor wording, and clarifies the effects of question order and answer format. It is a valuable and challenging add-on to further improve survey methodology.

Another highly innovative way of data collection in the social sciences is to collect medically relevant data (i.e. biomarkers) in an Internet survey (Chapter 15). Biomarkers have been used extensively before in numerous surveys, but the combination with an Internet survey is quite new. It raises medical ethical considerations, but the potential of combining biomedical research with socioeconomic research in one survey is very promising. As technological developments continue, the collection of biomarkers may become increasingly undemanding. Respondent burden is limited, and data are automatically transferred via Internet technology. These new tools allow for much more accurate and cost-effective measurement and experimentation than was possible in the past. Its practical applications and benefits are virtually infinite.

Summarizing, this book illustrates the feasibility and usefulness of Internet surveys for the social and behavioral sciences and tackles the central problems. The Internet as a mode for data collection should be taken seriously by social and behavioral scientists. It offers new and innovative ways of data collection.

The LISS panel was used as a tool to carry out several experiments. The way the panel is set up and the efforts that are put into the solution of known problems of coverage and self-selection are impressive. We hope more national Internet panels in other countries around the globe will follow. For cross-country or cross-cultural research in the social and behavioral sciences, having comparable or even similar Internet panels that meet high scientific and professional standards would be a golden asset. Of course, challenging issues remain in terms of methodology, design, and measurement. But solutions also become more available, and this books aims at doing so. One development is clear: Internet surveys are here to stay.

Author Index

A

B

C

D

E

F

G

H

M

N

O

T

U

V

Subject Index

D

N

O

T